Doing Family on the Move

Florian Tissot

Doing Family on the Move

Highly-Skilled Migrants in Switzerland and Germany

PETER LANG

Bern · Berlin · Bruxelles · New York · Oxford

Bibliographic Information published by the Deutsche Nationalbibliothek
The Deutsche Nationalbibliothek lists this publication in the Deutsche Nationalbibliografie; detailed bibliographic data is available online at http://dnb.d-nb.de.

Library of Congress Cataloging-in-Publication Data
A CIP catalog record for this book has been applied for at the Library of Congress.

UNIVERSITÉ DE NEUCHÂTEL
SWISS NATIONAL SCIENCE FOUNDATION

Book published with the support of the Swiss National Science Foundation and the Publications Commission of the Faculty of Humanities of the University of Neuchâtel.

cover image © Montri Thipsorn/Shutterstock.com

Printed by CPI books GmbH, Leck

ISBN 978-3-0343-3918-6 (Print)
E-ISBN 978-3-0343-3987-2 (E-PDF) • E-ISBN 978-3-0343-3988-9 (EPUB)
E-ISBN 978-3-0343-3989-6 (MOBI) • DOI 10.3726/b16724

PETER LANG Open

This publication has been peer reviewed.

Peter Lang AG
International Academic Publishers

Printed in Germany

www.peterlang.com

Contents

Empirical Part

Discussion Part

Acknowledgments

When I started this work, I was told that a dissertation is a lonely and yet a collective endeavour. Today, I understand the paradox of this statement and I cannot agree more. Thus, I want to warmly thank all the people and institutions who made this work possible, by their support, their help, and their advice.

First and foremost, I warmly thank all the interviewees, who, in the most literal sense of the term, made this thesis possible. I thank them not only for their time and for having accepted to share their stories but also for having opened the door of their home or their office, inviting me to restaurants for a dinner or a coffee, and for having trusted me. You are too numerous to be individually thanked but should you reads these lines, I want to express to you my deepest gratitude.

This research was made possible by the Université of Neuchâtel, where I was a teaching-assistant for the first years of my thesis, through gaining the grant Doc.Mobility of the Swiss National Science Foundation as well as the Goethe Universität Frankfurt and the Brandenburgische Technische Universität where I was welcomed to do my research during my stay abroad.

I would like to express my special thanks to my supervisors Prof. Gianni D'Amato (Université de Neuchâtel) and Prof. Anna Amelina (Brandenburgische Technische Universität), who gave me critical and encouraging feedback and who never let me down. This Ph.D. is the fruit of their collaboration and the constant criss-crossing of their comments. Thank you for organising meetings and research colloquium: they were each time a source of motivation as well as a moment to meet with other fellow Ph.D. students.

I salute the members of the jury, Prof. Eric Davoine, Prof. Yvonne Riaño and Prof. Tania Zittoun for constructive and critical comments. Thank you to have taken the time to read it through twice.

A special thanks to Vicky Woollard, Alexia Moyer, Laura Cameron, and Richard Cassidy who accepted to reread and clean my rusty English making my work more pleasant to the reader. I thank you all for your critical readings of the entire manuscript.

I want to sincerely thank the administrative staff of the University of Neuchâtel and the collaborator of the library who helped me in my research in many ways. Thank you to Nadja Rinchetti, Christine Diacon, Hoang-Mai Diep, and Aronne Watkins.

Many thanks to my colleagues of the Swiss Migration Forum in Neuchâtel for having discussed and read the former versions of some chapters: Denise Efionayi-Mäder, Rosita Fibbi, Marco Pecoraro, Noemi Carrel, Eva Zschirnt, Nicole Wichman, Jean-Thomas Arrighi de Casanova, Dina Bader, Johanna Probst, Ilka Steiner, Alice Milivinti, Salomon Bennour, and Irina Sille. I want to especially thank Didier Ruedin, Robin Stünzi and Christelle Maire who helped me to prepare my proposal for the grant.

I want to express my thanks to my sister, my parents, and my friends in Lausanne, Neuchâtel, Frankfurt, Bochum, and elsewhere. Last but not least, my personal gratitude to my wife for her attentive and insightful rereading of the manuscript. You are wonderful; you give me strength, faith, and hope.

Florian Tissot
September 2018

Abstract

This study analyses the division between the labour force work and the care work of couples of highly-skilled migrants settling in either the Lake Geneva region (Switzerland) and the Frankfurt Rhine-Main region (Germany). It combines Migration studies and Expatriation studies and adopts a critical and innovative theoretical framework. In order to develop such a framework, it does not only stress the "methodological individualism" and the "methodological nationalism" but also introduces the "methodological economism" to deconstruct an essentialised distinction between migration and mobility. Drawing on this framework and based on 36 qualitative semi-directive interviews with highly-skilled migrants and 8 problem centred interviews with key-informants, the current study deals with the construction of gendered hierarchies between partners who are repeatedly on the move for professional reasons. It shows various ways of settling in a new region after a relocation that I subsume under the concept of "doing family on the move". Specifically, the analysis reveals a form of settling which readily implies the possibility of a next move: a "motile" settling. This form of settling has serious consequences on the capacity of the partners to coordinate two professional careers. Through an analysis of the decision to move, the discourse about one's family and the strategies concerning mobility, the empirical part shows the gendered consequences of "motility". These consequences are articulated in a "mutually exclusive model" deepening the understanding of gendered hierarchies in career achievement, in the context of highly-skilled migration. While the male partners operate three parallel elements: an upward professional career, a family-life implying child(ren), and maintaining their availability to further unplanned relocations; the female partners can only coordinate two of these concurrently. This inequality exists in the way the partners divide the work between the labour force and the care work; as the male partners combine the three elements by extensively taking advantage of specific, and mostly invisible, care work that the female partner provides. This care work does not only include caregiving and housework but also what I call the "homemaking"; that is to recreate the necessary conditions for a family-life after a relocation. Furthermore, the study shows that the couples managing to maintain two professional careers while being on the move actively mobilise local childcare provision. Based on these empirical results, the conclusion of the study proposes practical recommendations to increase the capacity of highly-skilled migrants to coordinate both their professional and family-life.

List of Figures

List of Tables

1 Introduction

This study asks the question how highly-skilled migrants cope with professional careers on the one hand and family life on the other. To answer to this question, I conducted 36 interviews with highly-skilled migrants and seven other interviews with key informants in the Lake Geneva region, Switzerland, and the Frankfurt Rhine-Main region, Germany. The main finding resulting from the interviews is that highly-skilled migration has specific constraints, which are currently not assessed in the scientific literature. It is neither a "free movement in a flat world" (D'Andrea, Ciolfi, and Gray 2011, 150) nor a "frictionless mobility", but a mobility whose constraints are differently tracked (Favell 2014, 135). When at least one of the partners is mobile for professional reasons, I argue these constraints emerge for the other partner, as a consequence from the mobility of the former. By identifying which partner initiates a move, I developed a framework structured around two types of mover: the "primary-mover" (who takes the initiative of relocating) and the "secondary-mover" (who reacts to it). Through this model, I show not only that the female partners are more often the "secondary-movers", but also that the "secondary-movers" face unique challenges after a migration. This distinction is a useful tool to understand better the emergence of gendered gaps in achievement and wage. The experience of highly-skilled migration differs between men and women when it comes to combine (1) family life, (2) upward professional career, and (3) mobility (or, more precisely and as we shall see, "motility" (Kaufmann, Bergman, and Joye 2004; Flamm and Kaufmann 2006), which is the capacity to be mobile). While men can have them all, women can only have two of them simultaneously. It is the central insight of this study: to consider the construction of gender inequalities and gender hierarchies not only *per se* but through a mutually exclusive model.

To come to this result, I examine the decision and the consequences of the partners' (multiple) move(s) on their distribution of responsibilities between care work and work in the labour force, using the approach of "doing family" (Jurczyk, Lange, and Thiessen 2014; Baldassar et al. 2014). "Doing Family" is an approach which analyses the practical production and organisation of personal and affective relationships between the members of a family. This implies looking at the ways the partners divide the care work and the work in the labour force and the relationships of interdependencies linking different generations; relationships involved in care work such as emotional work or housework. According to this approach, families are (re)constructed and performed daily by their members in relation and in reaction to their environment, incorporating the social resources available, such as kindergarten.

As I will speak a great deal about families, couples, and skills in this work, it is useful to propose starting definitions of these terms which I can work on. These definitions are temporary; I shall refine and deepen them further in this work. I refer to highly-skilled migrants to underline either a tertiary educational achievement or a position in the labour force requiring it. Furthermore, what distinguishes a family from a couple are the intergenerational linkages between certain members and the relation of dependency between them. Thus, a family usually assumes the presence of children, implying care work. It raises acute questions of organisation in a mobile context. A couple does not imply the presence of children, but still implies coordination between the partners and care work, such as housework. The present study deals with the families and the couples of highly-skilled migrants adopting the approach of "doing family". For families and for couples, I pay special attention to the relationships between the partners and the different constraints which hinder and/or favour their mobility.

1.1 Relevance of the Study

Research in the field of highly-skilled migration often overlooks the link between mobility for professional reasons and family relationships. This study analyses this gap in the scientific literature. King et al. (2006), Kofman et Raghuram (2005), Lutz and Amelina (2017), Stark and Bloom (1985), and Riaño (2012) all underline the importance of researching on the family while studying migration. Taking the family into account requires embedding "social relations between individuals in kinship groups (e.g. families) [and] households" (Faist 2010, 60) into the study of migration. Such an inclusive perspective allows the study to shed light on a range of topics central to understanding the dynamics of migration. Thus, the way the partners develop specific "family-strategies" (Känsälä, Mäkelä, and Suutari 2014; Ryan et al. 2009; Shinozaki 2014), the way they perceive, present and display their family (Davoine et al. 2013; Finch 2007), and the way they prioritise, for instance, one professional career over the other (Liversage 2009; Meares 2010), acknowledge the centrality of family in order to understand the dynamics of highly-skilled migration. In fact, except for these studies and a few others (Bonnet, Collet, and Maurines 2011; Cooke 2008; Favell 2008; Iredale 2005; Kõu et al. 2015; Levitan, Zittoun, and Cangià 2018; Riaño et al. 2015; Wilding and Baldassar 2009), little is known about the ways highly-skilled migrants divide the work between the labour force and care work. Too little is known about the impact of repeated relocations on the capacity of the partners to maintain two professional careers. Equally too little is known about the development of gendered discrepancies during the "second period of life" (Kohli 1989, 2)[1] of highly-skilled migrants. The development of the "gender wage gap" (Blau and Kahn 2017; Schmid 2016) and the relationship between "gender and career outcomes" (Reskin and Bielby 2005) are quite well understood in a "sedentary" context, but there is still a lack of knowledge when it comes to understanding them in the context of highly-skilled migration. That is why some migration scholars call for "opening the black box of the family" (King et al. 2006, 254), while others ask to "go beyond the workplace" (Kofman and Raghuram 2005), in order to better understand in what the experience of highly-skilled migration differs between men and women. My work responds to these proposals. I show the heterogeneity of "family-strategies" that highly-skilled migrants develop while being abroad. By this I stress the challenges that mobility and "motility" raise while dealing simultaneously and collectively with mobile professional career(s) and care work.

To assess the relationship between highly-skilled migration, professional career(s), and care work, I bridge two fields of study, migration studies and expatriation studies. On the one hand, migration studies produce research on "transnational families" (Baldassar et al. 2014; Baldassar and Merla 2014, 2013; Bryceson and Vuorela 2002; Cieslik 2012; Kilkey and Palenga-Möllenbeck 2016; Reynolds et al. 2010; Ryan et al. 2009), though barely focusing on highly-skilled migration. On the other hand, research developing knowledge on highly-skilled migration barely focuses on the family (Blitz 2010; Boeri 2012; Chaloff and Lemaître 2009; Lavenex 2007). The bulk of studies dealing with highly-skilled migration do not contextualise the family as they mostly tackle the professional activity of the migrants (i.e. his or her inclusion in the labour force) (Chiswick 2011) or they produce large comparative analyses of migration policies (Mahroum 2001; Triadafilopoulos 2013). In the same vein, researchers in expatriation studies focus on professional mobility and the reasons for expatriation within multinational companies (Avril and Magnini 2007; Azar 2012; Bartlett and Ghoshal 1999; Ietto-Gillies 2012; Millar and Salt 2008; Salt and Wood 2012b, 2012a). While some studies focus on family and partnership, they specifically focus on expatriation (Black

---

1 For Kohli (1989) the life course is a social institution. He distinguishes three periods of life: the period of training, the period of activity, and the period of retirement. Each period corresponds to a specific set of welfare social protection, respectively and in broad outline education, unemployment insurances, and pensions.

and Gregersen 1991; Briody and Chrisman 1991; Lauring and Selmer 2010; Mäkelä, Känsälä, and Suutari 2011). Doing so, they leave aside cases which are not technically expatriation but very close to it. Cases of foreign employees of multinational company who decide to stay where they live are left aside, while their colleagues relocating on a regular basis are central to these analyses. The two employees of this example see each other every day and work together but refer to different fields of academic research. When scholars in expatriation studies consider these liminal cases, they use a terminology which hinders a discussion with migration studies (or is it the other way around?). The concept of "self-initiated expatriate" is, for instance, very close to the one of "highly-skilled migrant", but strangely, except in a few recent studies (Davoine et al. 2013; Joy, Game, and Toshniwal 2018), nearly no one, to the best of my knowledge, combines the strengths of the two disciplines (of migration and expatriation). It is therefore timely to begin this discussion and, another objective of my work, to build bridges between them. Bringing together sociology and management is a fruitful approach that has existed for some time. In 1960, Smith published an article called "Sociology and Management Studies" (Smith 1960). But bringing together expatriation studies and migration studies is innovative, as I am unaware of studies that explicitly combines them together. Thus, my study aims to understand the nexus of expatriation and highly-skilled migration in a single frame.

Furthermore, many private consultancy groups and international organisations produce, in the wake of management studies, reports which underline the gender gap in multinational companies (Johnson 2017), and stress the discrepancies between men and women in composition of the management boards (Shilling 2017), thus calling for a better understanding of the main factors leading to gender inequalities in the labour market (Hausmann, Tyson, and Zahidi 2009). All these studies could benefit from a sociological perspective explicitly studying the relationship between labour force work and care work in the context of highly-skilled migration, for researchers show that understanding the "gender wage gap" without acknowledging the arrival of the first child, for instance, overlooks the central factors that explain it (Kleven, Landais, and Søgaard 2018). My thesis tackles the dialectic relationship between care work and work in the labour force and offers deeper insights on the reasons leading to the discrepancies between men and women in the context of highly-skilled migration.

Thus, in the context of highly-skilled migration I focus on the ways the partners reconcile private and professional lives. The incentive of being mobile in highly-skilled careers is increasingly present in almost every professional field. This incentive combined with the rise of the overall qualifications of the workforce leads to an inflation of highly-qualified individuals moving for professional reasons. Conjointly, the political liberalisation of mobility in Europe renders highly-skilled migration smoother on the legal level. However it is, I argue, certainly not frictionless as other challenges emerge. Therefore, it is central to understand the dynamics surrounding highly-skilled migration as they become a frequent experience of contemporary life. The sociological approach invites us to focus on the social and family consequences of mobility and migration. It suggests questioning the power relations within families as well as the external support they receive and the environment they live in. This study pushes forward the scientific knowledge around this topic with an approach using the key concept of "initiator of a relocation", initially used to differentiate several forms of expatriation. Expatriation studies distinguish the "assigned expatriate" from the "(intra or inter) self-initiated expatriate" and the "drawn expatriate" (Al Ariss 2010; Andresen, Biemann, and Pattie 2015; Biemann and Andresen 2010; Cerdin and Selmer 2014; Suutari and Brewster 2001); showing the differences between a move initiated by the migrant, the employing company or a competing business. I develop further this distinction from a sociological perspective acknowledging the family and the couple, distinguishing the "partner-initiated mover" and the "partner-coordinated mover" (6.3 *Conceptualising the Professional Careers Coordination*, 125). These types underline the various ways the "secondary-movers" react to the migration of the "primary-movers". Doing so, I am able to tackle contemporary issues which still remain out of the scope of the scientific literature as they lie between migration studies and expatriation studies, so to speak.

Studying family and highly-skilled migration also helps to understand why the "secondary-movers" – most often the female partner – give up their professional career. It is a central concern because people, who are out of the workforce increasingly risk precariousness; especially migrants. They are less likely to have access to the same social welfare protection systems. Frequent professional mobility is challenging for families and divorces are not rare. Divorce and separation rates are apparently not higher amongst highly-skilled migrants but their social consequences are much more complicated (McNulty 2015). Therefore, it is essential to comprehend under what conditions one career is prioritised while the other is subordinated or even sacrificed, in order to develop policies which can counteract these effects when one partner loses her (or his) financial independence. I develop a better understanding of the process of subordinating or sacrificing one's career – this is also a grey-zone in scientific literature. For it is important to take into account in more depth the role of gender within the negotiation processes of mobility and settling. Besides, this may make it possible to prevent one central aspect of the shortage of skilled manpower, as a result of women giving up their careers. Certainly, there are other factors contributing to the shortage of skilled manpower in Europe, but – to some extent – improving the access to the labour market of female highly-skilled migrants, who are already in place, is one step forward to diminish the shortage and to use the available potential. This is not only a central topic for Switzerland and Germany which is strongly dependent on foreign (skilled) workforce, but also for other European states.

1.2 Structure of the Study

The present study is structured around four main parts: the theoretical, the methodological, the empirical, and the discussion parts. The two first parts are divided into two chapters each. The theoretical part deals with the review of the literature (Chapter 2) and the theoretical framework (Chapter 3). The methodological part outlines the research design (Chapter 4) and provides a contextualisation of the conditions of production for the study (Chapter 5). The empirical part focuses on three facets of "doing family": the consequence of a migration for professional reasons (Chapter 6), the narratives portraying family (Chapter 7), and the "family-strategies" (Chapter 8). The first chapter of the discussion part stresses the theoretical and empirical insights of this study (Chapter 9), while in the second I gives recommendations for practice (Chapter 10).

The theoretical part starts with the chapter presenting current thinking and debate (Chapter 2). The goal is not only to present the relevant literature, but also to develop a conceptualisation of highly-skilled migration, which I will rely on for the rest of my study. I show how the conceptualisation of highly-skilled migration, which starts by acknowledging specific patterns corresponding to migrants with a tertiary education, ends up creating a world view (*Weltanschauung*) which encompasses unquestioned assumptions. As such it is not problematic to differentiate a highly-skilled migration from a lower-skilled migration, as "thinking is comparing". The problem lies more on a set of unquestioned assumptions, which allegedly contribute to the differentiation between highly-skilled and lower-skilled migrants: the notion of skill becomes a proxy to import other forms of categorisation. The review of the literature stresses that highly-skilled migration studies and expatriation studies develop binaries opposing these unquestioned assumptions: economic versus social, temporary adaptation versus permanent integration, frictionless mobility versus controlled migration, productive versus reproductive, us versus them, and, ultimately, male versus female. I will refer to these binaries as the "migration binaries" (King 2002, 91) and the "gender binaries". These two binaries are the main theoretical insights of the review of the literature. They lead to my critic of some studies (though not all) and I shall show studies which reflect on these assumptions.

The second chapter of the theoretical part (Chapter 3) develops the theoretical framework itself: I propose a "decentred approach" based on the ideas of Derrida (1978). I present three "methodological premises" and show the biases each of them could entail, if they are not reflexively conceptualised. These three "methodological premises" are the "methodological individualism" (Mises 1999 [1949]), the "methodological nationalism" (Amelina et al. 2012; Amelina and Faist 2012; Chernilo 2006; Wimmer and Glick Schiller 2002, 2003), and the "methodological economism". The "methodological individualism" warns against the risk of conceptualising the migrants as individuals outside the social context they live in, pleading for a collective and dynamic approach of "doing family". The "methodological nationalism" refers to the risk of ignoring or naturalising the nation states, that is, through conceptualisation either forgetting the nation states or overemphasising the link between a territory, a state, and a culture. I stress how a method based on the "cities as entry point" (Glick Schiller and Çağlar 2010) can overcome this. These two first premises are already known and conceptualised in the literature. I propose a third one, the "methodological economism", to complement them. Through the term of "methodological economism", I stress the risk of opposing a "frictionless mobility" and a "controlled migration" (Favell 2014, 135). The former implies a "temporary adaptation" and the latter a "permanent integration". Such a conceptualisation fails to acknowledge various forms of "(im)mobilities after migration" (Wieczorek 2018).

The methodological and contextual part corresponds respectively to chapters 4 and 5. Based on the three "methodological premises", I show the research design in chapter 4 in which I emphasise my methods and the concrete way I construct this study. I review chronologically the whole process of creating the present study.; explaining how I accessed the field, what kind of interviews I carried out, who I interviewed, and how I analysed the transcripts of the interviews. In chapter 5, I propose an in-depth contextualisation of the study, that is situating the position of the researcher in the study and contextualising the two regions where the study takes place. As we shall see, chapter 5 is central in overcoming the "methodological nationalism" by acknowledging the nation-states without naturalising them.

The empirical part focuses on "doing family" and is composed of three chapters. The first chapter (Chapter 6) deals with the coordination of two professional careers abroad. I develop a "collective approach" acknowledging the specific situation of both partners after a migration. Through this model I establish the types of the "primary-mover" (giving the initiative for the move) and the "secondary-mover" (reacting to the move), each partner facing specific challenges. I show the negotiations between the partners and their impact on their daily lives and their professional careers. While the challenges that the "primary-mover" faces are quite well-known in the literature, as it refers to the whole literature of the "adjustment of expatriates" after a relocation; the challenges that the "secondary-mover" faces are understudied, except a few exceptions (I dedicate a section in the review of the literature on studies dealing with the adjustment of the accompanying partner). Thus, the second part of the chapter focuses on the different reactions that a "secondary-mover" may adopt after the "primary-mover" takes the decision to migrate. I especially focus on the factors that favour or hinder the inclusion of a "secondary-mover" in the labour force. Doing so, I present several types of moves corresponding to different types of reactions given by the "secondary-mover".

In chapter 7, I analyse the discourses of the respondents when it comes to "display their family" (Finch 2007) and show two narrative stances shaping how the partners divide the care work and the labour force work. Chapter 7 deals with the representations and the discourses of the respondents whereas the chapter 6 focuses on the practices and the decision-making process. If one wants to understand the process of "doing family" in depth, it is central to study the two of them. "Doing family" is not only about how the partners, for instance, divide the care work daily but also how they portray it. In this context, the concept of "motility" is key to understand why some partners develop a traditional and heteronormative organisation of the family while others are able to maintain a more equal division of the household tasks and care work. While displaying their family, some respondents stress the importance of being "motile", prioritising their professional career and its importance for the well-being of the family. Others underline the necessity to develop arrangement in which they can both have a position in the labour force, implying reduced availability to further migration. In other words, the ones developing a "motile" narrative stance usually follow a traditional model of the family which contrasts with those developing an anchored narrative stance. Furthermore, I show a discrepancy between the narratives and the practices, implying that the model of the traditional family, even though practiced, is not completely acknowledged by many of the respondents.

The last empirical chapter (Chapter 8) combines the insights of the two previous chapters of the empirical part to propose three types of "family-strategy". These three types are the main empirical insight of my work. I distinguish the "motile family-strategy", the "local family-strategy", and the "mobile family-strategy". I underline that these forms of "family-strategy" are flexible and can change or switch during the life course of the respondents. Each form of "family-strategy" corresponds to a specific way of "doing family" on the move. It is through these three forms of "family-strategy" that I stress the development of a "mutually exclusive model" of gender inequalities. I distinguish three elements which form the model: the capacity of the partners to raise children, the capacity to be mobile, and the capacity to maintain a dual career partnership. Each strategy favours only two of the three elements. I did not witness any empirical case in which the partners manage to combine all three simultaneously. Briefly, the "motile family-strategy" favours the "motility" and the children but not the dual career. Here only the male partners (as they are in most of the cases the "primary-movers") can have the three elements simultaneously because the female partners (the "secondary-movers") do the bulk of the care work. Collectively, the partners do not develop a dual-couple career, which enables the male partner to have a successful professional career. In fact, it is in the case of the "motile family-strategy" that I notice the most successful careers in terms of advancement in a company. Following this strategy, the "primary-movers" can reach the highest position in the company as they can focus solely on their professional career. The "local family-strategy" favours the children and the dual career couple at the expense of "motility". It corresponds to a controlled narrative stance towards "motility". The partners prefer to maintain their current position in the labour force, as they are both employed. This process happens at the expense of being ready and willing to take advantage of another opportunity abroad, which hinders their capacity to advance in their career. The partners tend to stay middle managers in their company, yet they are both employed in the labour force. The last type is the "mobile family-strategy" which favours "motility" and dual-couple career but at the expense of the children. The partners continue to work in the labour force and coordinate their family life through mobility; emphasising the type of the split-families. It is a type of "family-strategy" common at the beginning of the professional careers of the partners as they (still) do not have children.

I discuss in depth these results in the last part of my work: the discussion part. In Chapter 9, I propose a summary of the main theoretical and empirical insights, by answering the research questions and proposing implications for further studies. In Chapter 10, I give some recommendations for practice focusing on three aspects: the partners, the "local policies", and the employing companies.

I have shown in this introduction that more knowledge in the fields of highly-skilled migration and expatriation is needed as there is still a lack of understanding of the processes influencing family life and professional careers while migrating. Thus, my work raises the question: How do couples of highly-skilled migrants cope with professional careers on the one hand and family life on the other?

Theoretical Part

2 Moving with Skills: A Review of the Literature

In this chapter, I will present a state of the art on highly-skilled migration and expatriation, focusing on studies that tackle these topics from a gendered perspective. First, I will specify which facets of the literature I will review by setting out my temporal and conceptual limitations. Second, I will explain the concept of "polarisation of migration" to introduce how scholars become aware of the kind of human mobility which does not fit within "*normalfall* migration theories" (Bade and Oltmer 2004). I will present the "neoclassical theory of migration flows" and the "dual labour market theory" and will argue that both conceptualise the "polarisation of migration" through a binary of "high/low skill migration". Here, I will develop the "migrations binaries". Third, I will turn to a review of "expatriation studies", showing how they overcome an approach focusing only on the professional activity of the expatriate to take into consideration the family and the cultural context of a relocation abroad. Nevertheless, this strand of studies struggles with the conception of the family; I will thus argue that "expatriate studies" create a "polarisation of migration", too. This polarisation is of another kind, however, opposing a "male breadwinner" and a "female trailing spouse"; through this model, I will develop the notion of "gender binaries". Fourth, I will link the research on expatriation and highly-skilled migration with studies on gender and highly-skilled migration. I will show how some scholars overcome simple conceptualisations of "migrant families" and propose to analyse "family strategies" and the "transnational family".

2.1 Historical Overview

Research on highly-skilled migration is relatively recent, beginning only after the Second World War. The development of this field of study corresponds to three historical periods. Chronologically, the first period coincides with sporadic studies, from the 1930s to the end of 1940s. Blitz refers to "an early period, characterized by spontaneous and personal movements and motivated primarily by negative push factors as a result of international and intrastate conflict and foreign occupation" (2010, 3293).

This "early period" of highly-skilled migration is characterised by a small number of individuals (intellectuals, scientists, engineers) who were mostly

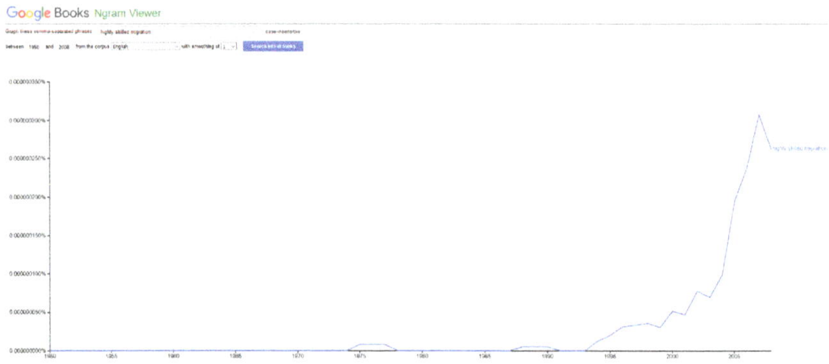

Figure 1 Frequency of the Term "Highly-Skilled Migration", between 1960 and 2008, in the Library of GoogleBooks. Source: Google Books Ngram Viewer (https://books.google.com/ngrams)

refugees fleeing Nazi Germany or the Soviet Union. Personalities such as Theodor W. Adorno or Stephan Zweig are well-known examples.

The second period tallies with the "*Trente Glorieuses*" (Fourastié 1979) and corresponds to "an industrial period, during which limited movements and state sponsored recruitment campaigns reflects the needs of growing industrial populations and state policies" (Blitz 2010, 3293). The "industrial period" is emblematic of the "brain-drain": it involved individuals coming mostly from low-income countries who had studied abroad and were hired within the industrialised "West". During this period, scholars began to conceptualise highly-skilled migration as a factor to foster growth. In Western Europe, the experience of brain drain was also one of European scientists and/or engineers leaving for the United States (Chorafas and Herbette 1969). These dynamics still exist today; yet they are characteristic of what Blitz, taking the example of the Indian doctor working in the British National Health Service, called the "industrial period" (2010, 3294). During the industrial period, migration flows were structured mostly by *bilateral* agreements between states.

The "global period" (Blitz 2010, 3293) started with the oil crises in 1973 and continues today: indeed, interest in highly-skilled migration is growing exponentially. There is an impressive extension of the literature dealing with highly-skilled migration between 1960 and 2008, as we can see with the example of *Google Books* (Figure 1). The "global period" concurs with structural and geo-political earthquakes such as the end of full employment in Western economies, the World Trade Organisation agreements, or the development of the European Union. New technologies of information and communication as well as a decrease in the costs of transportation have favoured a "globalised economy", in which multinational corporations, financial institutions, and non-governmental associations are the champions[2]. In terms of migration policies, the passage between the "industrial period" and the "global period" is a passage from bilateral agreements between states to multilateral agreements. The Schengen Zone in Europe is an example of such a multilateral agreement.

In these three periods, we see a qualitative and quantitative evolution of highly-skilled migration that has in turn inspired new approaches to studying this phenomenon. I will now focus on the third period, thus narrowing the scope of my literature review. Admittedly, this temporal distinction is somewhat arbitrary, since the circulation of elites existed long before the term "highly-skilled migration" was coined. Indeed, historians warn us against seeing the second half of the twentieth century as the only one to have witnessed highly-skilled migration (Braudel 1979; Green 2008); what we define today as highly-skilled migration is not a new phenomenon. Bankers, merchants, and intellectuals did not wait until the late twentieth century to move for work. For example, during the second half of the nineteenth century, a large share of the professors working at the Swiss Federal Institute of Technology in Zurich came from Germany, showing an early form of brain-drain (Urner 1976; Gugerli, Kupper, and Speich 2010). However, I focus on the literature published during the "global period" (Blitz 2010) of highly-skilled migration studies. Without such a restriction, there would simply be too much to cover. And yet even within these parameters, there is still too much material. Therefore, I also propose a second limitation—this time, a conceptual one.

2.2 Conceptual Overview

Koser and Salt (1997, 287) suggest that the interplay between three concepts – the migrant, the state, and the employer – structure the field of highly-skilled migration studies. The three concepts represent the three underlying perspectives of highly-skilled migration studies: a key to ordering this scientific field.

2.2.1 State

Some studies focus on highly-skilled migration from the "perspective of the state", analysing the "competition state" (Lavenex 2007) or the dynamics of

2 For an outline of the consequences of "globalisation", see Giddens (2009).

"brain drain" and "brain gain" (Boeri 2012). They shed light on the relationship between states[3] and highly-skilled migration. The structure of the labour force in the "global North" (Cochrane 2006; Söderström, Dupuis, and Leu 2013) is changing. In this context, politicians and policy makers recognise an increased demand for skilled workers. The attraction of skilled immigrants became and remains a strong trend of migration policies. Chiswick et al. (2011), for instance, analyse the different high-skill migration policies attempting to counteract the shortage of skilled workers in the "global North". This field thus develops international comparisons of the different state policies to attract highly-skilled migrants (Triadafilopoulos 2013). International organisations, such as the Organisation for Economic Co-operation and Development (OECD), produce knowledge from this perspective, too. By comparing migration policies, Chaloff and Lemaître (2009) show the relevance of language and active recruitment in attracting highly-skilled migrants. Most of these studies analyse highly-skilled migration from a 'stated perspective', using quantitative data in order to assess the effectiveness of various policies (Palmer and Pytlikova 2013) in 'attracting and retaining' highly skilled migrants.

2.2.2 Employer

Other studies focus instead on "the perspective of the employer", highlighting how multinational corporations (MNCs) deal with the mobility of their staff between their subsidiaries. In this context, managing staff internationally is part of a broader strategy to develop MNCs abroad. Other factors include the creation of a corporate culture or the rationalisation of production processes (Ietto-Gillies 2012). The new competitive environment, however, requires a modification in the ways companies are managed; Bartlett and Ghoshal (1999) offer a famous insight on the ways to transnationally manage a company in an international environment. Research in management studies or organisational sociology examine the internal organisation of MNCs (Eckert and Mayrhofer 2005; Hashai and Almor 2004; Johanson and Vahlne 1977). These studies question the internationalisation of MNCs, which have become border-spanning, employing thousands of people around the world.

For MNCs, human mobility – here mostly in form of expatriation – is a factor in implementing management strategies internationally. Thus, the literature deals with the role of intra-firm transfers. The main questions are: "Should we practice

---

3 It is always inconvenient to speak of the state as such, as if a state was a clearly defined entity.

intra-firm transfers at all given their cost?" and "What are the best "profiles" to be sent abroad?" Such research develops a utilitarian vision of expatriation. It focuses *stricto sensu* on MNC's mobile employees and managers within the realm of their professional activity. Examples of these studies would be the works of Salt and Wood (Salt and Wood 2012a, 2012b) and Miller and Salt (2008)[4] as they focus on "global staffing" – that is, intra-company transfers – and introduce "portfolios of mobility" to conceptualise the strategic use of mobility to fulfil different tasks within a MNC, such as "knowledge-transfer". Similarly, Harzing conceptualises the roles of expatriates in controlling foreign subsidiaries through three analogies: "Bears [to control and impose dominance] … bumble-bees [to] … create cross-pollination between the various off-shoots, [and] … spiders [to weave] … information communication networks" (2002, 6–8). This literature deals with expatriates *at work*. At the same time, it becomes clear that studies focusing solely on expatriate at work is insufficient. Scott notes that "[b]efore open system ideas, organizational scholars had concentrated on actors (workers, work groups, managers) and processes (motivation, cohesion, control) within organizations. Scant attention was accorded to the environment within which the organization operated" (2004, 5). He suggests a broader contextualisation to assess highly-skilled migration and expatriation. Expatriation as a "total phenomenon" produces the modification of one's life as a whole. Therefore, understanding expatriates at work implies embedding expatriation in the broader social context in which it occurs: it is not just a question of work, but also, for example, of families or couples.

2.2.3 Migrants, Families, and Couples

The third key to enter the field is the daily life of the migrants themselves. Mostly, this key refers to micro sociological studies dealing with the practices and representations of highly-skilled migrants, drawing on an emic perspective. In section 2.3, I will present studies dealing with highly-skilled migration. These studies propose theories and typologies assessing highly-skilled migration from the perspective of the migrants. But that is not all; as my work focuses specifically on highly-skilled migration and families/couples, I shall present studies crossing those two groups in sections 2.4 and 2.5. At the beginning of the introduction, I have already remarked a distinction between families and couples. I underlined the intergenerational nature of a family to

---

4 For a review of the literature on the topic see Collings, Scullion, and Dowling (2009).

distinguish it from a couple. To put it bluntly, a family implies children and the care work required to raise them (for a discussion of the notions of family and couple as well as my approach to them, see chapter 3.2 Methodological Individualism, 73). Thus, sections 2.3, 2.4, and 2.5 review studies based on the migrant – compared to the state and the employer – as they analyse the ways in which migrants as social actors deal with their environments, negotiate with their partners, and make decisions regarding the division of care work and work in the labour force.

2.3 Highly-Skilled Migration Studies

In this section, I argue that a "polarisation of migration" supports the establishment of highly-skilled migration studies. The ways to order, rearrange, and interpret scientific theories are numerous; yet a polarisation stresses the specificity of highly-skilled migration compared to other types of migration, I argue. A polarisation means the "division into two sharply contrasting groups or sets of opinions or beliefs" (OED 2018). My discussion primarily concerns "migration binaries" (King 2012b), which maintain an oversimplified categorisation of the topic. Favell (2014), for instance, criticises categories presupposing a fluid elite on the one hand as opposed to the "*Normalfall*" ethnic migration from places such as Africa and Asia on the other. Thus, critics like Bauman (2013) argue that such a polarisation implies different types of migration reflecting each other in a mirror image game (e.g., the expatriate and the refugee). This section subsequently explicates the roles of the many migration binaries, such as "high/low skill migration" or "professional/ethnic migration", in the construction of the field of highly-skilled migration studies. In the subsections that follow, I will argue that such a polarisation is present through two different processes.

2.3.1 Dichotomising Migration

I understand the expression "dichotomising migration" as referring to a group of studies that explicitly opposes two groups of people. I illustrate this process with two theories, namely, the neoclassical theory and the dual labour market theory. I argue that they both share a polarised vision of migration. While the neoclassical theory distinguishes between two patterns of migration which do not work under the same conditions, the dual labour market theory insists on a primary and a secondary job sector. In these examples, "polarising migration" happens through *dichotomising* migration, explicitly through creating frames.

a. Neoclassical Theory of Migration Flows

The neoclassical theory focuses on the economic aspects of migration, explaining them through a *macro* and a *micro* approach. At the beginning of the 1980s, it was the preponderant theory exploring the causes of migration and explaining the flow of international migrants. The neoclassical theory is also known as the "push/pull" theory.

For the *macro* approach, the labour markets are the main mechanisms to explain migration, as the economic differential between two spaces creates a migration flow. The economic differential establishes incentives to migrate from one space to another, ending once an equilibrium is reached between the two spaces. The macro approach proposes a model of economic development beneficial to all. The economic gap between spaces is supposed to decrease through "convergence" (Lewis 1954) because the "economic development" of the "poorest regions" will catch up with the "richest ones" through a phenomenon known as the "trickle-down effect". This theory's ideological standpoints are at the core of globalisation processes and do not focus on highly-skilled migration specifically. Its application is quantitative and its scope reflects needs to understand global economic modifications and how to justify them. The increase in international trade as well as the development of "global commodity chains" (Giddens 2009, 134) need standardisation and international norms. Thus, this theory manifests a technical imperative: the requirement of a commonly accepted framework which posits that globalisation benefits everyone[5]. Negotiating and legitimizing free-trade agreements requires a theory accepted by the different states in negotiation – a theory which justifies the neo-liberal political agenda. It is the theory of "the dominant", and in turn, "the dominant theory".

For the *micro* approach, the theory questions the motivation to migrate by conceptualising the expected outcome of migration (Todaro 1969; Harris and Todaro 1970). The migrant is perceived as a *homo economicus*[6] who valorises his or her own its human capital in an optimal way. S/he plays with the differential between spaces and moves for an expected superior wage. The migrant expects to maximise his or her utility, emphasized by the concept of "subjective expected utility model". When it comes to deciding whether or not to migrate,

---

5 The general agreement on trade and services (GATS) is an example and a consequence of this need.

6 Heterodox economists extensively criticise the way the orthodox model of economics conceptualises the individual as a rational and omniscient actor (Eymard-Duvernay 2006).

the micro approach underlines that highly-skilled migrants do a specific cost-benefit calculation because they possess a scarce human capital. As Massey et al. put it: "International flows of human capital – that is, highly skilled workers – respond to differences in the rate of return to human capital, which may be different from the overall wage rate, yielding a distinct pattern of migration that may be *opposite*[7] that of unskilled workers" (1993, 434). Scholars thus define a specific pattern of migration, accordingly highly-skilled migration. The neoclassical theory conceptualises two opposite groups, thereby drawing on the idea of a "polarisation of migration" alongside "high/low skill migration".

b. Dual Labour Market Theory

In contrast to the neoclassical theory, the dual labour market theory (DLMT) (Piore 1979; Berger and Piore 1980) explores the impact of globalisation from a critical perspective. For Berger and Piore (1980), migration is one of the structural modifications of "Western economies". They contest the neoclassical theory because, for them, migration is ultimately driven by "pull factors": international migration flows arise from "cheap labour" in the "Western economies". In other words, this theory offers a critical perspective on globalisation and gives another interpretation of migration. This interpretation leads Berger and Piore to describe a group called "the dominants" and to explain how they maintain their position. To put it figuratively, they claim to analyse the shape of the box – in other words, the so-called system and the ways in which "the dominants" carve it. Yet the DLMT implies a polarisation of migration by dichotomising it, too.

The DLMT considers the labour market within "Western economies" as being divided into a primary and a secondary sector[8]. The primary sector involves capital and offers well-paying jobs, providing positions for the "autochthone". The social security of the welfare state protects the primary sector. In sum, the primary sector offers income and protection. On the contrary, the secondary sector provides low-paying, unstable positions at the low end of the labour market to migrants. According to this model, migrants predominantly take the dirty, dangerous, and demanding jobs (the "3Ds" jobs) in the secondary sector. The

7 Own emphasis

8 The confusion is easy here and needs to be clarified. Classically, we speak of the third sector to refer to the service-oriented sector of the economy – compared to the secondary sector (the industry – manufactory work) and primary sector (the agriculture – farmland work), yet these three sectors are not the same as the two ones conceptualised within the dual labour market theory.

secondary sector provides jobs that no one (else) wants to do, but which fulfil crucial, unavoidable functions: "Jobs in the primary sector are largely reserved for natives, leading to a fundamental dichotomy between the jobs of migrants and the jobs of natives" (Morawska 2012, 58). In this context, highly-skilled migrants are outliers. They work in the primary sector, but they are migrants. They receive the income and the protection of the primary sector, the signs of financial and legal "inclusion" (Bommes 2012) as citizens of the "global North". And, highly-skilled migrants perform a trade or an occupation which is (at least) similar to the ones performed by the local population. Therefore, I argue, their status as migrants becomes invisible as they are incorporated, from a "Westerner's perspective", into an inclusive "us". To them, fluidity applies more than border-policing (Bauman 2013; Favell 2014). The DLMT, then, brings the question of inequality and power back to the core of the reflection on migration, opposing two seemingly homogeneous groups: "us vs. them".

The neoclassical theory and the DLMT both exemplify "dichotomising migration", the first process leading to the "polarisation of migration". We have seen how scholars describe highly-skilled migration in relation to other types of migration through two binaries: "high/low skill migration" and "us/them", introducing a polarisation through a dichotomy. However, I wish to distinguish a second process creating a "polarisation of migration". I call it "deepening migration".

2.3.2 Deepening Migration

In contrast to "dichotomising migration" (2.3.1), "deepening migration" focuses on highly-skilled migration as such, wherein the "polarisation of migration" is implicit. I will illustrate this point by pointing to the typologies of Iredale (2001) and Baruch et al. (2013) to refine the concept of highly-skilled migration. Both deal with the group they reify, thus leaving aside what they consider to be irrelevant. Certainly, one grand unified sociological theory able to consider everything is utopian and it is always easy to argue that some studies forget to focus on this or that, because saying something concrete simply implies making choices. Yet I use this critique as a tool to locate the blind spots in the literature; it helps to identify gaps.

a. Typologies of Highly-Skilled Migrants

The development of definitions and typologies is crucial work when scholars want to push forward a research agenda. It provides grounding concepts which help us to understand a complex phenomenon. Here, I focus on typologies which take up the broad conceptual base of the migrant, meaning they use the (professional) migrant her/himself as the unit of analysis. I have chosen to look at Iredale (2001) and Baruch et al. (2013) because they contain key elements to define highly-skilled migration. Iredale stresses factors leading to the "internationalisation of professions" (2001, 10), such as international agreements like the General Agreements on Trade in Services (GATS) or the "emergence of new skilled labour markets that are relatively free of national controls" (2001, 13). The "internationalisation of professions" requires new scientific tools, as the ones existing at that time were mostly focused on the nation states. Iredale therefore proposes five complementary typologies to enrich our understanding of highly-skilled migration and thus the mobility of professionals (2001, 16–20). She considers (1) the "motivation of migration" – is it forced or induced by policies designed to attract highly-skilled migrants?; (2) the countries of origin and arrival; (3) the "channel or mechanism" (she identifies three major channels: "the international labour market of MNCs, companies with international contracts that move staff to service their offshore work; and international recruitment agency"); (4) the length of the stay; and (5) the "mode of incorporation" (ibid). In so doing, she furnishes foundational concepts for the many studies that would come in the next twenty years. For Iredale, each typology corresponds to a particular "means of categorisation" (2001, 7), or to "ways of categorizing professional migrants" (2001, 16). Viewed together, the five typologies show that highly-skilled migration is inherently complex and diverse. These typologies are used theoretically to ground concepts such as the ones of self-initiated expatriates (2.4 Expatriation Studies, 43). They show the diversity of highly-skilled migration, thus paving the way for finer categorisations.

When it comes to "deepening migration", however, while the typologies of Iredale (2001) provide a thoughtful conceptualisation of highly-skilled migration taking into consideration factors outside the MNC, they remain "family neutral": they do not take into account the role of the family in shaping professional migration processes. In other words, Iredale's approach deepens our knowledge of highly-skilled migration *only* through the professional inclusion[9], as if the relevant topics in studying highly-skilled migration were restricted to professional migration. But since this is not the case, I propose that the typologies in fact hint at a migration binary: "work/family migration".

9 Truth to be told, four years later Iredale published an article that tackles gender (2005). Besides, the article of 2001 contains many references to gender discrimination. Yet, none of the six typologies deal with the dimension of the family.

The second typology focuses on different types of international career (Baruch et al. 2013). Though seven dimensions[10], Baruch et al. describe the twenty main patterns of international work. They show the heterogeneity of highly-skilled migration as it is diverse and encompasses many types of mobility including traditional corporate expatriation, short term assignments, globetrotting, virtual global employees, cross-border commuting, secondments overseas, and so on (Baruch et al. 2013, 2375). The research of Baruch et al. (2013) brings valuable insights for further empirical studies to the developing field of highly-skilled migration studies, as it refines the units of analysis.

Their typology exemplifies, however, another aspect of "deepening migration", in that they separate professional forms of mobility from "immigration", as if the two apply to different people. I argue that this categorisation implicitly opposes "international work" and "ethnic immigration". Two arguments illustrate my point. First, when we look at the table presenting the twenty main patterns of international work, the only two patterns which can be "illegal" are the two patterns labelled as "immigration" (namely "immigration – legal/illegal/asylum" and "temporary immigration" (Baruch et al. 2013, 2375). The 18 other types are "legal" or "legal; non-complex". From this perspective, highly-skilled migration is allegedly legal and frictionless, but essentially different from immigration. Second, their conception of the "cultural gap" reinforces the legal/illegal[11] distinction. Indeed, the two patterns containing the term "immigration" stress a high cultural gap for migrants coming "from 'the third world' to developed [sic.]" countries, although this gap is never described as "high" for other types of international work. Therefore, I argue that the patterns oppose the two groups. For highly-skilled migrants, race, ethnicity, and boarders do not apply, while they are deeply relevant to analysing "immigrants". Thus, the "polarisation of migration" by "deepening migration" is also about the perceived relevant analytical categories used to perform research. I propose that the typology of Baruch et al. (2013) contributes to developing a "migration binaries" present in many studies on highly-skilled migration structured along "economic/cultural migration".

10 The seven dimensions are the following: "Time exposure (short to very long-term foreign work)", "intensity of international contact (one to many cultures)", "breadth of interaction (predominantly work to holistic interaction)", "legal context (rights to stay/ work in country)", "predominant instigator (individual or organization-supported)", "cultural gap Job/role needs" (2013, 2375).

11 Strangely, the authors use the binary "legal/illegal" to ground their typology and not "regular/irregular" or "documented/undocumented". This choice is controversial as one could argue that no one is illegal; yet, someone can lack the "authorisation" to stay.

Nevertheless, Iredale (2001) and Baruch et al. (2013) improve our knowledge of highly-skilled migration. In sum, the two typologies map out a complex and multifaced social phenomenon. They place the foundation stones, and yet they fail to see that highly-skilled migration is also familial and cultural.

2.3.3 Intermediary Summary: Construction of a Polarisation I

In this section, I have presented theories and typologies dealing with highly-skilled migration. Despite the differences among these works, I argue that they all develop a "polarisation of migration", which refers to a specific interpretation of migratory phenomena, though four "migration binaries": namely (1) "high/low skill migration", (2) "us/them", (3) "work/family migration", and (4) "economic/cultural migration". As Favell (2014) suggests, the key to organising these binaries is an opposition between "a frictionless mobility [and] a controlled migration" (2014, 135). I will rely heavily on these "migration binaries" to develop the theoretical framework of this study. This interpretation introduces a sharp contrast between two groups: an economic, work-related, skilled, legally trouble-free group opposed to a cultural, non-work related, unskilled, potentially legally questionable group. Yet I argue that the polarisation of migration is part of a broader scientific process, moving from general to specific. The more numerous the studies, the more knowledge we have, and the more former all-encompassing categories are no longer sustainable – and then, the more further refinements are needed; an example of such a path would be in the evolution of terminology from expatriate, to self-initiated expatriate, to intra self-initiated expatriate (2.4 Expatriation Studies, 43). In a similar way, each new branch that grows adds complexity to a tree, but new branches can only grow out of existing branches.

After having critically assessed the underlying assumptions of studies dealing with highly-skilled migration, we can reverse the problem and see what these approaches may bring to the present study. Indeed, each single theory or typology brings its own insight. The neoclassical theory makes us aware of an important determinant in the motivations behind migration: the expected outcome. In other words, individuals inform themselves as they prepare to move, even though they may not have a perfect sense of what is going to happen. In this sense, professional migration is a question of income and career; this should not be overlooked. Then again, the dual labour market theory teaches us the "games of power" at play within contemporary societies: not all forms of migration are equal, because being mobile as such says nearly nothing about one's social position. It is biased to assume that highly-skilled migration concerns only a trouble-free, rich, elite class of businessmen. Hierarchies, inequalities, and social positions are still relevant when it comes to highly-skilled migration – another issue that is often overlooked. The typologies of Iredale (2001) and Baruch et al. (2013) provide first and foremost a relevant way to assess the empirical material by providing tools to categorise it. Indeed, the points these typologies raise are central to understanding highly-skilled migration – and so are those which are *not* raised. The blind-spots of these typologies deserve further exploration. In fact, the different theories and typologies discussed conceptualise vertical inequalities, like income, yet they do not have the tools to conceptualise "horizontal generator of inequalities (*Ungleichheitsgeneratoren*) [*i.e.*] gender, sexuality, age, ethnicity, nationality, and disability" (Lutz and Amelina 2017, 7) as well as "precarity" (Cangià 2018). In conclusion, these theories and typologies refine our analytical tools and, more importantly, open way to new questions, like: What about gender, ethnicity or age in the context of highly-skilled migration? What role do they play? Can some highly-skilled migrants be in a precarious situation?

2.4 Expatriation Studies

In this section, I will introduce the research on expatriation. I will use the same strategy again, presenting the major studies on the topic to critically assess their conclusions and to see what they can bring to the present study. I will make three points in this section. First, I will propose a definition of the term "expatriate", showing how such a definition emphasises the "us/them" binary. Second, I will define several other related terms such as "assigned expatriate" and "self-initiated expatriate"[12], arguing that they reinforce the "permanent/temporary" binary. Third, I will show how the private life of expatriates has come at the forefront of expatriate studies, by presenting two topics: the "cross-cultural adjustment" (Black, Mendenhall, and Oddou 1991) and the situation of the partner and the children in expatriation processes. Here, I will emphasise the opposition between "male breadwinner" and "female caregiver". Therefore, this section works as a bridge between studies which do not tackle the family and gender and the ones which do. Indeed, we will see how the human face lurking behind expatriation will force scholars to give attention to the social context surrounding professional mobility. Furthermore, highly-skilled migration studies and expatriation studies have failed thus far to speak with one another.

---

12 For a historical account of the use of the concept of expatriation, see Green (2009).

Putting the two fields in conversation can be very valuable in compensating for their respective weaknesses with their respective strengths, emphasising their complementarity.

2.4.1 Defining Expatriates

Let us start with an etymological clarification. The term expatriate is composed of the Latin roots *ex*, which means "out of", and *patri,* which means "native land". In other words, an "expatriate" is someone who is out of their native land. Moreover, *patri* comes from the Latin term *pater*, the father (Benveniste 1969, 217). The term is less neutral than it seems, as we can see a gendered dimension already in the terminology. It underlines a link between a person and their fatherland. It hints at people saying, "Look. I may be out of my home country for a time, but I intend to return to it or at least to maintain strong ties with it". In turn, the term raises questions about the "integration" of an expatriate in a new country. The bond that exists between the expatriate and his or her home country may remove any sense of urgency to "integrate" into the country of destination, precisely because the term implies that the person is already "integrated" somewhere else. To put it in Malkki's words: expatriates are not disturbing the "national order of things" (1995, 512) whereas migrants may very well be considered to do so.

McNulty and Brewster (2017) propose propose a stricter definition of the term expatriate. While dealing with the typologies of highly-skilled migrants (2.3.2 Deepening Migration, 39), I have shown the wide range of terms used to distinguish situations which are often similar. McNulty and Brewster (2017) also criticise this proliferation of terms ("flexpatriate, assigned traveller, self-initiated traveller, domestic international manager" [2017, 37], and so on) to name similar processes; it creates a fuzzy field of research, they argue. They suggest that this proliferation is due to the practical orientation of this field, which has led to a lack of studies engaging with theoretical considerations. To fill this gap, they propose the following definition: "We define 'business expatriates' as: legally working individuals who reside temporarily in a country of which they are not a citizen in order to accomplish a career-related goal, being relocated abroad either by an organization, by self-initiation or directly employed within the host-country" (McNulty and Brewster 2017, 46). The first part of this definition stresses that expatriates reside legally, temporarily, and for professional reasons in a country of which they are not citizens. I have already discussed the "documented/undocumented" binary in the previous section (2.3.2), and I will discuss in-depth the "temporal/permanent" binary in the next section (2.4.2). For now, let us focus on the integration of expatriates in the labour force. According the McNulty and Brewster (2017), the condition involves being "organisationally employed", regardless of the type of organisation. They argue that expatriates are not only employed by multinational corporations. Such organisations might also include non-governmental organisations such as the European Union in Brussels (Gatti 2009) or the United Nations in New York or Geneva, and to non-governmental organisations such as aid organisations or religious bodies as well as international sports and cultural associations. An expatriate might be "organisationally employed" by any of these groups. From this perspective, it seems that the "organisational employment" presupposes the skill level of the employees.

Thus, the three terms constituting McNulty and Brewster's definition of "expatriate" – legally, temporarily, and for professional reasons – tend to create an unproblematised definition of an expatriate as compared to a migrant. This anchors expatriation on the "frictionless side" of human mobility because it does not include the disruptive connotations used to depict a migrant. In other words, a migrant can clearly be "illegal" (sic.) (undocumented), permanent, and unemployed. An expatriate cannot. Unsurprisingly, McNulty and Brewster exclude migrants from the category of "business expatriate" (2017, 48). Thus, this definition contributes to create a "polarisation of migration" through the same process that I have shown in the first part of this chapter, namely by extracting professional forms of mobility from immigration, as the core of the definition is about being "organisationally employed".

Other researchers focus on the daily life of expatriates within the host-country. In *Transnational Lives* (2007b), Fechter analyses the presence and experiences of expatriates in Indonesia by using ethnographical methods. She develops the metaphor of "living in a bubble" (2007a, 167) to emphasise that transnational social spaces are not only spaces of fluidity and openness, but also conservative, rigid, and bounded ones. She underlines the intimate link between contemporary Euro-American expatriates in the "global South" and colonialism, pointing out that expatriation, transnational social spaces, and colonialism have a common history. In this context, the distinction between expatriates and migrants is rather clear. I quote this study because the "us/them" binary is only a step away from a racialised argument. This bias needs to be explicitly underlined and criticised. The argument goes as follows: an expatriate is a white male going abroad on a mission for a company in the "global South" whereas a migrant is "generic racialised and 'religionised' [sic.] being" coming to the "global North" for non-professional reasons. Thus, migration and expatriation respond to the "polarisation of migration" through the line of a "post-colonial world"[13], in turn reinforcing the "us/them" binary. Al Ariss (2010) speaks of the risk of a non-reflexive categorisation of the migrant and the expatriate. For him, this leads to a reproduction of biased categorisations: "when expatriates come from less-developed countries they are most frequently labelled as "migrants" or "immigrants". No rational theoretical or methodological foundation is given to explain such terminology. Instead, this terminological distinction comes to replicate and support a stereotyped image of migrants who are less advantaged in terms of their originating country and ethnic origins" (Al Ariss 2010, 80). This point is crucial to understanding that an unproblematised use of the term "expatriate" may lead to biased research.

The definition developed by McNulty and Brewster (2017) and the work of Fechter (2007b) are intended as tools to evacuate flawed understandings and misleading connotations of the term. In fact, the definition proposes a neutral stance when it comes to race and/or gender, as it is structured around three elements which attempt to narrow the scope of the field based on a valuable scientific argument. Furthermore, McNulty and Brewster propose a definition to clarify a field in which so many different concepts have appeared over the last few decades that it is sometimes difficult to understand who we are talking about. And yet the very endeavour of "extracting professional mobility from migration" contributes to producing the "us/them" binary. I do not say that there is "one best way" of doing it and my study should be seen as a reflection on this binary, but it remains problematic, I argue. I propose to include families and couples as units of analysis in order to circumvent this binary. We shall see that this approach, too, raises problems. In that sense, "our meanings and understandings are unstable and endlessly ambiguous" (Brinkmann 2017, 19) and social scientists are trapped in their own categories. I develop this argument in a later section on epistemology (4.1 Epistemology, 95).

2.4.2 Assigned Expatriate and Self-Initiated Expatriate

Beneath the broad definition of "business expatriate", the concepts of "assigned expatriate" and "self-initiated expatriate" are widespread in the literature. In fact, McNulty and Brewster (2017) include them in their definition when they emphasise various initiators of relocation: "by an organization, by self-initiation or directly employed within the host-country" (2017, 46). Thus, scholars agree

13 One could say a "Wallerstein's world" (Wallerstein 1974), where expatriates move from the "core" to the "periphery" whereas migrants travel the other way round.

on a distinction between "assigned expatriates" (Biemann and Andresen 2010; Dabic, González-Loureiro, and Harvey 2013) and "self-initiated expatriates" (Suutari and Brewster 2000). As we shall see, the distinction between a "self-initiated expatriate" and a migrant is blurry, too, as the concept of "self-initiated expatriate" beclouds the straight-line differentiation between expatriate and migrant. But what is a "self-initiated expatriate"? And how is he or she different from an "assigned expatriate"?

An "assigned expatriate" is sent abroad by – typically though not only – a multinational company; the company or other employing organisation[14] initiates the move. By contrast, a "self-initiated expatriate" takes the initiative to work abroad him- or herself. Moreover, an "assigned expatriate" has an employment contract located in his or her home-country while s/he works abroad. The contract, therefore, stipulates that the employee will be paid in the currency of his or her home-country. Typically, the contract also contains an "expatriate package", which includes support to settle and live in the new local space as well as other benefits, such as paid "home-leave" or a company car. On the other hand, a "self-initiated expatriate" has a local employment contract bounded in the legal framework of the country of arrival and receives less organisational support.

Cerdin and Selmer (2014, 1290) define "self-initiated expatriates" through four constitutive elements: they (1) take the initiative to relocate, (2) have a legal job or look for one, (3) wish to return to their home country, and (4) are skilled. For the authors, the wish to return to the home country is central to distinguishing between a "self-initiated expatriate" and a migrant. I argue that this is problematic, however. Although the definition is theoretically straightforward, it becomes confusing in the empirical world. Indeed, one may not know if one wants to stay in the country one is working in, or return to one's home country, or move on to a third country. In that sense, migration and expatriation are iterative processes. Hence, the notion of "wish to stay/wish to leave" is rather problematic and strongly dependent on context. External events can radically change the perspective of an individual.

Other research further refines the contrasts between these concepts. Andresen et al. (2014), for example, propose a typology of expatriation, distinguishing between (1) "assigned expatriate", (2) "*intra*- self-initiated expatriate", (3) "*inter*- self-initiated expatriate", and (4) "drawn expatriate". They construct

---

14 According to the definition of McNulty and Brewster (2017), the employer of an expatriate is not always a MNC. In the following, I will refer to the employer of expatriates as "employing organisation".

Table 1 Refining the Concept of Expatriate. Source: Own Elaboration based on the Results of Andersen et al. (2014)

	No Organisational Mobility: Work for the Same Company	***Organisational Mobility: Work for Another Company***
Move: Company's Initiative	Assigned Expatriate	Drawn Expatriate
Move: Own Initiative	Intra- Self-Initiated Expatriate	Inter- Self-Initiated Expatriate

their typology according to two factors, organisational mobility and initiative (Table 1).

First, when someone moves internationally within a single organisation, on the initiative of the employing organisation, the authors speak of "assigned expatriates". Second, it may be that the move is initiated by the employee him or herself, even as he or she continues to work for the same organisation: in this case, they speak of "*intra*- self-initiated expatriate". Both of these scenarios might occur if the organisation for whom the person works has an available position in another country and the employee applies for it internally. In both cases ("assigned expatriate" and "intra- self-initiated expatriate"), the employee continues to work for the same organisation. And yet, the "intra- self-initiated expatriate" mobilises the internal labour market of an organisation, in which employees apply for a new position while continuing to work for the same organisation. The difference between these categories is at the level of who initiates the move.

When a new employer is involved, the authors distinguish between the "*inter*- self-initiated expatriate" and the "drawn expatriate". As opposed to the "*intra*- self-initiated expatriate", the "*inter*- self-initiated expatriate" applies for a position in a new organisation abroad and quits his or her former position. The "intra-" and "inter- self-initiated expatriates" might not only work for MNCs, then – they can also be scholars or practitioners. Similar to McNulty and Brewster (2017), Andresen et al. (2014) go beyond the MNCs and include many people who would be called highly-skilled migrants in other fields. In other words, the research on "self-initiated expatriates" deals with the same people as the research on highly-skilled migrants, but uses different terms. The last case is the "drawn expatriate": an international hire. This typically happens when a head-hunter proposes a position abroad to someone on behalf of another employing organisation. In this case, the initiative comes from the company which wants to recruit somebody specific, such as a global top executive. The typology shows how the literature in management studies develops a refined categorisation of the different types of international moves possible between, within, and outside of an employing organisation.

The refinement of these categories, however, does not come without definitional problems. In a post-colonial vision of the world, it was easy to differentiate between expatriates and migrants, as I pointed out before. Yet new patterns of mobility have appeared over the last 25 years, and the "assigned expatriate" has become only one type of international professional mobility amongst others. As new forms of professional mobility appear, new denominations – such as "self-initiated expatriates" – follow[15].

a. Permanent/Temporal Migration Binary

With Cerdin and Selmer (2014) we have seen that those called expatriates – as opposed to migrants – are not considered through the lens of permanent settlement. It seems that expatriates need to adapt only temporarily. One assumes that everything will fall back into place once they return home. We can see how the binary "permanent and temporal migration" (King 2002, 93) is central to distinguishing between the two categories. In absolute terms, the permanent settlement of a migrant may be shorter than the temporal settlement of an expatriate. The outcomes of human mobility as an iterative process are difficult to foresee and recent research shows different "patterns of (im)mobility" after migration (Wieczorek 2018), thus overcoming the sedentary bias in migration studies. Conversely, I would suggest, we face a nomadic bias in research on expatriates. The distinction between migration and expatriation is based more on hierarchies of social classification than on questions of the intention to stay or to leave; or, more precisely, I argue, the intention to stay or to leave reflects hierarchies of social classification. Expatriation studies show how belonging somewhere else and having the possibility to return creates a "distinction" (Bourdieu 2012) between a migrant and an expatriate.

2.4.3 Expatriate Adjustments

Now that we have a clearer view of how expatriation is defined in the management literature, we can switch to a major topic it tackles: the "adjustment

15 Or is it the other way around? Can we only see what we can name? The epistemological question at play here is central. It shows how social agents (including social scientists) shape the reality they live in and in turn how this reality effectively takes place in our research. In that sense, (collectively) we discover what we are looking for. This becomes a way to classify the world with practical implications (Bourdieu 1983).

of expatriates" (Black and Mendenhall 1990a, 1990b; Black, Mendenhall, and Oddou 1991). Scholars working in this area measure the capacity of an individual to adjust to a new environment. Subsequently, they speak of high adjustment and low adjustment as they analyse how some people, in some places, under specific circumstances (like a strong "company culture" or a dedicated organisation support) are more likely to have a successful international assignment, with a lower rate of early returns and withdrawals. Centrally, they see three types of adjustment. Black and Mendenhall (1990b) define the "cross-cultural adjustment … in terms of the psychological comfort and familiarity an individual feels for the new culture" (1990b, 130). They propose a model of cross-cultural training (1990b, 127) to help expatriates to adapt to a new environment, as the aim of "cross-cultural training" is to soften the adaptation of expatriates when they arrive in a new affiliate by, for instance, diminishing the "cultural shock". The "cross-cultural adjustment model" highlights the centrality of learning the acceptable behaviours in a foreign cultural context. Black and Mendenhall argue that uncertainty about how to behave – "to perform one's role" – generates stress, thus leading to "cultural shock".

Black, Mendenhall, and Oddou (1991) further develop the concept of adjustment by bridging two bodies of literature: "international adjustment literature" (1991, 293) and "domestic adjustment literature" (1991, 295). While the domestic literature focuses on the adjustment process that an individual faces when starting a new job with little or no geographical mobility, the international literature focuses on the adjustment in cases involving international mobility. The two bodies of literature deal with changes and uncertainties in professional life. The domestic literature emphasises the ways organisations can foster the socialisation of new employees by implementing, for instance, an organisational culture. It stresses the "work factors" (1991, 295) which include clear definitions of the roles and tasks that a new employee must perform: the authors refer to the "work adjustment". Correspondingly, the international literature highlights the environment surrounding the professional activity that an expatriate must face while starting a new assignment abroad (food, climate, etc.), thus acknowledging expatriation as a "total phenomenon", modifying one's life at many levels: this is the "cross-cultural adjustment". There is also an "interactional adjustment", which refers specifically to the interactions with host-country nationals. Thus, by bridging the two bodies of literature, Black, Mendenhall, and Oddou distinguish three types of adjustment: (1) the adjustment to work, (2) the adjustment to activities outside of work, and (3) the adjustment to host-country nationals (1991, 304). In doing so, they examine the situation of an expatriate comprehensively and introduce a "framework of international adjustment" (1991, 303).

This framework highlights the various challenges (inside and outside work) that expatriates encounter when they arrive in a subsidiary abroad. In sum, the authors consider, within a single framework, the relevance of the professional environment *and* the centrality of other domains of life, such as the family, to assess professional mobility. The beginning of the 1990s is a turning point; before that, scholars accorded only scant attention to the environment within which expatriates evolved. The "framework of international adjustment" makes clear that the adaptations of an individual in a new environment cannot be understood outside of the social, cultural, and family context in which s/he lives.

I see complementarity between the way expatriate studies assess "adjustment" and the way highly-skilled migration studies tackle "integration". On the one hand, studies which use an adjustment model *de*politicise human mobility. Speaking of individual adjustment renders the topic more practical: it is a pragmatic approach aimed at facilitating the adaptation of individuals in a new environment. It becomes a technical problem and enables us to shift our focus to the concrete challenges faced by individuals in their everyday life abroad, bringing together the individual's situation and the challenges they encounter. On the other hand, the "integration" of migrants is a politicised topic and too often the concrete practices that either help or hinder their life in a new environment are hidden behind normative considerations on "cultural integration/assimilation".

Moreover, if "integration" occurs within the labour market (Bommes and Kolb 2006), then it is important to analyse how concretely one adjusts to a new workplace and how one copes, for instance, with a new environment. I argue that the "framework of international adjustment" (Black, Mendenhall, and Oddou 1991, 303) contains the necessary analytical tools to consider the complex relationship between professional mobility, work, and adaptation to a new environment. The strength of this model is also that it considers the ways in which the employing organisation must support its employee, for the adaptation is reciprocal and organisational support is crucial.

a. Partner and Family

So far, we have seen some definitional refinements of the concept of expatriation, and we have become acquainted with the "framework of international adjustment". Now, I will focus on how the studies of the "trailing spouse" [*sic*] have emerged. The term "trailing spouse" appears as the counterpart of a "breadwinner" implying a traditional conceptualisation of the family. The "breadwinner" brings money and "food" to the family while the "trailing spouse" follows and takes care of the domestic matters. Nearly always, the "trailing spouse" is a woman and the "breadwinner" is a man. For the most part, the literature focusing on the "trailing spouse" considers a traditional vision of the family: a vison where the wife follows the husband.

Several studies from the early 1990s focus on the ways in which the "trailing spouse" impacts the "breadwinner's" adjustment success. These scholars explore the adjustment of the "trailing spouse" because s/he increases the adjustment success of the "breadwinner". In this context, the "trailing spouse" is subsumed within the "spouse adjustment" of the "breadwinner" (Black and Gregersen 1991; Briody and Chrisman 1991). It is assumed that the successful adjustment of the "trailing spouse" increases the quality of the "breadwinner's" work in the labour force. Braseby (2010, 8) argues that the studies of Black and Gregersen (1991) or Briody and Chrisman (1991) conceptualise the "trailing spouse" as an independent variable to the "breadwinner's" adjustment. As the "family concerns" and the "spouse/partner career" are identified to be the main reason explaining "assignment failure" (Andreason 2008; Brookfield Global Relocation Services 2012, 14), the interest in the topic grows. In other words, it is because the "spouse's dissatisfaction" impacts the professional activity of the employees that more attention is paid to their specific situation. Scholars emphasise that the partner's satisfaction diminishes the risk of an early return to the home-country.

A semantic development in which the term "trailing spouse" is replaced by "spouse/partner" has taken place in the last decade. This is a welcome modification as it changes the unquestioned assumptions behind the terms and contributes to develop a more sensitive perspective acknowledging, for instance, the will of the partner to maintain a position in the labour force; it gives agency to the partner. Yet, the "female trailing spouse" and the "male breadwinner" are still gendered notions reflecting the empirical structure of the field of study. The "trailing spouse" and "breadwinner" correspond to the gendered binary of the "reproductive female" and "productive male"[16]. These gender binaries support strong narratives on masculinity and femininity and scholars are not immune to them. Research has struggled to overcome a gendered narrative conceptualising the "female trailing spouse" as a burden. It was not until 2010 that the first studies appeared analysing the supportive role that the partner not working in the labour force can give during an assignment (Davoine et al. 2013; Lauring and Selmer 2010). During the same decade, other researchers developed studies of the "emotional situation" (Cangià 2017) or the "precarity" (Cangià 2018) of the

16 I shall develop this crucial point in the next section on gender and highly-skilled migration for there is much to say.

"expat spouses", the importance of organisational support for the "accompanying partner" (Cole 2011; McNulty 2012), and the "career coordination strategies" of "dual career couples" (Känsälä, Mäkelä, and Suutari 2014; Mäkelä, Känsälä, and Suutari 2011). These scholars have also developed a reflexive use of the terms, thus overcoming the value-laden term "trailing spouse". In fact, in most of the existing research, the "trailing spouses" are seen as a burden, for this assumption is built into the term itself: "Although a number of investigations have included the potential negative influence of partners on expatriates' careers … few, if any, have focused on the positive role of the spouse for the expatriate career" (Lauring and Selmer 2010, 60). Lauring and Selmer (2010) look at the ways in which the partner not working in the labour force supports the partner working in the labour force abroad. In doing so, they manage to overcome a simplistic vision of the adventurous *pater familias*, supporting a family and a spouse abroad while continuing to work in the labour force, thus overcoming a conceptualisation implying that one of the partners is necessarily dependent on the other. In short, they envision the partners as a team and they analyse the ways in which one partner develops strategies to support the career of the other – for instance, by helping him or her to find professional opportunities in the new local space or back at home.

Similarly, Davoine et al. (2013) theorise three repertoires of the "supporting partner", which express the partner's positive impact on expatriation. The first repertoire highlights the assistance to the career as well as psychological support. The second repertoire emphasises the search for information on the new place where the partners will live. This includes developing a network in the new place. The third repertoire stresses the logistical support the spouse provides when it comes to the family. Thus, the authors show that the assistance of the "supporting partner" occurs at different levels, and they conceptualise him or her as far more than simply a burden.

Furthermore, Davoine et al. (2013) show differences in the mobilisation of the repertoire depending on the gender of the "supporting partner". They distinguish "frontstage activities" and "backstage activities" following a "Goffman's dramaturgical analysis" (2013, 18). "Frontstage activities" imply public representation while the "backstage" ones are done in private. Davoine et al. (2013) reveal perceived gendered expectations and how the actors deal with them. The male "supporting partner", for instance, tends to offer "backstage" psychological support, and yet it may be more complicated for them to perform "frontstage" activities, such as getting involved with the local expatriate community. In contrast, the female "supporting partner" is more at ease performing "frontstage" activities because these fit with the local "gender norm". In sum, this study stresses the gender differences in (1) the support provided and (2) the repertoires that the "supporting partners" mobilise. Although the structure of the field is gendered, since many couples of expatriates are indeed organised along traditional lines, the gendered assumptions of the researchers themselves have also made them blind to the active role the supporting partner may play.

Exploring the situation of the accompanying partner further, Cangià (2017, 2018) explores the burdens and challenges specific to their situation. Cangià (2017) focuses on the "emotional work" of the accompanying partner when they speak about their new environment. She considers especially the mixed feelings about the obligation they might feel to be excited about their international experience even while they face difficult personal situations (e.g., unemployment, loneliness, lack of social networks) that risk leading to intense suffering. In a subsequent article (2018), Cangià explicitly criticises the idea of "frictionless mobility", showing how the accompanying partners find themselves in a precarious situation. Through a reconceptualisation of precarity, she shows how people who could be seen as favoured are in fact in fragile and ephemeral situations. She underlines the price of an uncompromised focus on the career of one of the partners. The individuals who quit a position in the labour force to follow their partner abroad face a situation of precarity, defined here beyond solely socio-economic precarity: "Trailing in mobility creates a paradox in that, while being with the family can give the security and comfort for dealing with change both for the assignee and for the partner, it is the very choice of moving for the family that creates spouses' condition of precarity" (2018, 22). This situation is precarious because the accompanying partner must do the care work for the family while waiting for the hypothetical and yet very possible further relocation of the partner working in the labour force. The accompanying partner, in scholars' eyes, has changed from a "burden" to a source of support to individuals facing their own emotional challenges in precarious situations while on the move. It thus seems only logical that other scholars have paid further attention to the organisational support that can be offered to these couples and families (Cole 2011; McNulty 2012).

Cole (2011) and McNulty (2012) emphasise that the major sources of stress during a relocation abroad are the loss of professional activity, the personal stress, and the lack of adapted support to the accompanying partner. McNulty argues that "both career and relationship stress are two of the most common ongoing unresolved tensions encountered by the trailing spouse when moving into unfamiliar cultural environments" (2012, 421). Both McNulty and Cole emphasise the importance of "organisational support" for the accompanying partner. They show that the most common type of support is practical support (like finding accommodation), whereas the social and professional support still seem lacking in many organisations. McNulty gives a good idea of the wide range of support which could be made available to the accompanying partner: "Assistance in finding a job for the trailing spouse (e.g., obtaining work permits, using a career coach, updating a resume), helping them stay connected remotely to their career (i.e. through paid subscriptions, associations), and/or building a new career appears especially necessary (see, for example, Parfitt 1998). If employment is not an option or not desired, companies could help with the reimbursement of education-related costs to compensate for the loss of spousal income, or childcare to facilitate attendance at courses" (2012, 431). Actually, when we combine the results of Cangià (2017, 2018) and those of Cole (2011) and McNulty (2012), we see that the "burden" of an international relocation are not generally shared equally between the partners. The accompanying partner takes the larger share, especially if this person has to resign from a position in the labour force. Furthermore, Cole underlines that the partners making the decision to relocate are aware that one career will be prioritised: "expatriate dual-career couples make a conscious decision that one person's career will take precedence for the duration of the expatriate assignment. If so, spouses have already accepted the reality that their careers will be affected" (2011, 31).

The studies of Cole (2011) and McNulty (2012) both underline changing trends in the family organisation of expatriates. First, they have witnessed more male accompanying partners. In this context, Cole (2011) shows a gendered difference, as the female partner whose position in the labour force was interrupted because of a relocation will have higher cultural and interactional adjustment. This creates new challenges, as males have lower cultural and interactional adjustment than their female counterparts (which is coherent with the results of Davoine et al. [2013, 17], as traditional norms still prioritise the career of the male partner). Second, Cole (2011) and McNulty (2012) both refer to dual career couples as a more and more frequent form. McNulty found that 84 percent of the accompanying partners have a tertiary education and 79 percent have a career before the relocation, but only 36 percent continue to work in the labour force after the relocation (2012, 428). In light of these results, it becomes clear that reflecting upon "dual career couples" is a central topic when one deals with expatriate international relocation.

Känsälä et al. (2014) go one step further and focus specifically on "dual career couples", thus looking beyond the traditional model of the family. They analyse the different types of "career coordination strategies" and develop a theoretical framework, defining three strategies for coping with professional mobility and family life. The "hierarchical strategy" corresponds to the prioritization of one career over another. In most cases, the male career is prioritized while family responsibility and the care work lie with the woman: a “male breadwinner” and a “female supporting partner”. In the “egalitarian strategy”, both partners’ careers have equal importance, implying coordination and negotiation. In other words, family life, care work, and professional careers are equally important to both partners. The family tries to live in the same household, thus avoiding long-distance relationships. The “egalitarian strategy” expresses both an egalitarian approach to valuing the two professional careers and a vision in which work in the labour force and care work have uniform significance. In contrast, the “loose coordination strategy” emphasises equal investments in the careers and disengagement from the family. Both partners prioritise (equally) their careers and over their family and private life. They choose to favour their professional life over their family life. In sum, Känsälä et al. (2014) theorise the coordination strategies of expatriates and show the various models of family organisation.

2.4.4 Intermediary Summary: Construction of a Polarisation II

Section 2.4 deals with studies that focus on the relationship between professional careers and private or family life. Expatriation is essentially about professional mobility, yet scholars increasingly understand it in a broader context. In the latest studies, they have reconciled “labour migration” and “family strategies”. The most up-to-date research on professional mobility bridges the gap between the non-professional implications and the professional ones. Thus far, I have dealt with expatriate studies and assessed them critically. I pointed to definitional questions and indicated three main topics which can enrich the study of highly-skilled migration: the processes of adjustment, the specific (precarious) situation of the accompanying partner, and the coordination of two professional careers.

Nevertheless, most expatriate studies rely on “migration binaries”, and three of them arose in section 2.4: “us vs. them”, “temporal vs. permanent”, and “breadwinner vs. trailing spouse”. I argue that these binaries strengthen the semantic opposition between the expatriate and the migrant. The “polarisation of migration” has a performative impact in scientific research, too. There, too, it underlines the “migration binaries” between “us” and “them”, cutting human migration into two categories: “migrants” and “expatriates”. In crude terms, this approach assumes that expatriates bring science, growth, rationality, and development to underdeveloped countries while migrants disrupt the national order of the world (Malkki 1995) and bring problems to developed countries. This vision is a myth.

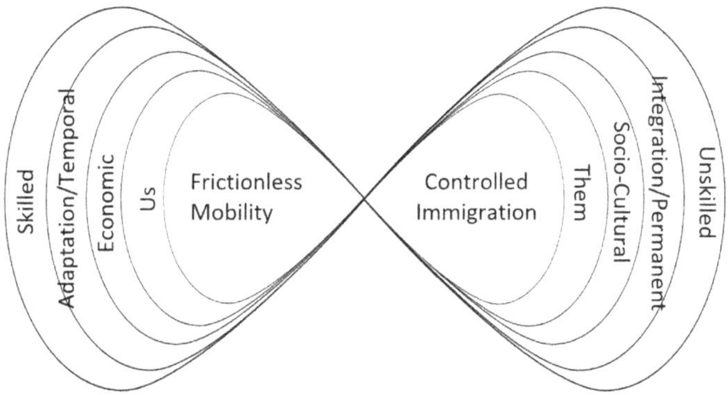

Figure 2 Migration Binaries. Source: Own Elaboration

The "temporal/permanent migration" binary shapes expatriation studies, too. It seems to justify the different social treatment of those who are seen to stay permanently – and who should integrate into the host society – and those who are only here temporarily – who just need to adapt for a time. Yet it is not clear how this distinction can be empirically justified, since human mobility is an iterative process. The line is blurry but taking it for granted can have strong performative effects on the lives of the migrants and the expatriates themselves. Thus, in the first part of this chapter, I have theoretically constructed what I will refer to as the "migration binaries" (Figure 2). In addition, I have described a gendered binary, which usually implies a "male breadwinner" and a "female trailing spouse", following the traditional conception of the family. I will deal with this topic in depth in the next section and construct a second set of binaries central for this work: the "gender binaries".

2.5 Gender and Highly-Skilled Migration

Up until now, I have pointed out that the "migration binaries" polarise migration, leading some scholars to biased categorisations. The present section is about gender and highly-skilled migration. I will introduce the "gender binaries" to develop further the "polarisation of migration" and more importantly to show how some researchers propose ways out. Then, I will address studies that use a "dichotomous variable"[17] to analyse gender and highly-skilled migration.

17 A "dichotomous approach" superposes sex and gender to compare the differences between men and women whereas a "relation and situational" approach considers

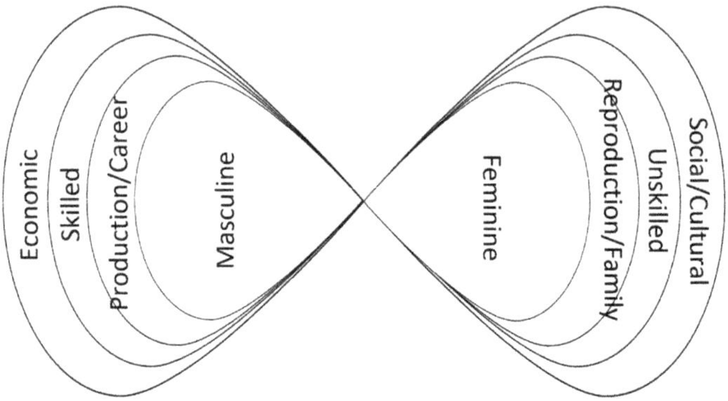

Figure 3 Gender Binaries. Source: Own Elaboration

After that, I will deal with research that stresses a "relational and situational" conceptualisation of gender, to finally argue that the study of gender and highly-skilled migration still lacks research that effectively tackles the images of femininity and masculinity when it comes to "families on the move".

2.5.1 Gender Binaries

The "gender binaries" express an opposition between narratives of femininity and masculinity. For example, they oppose a "female trailing spouse" and a "male breadwinner". Scholars in gender studies have developed this idea and spotted many mirrored images differentiating femininity from masculinity. The dichotomy opposes a productive, economic, skilled, work-oriented male to a social, cultural, unskilled, reproductive, and family-oriented female (Kofman and Raghuram 2006; Schaer, Dahinden, and Toader 2017) (Figure 3).

The "gender binaries" impact the topics addressed by scholars, which include highly-skilled migration studies and expatriate studies. I argue that highly-skilled migration studies mostly focus on the masculine side of the binaries as they deal with the professional careers of employed skilled migrants. In other words, the focus on the professional activity promotes research on highly-skilled migration from the masculine side of the binaries. For example, questions

gender as an everyday construct, thus reflexively conceptualising sex and gender (Donato et al. 2006).

around the wellbeing of the "supporting spouse" became relevant only when scholars acknowledged that the "dissatisfaction of the supporting spouse" leads the partner working in the labour force to break his employment contract and to return prematurely to his family in the home-country. Kofmann (2000) develops a similar point saying that highly-skilled migration studies overlook the female migrants. The women are invisible in highly-skilled migration studies, reducing the experience of highly-skilled migration to a generic gender-neutral professional experience.

The same argument the other way around also works: while highly-skilled migration studies are trapped in a gender-neutral paradigm, migration and gender studies do not tackle highly-skilled migration. According to Meares (2010, 473), the gendered experience of highly-skilled migrant women is largely ignored. Instead, she argues, the research focuses mostly on disadvantaged women, studying their family-relationships as well as social and cultural migration experiences of unskilled female migrants. In other words, research on gender, family relations, and migration has not tackled the topic of highly-skilled migration thus far, focusing more on the "feminine side" of the "gender binaries". This logic, Kofman (2005) argues, creates two strands of literature which are hermetic and blind to each other. Similarly, Schaer, Dahinden, and Toader (2017) emphasise this mutual blindness, stating: "Family migration, tied migration, and larger social networks have largely been ignored in this field of study [highly-skilled migration studies], while they have been extensively theorised and studied in the gender and migration literature" (2017, 1294). In sum, research on gender and migration scrutinises the feminine side of migration, while research on highly-skilled migration analyses the masculine side. The "gender binaries" provide a reading grid to assess migration and highly-skilled migration studies, I argue. Indeed, they lead us to see what has been and, more importantly, what has not been studied so far. In the last ten years, however, scholars have become more and more aware of this gap in the literature and they have engaged with it in two ways. A first way out consists in adopting a "crossing focus", analysing the specificity of the experiences of highly-skilled migrant women. In this context, scholars reconfigure the migration binaries by crisscrossing the "gender binaries" (Figure 4). In other words, this approach collapses the "male productive and female reproductive" dichotomy and focuses instead on the professional activity of *female* highly-skilled migrants – emphasised by the grey zones on the figure. A second way out is to question the family strategies and the family organisation comprehensively encompassing the binaries and analysing the impact of feminine and masculine narratives on family strategies and the migration decision.

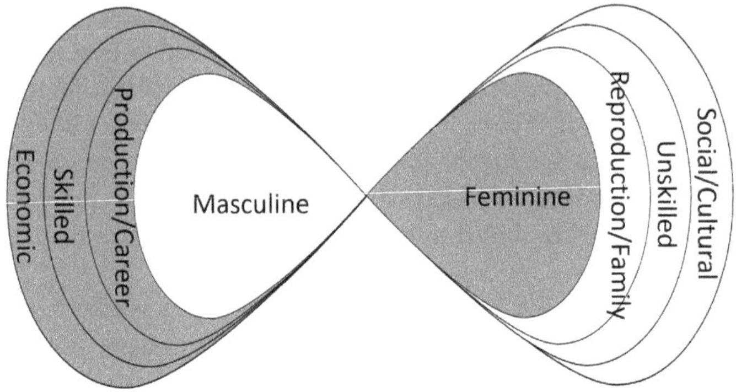

Figure 4 Gender Binaries II. Source: Own elaboration

2.5.2 Gender as a Dichotomous Variable

Studies using gender as a "dichotomous variable" (Donato et al. 2006) – that is superposing sex and gender – analyse discrepancies of income and career progression between men and women. They show the specificity of the experiences and the decreased "chances to succeed" of female highly-skilled migrants compared to their male counterparts. These studies focus on highly-skilled women and explain how the migration experience differs between men and women. The studies analysing the differences between men and women show that international migration tends to have a negative impact on the career of female highly-skilled migrants (Meares 2010, 473), whereas the impact is mostly positive for the men's careers. Research dealing with the professional integration of highly-skilled female migrants points out the reasons why they encounter more challenges than their male counterparts in finding a job that corresponds to their skills, if they find a job at all.

Adsera and Chiswick (2007) analyse also the difference that gender and skills make in the process of migration. They conduct a systematic analysis of individual earnings based on the 1994–2000 waves of the European Community Household Panel (ECHP). They test gender differences with other explanatory variables such as "marital status, number of children, education, experience, foreign birth" (Adsera and Chiswick 2007, 9) and develop arguments which provide better knowledge of the relationship between gender, highly-skilled migration earnings, countries of origin, and countries of arrival. Their results plead in favour of a better understanding of "intersectionality" (Crenshaw 1989) in highly-skilled migration, too. Indeed, the women from Latin-America and Eastern Europe are discriminated against two times in terms of income: first because they are women on the move and second because of their countries of origin, both times regardless of their skill level. This discrimination is also related to the difficulty they experience in getting their diplomas recognised.

Research using the "dichotomous variable" of gender uncovers four main factors (Liversage 2009) which lead to enhanced challenges for highly-skilled female migrants; they may even hinder international female highly-skilled migration. First, highly-skilled female migrants mostly have skills that are not as easily transferable as those predominantly held by men. Indeed, according to Cornelius et al. (2001), men possess more often technical, scientific, or managerial skills. Such skills are more in demand and easier to transfer than the skills of women, which tend to be in fields such as medicine and teaching. Second, the predominant type of migration into a new country differs between men and women. Women tend to enter more often as dependents or refugees while male entry routes are more oriented towards "work-migration", such as inter-company transfers. Because women move more often for non-professional reasons, they face greater challenges in finding a job, such as the lack of working-permit (Liversage 2009, 121). Further causes leading highly-skilled women migrants to encounter more hardship than men are related to causes outside the realm of migration studies. The gendered structure of the family, especially the gendered division of family tasks, is the third cause, while the discrimination women still face in labour markets is the last. These discriminations come from, for instance, the gendered orientation of the "welfare regimes" (Pfau-Effinger 1998). I shall come back to this central point in the next chapter. All in all, quantitative studies using a dichotomous variable of gender show that gender does make a difference when we speak of highly-skilled migration. Gender-neutral research is not sufficient to comprehend the phenomenon fully. And, as Liversage (2009, 122) argues, even studies using a dichotomous conceptualisation of gender do not help us to understand how discrepancies between men and women are produced and reproduced: another perspective is needed.

2.5.3 Gender as a Relational and Situational Feature

The relational conceptualisation of gender suggests that gender is an everyday construct, challenging the idea that it could be natural or biological (Butler 1990). Gender is "produced as a socially organised achievement" (West and Zimmerman 1987, 129). In order to operationalise these theoretical ideas, researchers take up a qualitative perspective to catch how gender is "done" (West and Zimmerman 1987), "undone" (Butler 2004; Deutsch 2007), and "displayed"

(Finch 2007) in the context of highly-skilled migration. This involves linking the "gender binaries" to assess how they "systematically" respond to one another. For this purpose, Kofman and Raghuram (2005) propose that further research on highly-skilled migration should go "beyond the workplace": "Virtually all the studies on skilled migration have concentrated on the workplace and on career trajectories, leaving aside the incorporation of familial relations and a wider social network" (2005, 151). Going beyond the workplace means analysing the relationships between professional careers and family life. In contrast to studies grounded on a dichotomous conceptualisation, the ones conceptualising a relational and situational perspective are more attentive to the social processes that constitute and reproduce gender. Yet studies using either a relational conceptualisation or a dichotomous one develop largely convergent results, showing that highly-skilled female migrants must face more frequently fearsome challenges, which may lead to painful shifts in their professional careers as well as fundamental identity ruptures.

a. *Women and Highly-Skilled Migration*

Studies analysing the biographies of highly-skilled migrant women highlight the moments which create or consolidate gendered hierarchies. Liversage (2009) uses the concept of "vital conjunctures" to refer to the options of an individual in a specific realm of structural possibilities during a period of uncertainty, typically "after" migration, thus having implications on the identity someone can claim. A "vital conjuncture" expresses what one can "do" after migration; and how one can protect and project their identity when one is confronted with structural barriers.

Liversage (2009) studies highly-skilled women who arrive in Denmark for non-work reasons and distinguishes the paths that her respondents take to find their way in the new labour market. She shows that the chances for highly-skilled migrant women to find a professional activity in Denmark hinge on the social structure in which they are embedded and the "marketability of their skills" (2009, 135). Some find a job in their field, going through the period of "vital conjuncture" quickly and without "migration de-skilling". Highly-skilled migrant women who are able to do so, she argues, are mostly the ones with "hard" skills, easily transferable, such a doctors or engineers. Others have to struggle to find a professional activity. These women often find looking for a job in a new country to be difficult. Nevertheless, some manage to attain the highly-skilled sectors. Liversage distinguishes three trajectories of highly-skilled migrant women able to attain the highly-skilled sector: (1) valorising their skills to find a professional activity with other migrants, (2) studying again, or (3) going back home (2009, 136). Those who do not find a high-skill job may accept an unskilled job, often implying painful identity reconfigurations. The ones who do not find a professional activity at all and the ones experiencing a migration "de-skilling" must find ways to cope with a "vital conjuncture", which makes the expectations they had when they arrived in Denmark "out of reach". A reason can be that their diplomas are not recognised. This shows the centrality of professional identity in contemporary societies and reveals that, in the worst-case scenario, its loss can "cast them back onto a gendered identity of being 'just housewives' with little life or purpose of their own" (Liversage 2009, 135).

Liversage (2009) also describes the paths of highly-skilled migrant women who change of country for non-work reasons. According to her, not only do women move more often than men for non-work reasons, but women also face stronger structural barriers than their male counterparts. For example, men are more likely to possess "hard" transferable skills, making it easier to find a job abroad. In sum, Liversage (2009) shows how the experience of highly-skilled migrant women is specific, thus pointing out the "blind-spots" of the gender-neutral paradigm of highly-skilled migration. A relocation is a key biographical passage, promoting the emergence of gender-based employment inequalities, especially when women follow men – which is, as many studies show, very often the case.

Similarly, Meares (2010) proposes an analysis based on biographical interviews of South African highly-skilled migrant women in New Zealand. She highlights the processes leading professionally successful women in South Africa to leave paid work in New Zealand, which include under- or unemployment or the absence of a working-permit in New Zealand. The transition between the two countries is problematic for many of her interviewees; indeed, it is accompanied in many cases by periods of unemployment, part-time jobs, or retraining. Meares (2010) focuses on the balance between work in the labour force and family life, analysing how it changes for highly-skilled migrant women after an international move. She emphasises two simultaneous movements which push highly-skilled migrant women back to the traditional role of the "supporting spouse". First, on the professional level, the hard times without a position in the labour force, the loss of money, the migration "de-skilling", and the subsequent identity shifts diminish a woman's chances to find a position in the labour force; and second, on the family level, the altered relationships within the family due to the geographical distance and the absence of a network of support increase the time the family requires in terms of care work. These concurrent processes make the time after migration, Meares argues, a risky biographical moment. Meares's study (2010) shows the "career damages" that her respondents experience. In sum, she explains the processes pushing highly-skilled migrant women towards the domestic sphere, all of which imply a painful identity cost and a total shift in the "vital conjuncture" (Liversage 2009).

Riaño et al. (2015) deal, also, with the specificity of the experience of highly-skilled migrant women, but they focus on the creation and/or the reproduction of gender inequalities. Their study highlights "critical moments" and "critical places" in the migration process by assessing the fissures in the biographies of highly-skilled migrant women. "Critical moments" are the birth of a child and/or the relocation of the family. "Critical places" are places where the "gender culture" (Pfau-Effinger 1998) remains traditional, such as the small town in Switzerland where the respondents of Riaño relocated. The nature of the location to which the highly-skilled migrants relocate does matter, as different places offer various degrees of institutional support. The type of "welfare regime" (Esping-Andersen 1990) – granting different lengths of maternity leave – or the support available for day care characterise a "critical place". Thus, not only does the breakage in the professional career through relocation and parenting contribute to gendered inequalities, but the very place where the family ends up offers various structural barriers. As Riaño et al. put it, "Parenthood is not necessarily the critical moment at which gender inequalities emerge. Migration of women from a country or area with a high level of gender equality to one with a more unequal system can be the turning point in inequality. In such cases, parenthood will only further reinforce inequality between partners" (Riaño et al. 2015, 162). Riaño et al. (2015) explain the processes by which gender inequality sneaks into families over time and through multiple relocations. These results corroborate the work of Aure (2013), who analyses highly-skilled female migrants who enter the labour market in Tromsø, Norway. Aure stresses that "labour market access is profoundly contextual – locally, socially, gender-wise, culturally and geographically" (2013, 282). In short, the complex interlinks between mobility, "critical moments", and "critical places" highlight the multi-faceted nature of gender inequalities. These three studies reveal that mobility involves serious challenges in terms of gender. Based on their results, we can distinguish three social spheres which shape gender inequalities: (1) the labour market, (2) the family-work balance, and (3) the gender culture of the environment. These three simultaneous social processes are the ones which lead to "patterns of downward mobility" (Chang 2014) of highly-skilled female migrants – or as Riaño (2016) puts it, the hardships of a "marginalised elite" (Cangià [2018] develops similar findings, see p. 54). Theoretically, the scholars in this section explicitly reverse the commonly unquestioned gender assumptions structuring research on highly-skilled migration to explore the impact of international migration on the careers of highly-skilled female migrants. While the odds are definitely not in women's favour, it is striking to see how the "gender binaries" impregnate the social world.

b. Migration Family Strategies

Researchers propose that another "way out" of the "gender binaries" is to encompass them in a framework which connects the "family-strategies", the individual professional careers, and the biographies of the members of a family. In the same framework, they put forth a conception encompassing international migration, work in the labour force and care work, developing a concept which is going to be central to my study; namely, the concept of "family-strategies".

In a study on Polish migrants in London, Ryan et al. (2009) examine the dynamic nature of "family migration strategies" (2009, 63). They define two broad types of "family-strategies". The first type maintains the unity of the household. The partners and the possible children move to London; thus, they may have less savings because life is more expensive, but they live together in a place where the quality of life is higher. The second type emphasises a split family in which the members of a family decide to live separately: one member goes alone to London and sends money back to Poland. According to Ryan et al. (2009, 65), it is usually the male partner who moves to London and sends back the money he earns to the female partners and the child/ren. In sum, Ryan et al. (2009) distinguish two main models: together or apart. "Family-strategies" do not provide a picture of a family at a given time, and they do not remain frozen in time; on the contrary, they evolve as constraints and opportunities (dis)appear. In brief, Ryan et al. further develop the concept of "family-strategies", arguing that a family's financial situation (standard of living) and lifestyle choices (quality of living) need to be accounted for. They underline the dynamic nature of "family-strategies" and they stress that an accurate conception of "family-strategies" needs to encompass not only work in the labour force and savings, but also the unpaid care work and housework.

Kõu et al. (2015) use a biographical approach and emphasise the dynamic nature of the "family-strategies", too; they focus on the "family-strategies" of highly-skilled Indians in the Netherlands. The authors incorporate a chronological dimension to the study of "family-strategies", meaning that the members of a family do not have to move together at the same time, but that they can plan different modes of living together or apart for a time. In addition, they argue that although the "family-strategies" of highly-skilled migrants contain a strong gender component, the female is not passive. In other words, it is not only about sacrifices but also about strategies and opportunities. Even though highly-skilled migrant women are more frequently on the move for nonprofessional reasons like marriage, they can also use this move as an opportunity to get a better position in the labour force or an additional degree; "they do not sacrifice but strategise" (Kõu et al. 2015, 1658). The authors do not reproduce a gendered binary implying a "passive female" and an "active male" in their study. As they speak of highly-skilled women on the move for family reasons – marriage – it would have been easy to conceptualise them as passive, following a non-reflexive categorisation of masculinity and femininity, but they consider other dimensions as well.

Another study reflecting the dynamic and gendered characteristics of "family-strategies" is that of Shinozaki (2014). She focuses on couples of highly-skilled migrants in Germany, contrasting different types of family migration strategies and highlighting the role of gender in those strategies. As in many studies, Shinozaki emphasises that the most common "family-strategies" are highly gendered, involving a "male breadwinner" and a "female supporting spouse". She points out the necessary support a "female supporting spouse" gives to her husband, whose professional mobility is possible only because she takes care of the family. In this case, when mobility is, for the male, a strategic way to progress in his career, it means for the female stepping back from her own professional career (Shinozaki 2014, 533). While she acknowledges that strategies can change over time and that the spouse does have agency, Shinozaki stresses that the gendered orientation of the family strategies is quite enduring. Indeed, the author introduces another migration "family-strategy" in which the partners shift the priority given to either one or the other professional career. In this case, the partners each make compromises for one another; however, Shinozaki shows that for the care work, the female partners rely on other female kin, like the mother-in-law, rather than the husband: "This way, Mrs. Ono-Roth did not have to directly confront her husband, letting his wish to have their baby taken care of by a (female) family member unchallenged" (2014, 536). In addition, Shinozaki (2014) analyses the case of dual career couple, in which both partners continue to work in their field. She notices particularities in these couples. The partners are specialised in fields which are flexible, and they possess transferable skills; as well, they carefully plan their careers, which is not the case in the other cases she witnesses. Moreover, they are able to transnationally mobilise their cultural capital through, for instance, professional networks. On the top of that, Shinozaki, emphasises the centrality of dual-career policies within the hiring organisation of one of the partners. Thus, Shinozaki shows that maintaining a dual career couple on the move demands a capital that can be hard to find and substantial institutional support.

In summary, Ryan et al. (2009), Kõu et al. (2015), and Shinozaki (2014) show the dynamic and temporal nature of family migration strategies. They also emphasise factors orienting the "family-strategies" towards a "traditional" organisation of the family for highly-skilled migrants.

c. *Gendered Image of Migration Family Strategies*

Additionally, scholars analyse the narratives of migrants in the development of "family-strategies" in order to determine the role gender plays in these narratives. Schaer, Dahinden, and Toader (2017) analyse the arrangements of young couples of academics and their partners on the move. They propose three ideal-types, each expressing the entanglement of gender and mobility (2017, 11). The first ideal-type, "from dual-career mobility to a conventional gender configuration", expresses the long-run impact mobility and gender can have on family organisation. It refers to moments in the biographies which modify the partner's role over time. Again, the birth of a child is an example of this process. In the long run, the "family-strategy" tends to follow a traditional division of the tasks. The lack of institutional support to do, for instance, the care work, the difficulty of transferring skills, the problem of diploma recognition, and "traditional" dichotomies between a public male and a private female, lead to such situations. Their second ideal-type reflects an unconventional pattern introducing a "female primary mover [and] male tied mover"; thus, it shows an atypical configuration in which the traditional gender roles are inversed. In this case, convincing the male partner to move seems to be linked with his own professional dissatisfaction or his capacity to transfer his skills. While this question has been ignored when it comes to the "trailing-wife" (and, ignored over more than 20 years of research), it is one of the first to be asked when it comes to the male partner. How can *He* give up *His* job for *Her*? Here, we see the strength of a gendered narrative. It underlines the value of paying special attention to gender when analysing highly-skilled migration. The authors develop a third ideal-type which speaks of the "male primary mover [and] female tied mover". This type falls back on the traditional construction of masculinity and femininity with a "male breadwinner" and a "female trailing spouse". The strength of this analysis is to show the ways in which narratives change according to who is the primary mover: "Men can adopt a rather protective – paternalistic – attitude towards their female partners' following them, whereas women can express concern – and even guilt – about their male partners doing the same" (Schaer, Dahinden, and Toader 2017, 12). These results complement the research done in expatriate studies. Earlier I discussed the study of Känsälä, Mäkelä, and Suutari

(2014), which distinguishes three types of career coordination strategies: hierarchical, egalitarian, and loose coordinated. They explain that female primary movers find it more difficult to negotiate with their partners than their male counterparts do. In light of the results of Schaer, Dahinden, and Toader (2017), we can better understand female primary movers feel obliged to offer additional narratives of justification. It seems "natural" for a male primary mover to ask his partner to leave her professional activity; when the roles are inverted, more justifications are needed. This is evidence of a powerful gender narrative surrounding the experience of highly-skilled migration.

Family migration strategies become even more complex when one uses a *flexible* conceptualisation of the family, encompassing both the "local-family" and the "transnational family". In the chapter 3.2.1, I will develop finer conceptual definition of the family. For the moment, let us say that – until now – I have dealt with "elementary families" composed of adults and children (procreated or adopted) and not with more encompassing concept of the family implying kinship. The above studies already pointed at this, and Wilding and Baldassar (2009) further stress the significant effects of the "transnational family" on "family-strategies". They underline recurrent cross-border practices of care work within families who span different countries, considering a broader concept of the family not limited to the "elementary family", as it encompasses close relatives, too. They consider kinship, too. To perform the care work efficiently, the authors show that the partners need both time and money; however, saving time to do the care work means a diminution in paid work: it is a zero-sum game. In addition, the members of a transnational family need to care about the "local family" and the "transnational family", which means that they face a supplementary challenge as they must care "multi-locally"; indeed, they must find a balance of care between the "local [elementary] family" and the "transnational family [implying kinship]" (Wilding and Baldassar 2009, 183). Similar to Shinozaki (2014), Wilding and Baldassar (2009) emphasize that family strategies demand demand resources that are hard to come by. In sum, Wilding and Baldassar (2009) are interested in the "work-family integration" (Halpern and Murphy 2005 cited by Wilding and Baldassar 2009, 185) of their respondents and how they develop coping strategies to deal with the need for money and the need for time to care. The authors consider both a masculine and a feminine way to do so. The masculine way to cope tends to increase working hours in the labour force in pursuit of a career in order to have enough money to delegate the care work. Males try to coordinate their professional activity with family visits abroad. In other words, males "use work to care for the family" (Wilding and Baldassar 2009, 183), as they tend to prioritize their career over family responsibilities. Correspondingly, the feminine way of coping is more oriented towards a "reduction of work to be with the family" (Wilding and Baldassar 2009, 180), sometimes for relatively long period of time when it comes to do the care work for an ageing parent back home. In brief, Wilding and Baldassar (2009) introduce different gendered images of "caring", as well as different perceived responsibilities toward that work. They stress that males and females tell different narratives, influencing both the "work-family integration" and the "family-strategies".

2.5.4 Intermediary Summary: Overcoming the Polarisation

In section 2.5. I showed how studies focusing on gender and highly-skilled migration overcome the "polarisation of migration", as these studies have proposed two "ways out". First, some "criss-cross" the "gender binaries" to assess highly-skilled migrant women. Scholars (e.g., Liversage 2009; Riaño et al. 2015) show how the feminine experience of highly-skilled migration is specific, and contains its own distinct challenges. Thus, they assert why the studies cannot be subsumed under a generic "gender-neutral" approach to highly-skilled migration. Second, other researchers (e.g., Shinozaki 2012; Schaer, Dahinden, and Toader 2016) tackle the "gender binaries" comprehensively, reconciling in a single analysis the interactions between highly-skilled migration and family migration strategies. They show the centrality of gendered narratives expressing and justifying the consequences of family migration strategies.

Having reviewed the most relevant literature on the topic and assessed its strengths and weaknesses, I will, in the next chapter, develop the theoretical framework that I will use to construct my own empirical analysis. This overview of highly-skilled migration and expatriation studies has revealed, above all, the centrality in existing research of "migration binaries" and the "gender binaries". Scholars struggle against these binaries; some manage to overcome them while others do no. The theoretical framework is therefore crucial, as the goal is to avoid conceptual "traps" which can lead to bias in the analysis.

3 Decentring the Research on Highly-Skilled Migration and Expatriation: Three Methodological Premises

3.1 Decentring and Deconstructing

In my literature review, I showed studies that analyse highly-skilled migration and expatriation from the perspectives of the migrant, the family, and the couple. I described two sets of unproblematised binaries: the "migration binaries" and the "gender binaries". In this chapter, I will dismantle these binaries to propose a "decentred analytical framework" that will allow for a more critical analysis of "highly-skilled migration". A "decentred analytical framework" deconstructs dominant discourses – which can delimit a more or less coherent field of study, such as that of "highly-skilled migration" – and creates space for a more focused discussion within that same field.

For scholars, the process of deconstructing discourses usually entails a critical and interpretative analysis revealing their unspoken, naturalised, and hegemonic assumptions (Hurlbert 2010). All forms of discourse – in any medium – can be deconstructed (e.g., scientific studies, newspaper articles, television shows, movies, and sociological interviews). Scholars of postmodernism create tools to deconstruct discourses in order to analyse the processes of power embedded in them. For Brinksmann and Kvale (2009), "A deconstructive reading tears a text apart; unsettles the concepts it takes for granted; concentrates on the tensions and breaks in a text, on what a text purports to say and what it comes to say, as well as what is not said in the text, on what is excluded by the use of the text's concepts" (Kvale and Brinkmann 2009, 230). Using the "migration binaries" and the "gender binaries", I will show what a non-reflexive use of the term "highly-skilled migrant" takes for granted – what the term says and does not say. I will deconstruct the assumptions that underlie such usage. This does not mean, however, forgetting the original concept and producing an entirely new theory. For Derrida (1978), deconstruction rather means to see these concepts as tools that one should use *à défaut de mieux*. It is about "conserving all these old concepts within the domain of empirical discovery while here and there denouncing their limits, treating them as tools which can still be used" (1978, 359). Thus, a "decentred analytical framework" not only deconstructs a non-reflexive usage of a concept, but also nuances it to create an analytical framework aware of the pitfalls implied by such a usage. A "decentred analytical framework" does not

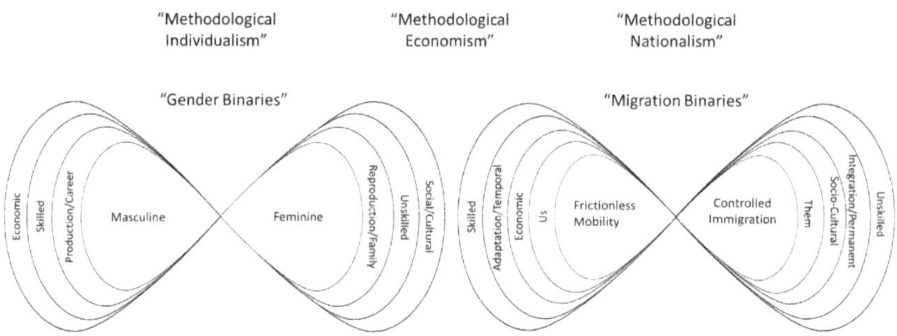

Figure 5 Gender and Migration Binaries. Source: Own Elaboration

dismiss the main positions of former studies as though they were now irrelevant or false, but rather focuses on the dominant mindsets they reproduce, showing how these mindsets create biases, in order to then create an approach able to tackle the same topic more reflexively. This implies looking specifically at the blind spots of the dominant mindsets. Metaphorically, the process is similar to moving a light source so that an object's shadow appears in a new place, and what was formerly in shadow comes to light. In sum, I develop an analytical framework to study highly-skilled migration by deconstructing the hegemonic discourse which the term sometimes implied.

I proceed in three ways in this chapter: (1) I deconstruct three core premises of highly-skilled migration and expatriation studies and propose a "decentred analytical framework" to overcome the biases they involve (which I refer to as "methodological premises"); (2) I develop an original "methodological premise", namely "methodological economism"; and (3) I articulate the analytical framework for my study. The three "methodological premises" are (1) "methodological individualism" (Mises 1999), which involves a blindness to the social context in which a highly-skilled migrant lives; (2) "methodological nationalism" (Amelina and Faist 2012; Wimmer and Glick Schiller 2002, 2003), which corresponds to the systematic superposition of national territory, people (*Volk*), and culture; and what I call (3) "methodological economism", which contrasts unproblematic and un-politicised mobilities with problematic and politicised migration. Each methodological premise is linked to one of the two binaries identified earlier, the "migration binaries" and the "gender binaries" (Figure 5). "Methodological individualism" concerns the "gender binaries", "methodological nationalism" concerns the "migration binaries", and "methodological economism" combines a critique of both.

3.2 Methodological Individualism

Intense and frequent international relocations influence both career path and private life. Moving is a key feature of many contemporary skilled careers: indeed, the requirement to be mobile is increasingly present in skill-demanding professional fields. Yet highly-skilled migrants also hold other social roles, as wives and husbands, mothers and fathers. Too often, they are only understood outside of their social and family context; this is what I call the "methodological individualism" bias. When they move, highly-skilled migrants are not individuals abstracted from their social milieu: their professional mobility has consequences for more than just them. Their partner, for instance, will have to decide if he or she will resign from a position in the labour force in order to possibly move, too.

Stemming from economics, "methodological individualism" (Mises 1999 [1949]) influences many studies on highly-skilled migration. It tends to obscure the social context surrounding the daily life of highly-skilled migrants. The problem of "methodological individualism" is not that it focuses on individuals as "the way to a cognition of collective wholes is through an analysis of the individuals' actions" (Mises, 1999 [1949], 42). The problem is rather the sole focus on the "masculine side" of the "gender binary" – in other words, the economic, skilled, and productive side, which ignores the conditions that make it possible. The "gender binaries" offer a specific way to categorise what is deemed relevant – the economic activities of men and women – leaving unquestioned what is deemed irrelevant – the necessary coordination of the work in the labour force and the care work, as well as the coordination between two professional careers when both partners work in the labour force. I argue that on the contrary, economic and care work exist in a dialectic relationship; one side cannot be understood without the other. An individual usually performs many activities related to both sides of the "gender binary" several times a day. The distinction is only a theoretical one, which has been constructed for practical and legal purposes, opposing, for instance, the public and the private life, the economic and the social realm, or the productive and the reproductive activity. A sociological approach focuses instead on what individuals do concretely in their daily lives; for example, they do not only go to the office[18]. Thus, I aim to decentre "methodological individualism" by systematically embedding the social and family relationships of highly-skilled migrants into my analysis. Many studies that focus on economic work do not pay heed to the division of the care work

18 As we shall see, this is a reason why one empirical chapter focuses on the daily-practices, emphasising a praxeological approach.

between the partners. In other words, in much of the existing research, the "masculine economic side" is essentialised and corresponds to the "natural" concern of highly-skilled migration studies. Decentring the analysis means questioning this presumed division; it implies that a study on highly-skilled migration should not only restrict itself to analysing the professional career of one of the partners – his or her productive activity – but should rather focus on the dialectic relationship between the work in the labour force and the care work, as well as the coordination between the two professional careers.

Through a decentred analysis of highly-skilled migration, I hope to overcome the "gender binaries". This involves revealing the collective social processes while also studying what is referred to as part of an individual economic process. Thus, my research answers the call to open the "black box" of the family in the context of highly-skilled migration (King 2012a, 23). Yet, I do not address the organisation of the family independently from the professional activity of the partners, which would only perpetuate the binary from the opposite side. Instead, I propose a single framework to study the professional and the family life. To explain and develop this framework, it is necessary to present a stronger conceptualisation of the family and the couple: I will briefly do so in the next subsection.

3.2.1 Defining the Family and the Couple

At the beginning of the introduction, I stressed a distinction between families and couples: families are intergenerational, while couples are not. While a couple must coordinate between, possibly, two professional careers and the care work (the absence of children does not mean the absence of care work), a family involves an extra layer of care work because of the presence of children and the need to raise them. At first glance, this distinction seems straightforward, yet it overlooks key aspects of my conceptualisation of the family and the couple. In the following, I will briefly define them, emphasising a distinction between "categories of practices" and "categories of analysis" (Brubaker 2013). Then, I will present the approach that I use to study families and couples in this work, namely "doing family" (Baldassar et al. 2014; Jurczyk, Lange, and Thiessen 2014).

Barry et al. (2000) define a "family" as a "group of people who are joined by consanguinity or by alliance" (2000, 725)[19]. Besides, Bryceson and Vuorela (2002) speak of "a feeling of collective welfare and unity, namely 'family-hood'" (2002, 3)

19 Ensemble des personnes apparentées par consanguinité et (ou) par affinité (Own translation).

Family: "a group of people who are akin by consanguinity or by alliance" (Barry et al. 2000, 725)

Elementary Family: "a cohabiting group composed of adults and their children who were procreated or adopted" (Barry et al. 2000, 725)

Couple: a voluntary union of two people by bonds of affection
→ **Unit of analysis**

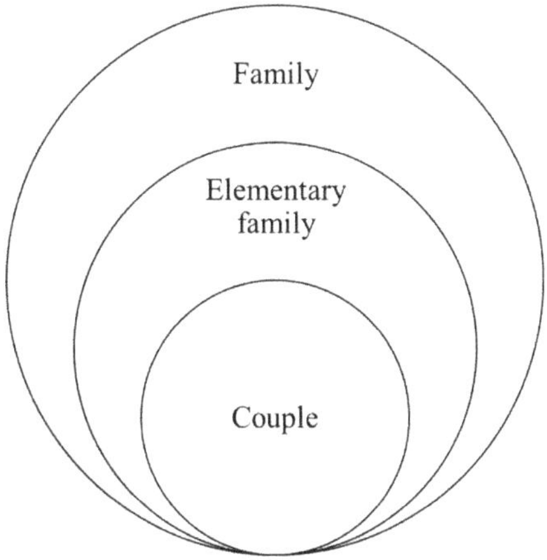

Figure 6 Family, Elementary Family, Couple. Source: Own Elaboration

while defining "family". Drawing on these two elements, I define "family" as a group of people linked by consanguinity or by alliance, sharing a feeling of collective welfare and trust, as well as a sense of unity and responsibility.

Furthermore, Déchaux (2010) defines the "elementary family" as "the residential group composed of adults and their children who were procreated or adopted" (2010, 2)[20]. Thus, "family" encompasses both the "elementary family" and the larger group united by kinship or by alliance. From this perspective, the "elementary family" and the "family" are different levels of analysis, as the "family" encompasses, arguably, a larger group (implying aunts, uncles, grandparents, cousins, etc.) than the "elementary family"; including the partners and their children.

The same can be said when it comes to distinguish the "elementary family" from the "couple". A "couple" includes only the partners. In other words, the intergenerational link is the key factor of distinction as a "couple" typically does not imply any. The "couple" corresponds to two persons "united by love or marriage"[21]. However, it does not exclude the embeddedness of the "couple" in larger groups: the partners forming the "couple" may very well have children. In fact, the concepts of "family", "elementary family", and "couple" correspond

20 Le groupe résidentiel composé d'adultes et de leurs enfants engendrés ou adoptés.

21 Truth be told, the *Oxford English Dictionary* defines a couple as "a man and a woman [sic.] united by love or marriage": an heteronormative definition.

to my "categories of analysis" (Brubaker 2013, 2). As categories of practice, the notions of family and couple are used by the actors in their everyday lives "to identify [themselves] and to identify others" (2013, 2). As "categories of analysis", the three concepts introduce different levels of analysis; implying different possible "units of analysis". My unit of analysis for this study is the "couple". In other words, when I speak of a "couple", I do not presuppose two partners without children, rather I indicate the focus on a specific level of analysis, namely the relationship between the partners – which may very well be at the same time parents, aunts, uncles, etc. Figure 6 illustrates the relation between different possible levels of analysis and my unit of analysis: the "couples".

Déchaux (2010) underlines the major transformations of the "elementary family" and the "couple" during the last decades. The freedom of choice in terms of sexual orientation freed many people to choose the affective life they desired. Though still suffering intense discriminations, LGBTQ+ communities have earned many rights over the last decades. Homosexual partnerships, marriages, and adoptions, for instance, have become legal in some countries. Furthermore, Giddens underlines that family ties are not naturally assumed anymore and have to be negotiated (2004, 122). As a result, divorces are more common, and children born outside marriages or partners deciding not to marry at all have increased, too. In sum, this emancipation process modified the ways of life of the "family", the "elementary family", and the "couple". For a sociologist, these transformations have to be analysed.

The "elementary family" does not equal what Parsons calls the "nuclear family" (1955) composed of two (heterosexual) spouses and their children. The larger group bound by kinship is excluded from the nuclear family, which is understood as archaic and not adapted to the conditions of modernity. In other words, the "nuclear family" exists independently from the notion of kinship (Déchaux 2010, 92). According to this (evolutionary) perspective, kinship will be, in time, replaced by the welfare state. This is somewhat reminiscent of Durkheim's distinction between a "mechanic" and an "organic solidarity" (Durkheim 1926). The basic idea is that "mechanic solidarity" – based on the proximity of individuals living in small community – will be replaced by an impersonal "organic solidarity" ruled by public institutions. The concept of the "nuclear family" has been roundly criticised by sociologists of the family because it ignores social context. Catherine Bonvalet (2003) shows, for instance, the persistence of the link between adult children and their parents. For her, kinship still offers concrete support, especially in difficult economic times[22]. Concretely, the support of

22 According to the Observatory of Emancipation almost 80 per cent of youth under 30

kinship means a "system of exchange of goods, services, and money" in a family (Déchaux 2010, 98). According to this perspective, adult children are not isolated from kinship, as they receive support, for instance, from their own parents.

3.2.2 The Hidden Economy of Kinship

Déchaux (2010) develops the idea of a "hidden economy of kinship" (2010, 99) to explore the support that exists among relatives. This support is structured around three elements: care work, access to others, and money transfer.

"Care work" primarily entails housework, shopping, cleaning, or caring for child or a parent. Déchaux (2010) argues that these services are mostly exchanged among the female generations; the "interchangeability of the females" (2010, 99) supports the "elementary family" – mothers, sisters, daughters, aunts or nieces. Interestingly, he stresses that "many of these services require geographic proximity" (Déchaux 2010, 99). He underlines that the care work is still predominantly done by women in contemporary families. As we shall see, this has deep consequences on the way in which partners prioritise their professional careers. Déchaux emphasises the necessity of considering kinship when analysing "elementary families" or "couples". The second element of the "hidden economy of kinship" is the "access to others" (Déchaux 2010, 99). One family member – usually a parent – mobilises their network to facilitate access to employment or to find accommodation for – most often – a child. According to Déchaux (2010), "access to others" involves the mobilisation of social resources (2010, 100). Finally, the third element refers to the money transfers. This implies not only inheritance, but any form of financial transfer (hand to hand, bank transfer, etc.). In this context, transnational studies show the relevance of "remittances" between the members of a family (see, for instance, Abrego 2009). Thus, the "hidden economy of kinship" proposes that "elementary families" and "couples" are not isolated. In a demographic study which took place in France, Bonvalet shows that half of the respondents of her study lives in the same commune[23] as a parent (2003, 38). She speaks of the local embeddedness of the family ("*famille-entourage local*") to express this idea. How does this support take place when an "elementary family" or a "couple" is recurrently mobile for professional reasons?

---

still live with their parents in Spain in 2014; retrieved August 3, 2018, from https://europa.eu/youth/es/article/38/23676_en 30.07.2018.

23 In France, a rather small territorial and administrative unit which can be translated as a community.

In summary, studies that focus on the "hidden economy of kinship" emphasise the integration of the "elementary family" and the "couple" within the "family".

3.2.3 Doing Family

Having defined the concepts, I still lack an approach within which to use them. In the context of highly-skilled migration, the approach emphasising "doing family" (Baldassar et al. 2014; Jurczyk, Lange, and Thiessen 2014) lacks the scholarly attention it deserves. "Doing family" – along with "doing migration" and "doing space" (Lutz and Amelina 2017) – are all socio-constructivist and praxeological concepts. They allude to the seminal work from the 1980s on "doing gender" (West and Zimmerman 1987). By "doing gender", the authors stress that gender is "a routine, [a] methodical, and recurring accomplishment" (1987, 126). In other words, the way gender is produced and exhibited in daily interactions creates a difference between men and women. The difference is socially constructed and not biological or naturally given. It is a way of defining the attributes of what is accepted to constitute men and women at a given time, in a given historical and geographical context. In this perspective, gender is always situated but "once the differences have been constructed, they are used to reinforce the 'essentialness' of gender" (1987, 137). "Doing family" underlines the same socio-constructivist logic, emphasising that "couples", "elementary families", and "families" are daily practices. For Jurczyk, Lange, and Thiessen, "doing family" is not only a socio-constructivist concept but also a praxeological one, because it "[d]irects the production and the organisation of personal relationships between generations and, where appropriate, between genders" (2014, 9)[24]. "Doing family" focuses on the way in which the partners practically construct their "couple", "elementary family", and/or "family". The collective decision-making process orients the actions of the partners, as most of the time they act in a way so as to maintain their personal relationship. The daily and recurring accomplishment of family goes in hand with the production of a discourse on the family. The partners give meaning to their practices. Thus, the socio-constructivist epistemology emphasises the processes by which a family is meaningfully constituted in a given context. It aims at overcoming a positivist and essentialist approach to the

24 "[Ein praxeologischer oder praxistheoretischer Blick auf Familie als Doing Family] fokussiert sich [...] auf die Praktiken der Herstellung und Gestaltung persönlicher Beziehungen zwischen Generationen und gegebenenfalls auch Geschlechtern". (own translation)

family which would consider the "nuclear family" as a "naturally" given form of organisation in which each gender naturally has his or her own role to play.

The children are often central actors within the process of "doing family". That being said, I do not specifically analyse them in the current study. I did not interview children but rather their parents. I shall show that the children are a central consideration for parents when developing "family- strategies", and are at the core of parents' way to "displaying family". I focus on the perspective of parents concerning their children and not on the perspective of the children themselves; my "unit of analysis" being the "couple". The work of Gaspoz (2013) explores the meaning of "geographic itinerancy" for teenagers. In a way, my work complements hers, as I focus on the parents and she focuses on the children. She analyses the institutional (school, hobbies, church) and interpersonal (friends, family) ruptures that teenagers in "geographical itinerancy" experience and I show the struggle of the parents to organise the institutional and social integration of their children.

"Doing family" refers to the ways in which partners co-create a feeling of collective welfare and unity daily within an "elementary family". It stresses how the partners do family (1) in practice, (2) in discourse, and (3) recurrently. First, "doing family" is a matter of practices. It is about the concrete consequences of the decision to migrate for an "elementary family" or a "couple", about how the partners recreate the fabric of daily life after a migration. Second, it is about the discourses they develop to present and portray their family, about how they justify their decisions regarding their daily organisation. Third, it is about how the practices and the discourses interact in the long run, as family is usually done over several years if not decades. In other words, it is not a fixed entity, but rather a dynamic among these three facets. Proposing a framework able to encompass the dynamics of "doing family" in the context of highly-skilled migration is the central ambition of my work. I propose to analyse the dynamics of "doing family" through three complementary perspectives which correspond to the socio-constructivist approach I developed earlier: the practice of the move, the narratives to display family, and the "family-strategy" that the partners adopt. The three facets cover three broad fields of sociological investigation: practices, discourses, and strategies. Each of these perspectives corresponds to an empirical chapter, as they each provide a specific perspective on "doing family". At the beginning of each empirical chapter I will propose a methodological clarification to show how I tackle the three facets of "doing family". Thus, the first element of my "decentred analytical framework" overcomes the "methodological individualism" by stressing the unquestioned and naturalised assumptions behind the "gender binaries".

3.3 Methodological Nationalism

The concept of "methodological nationalism" corresponds to another type of essentialising bias, this time concerned with the processes related to nation-states. I will use the same strategy that I used in the previous section, first presenting the problem and then proposing a decentred way to overcome it. The term "methodological nationalism" already lies at the centre of a large amount of literature (Amelina et al. 2012; Amelina and Faist 2012; Chernilo 2006; Wimmer and Glick Schiller 2002, 2003). In their seminal work, Wimmer and Schiller (2002, 2003) underline three forms of "methodological nationalism": ignorance, naturalisation, and territorial limitation. The first form overlooks a world structured around nation-states that have their own laws, institutions, and constitution; in other words, it ignores nation-states. The second form involves the naturalisation of "nationally bounded societies", implying a positivistic superposition of territory, people, and culture. On a nation-state's territory live culturally similar people; the assumption is that nation-states are internally homogeneous and naturally given – for instance, the French live in France. The third form implies the limitation of research to the territory of a single nation-state. Commissioned research paid for by the German government (mostly) deals with Germany.[25] Here, nation-states are conceptualised as independent boxes which can be studied as such. In sum, when it comes to "methodological nationalism", the path between ignorance and essentialism is short, as one must acknowledge the relevance of the nation-states (being complex entities acting at many levels) without naturalising them.

Interestingly, studies dealing with migration often emphasise the country of origin of the migrants. These studies construct their knowledge through an "ethnic" or a "national sampling" (Amelina and Faist 2012). This is much more rarely the case when it comes to highly-skilled migration and expatriation studies. While studies on migration tend to naturalise the nation-state, studies on highly-skilled migration tend to ignore it. Studies on highly-skilled migration and expatriation tend to refer to the larger frame of globalisation – arguably outside of the reach of the nation-states – while studies of migration focus on the "integration" of migrants in a national community. Thus, in many studies on highly-skilled migration and expatriation, the country of origin of the migrant is not specified. A non-reflexive use of the concept of "highly-skilled migrant" assumes a self-explanatory "us", the dominant group. I interpret these two fields

25 On this topic, Favell's (2001) "Integration policy and integration research in Europe: a review and critique" offers an extensive and insightful state of art.

of study as either focusing on "us" or focusing on "them" – which generally refers to the "global South". The approach focusing on "us" is not the same as the one focusing on "them"; this division highlights the relevance of the "migration binaries" in helping to spot unquestioned assumptions. Many of the studies that focus on ethnicity speak about "others", as if one could understand "them" better as a function of their national, religious, or ethnic belonging. Brubaker (2002) calls this "groupism": studying Italians assuming a cultural, social, and economic homogeneity among the members of the group created. In fact, studies on "ethnic migration" on the one hand and highly-skilled migration studies on the other develop, in parallel but opposite ways, a seemingly coherent discourse on the stratification of migration opposing an "elite" to "proles" (Amelina 2016). The model of the ethnically neutral highly-skilled migrant reproduces the dichotomy between the Western mobile professionals and the Southern desperate migrants. One way out of this problem would be to "ethnicise" highly-skilled migration studies – to analyse British highly-skilled migrants in Germany, for instance. A seminal study adopting such an approach would be that of Beaverstock (2005); yet he does not speak of "migrants" but rather of "British highly-skilled inter-company transferees". "Ethnicising" highly-skilled migration studies does not overcome the "migration binaries" but rather reverses them, just as studying only the family relationship of highly-skilled migrants (instead of focusing on their professional activities) only recreates the "gender binaries" in a reversed configuration. In order to overcome this conceptualisation opposing "us/them", I suggest changing the entry points of the study.

3.3.1 Changing the Entry Points

Overcoming "methodological nationalism" implies finding ways to acknowledge complex nation-states without naturalising them. Glick, Schiller, and Çağlar (2010) develop an approach to do so: I use their approach to establish a suitable framework for my study in the current chapter. In Chapter 5, I will contextualise the two regions investigated in this study and justify the relevance of this choice.

My work deals with migration for professional reasons, meaning that the respondents have, for the most part, a professional position in the country of arrival. Thus, they are embedded in different systems of social security. The region where they hold a professional activity grants them or their partner specific rights (e.g., maternity leaves) and offers specific opportunities (e.g., the availability of international schools) to coordinate the work in the labour force and the care work. These elements create specific realms of possibility for migrants in terms of their settling. I will discuss the case of a French pharmacologist taking a French maternity leave to be able to follow and live with her partner in Italy. This example shows how one's embeddedness in a specific welfare state offers various possibilities when it comes to coordinating the care work and the work in the labour force. The region where the respondents contribute towards social security, live, or are employed in the labour force matters. Thus, acknowledging nation-states means being aware of the variety of rights and social insurances in the different countries where the respondents contribute. The typology of "welfare state regimes" (Esping-Andersen 1990, 111) is useful in understanding these variations. Esping-Andersen (1990) proposes a typology to stress various forms of welfare states. The key variable in this typology is the concept of "de-commodification". "De-commodification" refers to "granting alternative means of welfare to that of the market" (1990, 105). The more a regime is de-commodified, the more the individuals outside of the labour force can maintain their standard of living. He differentiates between "liberal regimes", "corporatists regimes", and "socio-democratic regimes" (1990, 111–114), which all imply different relationships among the state, the market, and the family. In a nutshell, the "liberal regime" looks to the market to provide welfare, the "corporatist regime" encourages the traditional family, while the "social democratic" adopts a universalistic stance. Thus, the "welfare regimes" correspond to the configuration of social rights in different nation-states.

Further refining Esping-Andersen's (1990) model, Pfau-Effinger (1998) develops the concept of "gender culture" to show that the different "welfare state regimes" have cultural and normative assumptions. She focuses on the development of the various forms of "welfare state regimes", as well as their impact on the participation of women in the labour force. She underlines that the "welfare state regimes" are based on a certain idea of the "normal way" of "doing family" – in other words, a certain "gender culture". According to her framework, Switzerland and Germany are "conservative-traditionalist welfare regimes [in which] … a gender policy based on the male breadwinner/female carer family, [is] … least favourable for the labour market integration of women [compared to Scandinavian countries]" (1998, 162). When arriving in Switzerland or Germany, the respondents are confronted with these regimes.

The models of Esping-Andersen (1990) and Pfau-Effinger (1998) capture the structure of the "welfare state regimes" and explain institutional elements favouring or hindering the participation of women in the labour force. Yet they both understand the nation-states as homogeneous units. In this sense, these authors are still trapped in "methodological nationalism". Other authors stress that the "gender culture" and the structure of the "welfare state regimes" differs at the subnational level (Bühler and Meier Kruker 2002; Riaño et al. 2015).

The "gender culture" can change if one moves, for instance, from a metropolitan area to the countryside, from (in Switzerland) one *Bundesland* or *Canton* to another or from one linguistic region to another. Thus, the very region where the respondents live does matter, not only the country. In this context, Riaño et al. (2015) point out the different elements which constitute a "critical place" – that is, a place where it is especially difficult for the female partner to maintain a professional occupation after a relocation. These elements are "[the] geographical location, [the] availability of childcare facilities, ... [the] spatial mobility infrastructure, [the] labour markets, and [the] gender culture" (Riaño et al. 2015, 157). All of these elements play a role in explaining the division of tasks between the work in the labour force and the care work. The notion of "critical places" allows for a detailed conceptualisation of the national and the subnational variations of the "welfare state regimes", the "gender cultures", and the support available to highly-skilled migrants when they settle in a new location. This support does not have to be given by the state; I will show that many highly-skilled migrants mobilise privatised support such as international schools, private childcare facilities, au pairs, or nannies. Each region has specific constraints and opportunities, as they are embedded in specific "welfare state regimes".

Thus, the focus on regions rather than on nation-states acknowledges the inner heterogeneity of nation-states without ignoring their policies. Glick, Schiller, and Çağlar (2010) develop an analytical framework "using the city as an entry point"; this has the advantage of overcoming "ethnic lenses" (Schiller, Çağlar, and Guldbrandsen 2006), as the inquiry does not start by focusing, for instance, on the Turks in Germany but rather on the Frankfurt Rhine-Main region. The focus is not on one ethnic or national group or another, but rather on the processes that happen in given a city. Salzbrunn (2010) develops a similar argument, recommending that we start with the cities. In her view, "Focusing on localities rather than on specific groups based on national, ethnic, or religious criteria allow[s] us to go beyond methodological nationalism and to follow the actor's social practices, which extend beyond national frameworks" (Salzbrunn 2010, 189). She proposes to focus on more than a single city (in her case New York and Paris) to assess the ways in which migrants adapt their strategies according to the resources available in specific localities. Performing bi-local fieldwork allows for contrasts in the analysis, which in turn allow the researcher to assess the context in which the migrants live. I use a similar approach, though unlike Salzbrunn (2010) in her study, I do not develop a comparative research design. My goal is to reveal the differences between the two localities while studying while studying "doing family" on the move. In this way, it is possible to take seriously the warning against a "methodological nationalist" bias, by acknowledging nation-states without naturalising them – in other words, to assess the impact of policies (whether they come from the national level or the local level) and institutions on the daily lives of the respondents. This is crucial in my conceptualisation as the agency of the actors is oriented by these elements. Different cities, different "critical places", different regions offer different opportunities and constraints. Thus, doing my fieldwork in two regions allow me to contextualise and decentre the interviews, seeing the differences as well as the similarities in the daily-life of the respondents and producing a study aware of the role of the state in migration processes.

3.4 Methodological Economism

I develop the term of "methodological economism" to complement "methodological individualism" and "methodological nationalism". In a nutshell, I have proposed, thus far, to study how highly-skilled migrants are "doing family" in two locations in order to decentre "methodological individualism" and "methodological nationalism". "Methodological economism" aims to decentre the very concept of highly-skilled migrant. To do so, I examine the unquestioned assumption that highly-skilled migrants perform temporary moves by choice whereas lesser-skilled migrants are forced to move permanently. The consequence of this dissimilarity would be that highly-skilled migrants only need to adapt for a time in a new location while lesser-skilled migrants need to integrate for good. But I did not witness this contrast during my fieldwork. Thus, I hope to decentre the concept of highly-skilled migrant by "problematising mobility". I interpret this process as a corollary to "depoliticising migration" (Moret 2018; Wieczorek 2018) or, as Dahinden puts it, "de-migranticising migration" (Dahinden 2016).

3.4.1 Mobility and Migration

The concept of "methodological economism" follows Favell's critique (2014) opposing "frictionless mobilities" to "controlled migration". The problem with this conceptualisation is not only that it implies – once again – an opposition between "us" and "them", but that it suggests that mobility is frictionless. The superposition of the different binaries creates a worldview in which migration and mobility refer to allegedly different phenomena: "Among those moving across the borders of territorial 'container' states, there are the immigrants (e.g. refugees and the economically desperate), who are moved by forces beyond their control; and then there the others, most generally thought of as 'international travellers' (e.g. tourists, businessmen, expats, exchange students, retirees) who move by choice alone" (Favell 2014, 135). Favell shows yet another categorisation cutting the world into two: these are the "migration binaries". Favell argues that such a conceptualisation does not reflect the challenges that highly-skilled migrants may face in their daily-life. He points at the lack of empirical studies reflexively dealing with highly-skilled migration, underlining that "it is not frictionless mobility but rather differently tracked mobility with its own costs and constraints" (Favell 2014, 136). Highly-skilled migration studies should not presuppose an absence of constraints but should rather consider their possible existence as well as ways to track them. I will argue that the costs and constraints arise, for instance, in the coordination between the care work and the work in the labour force.

Questioning "migration" and "mobility" opens the topic of the nomenclature that I use in the current study. In this study, I have decided to use the term "highly-skilled migrant" and not "highly-skilled mobile professional" or "expatriate". Using the term "migrant" is part of the process of decentring the analysis. By underlining that the respondents of this study are migrants, I situate them in the field of migration studies. At the same time, placing them in the field of migration studies throws the whole field into question. Green (2008) develops this point while discussing the "migration of the elites":

> Thinking about the "migration of the elites" inserts this topic into the field of the history of migration, while nevertheless placing it at the margins of this field, margins that challenge the field itself. Performing greater mobility, business people are an extreme on the scale of migratory movements. Too rich, and they would be at the economic margins of the field as it was initially defined. The well-to-do migrants would be on the sidelines of a culturalist definition of the immigrant, too; they are often too close to the natives or, in any case, thanks to this social proximity, not seen as problematic. All of these criteria refer to the implicit delimitations of the field of migration studies that have given rise to a rich literature devoted to the migration of workers (Green 2008, 112; own translation)[26].

---

26 "Penser une 'migration des élites' insère cette histoire dans le champ de l'histoire des migrations tout en se plaçant à ses marges, marges qui interpellent le champ lui-même. Pratiquant une mobilité accrue, les gens d'affaires représentent un extrême sur l'échelle des mouvements migratoires. Trop riches, ils se situeraient également aux marges économiques du champ par rapport à la définition initiale. Les migrants aisés seraient également en marge d'une définition culturaliste de l'immigré puisque souvent trop proches des autochtones ou, en tout cas, grâce à leur proximité sociale, non perçus comme problématiques. Tous ces critères nous renvoient aux délimitations implicites du champ des études migratoires qui ont fait fleurir une riche littérature consacrée à l'immigration ouvrière".

Green (2008) decentres the history of migration by inserting the "migration of the elite" into the framework of migration – "too rich, and they would be at the economic margins of the field as it was initially defined". She points to the many unquestioned assumptions that I have presented in my theoretical framework, concerning, for instance, the "methodological nationalism" bias – "they are often too close to the natives or, in any case, … not seen as problematic". An unconsidered categorisation would be blind to the overlap between social class, gender, and ethnicity. Thus, using the term of highly-skilled migrant is a deliberate choice, as it reinserts these movers into the discussion on migration. Decentring the analytical framework is about precisely that: revealing the essentialised hierarchies of power, or moving the light to see the shadow of a concept. The term "highly-skilled mobile professional" does not insert the respondents into this debate; the light is metaphorically at its zenith and no shadow can be seen. It places the movers on the "frictionless side" of the binaries, coherently aligning race, gender, and class. Indulging in this assumption leads scholars to overlook the possible constraints that (multiple) relocations imply; it presumes a frictionless mobility.

3.4.2 Temporal Mobilities and Permanent Migration

Another binary within "methodological economism" opposes "temporal mobilities" and "permanent migration". I will use this binary to explain why I use the term "highly-skilled migrant" rather than "expatriate" in this study. Wieczorek (2018) argues that migration studies often fail to see mobility after migration. She develops three patterns of (im)mobility to analyse the various constellations of (im)mobility after initial migration. In her view, the "classic theories of migration" (e.g., assimilation and multiculturalism) assume that migration is mostly immobile, as the migrants are not thought to move again after their initial migration. She thus draws on "transnational studies" and on "mobilities studies" in order to develop other empirical patterns in which further mobilities (after migration) are investigated. In so doing, she underlines the diverse and complex mobilities of Polish migrants after their initial migration. Most studies of expatriation focus on a succession of short-term assignments and/or ultimately the repatriation. There is, however, a third possibility, which is to stay in the long-term in the new country of residence – what Wieczorek calls the "pattern of immobility" (2018, 101).

In the course of my own empirical work, I met people who had arrived in Switzerland or Germany as expatriates – having a position in the labour force before arriving in the country, most often in a multinational corporation – several decades ago. Since then, they have managed to stay on, either by convincing the employer not to relocate them anymore or by changing their employer. In such cases, the border between expatriation and migration is blurred. I already mentioned this point in my review of the literature, but I believe this point is central. The concept of expatriation falls short when the focus is on the biographical dynamics: some people decide to stay. As a result, it can be difficult to conceptualise the expatriate's inclusion in the country's "immigrant policies" (Hammar 1985) as well as their efforts to gain access to resources and privileges offered by, for instance, attaining a particular citizenship. It can also be difficult to resist conceptualising the expatriates as part of a "self-segregating" group (Fetcher 2007) who have no interest in the local population and do not learn the local language. I do not say that "self-segregating communities of expatriates" do not exist, as I witnessed some during my fieldwork. Rather, I wish to underline that these assumptions, related to the term expatriate, may blind the researcher to aspects of the study such as people saying that they are expatriates even though they have lived in Germany for 25 years. In this case, the "category of practice" may be expatriate but my "category of analysis" is "highly-skilled migrant". This choice is motivated by my explicit ambition to propose a "decentred analytical framework" that will allow for the analysis of liminal cases which do not really fit with the classic definition of expatriation but can still enhance our knowledge of the complexity of contemporary human migration.

3.4.3 Defining and Problematising the Skills

Choosing the term "highly-skilled migrant" also implies decentring the notion of "high-skill". The term underlines the educational achievement of the respondents and/or the level of skills required to occupy a position (OECD). Ryan and Mulholland (2014) stress that "[t]he term 'highly skilled' covers a diverse group, but the OECD and European Commission/Eurostat framework defines it as encompassing those who have either successfully completed a tertiary education and/or are employed in occupational roles normally requiring such qualifications" (2014, 6). Therefore, I deal with "highly-skilled migrants", a heterogenous group which is not constituted through race, ethnicity, or country or culture of origin, but through educational degree and/or the position hold in the labour force. Though straightforward, this definition is problematic because it refers to the binary opposing "high/low skill migration". This binary needs to be dissolved, as the notion of skill is often used as a proxy to refer to other forms of binaries. Higher skills are often linked, for instance, to the economic and productive side of the binaries; they create a "distinction"

(Bourdieu 2012) between individuals – and not only migrants. Higher skills are assumed to be central to judging the quality (or the value) of an individual in a society in which the labour market is a central institution (Bommes and Kolb 2006; Polanyi 2001). Yet many studies show the mismatch between a person's high educational achievements and a powerful position in the labour force. Riaño (2012) stresses that "[t]he presupposition by the human capital theory that educational attainment is rewarded with professional status does not apply to the case of migrant skilled women, especially when they originate from countries outside the EU" (2012, 16). Through an intersectional approach, she shows that the educational attainment alone is not enough to presuppose the position of an individual in labour market. Doing so, she "problematises" highly-skilled migration. She shows that a simplistic definition of the skills hides inequalities in terms of gender and countries of origin, referring respectively to the "gender binaries" and the "migration binaries".

Concerning the "gender binaries", Kofman and Raghuram (2005) argue that "the model of the rational and work-oriented male reproduces the dichotomy between economic man and social and cultural woman. … It supposes skilled migrants to always be men and women migrants to usually be less skilled" (2005, 151). They call for more studies on gender and highly-skilled migration precisely in order to deconstruct this assumption. They underline that studies adopting a gender-neutral perspective reproduce a hierarchy and a worldview: that of the dominant. The notion of skill contributes to the objectivation of a relationship of power, as usually a higher skill corresponds to a higher income and a higher social status. And women still face a "gender wage gap" (Blau and Kahn 2017); they earn less than their male counterparts with equal qualifications. On the top of that and in a migratory context, they also are discredited in their negotiations with the male partner concerning possible further professional migrations, as he already earns more: I shall show this in my empirical chapters. It follows that they are more often encouraged to resign in order to follow the male partner, and that they are then the ones who must face the difficult task of finding a position in the labour force after migration, not yet having a secured position in the country of arrival. Not having a secured job in the country of arrival is in turn a further risk of "brain waste and job-education mismatch", especially in the case of first-generation migrants (Pecoraro 2013, 10). In other words, many of the male respondents have a position in the labour force before moving, securing a relatively high income and recognition of their skills, while a lot of the female respondents, though they also have a tertiary education, struggle to find a position in the labour force corresponding to their skills and/or do not see their diplomas recognised. Though both are skilled, their lived experience of migration differs substantially. Sandoz

(2018) develops the concept of "migration channels" to express the differences in these experiences of migration. She distinguishes between different "channels of migration", or different ways of entering and subsequently settling in a new country. She defines the "channels of migration" as "Mobility pathways structured by different actors (states, profit-oriented actors, third-sector actors, and individual social ties) that create specific opportunities and constraints for migrants" (2018, 3). Based on this definition, she distinguishes four "channels of migration", each involving specific opportunities and challenges after migration: the "family-oriented channel", the "company-oriented channel", the "study-oriented channel", and the "protection-oriented channel". These four channels encompass the various ways someone otherwise categorised as "highly-skilled migrant" can enter a country. They stress different lived experience for the migrants. In my study, I deal with migrants entering through either a "family-oriented channel" or a "company-oriented channel". Very often, the female partner enters through a "family-oriented channel" while the male partner, already having a position in the labour force, enters through a "company-oriented channel". But an oversimplified definition of their skills can lead to an essentialisation of the "gender binary", as Kofman and Raghuram (2006) show; by decentring the "high/low skill binaries", using the works of Riaño (2012) and Sandoz (2018), I develop a more nuanced definition of "highly-skilled migration", showing that the term hides complex interactions among skills, work in the labour force, "migration channel", "doing family", and gender.

Concerning the "migration binaries" and according to the Database on Immigrants in the OECD (DIOC), the share of tertiary-educated migrants represents a non-negligible share of foreign-born individuals in Germany (14.9%) and Switzerland (23.7%). For the OECD, "population with tertiary education is defined as those having completed the highest level of education" (OECD).[27] However, there is no real overlap between the region of origin and the educational attainment. In other words, superposing "high/low skill migration" and "us/them" offers only a theoretical parallel. Table 1 shows that while women are nearly systematically discriminated against – having more often primary or secondary educational attainment – the share of highly-skilled foreign-born workers evolves in a complex dynamic that the "us/them" binary can only subsume with difficulty. There are still strong regional differences, too. 43.8% of

27 Definition available on the website of the OECD, retrieved April 13, 2018, from https://data.oecd.org/eduatt/population-with-tertiary-education.htm#indicator-chart

Region of birth	Men				Women				Total			
	Primary (%)	Secondary (%)	Tertiary (%)	Total (000)	Primary (%)	Secondary (%)	Tertiary (%)	Total (%)	Primary (%)	Secondary (%)	Tertiary (%)	Total (000)
North Africa	52.9	27.1	20.0	**1 993**	58.0	25.8	16.2	**1 643**	55.2	26.5	18.3	**3 636**
Sub-Saharan Africa	31.1	31.9	37.0	**1 509**	36.4	33.7	29.9	**1 432**	33.7	32.8	33.6	**2 941**
Asia	27.0	32.1	41.0	**7 770**	31.8	32.3	35.9	**8 381**	29.5	32.2	38.4	**16 151**
Latin America	56.1	31.2	12.7	**9 648**	51.5	33.2	15.2	**9 394**	53.8	32.2	14.0	**19 042**
Oceania	27.3	43.7	29.0	**541**	30.1	39.8	30.1	**570**	28.8	41.7	29.5	**1 111**
North America	18.9	35.0	46.1	**875**	20.0	38.2	41.8	**1 040**	19.5	36.7	43.8	**1 916**
Europe EU15	37.4	35.8	26.8	**7 252**	42.0	34.5	23.5	**8 114**	39.8	35.1	25.0	**15 366**
Europe EUA10	28.1	47.7	24.2	**1 684**	36.3	43.5	20.2	**2 068**	32.6	45.4	22.0	**3 752**
Other Europe	45.3	37.1	17.6	**4 805**	51.4	31.9	16.7	**5 103**	48.4	34.4	17.2	**9 908**
OECD	45.5	33.2	21.3	**16 521**	45.9	33.4	20.7	**17 221**	45.7	33.3	21.0	**33 742**

Table 2 Educational Attainment of the Foreign-Born Population in the OECD Area, by Region of Origin and Gender (percentage of the 15+ population). Source: OECD (2008, 88)

North Americans and 38.4% of Asians who move within other OECD areas have a tertiary education, while this figure is only 14% for Latin America.

"Methodological economism" thus corresponds to a third type of bias which opposes a skilled, frictionless, and temporal mobility to an unskilled, controlled, and permanent migration. These assumptions have important implications for the conceptualisation of studies, as temporal mobility requires adaptation and permanent migration implies "integration". Thus, "methodological economism" contributes to developing a framework that will not (re)produce hegemonic perspectives.

Each of the "methodological premises" I have outlined in this chapter offers a way to avoid specific biases in the research. "Methodological individualism" is a tool to deconstruct gender-neutral studies that look exclusively at the professional inclusions of male mobile professionals extracted from their social context. It stresses the necessity of taking into consideration the family-life and the professional-life concurrently. "Methodological nationalism" is a tool to acknowledge the role of the nation-states and their regional influences without naturalising them, by underlining the necessity of having more than one "entry point". And "methodological economism" is a tool to "problematise" highly-skilled migration by stressing that not all highly-skilled migrants are temporarily on the move for professional reasons and that their mobility is not "frictionless"; it is a tool to "problematise" highly-skilled migration. Finally, "methodological individualism" is the structuring concept of this study; I use it to divide the empirical analysis into three chapters and it provides me with the terms to ask the research questions.

3.5 Research Questions

The research questions (below) summarises the research questions. The first row of the table stresses the "main research question", while the three following rows all deal with thematic research questions. Thus, I propose a "main research question" that I subdivide to explore the different facets of "doing family" on the move. Each subset of research questions corresponds to an empirical chapter, and for each subset (i.e., each row of the table), I propose a "key concept" and a "conceptualised research question". At the beginning of each "empirical chapter", I define and conceptualise in depth the corresponding "key concept". For example, I define "displaying family" and "meaning pattern" at the beginning of chapter 7. The three "key concepts" have allowed me to develop a comprehensive framework to analyse "doing family". Thus, the middle column introduces each of these concepts – namely the practices, the narratives, and the strategies. I rework the "general questions" in the light of the "key concepts" to propose "conceptualised questions". These "conceptualised questions" are the ones I answer through the three empirical chapters. Chapter 9 offers a brief summary of all the answers. In other words, the "conceptualised questions" are reformulated research questions that take into consideration the main concepts that I use to develop my analysis. The second row focuses on the micro-level of the daily practices after a relocation (Chapter 6). The third row addresses the narratives of the respondents while portray or display their family (Chapter 7). And finally, the fourth tackles the strategies of the respondents on the long run (Chapter 8).

Table 3 Research Questions. Source: Own Elaboration

	General Questions	Key Concepts	Conceptualised Questions
Main Research Question	How do highly-skilled migrants and their families cope with professional careers on the one hand and family life on the other?	*Doing Family* **P+N+S**	How does "doing family" happen under the constraints and opportunities of frequent professional moves?
Research Questions for Chapter 6: ***Professional Careers***	How does the partners coordinate their professional careers when at least one moves for professional reasons? What are the individual consequences for their professional careers?	*Work in the labour force integration* **P**ractices	How do couples "integrate" two positions in the labour force when one has to move abroad for professional reasons? Is the "secondary-mover" facing specific challenges regarding their professional career? If yes, what are these challenges about?
Research Questions for Chapter 7: **Representing Migration: Between Motilities and Anchors**	What narratives do the partners develop when they are asked to portray their family? How do they talk about the division between the care work and the work in the labour force?	*Displaying Family* **N**arratives	What kind of "meaning patterns" do the interviewees produce when they "display family"? Does "displaying family" guide them in making decisions on their "care work integration"? If yes, how do they orient their actions while making these decisions?
Research Questions for Chapter 8: **Family-Strategies of Highly-Skilled Migrants**	Which strategies do the partners develop while settling in a new local space? How can they be conceptualised? Is the specific local space where the family settles important? If yet, in what respect?	*Family Strategies* **S**trategies	How can the "family-strategies" be conceptualised to study "gendered hierarchies" within families? What kind of model can I construct around them? What is the relationship between the "family-strategies" and the region where the respondents settle?

Methodological Part

4 Research Design

I will now focus on the methodological approach – corresponding to the research design (Chapter 4) and the context of the study (Chapter 5). The research design stresses how I tackle the research questions (the methods: my tools in this study) (Subchapter 4.2) and the justifications for using the methods I chose (the epistemology: the philosophical argument supporting the scientific validity of the methods chosen to construct knowledge) (Subchapter 4.1). Moreover, the present research is qualitative. Thus, I show that contextualising the conditions of production of the study is a necessity, because qualitative interviews are by essence heavily dependent on context. Therefore, the methodological part bridges the theoretical and the empirical parts, by explaining the epistemology, showing the methods, and contextualising the conditions of production of the study.

4.1 Epistemology

I use the qualitative methods of social science research (Beaud and Weber 2003; Becker 2008; Flick 2009; Lamnek 1993; Van Campenhoudt and Quivy 2011; Witzel 2000) and take inspiration from the "grounded theory", based on the ideas of Corbin and Strauss (2008). The underlying epistemological tenet of these methods is that a qualitative research design implies interpretative research findings: "unlike quantitative studies, where researchers claim to hold the objective perspective of the "disinterested scientist", qualitative researchers work from a tradition which recognizes that all research findings are interpretative and that the researchers are engaged participants" (Walsh 2003, 72). For most qualitative studies, the researcher creates his or her own empirical material in the field that he or she sees as relevant. A qualitative study is not "laboratory work" where the researcher controls all the factors influencing the study; or, if there is a laboratory, then the world itself is the laboratory. Thus, the epistemological foundations and the scientific validity of qualitative research lie in philosophical traditions other than the (neo-)positivistic leanings of (many) quantitative studies practised widely in the natural sciences. The principle of replicability is not attainable, as it is impossible to recreate the same study under the exact same conditions. In a sense, these conditions are gone forever, and no one will ever be able to replicate the context of Frankfurt am Main, for instance, during the warm spring of 2017 when I carried out interviews. Though conducting another study on the same topic is possible, the interviews and the whole manner of conducting it are going to be different. In fact, only the title may be similar. The experiment cannot be replicated.

Qualitative researchers do not work with "pure materials" (Becker 2008, 152). Geologists can measure, for instance, granite at different places, at different times, and will allegedly always find the same characteristics. Qualitative research does not work like this, as it relies on heavily contextually and relationally dependent material. In this context, Maxwell (1992, 279) quoting Bosk (1979) highlights the central question that researchers in qualitative science need to answer: "All field work done by a single field-worker invites the question, Why should we believe it?" (1979, 193) A qualitative answer to this epistemological question is that the more the reader understands precisely how, where, when, and by whom the study was conducted, the more the quality of the empirical material increases. In the absence of the possibility to replicate the study, the scientific validity is constructed around the capacity of the researcher to explain as precisely as possible how the research was conducted and constructed.

The central idea is that the qualitative empirical material is contextual and relational. Metaphorically speaking, there is no such thing as a "data tree" that the qualitative researcher finds in the "wilderness of the social world" to then collect the "authentic and unaltered fruits of knowledge". The conditions of production of the empirical material are, in fact, always relational because "whatever the configuration of the study, the researcher is, in practice, never absent" (Papinot 2014, 237)[28]. Thus, there is no data *per se,* as they are always produced in a relational context. Papinot (2014) quoting Bourdieu, reminds us that "real is relational" (Bourdieu 1994, 18 quoted by Papinot 2014, 238). The empirical material is nothing more than the result of the meetings between the respondents and the researcher in the context of a sociological interview. Yet, this encounter is by no means neutral. Reflexivity is therefore of the utmost importance. A reflexive approach requires that the researcher concretize how s/he gathers the empirical material (the "objectivation" in French). The goal is to overcome the naiveté of the positivistic "tree of knowledge" and – simultaneously – the pitfalls of a relativist approach in which no general knowledge is possible, as everything is unique and contextual. Though the situation of the interview is unique, it remains, nevertheless, a social interaction, in which the actors mobilise "schemes of meaning" or "habitus" (Bourdieu 2012) or "dispositions" (Lahire 2006) which are present before the interview. Language

28 Quelles que soient les configurations de l'enquête, l'enquêteur en pratique n'est jamais absent (Own Translation).

is an example of what is in place prior an interview. From this perspective, the matter of knowing whether or not respondents are telling the "truth", i.e., to know if the data collected by researcher are "pure" and "unaltered", becomes less important than understanding why respondents develop a particular discourse in a particular interview. From a reflexive perspective, the empirical material is not "self-sufficient" and needs to be interpreted and contextualised further in order to anchor its scientific value. What is at stake during this interview? Why do the respondents depict themselves or the family the way they did? What kind of power game did the researcher create by soliciting the interview? These are questions at the core of a study that reflects on the conditions of its production.

This imperative of reflexivity is central to the philosophies of qualitative research. Brinkmann (2017) – author of *Philosophies of Qualitative Research* – differentiates several epistemological "traditions" in qualitative research. These "traditions" each tackle the question of reflexivity and subsequently the way of grounding and justifying a scientific knowledge through a qualitative material in slightly different ways. My study mobilises a mix of two of them: the American tradition known as "pragmatism"[29] (Becker 2008; Dewey 1957; Goffman 1990; Rorty 1982; Thomas 1928) and the French one known as "post-modernism" (Derrida 1978; Lyotard 1979). Brinkmann (2017) summarises the American tradition through the following idea "*making the hidden dubious* implies a critique of the very idea that there are hidden dimensions of meaning behind our common superficial experiences and practices" (2017, 19). The major part of my empirical analysis is grounded on this idea. "Doing family" is ultimately a process that I can grasp through three concepts: the practices, the narratives, and the strategies. According to this tradition, (social) sciences do not reveal the "far side of the moon", but rather show the practices, the narratives, the representations, and the strategies of the actors – furthermore, doing so is a practice, too. For Dewey, a leading pragmatist figure, "the so-called separation of theory and practice means in fact the separation of two kinds of practice, one taking place in the outdoor world, the other in the study" (Dewey 1957, 69). The next subsection of the present chapter will describe how I conducted the study (4.2 Methods in Practice, 99). It allows the reader to understand how I practically (and pragmatically one might add) created the study. It is a first step to contextualising the

29 For Brinkman, these distinctions are just analytical ones to order various epistemological traditions. It does not mean that the "French" use only the so-called "French" set of theories while the "American" use only the "American" one. They are just labels based on the place where this tradition was originally developed.

conditions of production of the study: a necessary but insufficient step. Indeed, to understand the conditions of production of the study comprehensively, the reader needs to know more about who crafted this study (5.1 Contextualising the Researcher , 115) and the reason why the study took place in specific regions and not others (5.2 Contextualising the Lake Geneva Region and Frankfurt Rhine-Main Region, 118). The scientific justification of a study such as this one is not only grounded in the contextualisation of the conditions of production of the analysis; but also, in the contextualisation of the study itself. The researcher cannot be overlooked and should not be hidden, as he or she is a central actor of the process.

Brinkman (2017) characterises "post-modernism" as an extremely skeptical tradition when it comes to understanding the social scientist as a neutral producer of scientific knowledge on "society". "*Making the obvious dubious* implies an attempt to question what we take for granted to show that our meanings and understandings are unstable and endlessly ambiguous" (2017, 19). These ideas guide the state of the art (2 Moving with Skills: A Review of the Literature, 31) and the theoretical framework (3 Decentring the Research on Highly-Skilled Migration and Expatriation: Three Methodological Premises, 71) through the "migration binaries" and the "gender binaries". In these parts, I deconstruct and decentre the meanings and understandings of previous studies to reveal some of their non-reflexive arguments. Deconstructing and decentring other studies is one thing; doing the same in the process of the current study is another. In other words, decentring other studies does not protect my research from (re) producing non-reflexive assumptions and arguments. One method to control – as much as possible – the knowledge taken for granted is a recurrent toing and froing between the construction of the empirical material and its assessment. Thus, I use a "circular" model rather than a "linear" hypothetico-deductive model. The "circular" model relies on "feedback loops" (Van Campenhoudt and Quivy 2011, 209) between the empirical and the theoretical work to create knowledge which considers what the respondents have to say in the construction of the research. As a learning being, the researcher develops and sharpens his or her own understanding of the topic during the research. Not only does the theoretical work influence the understanding of the topic; but, during the fieldwork, the respondents give their perspective, underlining the challenges and the questions that are relevant to them. The respondents draw attention to topics that the researcher might overlook, leading the latter to reorient the study. Thus, the research design is open and flexible. Ultimately, it grounds the research in the discourses and the practices of the respondents, who are understood as the experts on their own lives. The sociologist does not know more than any of the respondents but knows what they all say, the collection of all discourses (Becker 2008, 123). Subsequently, he or she provides a respectful, yet critical, account of the respondents' discourses and practices. Practically speaking, it means reworking the core conceptualisation of the study based on the empirical material produced to analyse it. In sum, I develop a qualitative, empirical, reflexive, and circular study.

4.2 Methods in Practice

I repeat: the epistemology is the underlying philosophical argument justifying the scientific value of the methods. The methods are the tools to produce the empirical insights. As such, it is very difficult to present methods *in abstracto*, as they are, following a pragmatic standpoint, literally the practice of the research. Thus, the present subchapter (4.2) focuses on the methods in practice.

4.2.1 Accessing the Field

I will use the first stages of my fieldwork and the initial lack of access to the field as means of illustrating the circularity of the research process. At the start of this study, I wanted to analyse the "internationalisation processes of four multinational companies", focusing on the "role" of expatriates and human resources in the aggro-food business. In January 2014, I began looking for potential respondents. I sent requests to the companies and their employees for interviews; at first, I received no answer. When I received a response, it was a categorical "no go". The public relations representatives of the companies redirected me to their company website. The potential respondents systematically refused the interview, telling me that the information I was asking for was too sensitive. Besides, I needed to have the agreement of the public relations teams of the companies, they told me, which, of course, I did not have. In short, I could not access the field. Darmon (2005) stresses how the "refusals of fieldwork" ("refus de terrain" in French) and the "struggles to access the field" are valuable empirical material. Darmon's main point here is that the fieldwork does not start when the microphone is on and when the respondent starts to talk, but rather it starts even as the sociologist is negotiating access to the field. I wanted to enter a protected milieu, which generates a lot of money, and which feels threatened by many external actors. These companies aim to avoid "bad communication" with such actors. They had nothing to gain by accepting a study such as mine. For them, it implied only risks. Furthermore, had they wanted to know more about their "internationalisation processes", they would have investigated it internally. Their image is of the uppermost importance and they felt threatened because I wanted to analyse a critical, and yet crucial, aspect of their work. If I wanted to have access to them, I would need to present my research in such a way that it would not be perceived as a threat. My intention to study four specific companies increased their fears and thus raised the barriers to my entering. In fact, these companies are as afraid of seeing their company name appearing in a study as much as people studying them specifically. Such is the difficulty of studying multinational companies, as they restrict access to information concerning themselves.

One way to circumvent their fear was to change the "unit of analysis" of the study. Rather than analysing specific companies, I decided to study the "role" of the employees in multinational companies in general as well as their professional careers. In other words, the "unit of analysis" changed from the company to the migrants. A personal contact gave me four email addresses of potential respondents, whom she had known through her professional activity. This contact asked the potential respondents beforehand if I could send them an email. It is only when they accepted to be contacted that I sent them my requests. While I established that I was only interested in their personal experiences of migration and underlined that I would completely anonymise the interviews, only two of them accepted to meet for an interview. During the interview, the respondents did not fully trust me when I asked them questions about their employers. Their answers were brief and general. They were not at ease and defensively wondered at my questions. They did not know what to say when it came to the alleged employment strategies of their company. It is only when I started to ask personal questions about their private lives and the challenges they experienced during their various stays abroad that the respondents started to feel more confident. I felt a relief in their attitude when they understood that I was interested in their personal experience of migration. In the empirical analysis I will discuss further the fear of losing one's position in the labour force. Briefly put, the fear of saying something that could be used against the company and subsequently having consequences for the respondents themselves explains why many respondents were reluctant to agree to my first requests for interviews and why they felt so ill at ease speaking about their company as such. This line of questioning is also a matter of ethics as the researcher should not harm the respondents. Thus, these two first interviews were crucial to better understanding the people I wanted to interview.

The "feedback loops" between the theoretical work and the fieldwork imply that the latter influences the former. I transcribed the first two interviews and decided to approach them by asking myself which question these interviews answered – following the "trick of the trade" of Becker (2008, 196). I needed to account for what the respondents were telling me and not consider their discourse as irrelevant just because it was not what I wanted to hear. Analysing these first two interviews revealed that a central concern of the respondents was the coordination between care work and labour force work. I reworked the research questions and subsequently reformulated the way I was presenting my research to include this aspect. In doing so, access to the field became easier. I specifically explained in my requests for interviews that I was interested in better understanding the "work life balance" (Wilding and Baldassar 2009) in the context of highly-skilled international professional careers (Appendix 1: Contact Letter, 324). This way, I began to receive positive responses to my requests for interviews. Furthermore, the new interview grid (Appendix 2: Interview Grid, 325) focusing on the lived experience of migration was better understood by the respondents: they accepted the "contract" of a sociological interview (Kaufmann 2011) and began to share. The respondents did not necessarily speak without "filters" telling the "truth" about their "work life balance". Papinot (2014, 239) shows that such a naïve conception of the interview practice would mean that the moment in which the interview takes place would be out of the social, "floating in a social zero gravity zone". This was not the case. The respondents judged me, as well as the situation, judged my questions as well as the relevance of my study and presented me with a discourse they perceived relevant according to their judgement. Many of them told me before the interview that my study tackled a central concern for them. Changing the topic of the research, going in the direction of what the first two respondents were concerned about, made for a study that genuinely interested potential respondents. They not only felt less threatened but were also curious about my work. For me, it meant, that the respondents would agree to see me and to "play the game" of answering my questions.

4.2.2 Constructing the Interview Corpus

Overall, I did four waves of interviews, each time focusing on another characteristic of the interviewees, my goal being to maximise the heterogeneity amongst the respondents. Thus, I conducted the fieldwork between the Spring 2014 and the Summer 2017 in the Geneva Lake area, Switzerland, and the Rhein Main area, Germany. I ran semi-directive interviews with 36 skilled migrants, problem-centred interviews with eight key informers, and participated in three meetings dedicated to skilled migrants and expatriates. Table 4 describes the main characteristics of the respondents of the 36 semi-directive interviewees.

As Table 4 shows, the interviewees have some characteristics in common. In fact, these characteristics mirror the way I selected the respondents. They

Table 4 Interviewees Characteristics, Absolute Numbers. Source: Own Elaboration

	Number of respondents (N=36)		Number of respondents (N=36)
Gender		**Employer**	
Male	19	Consumer-good MNC	11
Female	17	Pharma MNC	9
Age (years)		Marketing MNC	6
25–29	1	University, Research	5
30–34	4	Finance MNC	2
35–39	4	Unemployed	2
40–44	7	Education	1
45–49	8	**Highest Qualification**	
50–54	9	Master's	24
55–59	1	Bachelor's	6
60–65	2	Doctorate	6
(Dual) Citizenship		**Family Situation**	
France	8	Married	22
US	8	Partnerships	6
Germany	7	Divorced	4
UK	4	Single	4
Indonesia	2	**Number of International Relocations**	
Netherlands	2	1	8
Austria	1	2	6
Brazil	1	3	6
Portugal	1	4	5
India	1	5	2
Israel	1	6	6
Italy	1	7+	3
Japan	1	**Children**	
Mexico	1	Yes, at home	21
Russia	1	Yes, not at home	3
South Korea	1	No	12

all have a university degree or equivalent; technically, they are all highly-skilled. They are all in the second period of their lifetime – what Kohli calls the "period of professional activity" (1989, 2), compared to the "period of education" and the "period of retirement" (ibid). Thus, none are retired, and all have completed their studies. Their ages show that they are most likely to be in this second period of life too as all are between 25 and 65 years old. Most of the respondents work in the labour force and most of them are employees of a multinational company. In fact, most of the respondents are part of the upper category of the middle management in multinational companies. I carried out the interviews in six distinct companies active in various sectors. Also, five respondents are active in research and one is employed in education; namely a specialised school. On eight occasions, I conducted interviews with four couples, each partner separately; which means I have the story from the perspective of each partner four times over. The two interviewees without a paid job were two (female) partners who – though they completed a university degree – stopped their professional activity for the sake of the (male) partner's work in the labour force. All the respondents were born outside of their current country of residence and all had lived abroad for at least two and a half years, which corresponds to the time spent abroad by the youngest respondent who was 28 years old. In fact, most of the respondents lived a least a decade abroad and some more than 25 years. To take an example from the interviews, Hannah left Britain at the age of 24, lived in Germany, Ukraine, Russia, and Turkey, and is now back in Germany at the age of 52, having thus lived abroad for more than 25 years. Thus, they all experienced professional mobility at least once. To conclude, it is important to underline that the respondents all correspond to a privileged group of professionals with relatively high financial means.

Though there are many similarities between the respondents, I maximised the heterogeneity of my sample. Many of the respondents had a position in the labour force before relocating, though with different types of contracts. Some had an "expatriate contract" and others were hired under a "local contract" – depending on the policy of the employer and the way they received the position – some applied abroad, others were transferred by their employing company. I also conducted interviews with people who relocated for the sake of their partner's professional activity and found a position after relocating. In the sample, the respondents' citizenships are as varied as their employment situations. This was a deliberate choice. My aim was to gather knowledge that overcomes "methodological nationalism" (Wimmer and Glick Schiller 2002) by treating nationality as one factor amongst others and in my cases not a determinant one. Their passport did not really play a role as most of the respondents come from the "global North": underlining once again their privileged status. Those respondents with passports from countries that posed barriers to settlement in Germany or Switzerland were for the most part supported by their employers. The procedure is straightforward as the status of being an "expatriate" employed by a multinational company unlocks residency and working permits.

a. Constructing the Corpus of Interviews

I collected the discourses in four distinct waves of interviews. The semi-directive interviews are the core empirical material of this study and are made up of 31 hours and six minutes of recorded, transcribed, and coded interviews. Two interviews were not recorded as per the respondents' request. It is important to note here that I proceeded through a "theoretical sampling" (Corbin and Strauss 2008, 144). Corbin and Strauss (ibid) compare the "theoretical sampling" to detective work. For each "feedback loop" the research uses the new data gathered to explore another understudied aspect of the topic, meaning, the people I was looking to interview changed slightly between each wave.

In spring 2014, and after the first two interviews, I conducted a first wave of interviews focusing on the mobile background of the respondents as well as their family relationships. I got in touch with the first respondents through the website *Internations*[30]. We met briefly at a meeting organised by the administrators of this website and agreed to proper interviews. After I did the interviews, one of the respondents showed interest in my study and acted as a "gatekeeper", as he gave me the contacts of four of his colleagues. During this first wave, I mostly got to know pharmacologists working in a middle-sized pharmacological multinational company. Most of the interviewees were pharmacologists who have a position in the research department or the regulatory division of the company. The policy of the company concerning the mobility of its employees is specific as none of the interviewees have an "expatriate contract". They all told me that the company does not offer this opportunity. Instead, they all have a "local plus contract" – a local contract with specific advantages for mobile employees such as tuition fees for the schooling of the children.

After the first wave of interviews, I looked for different profiles, diversifying the employing companies. During the spring of 2015, I carried out a second wave of 12 interviews. This time, I contacted the respondents not only via *Internations,* but also via *Facebook*[31] and *Glocals*[32]. The various entry points allowed me to get in touch with skilled migrants with positions in marketing and consumer goods

30 Website of Internations, retrieved April 13, 2018, from www.internations.org

31 Website of Facebook, retrieved April 13, 2018, from www.facebook.com

32 Website of Glocals, retrieved April 13, 2018, from www.glocals.com

companies. Once I completed the first interviews, I used the "snowball sampling strategy" (Atkinson and Flint 2001) to get in touch with more respondents. While some gave me an additional contact, one specific interviewee – a manager in a large consumer goods multinational company – organised four interviews with her colleagues. During this second wave, the profiles of the respondents were more diverse, emphasising the heterogeneity of the category of skilled migrant. I got in touch with skilled migrants working in research, education and/or in smaller companies too. I noticed that the way the partners divided the care work and the work in the labour force was a central topic of the interviews, and that I was lacking interviews with respondents working for large multinational companies under an "expatriate contract".

I prepared the third wave of interviews by modifying the interview grid and adding specific questions about the coordination between care work and work in the labour force. In Spring 2016, I started the third wave and contacted an organisation supporting dual couple careers. I did an interview with one of the persons responsible for the program. Thanks to this individual, I managed to get in touch with an employee of a consumer goods company who found employment in the labour force with the support of the program. This employee gave me the contacts of two of her colleagues and I launched the "snow ball sampling strategy". During the third wave, all the interviews were carried out in a large multinational company based in Lausanne. I managed to interview seven more employees in this consumer goods company. Many respondents emphasised their difficulty in finding day care arrangements for their children, this a hinderance to the possibility of dual careers. Many complained about the price and/or the lack of availability of such care in Switzerland.

Thus, the fourth wave of interviews stemmed from the necessity to explore the role of the locality on the corpus. Hence, I went outside the Lake Geneva region and chose the Frankfurt Rhine-Main region[33]. For this wave, I did not want a change in the characteristics of the people I was interviewing. Instead, I wanted to interview them somewhere else. I carried out these last interviews in the Frankfurt Rhine-Main region during the spring of 2017 in multinational companies active in consulting and marketing there. I activated a contact that a former interviewee in Switzerland had given me. I did six more interviews which allowed me to contextualise the data I gathered in Switzerland. I stopped doing

33 For the in-depth justification of the choice of these two regions, as well as the main differences between them, see the subchapter 5.2 Contextualising the Lake Geneva Region and Frankfurt Rhine-Main Region, p. 98.

interviews as I reached a state in which the new interviews were not providing any new information that I did not already know: what Bertaux (1981) and Pires (1997) call the "empirical saturation". In other words, it is not that I knew any more than any respondent on the topic but I knew what they all knew (Becker 2008, 150). Of course, each new interview would bring a specific configuration of the different elements of the former interviews, but each topic had already been covered at least once in a former interview. Thus, the whole process of gathering the material was deeply embedded in the analysis itself: the distinction is mostly theoretical as usually, after an interview, I started to transcribe it, analyse it and further develop my concepts. A circular model drives my research. For Corbin and Strauss (2008) this process takes shape as follows:

> Unlike conventional methods of sampling, the researcher does not go out and collect the entire set of data before beginning the analysis. Analysis begins after the first day of data gathering. Data collection leads to analysis. Analysis leads to concepts. Concepts generate questions. Questions lead to more data collection so that the researcher might learn more about those concepts. The circular process continues until the research reaches the point of saturation (Corbin and Strauss 2008, 145).

This quote summarises how I collected my material for this study. I did it hand in hand with the empirical analysis. Thus, I developed a "theoretical sampling" characterised by "feedback loops" between the fieldwork and the analysis.

b. Interview Grid

In conducting the interviews, I used an interview grid, which served me more as a guide than a strict list of specific questions to ask. More than strictly following the interview grid, I focussed on what the respondent was saying, encouraging him or her to develop and to explain concretely his or her answers. Following the method developed by Kaufmann in *L'Entretien compréhensif* (2011), the goal is that the respondent feel at ease in front of the interviewer, the researcher encouraging him or her to speak freely. This approach does not neutralise the power play during the interviews. In an effort to do so, I used a grid which was a combination of an open-biographical question and semi-directive questions. I systematically started with the question asking: *How did it happen that you are in Germany (or Switzerland) now?* The open question was aimed at eliciting a narration on the part of the respondent about his/her journey to the place he or she was currently living in, getting relevant information on the mobile background of the interviewees and their families. It was also an attempt on my part to disrupt the "question answer model" in which the respondent gives short answers. The goal was to encourage him or her to speak. The first part of the interviews consisted of the respondents' story and lasted approximatively 20 minutes in each interview. After the first part, I switched to the semi-directive questions, which composed the second part of the interview. I organised the semi-directive question through different topics: the choice of the country of destination (and who made that choice), daily life in the new place, the partner's situation and his or her activity, the "work care integration" of the partners (Halpern and Murphy 2005), the schooling of the children, the social life of the partners, the support of the company, the formal and informal support, the relationship to the different state bodies, and questions regarding self-identification. Thus, the interviews encompass both the trajectory to today (the social processes and physical movements of the respondents) and specific questions about the subjective experience of expatriation abroad (Appendix 2: Interview Grid, 325).

4.2.3 Analysing the Interview Corpus

So far, I have explained how I created the corpus of interviews. In this part, I will show how I analysed it through three angles, each corresponding to an empirical chapter. I conducted the analysis of the corpus using the free software for qualitative research, Sonal[34]. The strength of the program is that it proposes an "all integrated" solution to analysing qualitative data; from transcribing to coding audio files and later text documents.

a. Objective Data

Yet, the tool does not make the research. The first part of the analysis was about organising the data. To that purpose, I completed the corpus of interviews with "objective data". At the end of each interview, I asked the respondents to fill in a form in which I asked for basic sociodemographic data: the country of birth, the nationality, the highest qualification achieved, the marital status, the children (if any), the current place of residency of the partner and the year of birth (Appendix 3: Data Sheet, 331). I also used the LinkedIn profile[35] of the respondents and I combined it with the data of the interviews to recreate the mobile background of each respondent. Thus, I could see the professional career of the respondent (the succession of positions in the labour force) (Baruch 2006). Furthermore, I combined the objective data of the respondent with the situation of the partner and the children to get an overview of the family-strategy

34 Website of Sonal, retrieved April 13, 2018, from www.sonal-info.com
35 Website of Linkedin, retrieved April 13, 2018, from www.linkedin.com

of the partners over time. In order to do so, I use another free software called FreeMind[36] to create a map for each interview. The map below is the example of John and Aurelia. I conducted the interview with John at his office and recreated his background as well as Aurelia's on this map, crossing the information from the interview, the data sheet and his LinkedIn profile. These maps would be central to understanding the family dynamics in the long run. The circle at the middle of the map summarises basic sociodemographic information about John. The numbers symbolise the different professional moves. The right-hand side of the map emphasises John's background while the left-hand side of the map highlights Aurelia's background.

The map (Figure 7) helps to illustrate the impact of one partner's career on the other partner, as well as the "family-strategy" that the partners develop: in this case, we shall see that the "family-strategy" is gendered as Aurelia consented to moving to follow John and to do the care work for their children. In other words, her professional career was strongly impacted by her move with her future husband and by the eventual arrival of their children. John's career has not been similarly affected.

b. *Subjective Data*

The bulk of the data is composed of transcribed qualitative interviews. I systematically coded the interviews by using a list of pre-set codes and developed a list of emergent codes (Appendix 4: Code Book, 332). The list of "pre-set codes" (also known as "*a priori* codes") corresponds to the codes that I developed before assessing my data. These codes in fact came from my conceptualisation and my research interests. They corresponded to what I was looking for. I prepared the list, as the name suggests, before assessing the interviews. Examples of "pre-set codes" are: professional career, support of the company, support of the state, private life, self-identification, etc. The list of "pre-set codes" was mostly a tool that I used between the different waves of interviews. It allowed me to see if my conceptualisation fit with the interviews, or if I needed to change my conceptualisation and rework my interview grid. It was a controlling tool to anchor the study in the interviews, to avoid the risk of over-conceptualisation. Thus, it created a discussion between the fieldwork and the analysis, allowing for the construction of a study that takes advantage of the information gathered during the fieldwork. This is a strategy to enrich the study and increase its

36 Website of Freemind, retrieved April 13, 2018, from www.freemind.sourceforge.net

Figure 7 John's and Aurelia's Mobile Background. Source: Own Elaboration based on the free software Freemind (www.freemind.sourceforge.net)

Selective Coding	Axial Coding (Grouped Open Codes)	Main Idea (of the Research Notes)
200 Family Strategy		Doing family: Dynamic primary <-> secondary mover
	201 Family Strategy: Being divorced	A new organisation needed
	217 Family Strategy: Marriage	To make it work, I accept sacrifice
	212 Family Strategy: Discussion	Negotiation, Rupture, and Power - I will not stop working for you!
	218 Family Strategy: Division care-work	Egalitarian Families and Patriarchal Families
	202 Family Strategy: Settling	Difficulties to settle when arriving in a new place
	203 Family Strategy: Supported by migration industry	Different types of support - Heterogeneity of MI
	204 Family Strategy: Not supported by MI	Local Move - Do it yourself
	205 Family Strategy: Accomodation	Where they live
	207 Family Strategy: Local oriented	The wish to stay
	208 Family Strategy: Motility	The perceived likeliness and possibility of a further move
	216 Family Strategy: A relocatable unit	Motility - We move when we want - patriarchal family
	215 Family Strategy: Maintaining ties	Boomerang to maintain friendships
	213 Family Strategy: Mobility	Mobility as a strategy!
	206 Family Strategy: Children	Organising the care-work
	209 Family Strategy: International School	Types of Schools
	210 Family Strategy: Local School	Types of Schools
	211 Family Strategy: Boarding school	Types of Schools
	214 Family Strategy: Path-dependency	Language of education for the children -> path dependency

Table 5 Example of a List of Codes. Source: Own Elaboration

quality. Thus, the pre-set codes are crucial to recalibrating the interview grid after having carried out a wave of interviews in order to explore new dimensions in the following wave.

An "emergent coding" (also known as inductive coding) develops the empirical analysis based on the content of the interviews. As its name suggests, the codes emerge out of the interviews. In other words, the researcher creates the analytical categories through codes coming from the data. Furthermore, the research notes, the memos are an important tool to develop the "open codes" as they contain a multitude of thoughts, "hypothesises", ideas, and notes taken, for instance, just after an interview. Strauss and Corbin insist on the importance of this tool (2008, 164). The goal of using "emergent coding" is to stick as much as possible to the content and the context of the interviews. It is about developing codes based on the interview and the research notes. The first step is to develop "open codes", that is a significant list of codes close to the text, describing and pointing at specific processes and topics developed by the respondents. "Open coding aims at developing substantial codes describing, naming, or classifying the phenomenon under study" (Flick 2009, 309–10). To illustrate this method, I present in Table 5 a part of my code book. In this example, the "open codes" are: being divorced, marriage, discussion, division

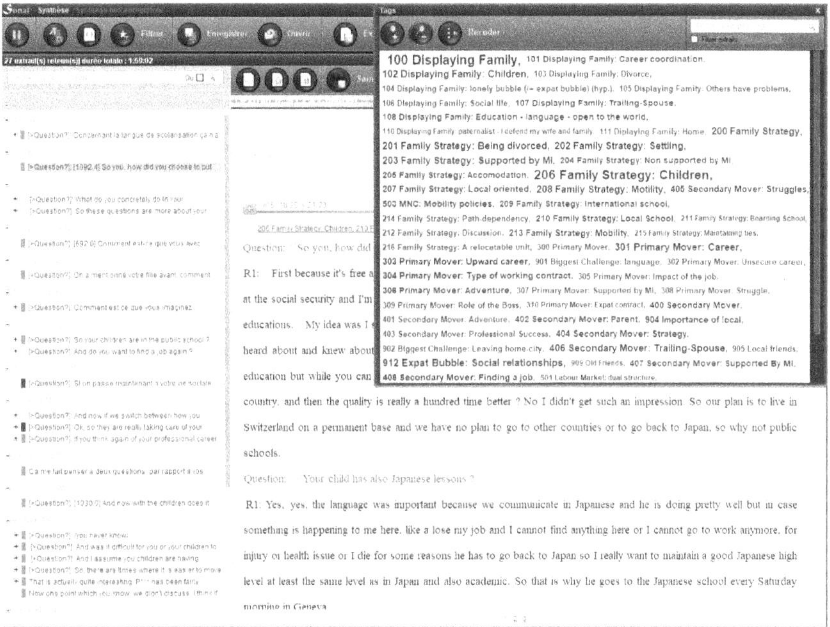

Figure 8 Open Codes and Excerpts. Source: Own Elaboration based on the free software Sonal, www.sonal-info.com

of care work, etc. They correspond to various excerpts of the interviews and I linked them to research notes and memos that I collected during the research process. In the list of code, I summarised the main idea of the research note.

Each "open code", corresponds to parts of the interviews in which the respondents talk about a specific topic. Thus, the process of developing and arranging the "open codes" is the engine to develop the empirical analysis. Figure 8 is a screenshot of the program I used to transcribe and code the interviews. Concretely, I coded the entire cursus of interviews. The right table entitled "Tags" refers to a part of the list of "open codes". In this example, I selected the code "206 Family Strategy: Children" which corresponds to 27 extracts; then, I selected the interview with Yuna in which she describes the challenges she faces raising her five- year-old boy while living in Switzerland. The advantage is that I can focus on a thematic rather than an interview as a whole as it is possible to see all the excerpts corresponding the "open code: children".

The second step regroups the "open-codes" into key categories, through a process called "axial coding". "Axial coding" involves coding the codes, regrouping the dozens of "open codes" into meaningful categories and creating connections between the codes. It is a tool that ultimately creates meaning out of the multiple anecdotes, lived experiences, and memories shared within the interviews. It allows the researcher to focus on the main topics of the analysis by regrouping for instance all the codes related to "professional career", or "family-strategy". In Figure 8, the process of "axial coding" corresponds to the way by which I group all the "open codes" in the category "family-strategy".

The last step is the "selective coding" which refers to the selection of the core analytical categories for the study. While presenting this method, Flick (2009) speaks about "the categories that are most relevant to the research question" as being "selected from the developed codes" (2009, 312). The "selective coding" refers to the way the researcher selects the core categories which are going to structure the research. They are going to be the core material of the following three empirical chapters. In the list of codes in Figure 8 (the window "Tags" on the screenshot), three groups of codes can be distinguished. I distinguish three analytical categories that correspond at the same time to the last step of the coding and to the structure of the empirical analysis. These three analytical categories are namely the 300s and 400s codes called "primary-movers" and "secondary-mover", the 100s codes, "displaying family", and the 200s codes, "family-strategies". These three groups of codes correspond in turn to three concepts that I made reference to while presenting the "methodological individualism": the practices, the narratives to "display family" and the "family-strategy" that the partners adopt. The first chapter of the empirical part (Chapter 6) deals with a typology of moves and movers based on the concept of initiative. It distinguishes the partner who initiates the move (the "primary-mover") and the possible reactions of the other partner (the "secondary-mover"). It adopts a collective perspective encompassing both partners, not just one of them, to understand the various motivations and the consequences of a professional move. The second chapter focuses on "displaying family" (Finch 2007) and deals with the narratives employed to present and justify decisions made regarding the organisation of the family. It shows that while the discourse regarding the traditional heteronormative family with a male breadwinner and a woman doing the care work is rejected by the respondents; it nonetheless corresponds with their own practices. The third chapter stresses the development of "family-strategies" in the long run and develops different types of "family-strategies" allowing for a better understanding of the interplay between professional migrations and the organisation of the family. Before switching to the empirical part, I will present the two central epistemological foundations of my work. I will show that both epistemological foundations underline the necessity to situate the researcher in the context of the study he or she is producing. The next chapter concerning the methodology gives information about the researcher who conducted this study as well as the regions where this study was conducted.

5 Contextualising the Study

5.1 Contextualising the Researcher

By presenting my position as a researcher, I contextualise and objectify the conditions of elaboration of the study. The researcher undertaking fieldwork is not neutral. Rather, he or she influences and learns from the empirical material produced. This point is central. It not only justifies the "feedback loops" between the fieldwork and the analysis but also stresses that the same respondents would probably have answered differently to another researcher, in another place, at another time. Thus, the material collected in qualitative studies is highly contextual and relational. In this context, the researcher needs also to be contextualised. His or her endeavour to deconstruct or decentre cannot be fully understood without knowing from where he or she speaks. "What is his or her position?" and "who is he or she?" are central questions that once answered give the reader an opportunity to understand the context and the person creating the perspective of the deconstructive and decentring processes. Here, the researcher is historically, geographically, and socially situated. There is no such thing as a "disinterested researcher" floating above the world creating a "pure theory". The researcher is part of the world and what he or she thinks is subordinated to his or her historically- and contextually-situated knowledge.

Doing this research implied moving. Being on the move myself certainly led me to better understand the challenges of coordinating family life and a professional career. I lived in different places in Switzerland and Germany during the time of this research, namely Neuchâtel, Lausanne, Frankfurt, Bochum, and Nurnberg. I moved for my own research, but also to live with my partner and then for the sake of her career. Thus, my partner and I faced some of the challenges that my respondents faced: finding a new flat in cities we did not know, discussing our next steps, our possible next move. Were we going to move if I found a position abroad? My personal situation helped me to understand the topic I was investigating from a subjective perspective. The down side of it is that I may see the world only for its migrants, those people who move for professional reasons, while such moves are not, in fact, the norm. In order to overcome this possible bias, I developed the term of "secondary-stayer" and referred explicitly to the term of "(im)mobility" (Wieczorek 2018). However, my empirical analysis strongly focuses on the people who move, which is a direct consequence of studying highly-skilled migration. Yet, it is important to remember that the bulk of the world is "sedentary" – only 7.5% of the total OECD countries was foreign born in 2000 (OECD 2008, 13). My study deals with a share of this population, namely the ones with tertiary education. That is, my study deals with an exception.

Furthermore, I am a Swiss national and a white male moving between Switzerland and Germany. My citizenship, my gender, and my ethnicity mean that I occupy a privileged position. Thus, I did not encounter administrative difficulties while settling into any place I chose to live. Also, I did not encounter the "controlling policies" of the nation-states; neither are visible in my work. In fact, for many of the respondents, such policies did not come up either, as most of them have a passport from a country of the "global North" and are white. This study is a study done by a privileged person on privileged persons. Yet, it is not only a question of privilege but also a question of power. For the most part, the respondents are powerful, in their organisation but also in the social world. In fact, their privileges are a mark of their power. Their economic capital, their position in the labour force, and their "family-strategies" all show that people around them often do what the respondents want. By decentring the analytical framework and the empirical analysis, I take this point into account. During my fieldwork, I systematically asked questions regarding the relationship with various state-bodies (Appendix 2: Interview Grid, Relationships with State-bodies, 329). The respondents did not really understand my question and were answering succinctly referring to a straightforward process. For the privileged ones, the "controlling state" is more a "welcoming state": they are "wanted and welcome" (Triadafilopoulos 2013). It is important to remember that amongst the foreign-born population only a small portion is "wanted and welcome": again, my personal situation and the situation of most of my respondents cannot be generalised and needs to be contextualised. I did not encounter a "frictionless mobility". Other constraints, as I will show, emerged. In their case, however, the "controlling state" is mostly absent. As soon as we diverge a little from this pattern, the constraints of the "controlling state" appear. I interviewed respondents from Indonesia aiming to stay in Switzerland for the long term. In their case, the constraints imposed by a "controlling state" appeared in the interview; they are struggling, for instance, with the renewal of their residency permit, which will not be granted if they want to travel back to Indonesia. Otherwise, they run the risk of being refused at the border on their return to Switzerland. This challenge is beyond the scope of a lot of the other respondents.

The same can be said about discrimination, xenophobia, or racism: I do not face them personally in my daily life, and the same is probably true for many of the respondents. I asked questions about discrimination and xenophobia in the interviews. Some interviewees were shocked by the xenophobic rhetoric in many Swiss electoral posters but were also saying they did not feel targeted by these posters. The "migration binaries" act as a "category of practices" (Brubaker 2013) in which the respondents imply that they are part of the "us", a form of "temporal adaptation" in Switzerland. Furthermore, their presence benefits the country, they argue. As soon as we diverge a little from this pattern, some respondents say they are victims of xenophobia. The respondents from the "global South" who are not embedded in a multinational company seem the most affected by it: for example, the partner of a Russian respondent who was asked to "go back home" in a supermarket. For those working for a multinational company, they are systematically referring to the "truly international ambiance" of their workplace and their lack of contact with the "local population". Their partners, however, more often experience xenophobia and racism. This might explain why the "expat bubble" (Fechter 2007a) is so important to some of the respondents. It acts as a barrier against the xenophobia and the discrimination they could face in a new local space. Although I do not investigate this topic here, there is a lack of research dealing with the racism that highly-skilled migrants from the "global South" face while relocating to countries like Switzerland and Germany.

Another element which could influence the insights of this study is my position as a researcher in the field. I am not a colleague or a friend of the respondents but a student in sociology, specifically studying family relationships amongst couples of highly-skilled migrants. In chapter 7, I will discuss the discrepancies between the discourses and the practices of the respondents when it comes to displaying their families. I will interpret these discrepancies as the development of the respondents' notions of what a "family should be" in 2018. Yet this insight shows an attempt on their part to provide a "good answer" to a sociologist working on family in 2018. Garfinkel notes that individuals (which includes those agreeing to participate in a sociological study) are not "cultural idiots" (Garfinkel 1986). I made a similar point with Papinot (2014) earlier. The moment of the interview is not "floating in a social zero gravity zone". The respondents knew well with whom they were speaking. They knew from the moment they received the contact letter (Appendix 1: Contact Letter, 324). Thus, it may be the case that they "prepared" a discourse specifically adapted to answering the questions of a sociology student. Furthermore, I have my own opinions, in part, because of what I studied: sociology, and what I did not study: law, for instance. Therefore, I also have an idea of what "a good family should be". In this work, I aim (as best as possible) to suspend my own judgement while developing the empirical analysis; however, it would be misleading to suggest that judgement didn't enter into my work. The first empirical chapter, for instance, focuses on the work in the labour force of both partners, implying, in part, my normative conception of "what family should be": that the two partners should work in the labour force. It replicates the same image of the family that some of my respondents provided during their interviews.

The following four points might influence the respondents' discourse as well as the study as a whole. First, the matter of "nomadism", as I call it, implying as it does that the whole world migrates, which is empirically not the case. My study deals with a specific population, which is not representative of the whole population. Not everyone is on the move. The second point refers to my experience of being a privileged person while moving from Switzerland to Germany and living in both Switzerland and Germany. The ease with which such moves were carried out might lead to an ignorance on the part of the researcher of the "controlling nation-states" when it comes to migration: a form of "methodological nationalism". In this study, nation-states seemingly do not control or do not attach much importance to controlling privileged migrants. I see two reasons for that. It stems out of a political choice formalised in multilateral agreements like Schengen and the very conceptualisation of the study itself is a proposition to deal with privileged migrants. The third point deals with the other side of the coin, so to speak, concerning discrimination, xenophobia and racism. The fact that they are absent from this study does not mean that I did not ask the question. Furthermore, the fact that many respondents did not feel as though they were victims of racism, xenophobia, or discrimination tells us something about the structure of domination in contemporary societies. In this context, I have also suggested that the "migration binaries" are a "category of practice". In other words, this point underlines my privileged position as well as the one of the respondents emphasising the need to deconstruct these categories as they convey a strong normative load. The fourth point refers to the fact that I presented myself as a researcher in sociology while asking for interviews. The respondents may have seen me as someone to whom "good" answers should be given and produce a particular discourse accordingly.

5.2 Contextualising the Lake Geneva Region and Frankfurt Rhine-Main Region

I decided to change my access to the field. Instead of focusing on four multinational companies, this work deals with the experience of highly-skilled migrants. Yet, an approach starting with the migrants themselves required another conceptualisation than, for instance, the "ethnic lenses". In the theoretical part (3.3 Methodological Nationalism, 80), I showed the advantage of using the "cities as the entry points" – understood as "critical places" (3.3.1 Changing the Entry Points, 81) – to overcome the array of biases summarised under the term "methodological nationalism". One of the keys to conceptualising my study is the process of "decentring". Following this logic, I focus not just on one region but two, developing a study in which the knowledge of one region is "decentred" by another perspective, namely a second region. Thus, this study deals with the Lake Geneva region, Switzerland and Frankfurt Rhein-Main region, Germany. Though I conducted the bulk of the interviews in the Geneva region (30 interviews), I completed the corpus by undertaking six more interviews in the Frankfurt region. These last allowed me to see what is specific to the Lake Geneva or the Frankfurt Rhein-Main regions as well as what they have in common; the experience of highly-skilled migrants may differ, in some respects, when we change the place of investigation. I developed a "bi-local fieldwork" to be able to contextualise these differences. The "bi-local fieldwork" creates a more heterogeneous corpus of interviews. However, I do not develop a formal comparative analysis, but rather "decentre" my study to escape from the traps of "methodological nationalism". Yet, the fact that I will not analyse the qualitative data in a comparative design does not mean that the sites where the respondents live at the time of the interview do not play a role. In fact, acknowledging the sites where the respondents live, addressing the central characteristics of these regions, and showing how they differ help to situate the conditions of production of the qualitative material. To present the context of the study, I will first paint a broad socio-economic portrait of these two regions. Then, I will focus on the "family policy" in these two regions, as the capacity of partners to arrange childcare after a relocation is central to understanding the "family-strategy". In the discussion part (Chapter 10.1), I will rely on the elements I develop in the current chapter to show the differences between these two regions in terms of childcare and "family policy".

The three maps show the two regions where I conducted this study. First, Figure 9 is a general map of the "centre of Europe" showing Eastern France, Southwestern Germany, Switzerland, Luxemburg, Liechtenstein, and a part of Austria, Belgium, and Italy. The Lake Geneva region (later on called the Geneva region) is in the western, French-speaking part of Switzerland, on the northern shore of Lake Geneva. It is the "metropolitan area" between Geneva and Montreux (Figure 10) and is made up of the Geneva and Vaud *cantons*. The Frankfurt Rhine-Main region is in Southwestern Germany. The official language is, unsurprisingly, German. This region (later on called the Frankfurt region) is comprised of the "large metropolitan area" of Frankfurt (Figure 11) and includes the cities of Frankfurt am Main, Darmstadt, Mainz, Offenbach, and Wiesbaden. Thus, the "large metropolitan area" of Frankfurt spans the German

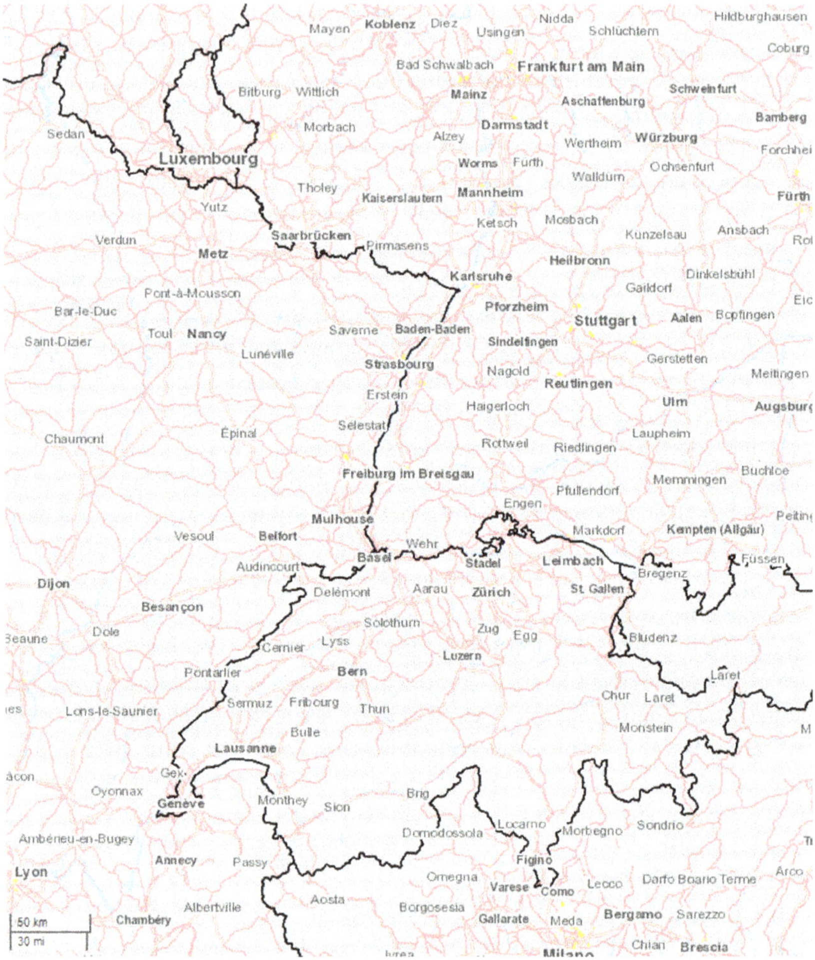

Figure 9 General Map Situating Frankfurt am Main and Geneva. Source: Eurostat (2017c)

Bundesländer of Hesse, Rhineland-Palatinate, and Bavaria. The city of Frankfurt am Main itself is the regional capital of Hesse. According to the definition of the Organisation for Economic Co-operation and Development (OECD), "metropolitan areas" and "large metropolitan areas" are "functional urban areas" [FUA] with, respectively, "a population between 500'000 and 1.5 million people [for the

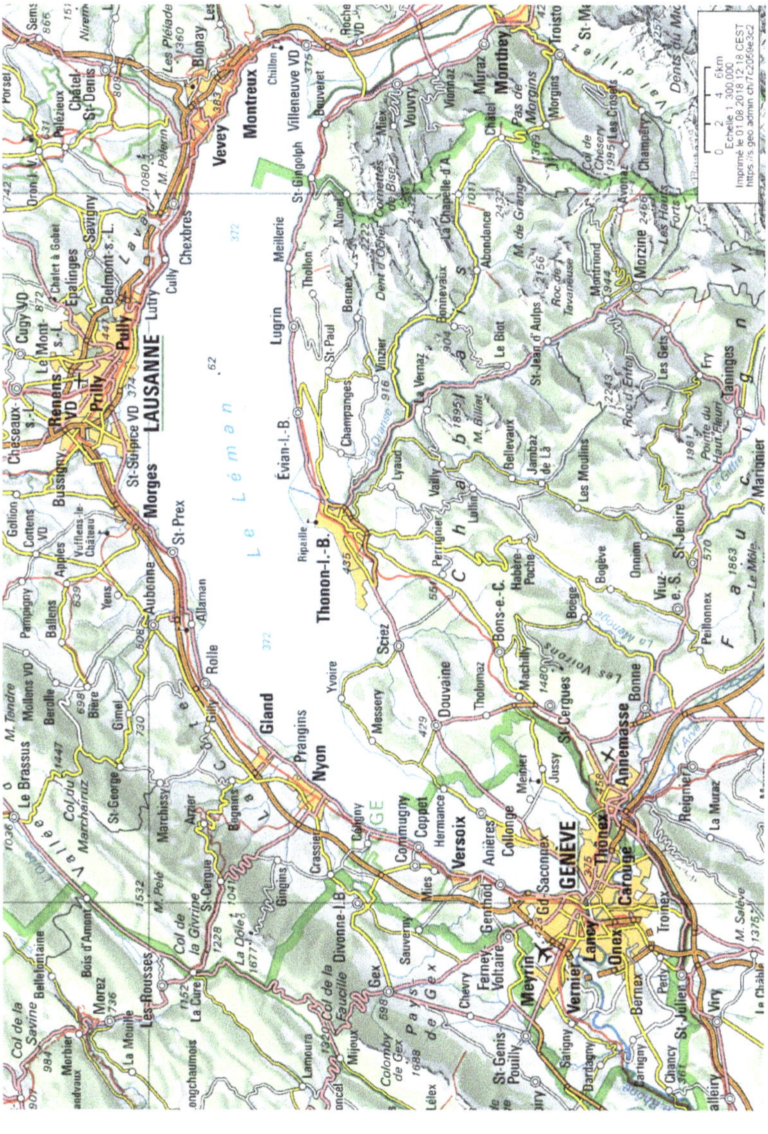

Figure 10 Map of the Geneva Region. Source: Office fédéral de la topographie (2018)

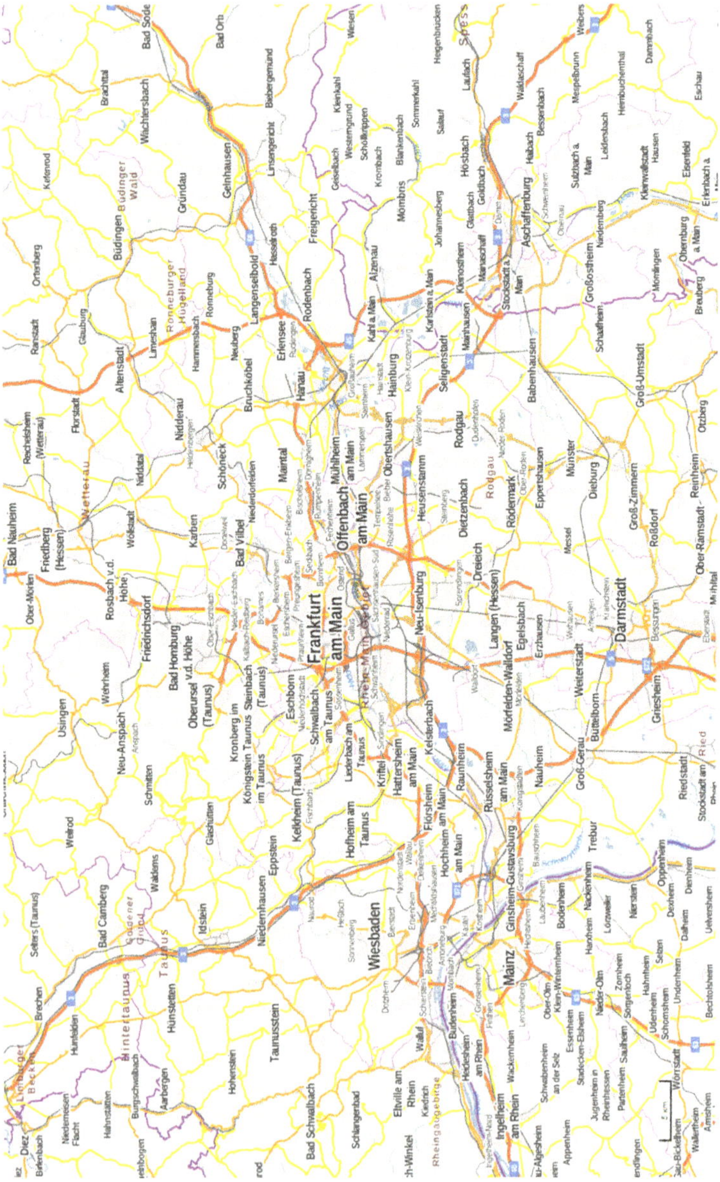

Figure 11 Map of the Frankfurt Region. Source: Google Maps (2019)(https://www.google.com/maps)

"metropolitan areas"] and a population of 1.5 million people or more [for the "large metropolitan area"]" (OECD 2013). Furthermore, a "FUA consists of a city plus its commuting zone" (Eurostat 2017b) and a "commuting zone contains the surrounding travel-to-work areas of a city where at least 15% of their employed residents are working in this city" (Eurostat 2017a). In other words, the two entry points of this study are the "metropolitan area of Geneva" and the "large metropolitan area of Frankfurt". Geneva and Lausanne actually represent two specific FUA, according to the conceptualisation of the OECD, but scholars in urban development refer to a single "metropolitan area" (Dessemontet, Kaufmann, and Jemelin 2010, 2975).

In 2014, out of the 1,238,831 inhabitants living in the Geneva region, 36.1% were foreigners (Rietschin and Imhof 2017, 4). Furthermore, for the same year, 42.8% of the total immigrants arrived for professional reasons (ibid). The Frankfurt region corresponds to the "Frankfurt Rhein-Main Metropolregion", in which 5,525,603 people were living in 2009 (Bürgeramt, Statistik und Wahlen 2016, 43). Amongst them, 12.2% were foreigners (ibid). Both regions are characterised by the presence of international organisations (The UN in Geneva and the European Central Bank in Frankfurt) and multinational corporations (L'Oréal, Nestlé, Monsanto, Rolex, etc. in the Geneva region and AEG, Deutsche Bank, PwC, Lufthansa, etc. in the Frankfurt region). The two regions offer many professional opportunities for highly-skilled migrants, as both are well known economic hubs in Europe and the world. As is the case for the Geneva region, the Frankfurt region is richer and more expensive than the rest of the country. According to the Reports on prices and earnings (Höfert and Kalt 2015), the "net annual income" is higher in the Geneva region (128.3) than in the Frankfurt region (97.0) (100 being New York City [NYC]); yet, the prices (including rent) are also higher in the Geneva region (91.8) compared to the Frankfurt region (55.1) (100 being NYC) (2015, 6 – 11; thus, both regions provide a high "domestic purchasing power" to highly-skilled migrants. The professional opportunities and the relatively high standard of living render them attractive to highly-skilled migrants. Another similarity between the two regions are the economic promotion policies they use to attract foreign investment and to favour the settling of multinational companies in their territory. For the Geneva region, a whole network of private and public organisations develops the economic promotion (e.g. the "Greater Geneva Bern Area" (GGB) and the "*service de la promotion économique et du commerce Vaud*" [SPECo]). In Germany, similar organisations can be found such as the "*FrankfurtRheinMain GmbH*" responsible for the economic marketing of the region or the "*Wirtschaförderung Frankfurt*" in charge of economic development. Furthermore, both regions have an international airport and are "mobility nodes" with intercity trains reaching most of Western Europe.

5.2.1 Family Policy in the two Regions

In chapter 3, I decentred the research on highly-skilled migration through three "methodological premises". When it comes to the "methodological nationalism", I emphasised the necessity to acknowledge the nation-states without naturalising them. In this chapter, I have quoted the studies of Pfau-Effinger (1998) and Esping-Andersen (1990) to show that various "welfare state regimes" provide different types of support favouring or hindering the participation of women in the labour force. Doing so, I showed the relevance of considering the inner heterogeneity of "welfare state regimes" pointing to their subnational variations (Bühler and Meier Kruker 2002; Riaño et al. 2015). While chapter 3 was theoretical and aimed at developing a suitable approach to overcoming the "methodological nationalism", the present section (section 5.2.1) is contextual and focuses on the support effectively available within these two regions. To do so, I will focus on the "family policy" in the two regions. Neyer (2003) defines the "family policy" as:

> Policy that targets parenthood (…) most closely related to fertility: maternity policies, parental-leave policies, childcare services, and child benefits (Neyer 2003, 8).

I will present these policies at the national level, using the "OECD family database"[37] and the country reports of Germany and Switzerland published by the Population Europe Resource Finder and Archive (PERFAR)[38]. To further contextualise my study, I will also focus on the specific *Bundesländer* and *Cantons* where this study takes place, by presenting the support concretely available in the two regions. To refer to the "family policy" in each specific region, I will speak of the subnational variation of the "family policy". In other words, I will look at the possibilities – in terms of the support to the care work required to raise a child – highly-skilled migrants have when they settle in a local space after a relocation.

Harrison Villalba et al. (2012) distinguish "formal care", "non-formal care", and "informal care" (2012, 14). They define "formal care" as the "organized structure with qualified staff, at a day care centre or at an organized family day care"

37 Website of the OECD Family Database, retrieved August 6, 2018, from http://www.oecd.org/els/family/database.htm

38 Website of the Population Europe Resource Finder & Archive (PERFAR), retrieved August 6, 2018, from https://www.perfar.eu/

(ibid). "Non-formal care" implies "no organized structure and no notion of qualified staff, parents arrange for and pay the services directly to the nanny or caregiver" (ibid) and "informal care" corresponds to the "unpaid care provided by family and friends" (ibid). I will start by presenting the "family policy" and the "formal care" in the regions of Frankfurt and Geneva, then speak briefly about the "non-formal care" and "informal care" in these regions. In the last part of this subsection, I will propose the idea of "privatised formal care" to refer to international (semi-)privatised (pre-)schools. Over all, I ask the following question: what is the structure of the childcare in these two regions and what are the differences between them?

a. Formal care

Quoting Pfau-Effinger (1998) and Esping-Andersen (1990), I said that Germany and Switzerland have similar "welfare state regimes", namely a "conservative-traditionalist welfare regime" (1998, 162). While the concepts they develop are going to be central for the next decades of research on the topic, the studies as such are quite old. Besides, the "welfare state regimes" encompass more than the family policy. In this subchapter, I specifically focus on the "family policy" and some of its elements, which have changed since then according to more recent studies. Andersen (2009) and Ferragina and Seeleib-Kaiser (2015) speak of the silent – yet incomplete – revolution of the family policy that has occurred in the last twenty years, in rich OECD countries. Ferragina and Seeleib-Kaiser (2015) stress the expansion of "family policy," "leading to a socialisation of family care responsibilities, traditionally disproportionately performed by women" (2015, 23). They analyse the family policy in rich OECD countries and show that Germany undertook significant changes during the last two decades, emphasising an important increase in the public provision of childcare with consequent parental leaves (2015, 14). The "family policy" in Switzerland did not change significantly, constituting an exception amongst rich OECD countries. The Swiss family policy remains conservative with short maternity leaves, no paternity leave, and low public investment in childcare (2015, 16). Ferragina and Seeleib-Kaiser (2015) underline significant differences between Germany and Switzerland when it comes to the family policy. In the following paragraphs, I will show with examples what these differences are all about, focusing on the childcare provision, the parental leave system, and the schooling system available to highly-skilled migrants.

The childcare provision corresponds to the services provided to parents to ease the coordination between being at work in the labour force and doing the care work. It includes day nursery, kindergarten, pre-school, out of school care, etc. In Germany, children from age one are entitled to childcare, according to the Federal Social Security Law (*Sozialgesetzbuch (SGB) - Achtes Buch [VIII]*)[39]. The effective attendance of children at day care (*Kindertagesbetreuung*) varies between the *Bunderländer*, because of historical reasons (the former socialist East has a more extensive day care program for young children). According to Federal Statistical Office of Germany (Destatis), in Hessen (which is in the former West Germany), in 2013, 25.7% of the children between zero and two years old and 93.1% between three and five attend a day care centre (*Kindertageseinrichtungen*) (compared to respectively 57.7% and 95.5% in Saxony-Anhalt (a former East socialist *Bundesland*) (Destatis 2014). Radenacker (2014) stresses that these numbers hide the fact that the vast majority of the children attend day care on a part-time basis. In fact, 75% of the children attending day care spend less than seven hours per day in day care (Radenacker 2014). As we shall see, the possibility of having parental leave influences the rate of attendance of young children.

In Switzerland, unlike in Germany, there are no legal provisions to enforce day care. At the federal level, only a federal law gives an incentive to the *cantons* to develop day care solutions on their territory. It is called the Federal Law on Financial Aid for Non-Family Homes for Children (*Loi fédérale sur les aides financières à l'accueil extra-familial pour enfants*)[40]. Article 1 paragraph 1 of this law aims at "favouring a better coordination between family life and professional life or studies". This law does not create any legal obligation to the *Cantons* but rather gives incentives to develop better day care solutions throughout the country. The *Cantons* are responsible for implementing the day care solutions. For historical reasons, the *Cantons* are responsible when it comes to education: the Swiss constitution safeguards the prerogative of the *Cantons* to organise public education, including day care. The result is that there is no harmonised policy at the national level. Zufferey and Widmer (2014) note that parents across Switzerland do not have equal access to childcare. In the Canton of Vaud 27.2% of the children between zero and four years attend a preschool day care centre, in 2017. It is 7.2% more than in 2010, showing that the development of preschool day centres is an important aspect of the Canton of Vaud's family policy.

---

39 Sozialgesetzbuch (SGB) - Achtes Buch (VIII) - Kinder- und Jugendhilfe - (Artikel 1 des Gesetzes v. 26. Juni 1990, BGBl. I S. 1163). Retrieved August 6, 2018, from https://www.gesetze-im-internet.de/sgb_8/BJNR111630990.html

40 Loi fédérale du 4 octobre 2002 sur les aides financières à l'accueil extra-familial pour enfants (LAAcc) ; RS 861. Retrieved August 6, 2018, from https://www.admin.ch/opc/fr/classified-compilation/20020609/index.html

Furthermore, 14.5% attend an out of school day care centre (Statistique Vaud 2017). In Geneva, the numbers are similar (30.9% for the children between zero and four years attend a preschool day care centre, in 2017) (Statistique Genève 2017). This rate is on the rise, too. Still, the Swiss figures are significantly lower than the German ones, especially if, as we shall see, parental leave is taken into consideration. In fact Switzerland has the third lowest enrolment rate for pre-primary education for three to five year old children amongst all the OECD countries (just above Greece and Turkey) (OECD 2016, 6).

There is not only the enrolment rate but also the costs for the parents as well as the waiting period for access to any form of day care support. The figures of the OECD are striking in this regard, as the "Gross fees for two children (age 2 and 3) attending full-time care at a typical childcare centre, as % of average earnings, in 2015" is 70.3% in Switzerland against 10.5% in Germany (OECD 2017a)[41]. In other words, it is comparatively much more expensive to send children to a day care centre in Switzerland than in Germany. Furthermore, the waiting time reflects an insufficient offer in terms of day care services. According to a study of the Swiss Graduate School of Public Administration, in the Canton of Vaud, 21.2% of the demand for day care centre is not satisfied in the city-centres, in 2012 (Bonoli and Vuille 2013, 47). This figure reaches 32.1% for children under 2 years old (2013, 48). In Germany, 13.3% of the demand is not satisfied, in 2016 (IWD 2017). In Hesse, 13.7% of the children under the age of three did not find day care though their parents were actively looking for one (ibid). It means 293,486 missing places for the country and 23,049 in Hesse (ibid). All in all, there are significant differences between the two regions. The Frankfurt region has a higher enrolment rate for preschool day care centres than the Geneva region, and it is cheaper for the parents to send their child there. Though the figures show an increase of available places in the Geneva region.

Concerning the parental leave system, the differences between the two regions are striking. In short, the parental leave system is more developed in Germany than in Switzerland. The results of Ferragina and Seeleib-Kaiser (2015) reflect these difference. The OECD (2017b) distinguishes several forms of parental leave. The most current forms of parental leave systems are the maternity leave, the paternity leave, and the parental leave. The maternity leave corresponds to the "employment-protected leave of absence for employed women at around

41 These statistics are for Zurich in Switzerland and Hamburg in Germany. Thus, they are not completely accurate for the Geneva region and the Frankfurt region but rather gives some idea.

the time of childbirth, or adoption" (OECD 2017b, 1); the paternity leave refers the "employment-protected leave of absence for employed fathers at or in the first few months after childbirth" (ibid); and the parental leave is defined as the "employment-protected leave of absence for employed parents, which is often supplementary to specific maternity and paternity leave periods, and frequently, but not in all countries, follows the period of maternity leave" (ibid)[42]. Switzerland has a statutory maternity leave arrangement of 16 weeks, 14 of them being paid at 80% of the last income up to a ceiling of 196 Swiss francs per day (OECD 2017b, 16). In Switzerland, there is neither paternal nor parental leaves, or to put it in the OECD's language: "no statutory entitlement" (ibid). In Germany, the system proposes more possibilities for the parents. The idea is that the parents can freely share the 12 months they are entitled to after the birth of a child (BMFSFJ 2017). In fact, if they decide not to share, the mother receives 12 months and if they do share the care it can be divided between 14 months. This system is called the *Elterngeld*. Another option is the *ElterngeldPlus*, which is longer and offers parents the possibility to reduce their work week and to receive the insurance for the day spent doing care work for the child. Thus, while both possibilities maintain the working contract, the basic *Elterngeld* implies a concrete break from the labour force to fully undertake care work for the child/ren: a 100% break for at least a month, so to speak. The *ElterngeldPlus* offers the possibility to work part time in the labour force and receive benefits to compensate for the reduction of professional activity. In other words, the partners can divide the care work between them, reducing their activity in the labour force without fully stopping it[43].

Such programs do not exist in Switzerland. Here, (a lack of childcare provision combined with nearly non-existent parental leave), it is the women who most often do the care work for the children. The lack of available places in day care centres combined with a weak maternity leave system, and non-existent

42 What is important in law is relatively easy. The specifics of these maternity, paternity, and parental leave systems are, however, complex and involve a lot of actors, covering a lot of individual cases. One could write a whole dissertation on this topic. For the present work, I made the decision to present only the general aspects of these systems.

43 For more information on the parental leave arrangements possible in Germany, see *Elterngeld, ElterngeldPlus und Elternzeit: Dans Bundeselterngeld- und Elternzeitgezetz*, (2018) Bundesministerium für Familie, Senioren, Frauen und Jugend. Retrieved August 6, 2018, from https://www.bmfsfj.de/blob/93614/883f631806ac368da9d4a5a1cce66aa8/elterngeld-elterngeldplus-und-elternzeit-data.pdf

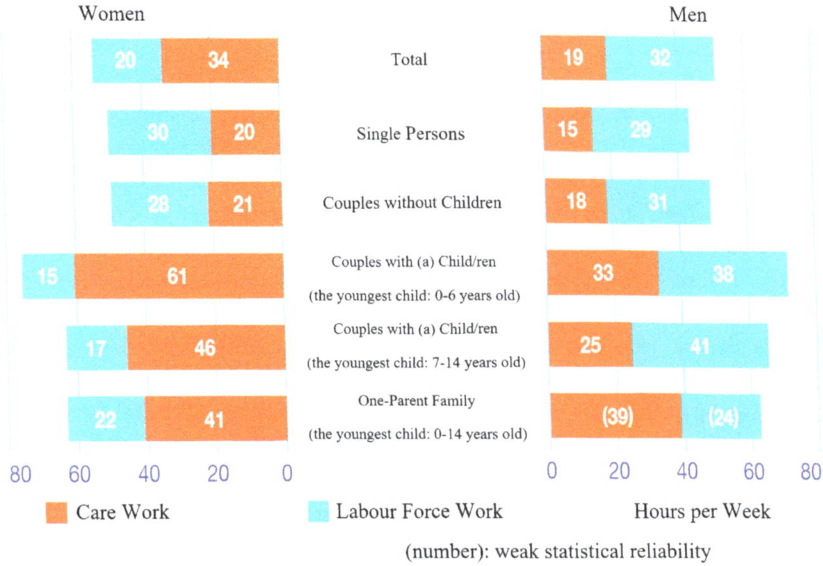

Figure 12 Average Time Spent on Work in the Labour Force and the Care Work in the Canton of Vaud, in 2013 (only includes people working in the labour force): Source: Imhof (2015, 33)[Data: OFS, ESPA](Own translation)

paternity and parental leave systems impact mostly on the female partner, as she is the one who does the care work in the absence of day care arrangements and support from the father. In these conditions, the male partner is free to continue his professional career.

Based on statistics of the Canton of Vaud, Figure 12 exemplifies that with the arrival of a child care work is predominantly undertaken by women. Thus, women raising a child between zero and six years old spend 61 hours per week doing the care work: twice as much as their male counterparts who spend 33 hours. The difference works the other way around, as men with a child between zero and six years old spend 38 hours per week in the labour force. More than twice the time that women spend (15 hours). But that is not all, as – according to the same study – many women doing care work say that it restrains their professional activity. In fact, according to Imhof (2015, 33), 38% of them say they are restricted in their professional activity because they do the care work for the child/ren. They would prefer to have access to day care. Comparatively, the figure is only about 10% for men (2015, 33). These statistics show that the lack of day care options in the Geneva region predominantly impact the professional activity of the women. It is primarily they who do the care work until a day care solution is found, not the men.

In sum, the family policy – grounding the "formal care" – is more developed in Germany than in Switzerland, introducing an important distinction between the Frankfurt and the Geneva regions. However, highly-skilled migrants arriving in a new country typically do not have access to the full package of "formal care". The access depends on multiple factors, such as the country of origin, where the person already contributed, etc. While presenting the "dual labour market theory" (Piore 1979; Berger and Piore 1980), I showed the distinction between the "primary sector" and the "secondary sector" of the labour market. According to this theory, migrants typically hold positions in the "secondary sector". Highly-skilled migrants are a liminal case, as they usually have positions considered to be in the "primary sector". The fact that they are a liminal case raises questions that my study seeks to clarify. One could ask, for instance, how does the "formal care" happen under the conditions of repeated professional mobility? When one partner resigns to follow the other partner for the sake of his or her professional activity, is this person going to receive "formal care" services? If not, how does the partners coordinate and organise the care work? As we shall see in the empirical part, the individual situations are diverse, and it is difficult, if not impossible to bring clear cut answers to these questions. It will depend on the "family-strategy" that the partners adopt while settling in a new local space, I will argue. However, the local conditions and the access to "formal care" is a central consideration for partners making decisions concerning the division between the work in the labour force and the care work.

b. Informal and Non-Formal Care

In the context of "informal care", I have shown the relevance of the "economy of kinship", yet this once again replicates gender hierarchies, as it is most often the female relatives who contribute to the care work. I have already mentioned this in the previous chapter (3.2.2 The Hidden Economy of Kinship, 77). In the empirical chapters, we shall see the difficulty of developing "informal care" practices for families who are frequently mobile for professional reasons. Relating to "informal care", the relevance of the so-called "expat bubbles" may correspond to practices of "informal care", whether it is in the Frankfurt or the Geneva region.

When it comes to the "non-formal care", the partners can find "private care arrangements". There is the possibility to hire an au pair or a nanny. We shall see in the empirical part that it is a common way to compensate for the lack of "formal care" when both partners want to continue to work in the labour force.

These practices are, however, not specific to highly-skilled migrants[44]. Websites such as *Motherworld*[45] in Germany or *Ma Nanny*[46] links potential employer and employee for the provision of child care. There is also the possibility to hire an au pair. This possibility is limited due to the need to speak the language spoken in the region; that is French in the Geneva region or German in the Frankfurt region. It is difficult to spot differences between the Frankfurt and the Geneva regions when it comes to the "non-formal care".

c. *Privatised Formal Care*

Another possibility is to mobilise organisations dedicated to highly-skilled migrants, namely a specific form of "migration industry" (Groutsis, Broek, and Harvey 2015). For Hernández-León, a "migration industry" corresponds to "the ensemble of entrepreneurs who, motivated by the pursuit of financial gain, provide a variety of services facilitating human mobility across international borders" (2013, 156). Thus, they are "private organisations" facilitating settlement in a new local space after a relocation. Initially, the concept of "migration industry" was mostly used in the context of "undocumented migration" (Gammeltoft-Hansen and Sorensen 2013; Hernández-León 2013; Salt and Stein 1997). Scholars have only recently started to study it to better understand the nexus of organisations surrounding highly-skilled migration such as relocation offices, outplacement agencies, and international schools (Groutsis, Broek, and Harvey 2015; Tissot 2018). Both the Geneva and the Frankfurt regions offer international schools, European schools or non-German or -French speaking (semi-)private (pre-)schools. An advantage of these schools and pre-schools is that some offer an education in English or another non-local language, though English is the most common. However, private international (pre-)schools are expensive and without the support of the employing company, difficult to afford. The annual gross fees for a child (age two and three) attending full-time care at a private childcare centre is 18,860 euros at the Frankfurt International School[47].

---

44 This topic corresponds to the "global care chains" developed by, amongst others, Amelina (2016) or the "transnational care work" developed, amongst others, by Shilliger (2013). These studies focus on migrants doing the care work in Western Europe.

45 Website of Motherworld, retrieved August 6, 2018, from www.motherworld.de

46 Website of MaNanny, retrieved August 6, 2018, from www.ma-nanny.ch

47 Website of the Frankfurt International School, retrieved August 6, 2018, from https://www.fis.edu/page.cfm?p=945

In the International School of Geneva, the annual tuition fee for one child between the age of two and three is 27,060 Swiss francs[48]. In both regions, what I call the "privatised formal care" is expensive. In fact, the international schools are amongst the most expensive while other schools such as the European school in Frankfurt is more affordable[49]. In the Geneva region, the network of private school is – for historical reasons – quite developed. Nevertheless – and as we shall see in the empirical part – these schools are often full, or at least a place for the children is not necessarily immediately available: in other words, these (pre-) schools have waiting-lists, too. For many respondents, finding a day care centre or a school for the child/ren after a relocation is a major challenge, regardless of the kind of care they are looking for. In fact, they often take what is available.

Although, the two regions share large socio-economic similarities, when it comes to the "family policy", I see significant differences: it is a key reason why I chose them. The Frankfurt region has a more developed "family policy" than the Geneva region. In these conditions, I expected it to be easier for the parents to find suitable day care arrangements in the Frankfurt region than in the Geneva region. I have not developed a comparative study which would imply a systematic review of the samples, but rather I used the region of Frankfurt as a "shadow case" to have another point of view on my data. Though both regions offer many professional opportunities for highly-skilled migrants, the differences between them can be found at the level of the "family policy". Thus, by having two entry points in two regions which have different "family policy" is a way to decentre my study as I can conceptualise the nation-state in which the migrants are embedded without naturalising it. This allows me to grasp the contrasts between the two localities. Spotting similarities and differences between the lived experiences of highly-skilled migrants in two regions strengthens the results of the study, as similar social processes in two localities are less likely to be only typical for the very location the investigation takes place. The recurrence of similar challenges in the two localities speaks in favour of a phenomenon less likely to be typical of one location. In other words, using two cities as entry points broadens the relevance of the results as it allows the researcher to take a greater distance with the singularity of each city. By doing so, I am able to reassess and contextualise the

48 Website of the International School of Geneva, retrieved August 6, 2018, from https://www.ecolint.ch/admissions/tuition-and-fees

49 Website of the Europäische Schule Frankfurt am Main, retrieved August 6, 2018, from https://www.esffm.org/fileadmin/downloads/infos/schulgeld/Info_School_Fee_18-19_EN.pdf

interviews. These two cities allow me to produce a more solid theoretical framework that deploys a broader empirical scope, enhancing the validity of my results (by overcoming methodological nationalism) and broadening the scope of my research (by a bi-local framework). In the methodological section, I have not only contextualised the study itself, but I have shown how I developed the structure of the empirical part around three chapters: the practices, the narratives, and the strategies.

Empirical Part

6 Professional Careers Coordination

The present chapter analyses the decision-making process involved in migrations for professional reasons. The analysis revolves around the question of who provides the initiative for such a migration as well as the consequences awaiting the partners involved. Indeed, I take into consideration both partners rather than only the isolated individuals. In the review of the literature, I mentioned that the possibility of overcoming the "gender binaries" does not mean forgetting about the partners' professional activities and focussing only on the division of the care work. The division of care work is of course important but so are the ways in which the two partners (try to) coordinate their professional careers through a migration for professional reasons. Thus, this first empirical chapter focuses on the initiating of a migration for professional reasons and on the ways this migration reorganises the partner's coordination of their professional careers. It is composed of three main parts. I start the analysis by using a framework drawn from Expatriate studies (Al Ariss et al. 2012; Andresen et al. 2014) – that I call an "individual approach" – in order to spot the initiator of a migration as being either the employee or the employing company. In the second part, I present a model – that I call a "collective approach" – meant to grasp the coordinating of the professional careers in a partnership by differentiating the "primary mover", who takes the initiative, from the "secondary mover", who responds to that decision. The "collective approach" simultaneously complements the framework provided by Andresen et al. (2014) – the "individual approach" – and emphasises the range of differentiated consequences for the partners who initiate or respond to a family's migration for professional reasons. In the third part, I explore the professional consequences of such migrations for the "secondary movers". Doing so, the objective is to decentre the studies focusing solely on the professional career of the "primary mover" (whom is conceptualised there as an "expatriate" or an "highly-skilled migrant") while considering the "secondary mover" (seen there as a "trailing-spouse" [sic.]) only as a passive "burden". Though not every "secondary movers" I interviewed maintained a position in the labour force, my analysis here will focus on the ones who did or at the very least wanted to do so: so goal being to adopt a decentred perspective.

6.1 Migration Triggering: An Individual Approach

In the review of the literature, I presented Andresen et al.'s (2014) study, in which are articulated different types of expatriation according to whether the subject is or not the initiator of the move[50]. Thus, Andresen et al. (2014) focus on the concept of initiative. Yet, they analyse who between the expatriate or the employing company and even a third company gives this initiative. This approach allows Andresen et al. to differentiate an "assigned expatriate" from a "drawn expatriate", and "intra" from "inter self-initiated expatriates". While this approach provides a relevant way to make sense of decisions to migrate, it fails to acknowledge the relationship between the partners. Let us still give flesh to the bones of these four types of expatriates by presenting four empirical cases each exemplifying one of these types.

6.1.1 Assigned Expatriate

In the case of an "assigned expatriate", to whom the supervisor offers a new position abroad, the initiator of the relocation is the employing company. Katia and Dennis' case[51] illustrates this. Katia and Dennis are both German. They have three children. Katia does not work in the labour force anymore, but Dennis has worked for the same multinational consumer goods company for more than twenty years. Having completed a degree in management, he started working for this company in Germany in 1996. Since then, the company has reassigned him to the United States, Italy, Indonesia, Hong Kong, and lately to Switzerland. Altogether, Katia and Dennis have relocated to three continents and five countries for the sake of Dennis' professional career. They had lived in Hong Kong for five years and really "loved it", Dennis told me. As his posting in Hong Kong was coming to an end, his supervisor proposed that he relocate to Switzerland. Dennis and Katia wanted to stay in Hong Kong though, and he looked for another position there – both within the company and outside it – but did not find any. He reflects that while one can always refuse to move, once the opportunities have been exhausted, one has relatively little choice:

---

50 Working within the larger framework of Expatriation studies, Andresen et al. use the term "expatriates". I have already shown why I prefer the term "highly-skilled migrant" for the current study. Still, one of my objectives is to build bridges between Migration studies and Expatriation studies, given that they both deal with similar topics. I will stick to the term "expatriate" in the first part of the analysis, before going on to present concepts that will serve to link these two fields of study.

51 All the names have been changed to protect the privacy of my interviewees.

> Well, the final decision was that my job in Hong Kong was over and that the new job was here [in Switzerland]. … So, that is why, in the end, when all options had been exhausted, we simply had to go (Dennis, 49yrs, married).

Favell (2014) underlines that highly-skilled migration may have its own constraints which this quote provides us a way of tracking. Indeed, it shows the irony that a well-to-do family living in Hong Kong and wanting to stay may yet be unable to do so. Neither a forced migration exactly, nor a desired migration for that matter, we should perhaps speak here of an unwanted professional migration? A kind of disguised dependency, Dennis and Katia's livelihood is fragile in the sense that it remains contingent on where the company wants him to go. Thus, the initiator of the relocation is the company that employs Dennis who, in turn, sees the relocation as the condition of his staying employed. The company led the move and assigned Dennis a new position. The decision-making process is a professional one which Dennis was not, however, really in control of. The employing company gave him a new assignment, just as they had already done four times before. In sum, Dennis would have resigned if he had found something else in Hong Kong, but he did not and could not, therefore, which underlines the assigned character of this type of migration.

6.1.2 Drawn Expatriate

A "drawn expatriate" is hired abroad by an as yet unrelated company (Andresen et al. 2014). In many cases, a head-hunter calls the (soon to be) "drawn expatriate" and says, "Listen, company B has an opportunity for you. Would you be interested? The job is in Geneva, Switzerland". This other company then hires the "drawn expatriate", and thereby initiates the migration. Most "drawn expatriates" possess "hard-skills", like managerial, scientific, and technical skills, which are more easily transferable than such softer skills as proficiency in a given language (Cornelius et al. 2001; Liversage 2009). Gabriel, for example, studied in Paris and holds a Ph.D. in chemistry. He is French and has worked in industrial pharmacology for more than twenty years now. Unlike Dennis, he has changed employers several times during the course of his career. He was then contacted by a head-hunter who offered him a position in another company. This is how he tells the story of how he started working for this other company:

> At the time, they [the people hiring him] wanted to develop [in their subsidiary] a function similar to the one I had created in Basel, where I was one of the two leaders of the group. I had created that function (Gabriel, 54yrs, divorced)[52].

52 Un chasseur de tête, à l'époque, ils voulaient monter ici en Suisse une fonction similaire

The quote highlights the competitiveness of the pharmaceutical sector[53]. Gabriel's new employer asked him to recreate the system he had developed for his former employers. Gabriel is thus a typical example of a "drawn expatriate", illustrating a social process that combines "hard-skills", a competitive environment, and the involvement of head-hunters. The initiative of the move comes from a competing company that wanted to hire Gabriel away from the company he was already employed by.

6.1.3 Intra Self-Initiated Expatriate

The initiator of the move can also be the individual herself. There are two types of "self-initiated expatriates". Some of them move but remain within the same company – these are the "intra self-initiated expatriates" – while others, the "inter self-initiated expatriates", move as a result of their switch to a new company.

The "intra self-initiated expatriate" is someone, like Carlos, who takes the initiative to move but continues to work for the same company. Carlos was born in Mexico to a German father and American mother. He studied marketing in Mexico City. His career started in the marketing industry in Mexico. After a few years, his employer offered him a position in the Dominican Republic, which lead to an "assigned expatriation". Carlos spent a few years there until he began to feel stuck in his position. He did not see himself being able to move further in his career so long as he stayed in the Dominican Republic. He needed a change. He took the initiative, organizing the next relocation because there were no opportunities for him to grow in the Dominican Republic. He told me about his feeling of having been forgotten by the company for whom he worked as a director of the national subsidiary:

> You just know from a professional point of view that the corporation has said: 'We cannot move you further. This is where you will end up' (Carlos, 44yrs, partnered).

When Carlos told me of his experience in the Dominican Republic, that feeling of being left alone was striking. These difficulties almost made him quit and return to Mexico without having found another job. Things changed, though, when he met one of the directors of the company's European subsidiary in a

---

à celle que j'avais créé à Bâle. J'étais un des deux responsables de ce groupe. J'avais créé la fonction quoi (Own Translation).

53 I interviewed Gabriel at his workplace. He opened the door to the conference room with a retinal scanner. Clearly, the security of intellectual property is very important in this sector. Even just getting the interview set up was the result of a long process made all the more difficult by the challenge simply of finding Gabriel's email address.

"global meeting" at the headquarters. In conversation, this director told him that they might have a position for him at the European headquarters. Soon after that meeting, Carlos quit his position in the Dominican Republic. This is how he tells of the episode:

> If I had not been there, that May in ***, and had not met ***, then probably the network would have left me in the Dominican Republic until I died, so yeah, I mean I am really grateful, that *** was there and that the stars aligned in my favour (Carlos, 44yrs, partnered).

The difference between the "intra self-initiated expatriate" and the "assigned expatriate" is a matter of who initiates the move. Nobody in his company had wanted to move Carlos ("[they] would have let me there until I die"). Carlos was lucky to have been in the right place at the right time, though. He found an opportunity abroad within the same company, although he could easily have stayed in the Dominican Republic. He relocated as an "intra self-initiated expatriate", unlike Dennis (above) who very much wanted to stay in Hong Kong and only left due to the lack of opportunities there. Dennis' only remaining option, after his unsuccessful search for other positions in Hong Kong, was to accept what the company had offered him in Switzerland. By contrast, Carlos very much wanted to leave the Dominican Republic and so found for himself another position in Germany. Still, both moves take place within the same company.

6.1.4 Inter Self-Initiated Expatriate

The case of Emma, finally, describes expatriates who decide to move over to a new company after having made their own application to a new position. Emma is an engineer who worked in France for some years after her graduation. After temporarily ending a relationship with the man who would later become her husband (they met, got together, separated, got back together and got married), she replied to a call for applications in Switzerland and was hired there:

> In fact, we met at work and then we broke up, which is also the moment when I first came across the announcement in *** to which I responded. Only once I applied for and accepted the position did we get back together (Emma, 37yrs, married)[54].

54 En fait, du coup, moi, je suis, on s'est rencontré dans le boulot pis après on s'est séparé et du coup c'est le moment où je suis tombée sur l'annonce à *** que j'ai postulé, que j'ai accepté le poste et une fois que j'ai accepté le poste ben on s'est remis ensemble (Own Translation).

In Andresen et al.'s typology (2014), Emma is an "inter self-initiated expatriate", given that she took the initiative to simultaneously move abroad and switch companies. She came to Switzerland with an employment contract that had been signed prior to the relocation. Being single was one of the factors that motivated her to seek a position abroad. For her, it remains clear that she would not have moved if she and Blaise – now her husband – had not been separated at the time:

> Yes, yes, of course, otherwise I would not have left. I had been in Grenoble for 10 years. It wasn't so bad. The fact that we broke up and the feeling that I did not have much to lose any more in Grenoble [convinced me]. So, I left (Emma, 37yrs, married)[55].

So, she decided to move to Switzerland. Being single was not seen as a hinderance in this decision-making process. After they had made up a short while later, as Emma was already working in Switzerland, Blaise joined her there. Once in Switzerland, he sought employment in the labour force and found a position at a research institute. They got married and have a child now.

What, then, is Blaise's role in the initiation of the move? In the typology presented by Andresen et al. (2014), Blaise is an outlier. He could be conceptualised as a "inter self-initiated expatriate", but he did not have a work contract prior to arriving in Switzerland, which blurs the boundary between expatriation and migration. Furthermore, the centrality of his feelings for Eva in his decision to move would be lost if we focussed only on the professional aspect of Blaise's move. While he is the initiator of his move, he was motivated by personal rather than for professional reasons. Nevertheless, he found a position in the labour force corresponding to his skills. He makes the decision to move for sentimental reasons. Such a family sensitive approach, I argue, completes the typology provided by Andresen et al. (2014), and allows me to develop a better understanding of Blaise and Eva's situation, in which a migration for professional reasons is followed by a migration for sentimental reasons.

6.2 Migration Triggering: A Collective Approach

A "collective approach" is one which allows us to assess the perspectives of both partners who work at maintaining their relationship while at least one of them moves for professional reasons. Thus, I propose to interpret the initiation

55 Oui, oui, bien sûr, sinon je ne serai pas partie, ça faisait 10 ans que j'étais à Grenoble, je n'étais pas si mal, le fait qu'on ait rompu et que j'avais l'impression que je n'avais plus grand chose à perdre à Grenoble, donc je suis partie (Own Translation).

of a move from the perspective of the coordination of two professional careers. From this perspective, the decision to move proceeds from one of the two partners; which we can grasp by using the analytical distinction between a "primary-mover" and a "secondary-mover". *One provides the initiative; the other one reacts to it.* This configuration introduces a model with two types of movers. I draw on the work of Schaer, Dahinden and Toader (2017, 1298). They use a distinction between a "primary-mover" and a "tied-mover", wherein the "primary-mover" provides the imperative to move by accepting the position abroad and the "tied-mover" reacts to it. My conceptualisation considers the "tied mover" as one specific type of what I call "secondary-movers". Empirically speaking, the reaction of the "secondary-mover" to the impulse of the "primary-mover" is not always to follow. The partners might decide to live apart temporarily, for example. I understand the "tied-mover" as only one possibility amongst others, underlining the fact that the "secondary-mover" is not, and should not be conceptualised as, simply passive. The "secondary-mover" is an active member co-producing "family-strategies". Such an understanding provides grounds for deconstructing the "gender binaries" that over-determine Expatriate studies, allowing us a better understanding of the negotiation and coordination of the partners considering both their personal relationship and professional career.

6.2.1 Primary-Mover and Secondary-Mover

The odds are low that both partners receive a job offer at the same place at the same time. Even in this unlikely case, we are still able to identify a "primary-mover" and a "secondary-mover". Lynn and Alex, for instance, moved together from the United-States to Germany fourteen years ago. At that point in time, they had just got engaged and wanted to start a family. They were about "to be married the following year, in May, and so [they] moved in January" (Alex, 52yrs, married). Lynn, who was working for a multinational marketing agency received an offer in Frankfurt first. She remembers the conversation she had with the director of the department:

> I said: 'Well, I am interested in going but I am kind of a fiancé now. So, I have to think about that' And I added: 'Actually, he works here.'
> He said: 'He does? Who is he?'
> I said: 'Alex, Alex *** [last name]'
> He said: 'Is that the same Alex *** that I worked with on *** [name of a company]?'
> I said: 'Yes'
> He said: 'He has a job, too!'
> I mean that was so lucky, so lucky (Lynn, 51yrs, married).

Obviously, her director had already worked on a project with Alex, a creative designer. Alex had been working as an external contractor for the same marketing agency and, as a result, the director was able to offer him a position in Frankfurt also.

> I was not with *** [name of the company] but I met my wife at the agency and one night we went out to dinner and she said: 'They offered me this one position and you this other one. Do you want to move to Germany?', to which I just said: 'Ok' (Alex, 52yrs, married).

Even when both partners get simultaneous job offers from the same company, it is usually one of the two who provides the initiative for the migration. In the case of Lynn and Alex, the company offered Alex a position because they wanted very much to transfer Lynn. In most cases, however, the distinction between the "primary-mover" and the "secondary-mover" is clearer. In the four cases used above to exemplify the "individual professional approach", the "primary-mover" and the "secondary-mover" are easily recognisable. One of the two partners receives a job offer and seriously considers accepting it, and speaks with her or his partner about it. Thus, in addition to the "individual professional approach", I also introduce the distinction between two types of movers within a couple: the "primary" and "secondary" mover, that I call a "collective approach".

According to Andresen et al.'s framework (2014), Lynn is strictly an "assigned expatriate". She works for a company that has offered her a position in Germany. From the perspective of the "collective approach", however, she would be the "primary-mover" who provides the initiative for her and Alex's move. We might even say that it is not she, but her company rather that provides such initiative. Thus, I argue, the notion of the "initiator of a relocation" is multi-faceted and very much dependant upon the perspective adopted by the researcher. The two approaches, moreover, are not mutually exclusive. In Lynn's case, she can just as well be described as an "assigned expatriate", because she accepts a position abroad within the same company. At the same time, she is the "primary-mover" of her partnership, because her husband (then fiancé) moves with her to Germany.

What though is Alex's place in this schema? From a "collective perspective", he is admittedly a limit case of a "secondary-mover" for he does not initiate the move. From an "individual perspective", his case corresponds to a "drawn expatriate" as he had been working for the agency on a contractual basis but was then offered a full-time job elsewhere. According to the "individual professional approach", the initiative to move comes either from the company or the employee him- or herself. Thus, Alex and Blaise's cases were strictly speaking difficult to categorize because the initiative to move ultimately came from their respective partners, Lynn and Emma, rather than from the companies involved. Taking a "collective perspective" into account, though, Alex and Blaise differ from the strict definitions of the "drawn" and "inter self-initiated" expatriates given that their moves were *partner-initiated*.

I argue that such a "collective perspective" complements and strengthens the "individual perspective" articulated by Andresen et al., where the former stresses the coordinating of two professional careers in a way that the latter cannot account for. In this context, I introduce the concept of "*partner*-initiated mover", which differs from the other types schematized by Andresen et al. (2014), for how it underlines the importance of the relation between the partners in the process of their relocation. The notion of "partner-initiated" does not reflect the process we have seen, for instance, in the case of Emma seeking employment in a foreign labour force. She applied abroad because one of her friends showed her a call for applications: this is the classic "self-initiated expatriate", relocating to where the work is. Yet, Blaise – her eventual husband – sought a position in the labour force in Switzerland because Emma already worked there. In brief, the concept of the "partner-initiated mover", underlines that the initiative of the move resides in the professional career of the other partner. What is specific to the situation of the "partner-initiated mover" is, I argue, the scope of the choice. A "partner-initiated mover" will neither choose the country, nor the length of the stay. This is a very common situation among my sampling of cases. The distinction between "self-initiated, assigned, or drawn expatriate", on the one hand, and "partner-initiated mover", on the other, underlines the different challenges involved in a move; and together this set of different individual situations call for the development of a broader "family-strategy" framework. Let us look then at what I call a "family-strategy", for it is a central concept of this study.

6.3 Conceptualising the Professional Careers Coordination

I just presented a distinction between "primary" and "secondary" movers. This distinction has deep consequences on the way we assess the decision-making process involved in a move, for there is not only the relationship between an employer and an employee to consider but the fact also that changes in the employment of one of the partners can trigger the movement of the other. How is it possible then to further conceptualise this seminal distinction?

Research by Halpern and Murphy (2005), which addresses the partners' "family-work integration" (2005, 29), a concept discussing the integration between the care work required in the sphere of the family and the work in the labour-force, offers an effective way to further develop the relationship between the "primary" and the "secondary" movers[56]. Indeed, their call to replace the notion of "family-work balance" with the concept of "family-work integration" is helpful. The notion of "family-work integration" refers to the ways in which the two partners coordinate their place in the labour force and, simultaneously, struggle to efficiently divide up the time spent doing the necessary care work at home. This definition implies many potential points of tension between the partners on the one hand, and between the partners and their respective employers on the other. Sharing the care work equitably requires making arrangements that allow the partners to find an equilibrium between the time and the energy they invest both in the labour force and in the care work. Finding this equilibrium may lead to conflicts between the partners that can be better accounted for by the concept of "work-family integration" than by the supposed "balance" between the two times of day spent on work and home. The notion of "work-family balance", in this sense, implies a zero-sum game that seems unhelpfully unrealistic. By contrast, "integration" implies that the partners can find a *more or less efficient* combination of working in the labour force and care working, for example through the use of a home office or day care centre at the workplace. The concept of "integration" moves us beyond the strictures of the zero-sum game of "balance". I prefer the term "integration" to "interaction", moreover, because the latter implies dealings between two spheres of life, as opposed only to a strategy meant to cope with two separate spheres simultaneously. Integrating does not refer to a zero-sum game nor a mere interaction but rather to a larger "family-strategy" that the partners develop together for their specifically situated case. This "family-work integration" model underlines that dealing with work in the labour force and care work is a collective and reflexive process. Wilding and Baldassar (2009), for instance, make the same argument where they note that "rather than trying to devote balanced time of each day, week or even year to the pursuit of employment or the care of family members, the participants in our study instead aimed to find an appropriate integration of work and family activities" (2009, 185). Thus, the "work-family integration" aims at overcoming the "gender binaries" by looking at the reciprocal impacts of work in the labour force and care work. In my study, migration for professional reasons complexifies the "family-work integration" even more.

56 Truth be told, Halpern and Murphy (2005) speak mostly of "family-work interaction"; yet, they do refer to the concept of integration, also, which I am privileging here. Furthermore, I understand the concept of "family-work integration" as an abbreviation of "care work for the family – work in the labour-force integration".

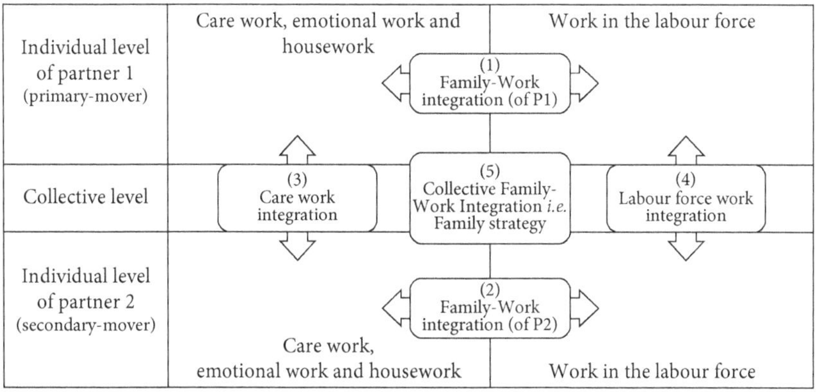

Figure 13 Family-Strategy. Source: Own Elaboration

In Thus, the "work-family integration" aims at overcoming the "gender binaries" by looking at the reciprocal impacts of work in the labour force and care work. In my study, migration for professional reasons complexifies the "family-work integration" even more.

Figure 13, I propose a model that conceptualises these multiple interactions; an analytical tool allowing us to study the "family-strategy". I construct the model by bringing both an individual and a collective level of analysis to the spheres of work in the labour force and the care work (where the work encompasses both emotional labour and housework). The levels of analysis are both individual and collective; the spheres of analysis are work in the labour force and care work. The individual "family-work integration of Partner 1 or Partner 2" (1 and 2) refers to the way each partner copes, individually, with the different demands of the labour force and care work. It represents an abstraction focussed on their individual situation. The "care work integration" (3) refers to the ways the partners share the care work (if they do share it at all), that is to say the care work concerning the housework, the emotional work and care work for the children as well as, in some cases, care for their parents. The "labour force work integration" (4) focuses on the arrangements made by the partners to coordinate their two paid positions in the labour force, independent of the care work. A "family-strategy" or "collective family-work integration" is defined, finally, as the negotiations engaged in and decisions made by thc partners after one of them accepts a relocation abroad. It refers to the ways the partners cope simultaneously with all the elements of the model. The model highlights the simultaneous search of a new integration of both their professional work and care work. It provides a way of studying the tensions and the conflicts felt by the partners as well as the solutions developed.

In this study, the professional move of at least one of the partners augments the complexity of the "family-strategy". In other words, at the core of their "family-strategy" lies a tension between mobility and mooring. I understand mobility as an asset in the labour force, as it facilitates an upward professional career, but as a socially disruptive force at home, where it compels the partners to reconfigure the "family-strategy". For example, if one of the partners accepts a position in which he or she will lead the national subsidiary of a multinational company abroad, the other partner also has to make a decision. The options are basically either following, staying, or finding some middle way. The mobility for professional reasons of one of the partners raises questions about the professional activity of the other, especially where the chances that both may find a professional position in their respective fields within the same local space is limited. Thus, mobility is a double-edge sword, both rewarding and disruptive at the same time. It is ambivalent.

Through the family-strategy model, however, we can better parse the constituent elements of that ambivalence and analyse its different facets separately. In the next part of this chapter, therefore, I will focus on the right-hand side of the model, that is, P1 and P2's work in the labour force, as well as their "labour force integration" (4), by which I mean the experiences and strategies of the partners who both work in the labour force when at least one of them moves for professional reasons. Of course, there are cases in which one of the partners stops working in the labour force: I will deal with these cases in the next chapters. For now, I will analyse the consequences of a decision to move through the various reactions and challenges faced by the partners. Indeed, how do the partners integrate two positions in the labour force when one has to move abroad for professional reasons? What are the individual consequences on their respective professional careers?

6.4 Primary-Mover

Let us start with the "primary mover's" place in the labour force, found in the top right corner of Thus, the "work-family integration" aims at overcoming the "gender binaries" by looking at the reciprocal impacts of work in the labour force and care work. *In my study, migration for professional reasons complexifies the "family-work integration" even more.*

Figure 13. The "primary-mover" holds a position abroad in the labour force for a certain time *under certain conditions.* In my conceptualisation, the "primary-mover" is the one who initiates the move; meaning that he or she already has an employment contract before arriving in the new country. I argue that the employment contract is one element among many to give meaning to a relocation, as not all relocations are perceived equally. Below, I distinguish between two types of moves, which typically require two kinds of employment contracts: the expatriate contract and the local contract. The partners' interpretation of the "primary-mover's" position in the labour market plays a significant role in the "family-strategy" as a whole. In other words, the way he or she perceives a relocation affects the "family-strategy".

6.4.1 Expat-Move

The "expat-move" can be characterized by the following three key components. (1) The company supports the partners. (2) The support maintains the "motility" (Flamm and Kaufmann 2006) of the "primary-mover". (3) The members of an "elementary family" or a "couple" are in a "liminal state" (Van Gennep 1960; Turner 1967), trapped between "here today" and maybe "there tomorrow".

a. Knowing What the Support is About

The "expat-move" is the kind of relocation in which the employing company provides financial and organisational support to the incoming employee as well as to potential partners and children. The expatriate contract formalises this extended support with the aim of facilitating the relocation. The case of Kim and Laura illustrates this. They have been married for 22 years. He is Dutch, and she is British. They have four children together. As a child Kim, moved back and forth between Switzerland and South Africa, before he began studying in Belgium. He has worked for a multinational consumer goods company for the last 25 years. Laura does not work in the labour force anymore, as she does the care work for the children. Altogether they have relocated eight times, all for the same company and each time with an expatriate contract. Frequent relocations are part of Kim's career path for he uses mobility to climb up the company's hierarchy. He is now the director of a worldwide promotion program. At the beginning of his career, he was an "assigned expatriate", relocated as he was to work where the company needed him. In the course of his career, as he climbed up the ladder of the company, he asked to come to Switzerland as an "intra self-initiated expatriate" and in doing so gained the power to negotiate within the organisation. In this context, his employment contract has been combined with an expatriate contract and includes specific clauses to support mobility. It formally articulates the type of support Kim, Laura and their children are to receive:

> I mean when you move, you know exactly (…) what are your housing allowances, whether you get the trip paid back home, whether you get entitlement for a car, schooling. It's all black and white there. So, I think that makes it very easy. I mean 90% of your next position is a situation, you know (Kim, 49yrs, married).

In other words, the company sends them all around the world and provides support for this. The challenges of the relocations remain in the background, because the company backs Kim, Laura, and their children. Respondents doing this sort of "expat-move" conceive of migration as a straightforward process. They perceive a move as a matter requiring a particular kind of service: for a broken sink, we need a plumber; for a relocation abroad, a relocation office. The organisational support extends beyond the professional activity of the "primary-mover" and provides assistance to the whole family. When needed, the company will pay for language lessons or for the services of an outplacement agency for the "secondary-mover" as well as for an international school for the child to attend. Centrally, I understand an "expat-move" as a relocation in which the company provides financial and organisational support, and promises a "frictionless mobility". As we have already seen, the constraints may very well be found elsewhere. In the third empirical chapter, I will show concretely what kind of support the companies actually offer (8.2.3 Company's Support, 220).

b. Not Knowing When and Where the Next Move Will Be

Another characteristic of an "expat-move" is the high possibility of a further relocation. Stefan and Caroline are married. He is Austrian; she is German. They have three children. While Caroline does not work in the labour force anymore, Stefan directs the financial operations of a multinational consumer goods company. Though he worked only in Europe, he was on an expatriate contract as he relocated frequently between and within Germany, Austria, and Switzerland. When I asked him about his plans to remain in Switzerland, he told me that he does not know. "Being ready" for a relocation is simply part of the job:

> We don't know actually very exactly, it can be either here or somewhere abroad. Most likely abroad, but we don't know well. I mean mainly in the region of Europe, because I am not going anywhere else (Stefan, 48yrs, married).

Stefan perceives his stay in Switzerland as being for a limited time; yet, he does not know for how long. He has some conditions, like refusing to relocate outside of Europe, but he also does not know where he will be posted next. The company has offices in more than 15 different cities, from Lisbon to Moscow. Stefan's willingness to relocate – at a time and a place he does not know – has a price. Thus, the employing company pays for the international school attended by the children, for the apartment they rent, as well as for any trips back home. In fact, the company pays for the family's settlement in a fashion that supports Stefan's "motility". "Motility" can be understood as an "how individual or group takes possession of the realm of possibilities for mobility and builds upon it to develop personal projects" (Flamm and Kaufmann 2006, 168). Thus, "motility" not only refers to the mover's capacity and the potential to be mobile, but also includes his or her acceptance and will to move again.

"Motility" implies financial and organisational means. The company pays to support Stefan's career, so he can remain open to mobility. Caroline too pays a price: an inability to maintain her own position in the labour force while she follows Stefan and takes on the family's care work. Thus, Stefan's "organisational means" not only refer to his relationship with the employing company but also and more centrally to a division of the tasks in which Caroline provides the care work. In other words, company support and Caroline's care work maintain Stefan's "motility", by facilitating the settling of the "elementary family" as a whole. If Caroline and their children are "motile", it is because Stefan's "motility" requires it. Stefan and Caroline develop a "motile mobility", as the purpose of an "expat-move" is maintaining an employee's "motility". In that sense, their "motility" is oriented towards his professional career; later on, I will take up this matter of his being the depository of the family's "motility" (7.3.1 Ignoring Motility, 208).

Furthermore, Stefan's "motility" profoundly affects Caroline's capacity to maintain a position in the labour-force, because she does not choose when and where to move. In fact, neither Caroline nor Stefan know where or when they will relocate. Yet, their respective positions differ. Though Stefan does not know where and when he will move again, he knows that he will move for the sake of his professional career and will have a position in the labour force after the next relocation. In other words, their "motility" favours his professional career while hindering hers. "We thought we would need to move so she did not start [to look for paid work in the labour force]" (Stefan, 48yrs, married). This quote gives a clue as to how the will toward and the acceptance of further mobility is constructed as well as its possible gendered consequences. Stefan does not seem to question the division of labour: because *they* thought they might move again for the sake of *his* professional career, *she* did not start to look for employment. His argument implies a strong hierarchisation between the partners. I will analyse this process in depth in the next empirical chapter (7 Representing Migration: Between Motilities and Anchors, 183). In sum, the concept of "motility" accounts for this extraordinary situation in that it has a deeply gendered impact on the "family strategies", explaining, in part, why Caroline does not work in the labour force but does the care work.

c. *From an Expatriate Contract to a Local Contract*

The "expat-move" requires the support of both the employing company and the "secondary-mover" to maintain the rather expansive state of "motile motility". It calls attentions to the "state of liminality" (Van Gennep 1960; Turner 1967) implying a tension between "here" and "somewhere else". A "state of liminality" is a transitional period. Being in a liminal state between "here" and "somewhere else" has gendered consequences, as we have just seen with Stefan and Caroline. Furthermore, expatriate contracts provide benefits for a limited number of years, generally between three and five years depending on the company – in case there is no further relocation. Companies create expatriate positions under expatriate contracts, despite their costs, in order to have a "motile" workforce. Multinational companies need a pool of highly-skilled migrants who can move easily and quickly. Thus, the expatriate contract formalises the support for a succession of relocations. It is the case for Kim, who has worked for the same company for 25 years and relocates every three to four years. Conversely, the company downgrades the expatriate contract to a local contract once the employees have stayed in the same place for three to five years. This happened to Nick, who is now the executive creative director of an international marketing agency in Germany. He relocated three times during his professional career as he moved from The Netherlands to Belgium, then to France, and finally to Germany. His last relocation was under a local contract, which implies less support:

> F.T.: What kind of support does the company offer?
> Nick: It is only the school, no housing, no nothing, I am actually on a local contract here.
> F.T.: Were you once on an expat contract?
> Nick: Because my expat contract expired when I was in Belgium, because an expat contract is three or five years after the move, but I stayed longer when I was in Belgium, about six and a half years. So, one and a half years too long. So, my contract was already transmitted to a local contract in Belgium (Nick, 54yrs, married).

An "expat-move" is not only about relocating in the sense of being mobile, but rather about giving the mover the capacity to relocate *frequently* in the sense of being "motile". To that end, the partners are supported by the employing company. When a relocation lasts longer, the employees are downgraded to a local contract. In conclusion, I propose three constituting elements of an "expat-move" as (1) the financial and organisational support of a company to a family, (2) the maintenance of the "motility" of a family for the sake of the "primary-mover", which introduces (3) a liminal settlement between "here" and "somewhere else".

6.4.2 Local-Move

A "local-move" creates more bonds between a highly-skilled migrant and the country of relocation than an "expat-move", because the former includes less assistance or none at all. International schools, outplacement agencies, and relocation offices are not part of the service granted by a "local contract". Neither does such a contract include financial incentives, like paid home-trips or organisational support provided by the local administration. To put it bluntly, a "local-move" implies a local contract with no additional support concerning settlement and mobility. The interviewees, who are employed on a "local contract", need to sort out the challenges of a relocation by themselves. They are alone in finding, for instance, an apartment or a kindergarten. The lack of support implies that the move is more anchoring; it impacts the current move as well as further possible moves. It is an "anchoring move".

a. Settlement Struggles

Emma, whom I introduced earlier as an "inter self-initiated expatriate" (6.1.4 Inter Self-Initiated Expatriate, 141)[57] relocated to Switzerland on a "local contract". She moved alone to Switzerland and struggled to find accommodations right away as she did not receive any support from the company that employs her, even though this company is a widely known multinational pharmaceutical company. Not having found an apartment right away, she thus lived at her uncle's place for two months, which was more than two hours away from her workplace. She struggled between working, commuting and searching for accommodation. Once she settled, she therefore wanted to remain in the same place for a while. Emma has since found another position in another region of Switzerland and intends to remain there. Interviewees moving locally regard a relocation as a challenging process, as opposed to those performing "expat-moves". The former express a desire to stay longer given the challenges they have overcome while settling in a particular location. Others, however, switch to a local contract when their stay exceeds a few years, as is the case with Nick who was transferred into

57 When I refer to the respondents I have mentioned earlier, I will point to the chapter where the context of their migration can be found so as not to be repetitive. Furthermore, the appendix 5 (p. 338) contains the lists of all the respondents used in the empirical analysis.

a local contract. These are two particular situations leading to the same outcome: Nick and Anouk and Emma and Blaise relocated under the conditions of a local contract, which implies less support.

b. Localising the Home-Base

The localisation of the employee's "home country" is another element which creates bonds with a local space by that expressing the wish of an "anchoring mobility". Some of my interviewees have asked to change the "home country" on their contract in the case they have to relocate abroad, so that they might eventually return to the country they have chosen to settle in permanently. Julia is a good example of this: not only did she ask to be transferred on a local contract, but she also asked her company to change her contract's "home country". She is a British citizen and a senior manager in an American pharmaceutical company in Switzerland. It was important for her to be on a local contract so that she might continue to see her daughter after her divorce:

> I might have to leave for a few years, but I've asked the company to consider that Switzerland as my home country to expatriate me out to come back. Not to consider the UK as my home country and take me back there (Julia, 42, divorced).

Julia strategically uses the "home country" to maintain strong ties with Switzerland, her adopted "home country". Yet, the decisions that Julia has made concerning her work in the labour force – see the upper right corner of Thus, the "work-family integration" aims at overcoming the "gender binaries" by looking at the reciprocal impacts of work in the labour force and care work. In my study, migration for professional reasons complexifies the "family-work integration" even more.

Figure 13 – remain unclear, until we learn of her need to integrate work in the labour force and family. The work in the labour force influences and is influenced by the "work-family integration". Julia's daughter is in a Swiss private school rather than an international school. Julia, together with her former husband, decided to raise their daughter in Switzerland, which means that Julia wishes to stay in Switzerland in the long run. Julia's situation illustrates that a "local-move" anchors her more to the country and she makes strategic use of it. This kind of move thus does not necessitate as much "motility" as an "expat-move" would.

In sum, the "local-move" is a different way to experience a migration for professional reasons. Here, migrating employees do not usually receive support from the company and may therefore struggle as they settle in their new location. Furthermore, a "local-move" requires less "motility" usually in keeping with the partner's wish or need to stay longer in the same local space.

6.4.3 Continuum of the Primary-Mover

I understand the "expat-move" and the "local-move" as two types of moves that a "primary-mover" performs, which influences the settlement of the family as a whole. The "expat-move" and the "local-move" correspond to the two ends of a continuum[58], symbolising two plain forms of mobility. While the "expat-move" introduces "motile mobilities", the "local-move" emphasises "anchoring mobilities". The expected frequency of further relocations is higher for "expat-moves" than it is for "local-moves". The two types represent two internally coherent forms of mobility. In that sense, the "types" are sociological tools, useful in structuring our understanding of the social world. I argue that some moves create more "anchors" to a local space, while others enable families to be "motile", yet they introduce different "family strategies".

a. Relocation of Headquarters

Sometimes, companies use "expatriate contracts" when they relocate their headquarters. In this case, they are not necessarily using such contracts to enhance the "motility" of their employees. Manon, who was married to Charles, works in the pharmaceutical industry as a national product manager, while Charles is a senior manager in the aggro-food industry. Both are French; they have three children together. When the company headquarters employing Charles were moved from France to Switzerland, the company proposed "expatriate contracts" to all headquarter employees in order to support their relocation. The company was not seeking here to maintain a high "motility" for these employees. On the contrary, the goal was to make sure the employees settled in the best conditions possible in Switzerland, so that they would stay there:

> I think that initially the idea was to have an expatriate contract for three years and then switch to a local contract. It meant changing my husband's contract from expatriate to

---

58 I speak of a continuum because my empirical cases are usually between two extreme poles. A "local contract" sometimes offers "expatriate benefits", like paid language lessons or paid "home-leaves" for the whole family – known as a "local plus contract". Indeed, some companies do not offer "expatriate contracts" and work only with "local contracts", which does not mean that they do not provide any support in maintaining the "motility" of their employees. Thus, a "local contract" does not systematically mean a "local-move". Furthermore, it may be more advantageous to be on a "Swiss local contract" and to receive the salary in Swiss Francs than to receive an American salary, in American Dollars, in Switzerland. The companies' policies regarding the mobility of their staff vary considerably.

> local. This relocation concerned many employees, because the *** headquarters were moved from *** to ***. So, it was not just for my husband. It was for many of them and they absolutely needed these top managers. They moved them and they knew that / my husband might have moved for a few years, had I not found [a position] … Well. Then, maybe my husband and I would have returned [to France] (Manon, 55yrs, divorced)[59].

A broader program to relocate the headquarters of the company triggered the relocation of its employees. It was part of the "grand strategy" of the company induced as they were by what Switzerland, which seeks to attract headquarters of multinational companies, had to offer. Management deciding to move a company as such may decide to relocate the whole staff as well. This case illustrates the complexity and the variety of factors involved in migrating for professional reasons: that is why I opt for a continuum which is a flexible tool to conceptualise these different experiences of migration.

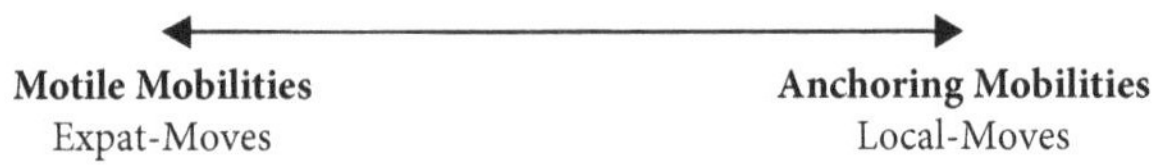

Figure 14 Continuum of Relocations of the Primary-Mover. Source: Own Elaboration

For all these reasons, an expatriate contract does not always overlap with an "expat-move", neither does a local contract overlap with a "local-move". I have presented two typical moves precisely to avoid a rigid structure while still underlining different orientations in the way highly-skilled migrants relocate. The types of moves and the continuum, structuring their relationship, highlight the centrality of "motility" in making sense of professional relocations. Even if Charles had been on an expatriate contract, he underwent a more locally-oriented move. Thus, the distinction between an "expat-move" and a "local-move" shows different conditions for moves, in which "motility" is more or less supported. I refer here not only to the type of working contract, but rather to the importance given to further mobilities, and thus, "motility", during a relocation. In

59 Je pense qu'au départ dans l'idée c'était d'abord d'avoir un contrat d'expatrié pendant trois ans et puis après d'avoir un contrat local de passer mon mari en contrat local. Cette mutation s'est faite bien pour beaucoup de salariés parce que le siège social de *** bougeait de Paris à Lausanne. Donc, ce n'était pas que pour mon mari! C'était pour un certain nombre d'entre eux et ils avaient absolument besoin de ces cadres dirigeants, de les déménager et ils savaient que voilà/ parce que mon mari aurait peut-être déménagé pour quelques années mais si moi je n'avais pas trouvé bon ben peut-être qu'ils seraient revenus (Own Translation).

sum, the two types of moves – the "expat-move" and the "local-move" – express a central qualitative difference between the relocations of the "primary-movers" (Figure 14). Some are more "motile", others more anchored, but – as I understand it – all are mobile.

Some "primary-movers" are "ready to move" (i.e., they face uncertainty about what is going to be the next step), while some others become more anchored to a local space. For the "primary-mover", these situations do not imply much uncertainty, because – from a professional perspective – the move makes sense. The "types of move" undertaken by the "primary-mover" has consequences for the "family-strategy" and on the organisation of a family. The "family-strategy" depends – *in part* – on the way the partners perceive the move of the "primary-mover". However, it is not a one-way street because the strategies regarding the labour force work are – *in turn* – influenced by the need to "integrate" them with care work, as in the case of Julia who intends to stay on in Switzerland due to the shared custody of her daughter with her former husband.

6.5 Secondary-Mover and Secondary-Stayer

Attentive readers may have noticed that many female partners of the "primary-mover" do not work in the labour force anymore. Through a "collective approach", I can trace how the constraints of a so-called "frictionless mobility" appear. In this part, I analyse the various reactions of the "secondary-mover" to the relocation of the "primary-mover", highlighting the relationship between them. One day a (soon to be) "secondary-mover" learns about an opportunity abroad for his or her partner i.e., the "primary-mover". A decision needs to be made quickly; the partners decide to accept the offer. Once they accept, discussions about what to do next begin. At that point, the partners need to coordinate anew to find another "family-strategy" that corresponds with their new living situation. Here, I focus on the "secondary-mover" in the labour force – the bottom right corner of Thus, the "work-family integration" aims at overcoming the "gender binaries" by looking at the reciprocal impacts of work in the labour force and care work. In my study, migration for professional reasons complexifies the "family-work integration" even more.

Figure 13 (6.3 Conceptualising the Professional Careers Coordination, 145) – and the integration of paid work with the paid work of the "primary-mover": what I call the "labour force work integration". This is part of creating an analysis adopting a decentred standpoint. Does the "secondary-mover" face specific challenges that the "primary-mover" does not experience when it comes to their place in the labour force? If yes, what do they look like? Does the "secondary-mover" try to maintain a professional activity? If yes, what is specific about this situation?

I analytically differentiate between two types of moves for the "secondary-mover": the "total-move" and the "half-move". The "total-move" implies a uni-local following-strategy to the new local space while the "half-move" refers to bi-local or multi-local coordinating-strategies. In the latter, the "secondary-mover" maintains sustained ties with several local spaces other than the new location. On top of that, I will present a third possibility in which the "secondary-mover" is in fact a "stayer" who does not move. Yet, not every "secondary-mover" works in the labour force; I will address the "family-strategy" of couples adopting this configuration in the chapter 8.

6.5.1 Total-Move of a Partner-Initiated Mover

I speak of a "total-move" when the "secondary-mover" leaves country A – and resigns as the case may be – to follow the "primary-mover" to country B. The place of residence, the place of work, and (if so) the place of the children's schooling change. A "total-move" implies that the "secondary-mover" relocates from one place to another without maintaining bonds with the former country of residence[60]. The partners move together to a new local space; avoiding split-families, long-distance relationships and frequent international commutes. When the "secondary-mover" agrees to a "total-move", I speak of the "partner-initiated mover", a notion that stresses the "primary-mover's" role in initiating the move. How does a "partner-initiated mover" react professionally when accompanying the "primary-mover" abroad?

a. Coordinating before Relocating

In rare cases, both partners manage to find employment in the same new place prior to the move; as Lynn and Alex's case (6.2.1 Primary-Mover and Secondary-Mover, 143) illustrates. They both moved from the United States to work in Frankfurt, Germany. During the interview, Lynn mentioned that they were "so lucky" since they both obtained positions at the same place, in the same company. Strikingly, they did not relocate for 14 years, even though they received some

60 Transnational studies and mobility studies show that there is no such thing as a "one-way ticket" in contemporary migration processes (Wieczorek 2018). A "total-move" does not imply that the partners totally cut ties with the country they formerly lived in but rather that the ties in the former country are not regularly activated to develop the "family-strategy".

concrete offers abroad. They only relocated once. Some offers were more interesting individually, but they were neither at the same place nor at the same point of time. Such a situation clearly shows the difficulty in developing a "family-strategy" in which both partners move, work and live together. Interviews with Alex revealed that they do not see how they could increase their financial and professional situation *as a family* by relocating again. "One of us", he told me, "would certainly not find a position as good as we currently have" (Alex, 52, Married). The "labour force work integration" stresses how the partners concretely cope with two professional careers. Alex is the "secondary-mover" performing a "total-move". He is a "partner-initiated mover", emphasized by his role in relocating in response to Lynn's initiative without keeping any professional bonds with the United States. Both moved together and then have since refused to move again in order to secure both their professional positions.

Lynn and Alex's case corresponds to a "total-move": *the "secondary-mover" follows the primary-mover to the new local space.* Their case also shows that making multiple relocations for the sake of one professional career is a risk that some do not want to take. Lynn and Alex feel both lucky to have good positions. The "family-strategy" they develop, in which both partners find a professional activity before relocating, is indeed a rare one.

6.5.2 Unique Challenges of a Partner-Initiated Mover

For most of the "partner-initiated movers", relocating with their partner implies quitting their position in the labour force and starting to look for a new one once they arrive abroad. This approach differs from the "family-strategy" that Lynn and Alex have developed. When a "partner-initiated mover" seeks employment abroad, he or she faces challenges and difficulties, which often requires a rearrangement in terms of his or her professional career. Three elements of this type of migration can be identified: (1) a gender imbalance, (2) a "new start", and (3) concretely seeking work in the labour force abroad.

a. Gender Imbalance

Many "partner-initiated movers" are women whose specific situation promotes a dynamic in which they are often sent back to the "domestic sphere". In other words, the "partner-initiated movers", who want to continue to work in the labour force need to fight against the pressures of "house-wifing", i.e., when care work is considered the most "reasonable" choice. Indeed, when one's partner already has a position in the labour force, a mobile and successful professional career in a multinational company, why would one - read *she* - have to look for paid work?

She can very well take care of the family. François and Lara both work in multinational corporations in Switzerland: they are married and have two children. Lara is a "partner-initiated mover" who followed François to the different countries where he worked. For each relocation she looked for an employment in the labour force and actually found a job in Switzerland, though she has to commute more than one hour a day to get to her workplace. On one occasion, while she was seeking a position in the labour force in Switzerland, a recruiter implied that she should not work:

> It was suggested to me that it was a little bit strange that I work instead of taking care of my children (Lara, 61yrs, married)[61].

She speaks about the social pressures and the necessity of resisting them if one wants to find a job as a "partner-initiated mover" with children. The "partner-initiated movers" quite often stop working in the labour force and this process of "house-wifing" explains in part why[62]. I understand the process of "house-wifing" as a process by which women, all women, have to face remarks, suggesting that they would be better off at home doing the care work for the children rather than looking for a position in the labour force. It is a problematic situation if this person happens to be a possible future employer. Finding a position in the labour force is rendered more difficult by those employers who are reluctant to hire women who are also mothers.

Yet, I believe that "house-wifing" is not specific to the situation of "partner-initiated movers"; still it is an important element for those I interviewed. The specificity of their position results from the fact that "primary-movers" begin their new professional activity without delay while the "partner-initiated mover" needs to find one first. Furthermore, not only do they have to find a professional activity first, very often they have to make arrangements regarding the care work before starting to seek employment in the labour force. Thus, the situation becomes even more challenging for the "partner-initiated movers" who have children because of the need to find new day care arrangements or a school. Even though the "primary-mover" and the employing company offer support. It is often the "partner-initiated mover" who maintains or even rebuilds the arrangements regarding the care work in a new local space. Only then, can the "partner-initiated mover" begin to seek work in the labour force. Often this

61 On m'a fait comprendre que c'était un peu étrange que je travaille au lieu de m'occuper de mes enfants (Own Translation).

62 In this case, the "partner-initiated mover" is pejoratively referred to as the "trailing-spouse". In chapter 8, I will return to this "family-strategy".

situation is not questioned by the respondents as it seems logical to them that the one who works in the labour force should focus rather on office-related duties. Thus, the one who seeks a position in the labour force after the migration does the care work and looks for care arrangement as – so it is often said – the "primary-mover" does not have time to do it, neither does he – it is often the male – feel responsible. The "primary-mover", working full-time, does not perceive rebuilding care work arrangements of the family as his task. These responsibilities and, accordingly, delays, partly explain why so many "partner-initiated movers" do not work in the labour force anymore, as (re-)constructing the care work arrangement of the family can be extremely time consuming. Certainly, the phenomenon of "house-wifing" combined with a situation in which the "partner-initiated movers" do the care work just after a relocation are two powerful elements which hinder the search for a position in the labour force in a country they do not know.

The distribution of the responsibilities related to "family-strategies" between the "primary-mover" and the "partner-initiated movers" is thus imbalanced as the latter face more challenges and take on more responsibilities regarding care work than their partners. The situation is stressful for them and leads to many anticipated returns. A way to analyse this situation is to conceptualise three "pillars" which maintain the sustainability of a "family-strategy": if the "partner-initiated mover" does not find work in the labour force (1st pillar), does not speak the local-language (2nd pillar) and does not find satisfactory care work arrangements (3rd pillar), then the "family-strategy" does not work[63]. Once the three "pillars" break, the partners are not able to integrate work and family in a satisfying way. In such a configuration, the odds for the "partner-initiated mover" to be cast back in the "domestic sphere" are even higher. When she (or, in rarer cases, he) refuses this arrangement, disagreements and dissatisfaction, anticipated returns and even divorces may arise.

b. Starting from Minus Zero

Right after a relocation, the "partner-initiated movers" typically do not work in the labour force but have to seek employment: a process which can be long and painful. It is especially complicated for those whose absence from the labour force work is combined with a huge load of care work – mostly because of parenting,

63 It is one of my interviewees – Thomas – who told me about the three pillars metaphor, which I later noticed in the interviews. It corresponds to the three most recurrent challenges of the "partner-initiated mover" when they arrive in a new local-space.

as we have just seen. In that sense, these mothers (and fathers) "start from minus zero" as "starting from zero" would imply arriving and starting to look for employment in the labour force directly. The "primary-movers" already hold a working position and are basically facing a familiar work environment though in a different location. Metaphorically speaking, they still use the same log-in to start their computer in the morning. When it comes to the "partner-initiated movers", the situation is completely different. The case of Sara exemplifies this challenge, in opposition to John, her husband and the "primary-mover". Both are in their early 30s. They do not have children, which gives them more time to focus on labour force work. Still, their individual professional situations and their experience relocating to Switzerland vary extensively. Sara comes from the United States. After her bachelor's degree, she decided to move to Israel to obtain her master's degree in the social sciences. There, she met John, whom she married. During her studies in Israel, she started to work for different NGOs while John, in the meantime, found employment in Switzerland as an engineer. She perceives the relocation to Switzerland as a disruption of her former life:

> I was very happy with my life and I had a lot of friends and I knew exactly where I wanted to go with my career after completing my masters. The network that I had and contacts and the organisation I wanted to work for meant that coming here was like starting from zero in every way. … It was a big step forward for his career which came with a big increase in salary. Plus, [John] had been living in the same place for a long time and he wanted a change (Sara, 32yrs, married).

Sara moved for John, who is the "primary-mover" and a "drawn-expatriate", as she quit her position in Israel to follow him because: "in marriage, in the end, you have to make a couple" (Sara, 32yrs, married). She relocated for him and now she faces the challenge of developing her own professional project – starting, as she says, "from zero in every way" (ibid). The relocation to Switzerland makes sense for her husband and his career; but not necessarily for her. The only reason for Sara to be in Switzerland is their marriage. The relocation disrupts her life in every way: she has to find ways to meet new people in order to create a professional network while she seeks employment. John's company does not provide support to partners. Besides, she is alone, as she told me, the whole day, as John works full time. On top of that, she does not speak French and lives in a remote area in the countryside, so they can be close to her husband's workplace. This case emphasises the accumulation of specific challenges faced by the "partner-initiated movers".

The "primary-movers" do not face a situation in which the new local space feels alien to them as is often the case for the "partner-initiated mover". In Sara and John's case, the specific place refers to a remote village in the Swiss countryside. Actually, Sara and John had at least two choices for their move: Switzerland and Spain. They decided to relocate to Switzerland because they thought it might provide more in the way of professional opportunities for Sara than Spain[64]. Sara's relocation to Switzerland emphasises that the "partner-initiated movers" move where their partner finds work. In other words, Sara would never have had the idea to come there. For them, a "total-move" is also a "bonded-move": *eine unbewegliche Bewegung*. Moreover, the place of relocation is often irrelevant as far as their own professional projects are concerned and they cannot move elsewhere as long as their partners remain employed – unless they do, which raises the question of power within couples. I will deal with this central topic in chapters 7 and 8. Meanwhile, the "partner-initiated movers" face increasing challenges finding employment. It is not only about starting from zero; but starting from zero in specific conditions, at a specific place, at a specific time which may be suboptimal for their own professional careers. One might even suggest that they start from *minus* zero, particularly for those who have to find new support regarding care work before they can seek work in the labour force.

c. Seeking Employment Abroad

Seeking a position in the labour force abroad is already a challenge *as such*; as a whole array of migration studies shows (Bommes and Kolb 2006). In my cases, it is a symptomatic challenge for the "partner-initiated movers". They move for their partner who already holds a paid position, leaving it up to them to find a position in the labour force. While the idea is to maintain a sense of "familyhood", this task is often left to the "partner-initiated mover". Maintaining a career thus requires a lot of perseverance as well as a strong capacity to resist such social pressures as "house-wifing", I argue.

Some of those who found a position in the labour force after a relocation perceive it as an exhausting adventure, requiting a significant personal investment. Yet, this adventure is not entirely unpleasant. Interviewees have said that it broadens their perspectives, offering them an opportunity to work in a different sector or for a different company. Maria and Franz both studied management in Germany and both are German. Franz has worked for the same consumer goods company for almost fifteen years and Maria also worked for this company for

64 When I checked Sara's *LinkedIn* profile a few months after the interview, she mentioned having moved to New York, where she found employment, which begs the question as to what has happened to their marriage.

six years. In fact, this is where they met. Then, Franz received an offer to go to England and they decided that Maria would resign and follow him. Since then, they have relocated four times: from Germany to England, to Italy, to Japan, and to Switzerland. Maria found employment after each relocation; yet, Maria and Franz do not have any children which is, I argue, what makes the difference. I develop this point further in the chapter 8. For the moment, it suffices to say that in nearly all my empirical cases the female "partner-initiated movers" either have a position in the labour force or they have children: maintaining both simultaneously seem to be extremely rare in the context of frequent migrations for professional reasons.

For some relocations, Maria performed "half-moves"[65] and for others "total-moves". Here is how she recalled her first relocation as a "partner-initiated mover" performing a "total-move":

> The first move was maybe one of the most difficult ones, because at that time I did not have any intention to leave the company. I knew it was going to be difficult to enter *** in the UK because it was a very small office at the time there and I also loved my job and had no / yeah / there was no reason for me why I should leave, but we also knew that we both wanted to move on and it was a good opportunity for my husband and London offers a great range of opportunity for workers, for employees. So, in the end I took it as a chance to learn something new and to get to know a different company (Maria, 51yrs, married).

Another specificity of the "partner-initiated mover" is, as the quote indicates, to quit a possibly rewarding position due to the relocation of the "primary-mover". Maria is very clear about her motivation: she does it for her husband and more especially for his professional success. The situation is similar to Sara's, who moved with her husband to "make a couple" (Sara, 32yrs, married).

Thus, the "partner-initiated mover" needs to re-enter the labour force in a foreign country. Truth to be told, they do not always perceive it as a sacrifice, as Maria, for instance, described, but as an opportunity rather. She worked in different sectors, on different continents, supported start-ups, worked as a creative writer, as an account manager or a project manager. Today she is the leader of a strategic project within a multinational consumer goods company. While some "partner-initiated movers" perceive the relocation as a professional opportunity, it implies an important professional risk for them. The choices of the "partner-initiated movers" regarding where they will live and when they will move are restricted. This hinders their professional career. Nevertheless, in some cases,

65 I develop the concept of "half-move" in the second part of the present chapter.

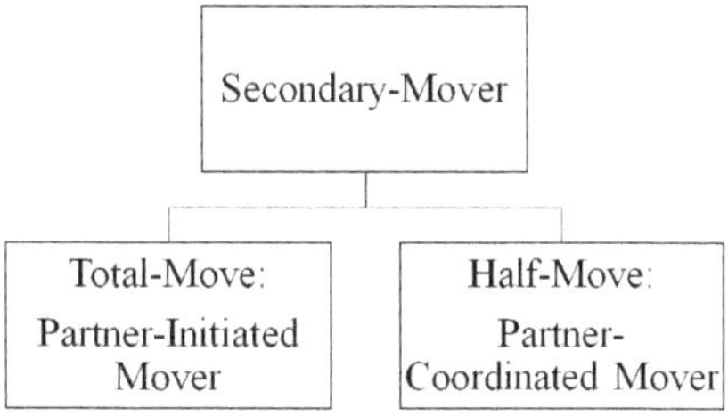

Figure 15 "Total-Move" and "Half-Move". Source: Own elaboration

their professional path can be made all the more rewarding and interesting; a point that Maria expresses many times during the interview. She also expresses how utterly exhausting it is to do so. The "partner-initiated movers" consent to move for the sake of their partner and spend a lot of time and energy doing so; which is something the "primary-mover" does not experience as such.

In sum, the "partner-initiated movers" face unique challenges in the course of a "total" move. They are very often women who seek employment in the labour force in a place they did not choose after having found day care or schooling arrangements for the children. From a professional perspective, the place of relocation may be irrelevant for them. Thus, a "total-move" often means a risky professional move for the "secondary-mover". Here, I focus on their labour force work, but in many cases the "partner-initiated movers" do not even work anymore, due to the challenges I have pointed out. The "secondary-movers", who continue to work after a relocation, use such other ways integrating their own and their partner's place in the labour force as, what we call, "half-moves".

6.5.3 Half-Move of a Partner-Coordinated Mover

Most of the "secondary-movers" – who stay employed in the labour force – perform "half-moves", which enable them to circumvent the unique challenges faced by "partner-initiated movers". Rather than follow the partner initiating the move and resigning from their own professional activity, these "secondary-movers" find ways to coordinate their own professional activity with their partner's migration. They perform a "half-move", meaning that they follow the "primary-mover" only partially, maintaining professional ties with the former country of residence. Thus, the "*partner-coordinated* mover" refers to a "secondary-mover" performing a "half-move" (Figure 15). According to this configuration, the "family-strategy" is bi-local (if not even multi-local), meaning that the partners continue moving back and forth between the former and the new countries of residence. A "half-move" can take a variety of such concrete forms as teleworking or commuting. Centrally, a "half-move" is an attempt to compensate for the drawbacks of the migration of the "primary-mover", whereby the "secondary-mover" uses mobility as a strategic means of maintaining their place in the labour force. In other words, the "secondary-mover" maintains their bond with the former country, coordinating, rather than subordinating, their own career with that of the "primary-mover". From the collective perspective, I refer to this phenomenon as a "half-move", because only one of the partners has completely relocated, at least initially. In other words, the "primary-mover" relocates, let us say, to country B while the "secondary-mover" maintains links with the place they had lived in before; i.e. country A.

a. Commuting between the Workplace and Home

Some "partner-coordinated movers" decide to maintain professional activities in country A while relocating to country B with the "primary-movers". In this case, the "partner-coordinated movers" commute internationally, creating a specific "family-strategy", in which the "labour force work integration", post-relocation, is maintained by frequent mobilities. The couple relocates to country B, but the "partner-coordinated mover" continues to work in country A. Such a strategy implies a strong coordination between the partners, as between Julia and her former husband, Jack, when they moved to Geneva (Localising the Home-Base, 134). She commuted between London and Geneva in order to work in England and spent the rest of her time in Switzerland with Jack:

> I was working for a company called ***, which is an American company in the UK, in the European headquarters, which are based in London while my ex-husband was working for a Swiss pharmaceutical company called ***, based in Geneva. He was relocated to the global or the international office in Geneva and so I came with him as his spouse, which meant that I was then living in Switzerland and commuting back to London for my European job, which was fine, because my job involved a lot of travel anyway (Julia, 42yrs, divorced).

Julia and Jack integrated their careers with their family in a way which required extensive commuting between Julia's workplace in London and their new home-base in Switzerland. When their son, Ben was born, they needed to simultaneously coordinate their two professional careers and the care work, which required a lot of organisation. In fact, both Julia and Jack were constantly juggling the need to have at least one of the parents doing the care work for Ben while the other one was working in the labour force. This required – according to Julia – a lot of organisation:

> I was travelling with my job and my husband was travelling with his job so what we would do is to sit down with the diary every month and say: 'ok, I am travelling ta ta ta and you are travelling these dates and so one of us be here all the time' (Julia, 42yrs, divorced).

Couples usually live together and commute frequently for their professional activity when there is a child involving care work, while they more often do not mind living apart when having none. In Julia's and Jack's case, frequent mobilities were needed because someone had to do the care work. One way of "integrating the professional work" of both partners is to intensively use international mobility, that is international commuting in their case. It implies a stronger coordination between the partners when it comes to being present for the care work that a child requires. In chapter 8, we will see that such a "family-strategy" does not, usually, last in the long run.

b. Teleworking

Similarly, other "partner-coordinated movers" decide to follow the "primary-mover" to country B *and* to continue to work for their company in country A, without for that matter commuting between A and B. In other words, they find arrangements with their employers that allow them to work from abroad, which is known as teleworking. This was the case for Maria (Seeking Employment Abroad, 163), who continued to work for her employer in Italy while living in Japan:

> In Italy, I worked for an online company. It was an online business and they allowed me to work from Japan. So, I worked remotely for the Italian company in Japan. It was not easy, which is one of the reasons why I quit after two years. (…) So, I ended up working from 4 pm in the afternoon until midnight which didn't really fit my schedule. I was just too remote, because it was just me in this time zone (Maria, 42yrs, married).

Though Maria is physically not mobile on a daily basis to do her work in the labour force, the mobility of information flows remained a prerequisite to her professional activities. New information and communication technologies allowed her to work in Italy while living in Japan as information is constantly shared and transferred between both countries. However, she developed a "labour force work integration" that was quite difficult to maintain in the long run, given that the working conditions were rather exhausting, she explained. After two years, Maria resigned from the Italian company and found a new position in Japan in a start-up, however on a volunteer basis only. After each of her husband's relocations, she managed to find a way to continue working in the labour force. Still, she paid a high price for *his* frequent relocations, given that she was not able to rise through the hierarchy of any company, as he did. Approaching the relocation of her husband with a "half-move", Maria circumvented the challenges of a "total-move" by continuing her former professional activity in the former country for a while. Indeed, she started seeking employment in Japan, two years later, but only once the couple had settled. Maria started out as a "partner-coordinated mover", working for an Italian company while living in Japan. After she resigned and accepted a voluntary position for a start-up in Japan, becoming a full-fledged "partner-initiated mover" but losing her income in the process and having to face the range of challenges inherent to this situation.

Maria's case emphasises how a "partner-coordinated mover" can continue to work in the labour force while the "primary-mover" relocates. It highlights a variety of ways that mobility is used to integrate two professional careers and it underlines the dynamics relating "partner-coordinated movers" and "partner-initiated movers". Truth to be told, Maria and Franz do not have children, which greatly facilitated their version of "work-family integration". Moreover, Maria started working in an unpaid position, which is usually easier to find than a paid one. The fact that Maria could even consider an unpaid position shows the couple's high social and economic status: not everyone can afford to accept an unpaid job.

c. *Maternity Leaves*

Others decide to temporarily stop their professional activities in country A, using maternity leaves or sabbatical as a means of following their partner to country B. Manon (Relocation of Headquarter, 155), working as a pharmacologist in the pet-food industry, has made this choice:

> My husband had been transferred by *** to Italy to lead the Italian subsidiary, and, at that time, I was pregnant with my third child and so I said: 'I will take a parental leave for two years'. So, for two years I stopped working. In fact, I followed my husband to Italy (Manon, 55yrs, divorced)[66].

The insurance and/or paid leave programs provide a support mechanism, which enables temporary "family-strategies" as the "partner-coordinated movers" reduce the "career cost" of the migration of their partner. The embeddedness in the French "welfare regime" was a crucial element of Manon's strategy as it is

66 Mon mari avait été muté en Italie par *** pour diriger la filiale italienne et à ce moment j'étais enceinte de mon troisième enfant et donc je me suis dit: 'pourquoi pas? Je vais prendre un congé parental pendant deux'. Donc pendant deux ans je me suis arrêtée de travailler, enfin j'ai suivi mon mari en Italie (Own Translation).

only because her position and her income were secured by the maternity leave that Manon accepted to move with Charles. Thus, the individual strategies are oriented by the opportunities and constraints that the structure of different "welfare regimes" produce. Manon did not resign from her position in the labour force. However, it is only a matter of time until the need for a new "family-strategy" arose. As Manon's maternity leave was ending, she refused to remain in the "domestic sphere" any longer than necessary. As she put it several times during the interview: "I refused to stop working" (ibid)[67]. When she did not find employment in the labour force in Italy and felt that her options there were limited, she told her husband that she was going back to France as she would still have a position there after her maternity leave had ended. Throughout her stay in Italy, Manon maintained strong ties with France, as she kept her income and her employment there; exemplifying what I describe as a "half-move" and a "partner-coordinated mover". This contrasts with Maria's case, who resigned from the company in Italy to accept a volunteer position in a Japanese start-up. Losing her own income, Maria had subordinated her career to that of Franz. Manon, on the other hand, refused to subordinate her career to Charles even when it became clear that opportunities for her were running low in Italy. Instead of staying, she *initiated* her own relocation to come back to France, becoming the couple's "primary-mover" in her own right:

> So, I came back and [Charles] followed me six months later, he was back to France, too (Manon, 55yrs, divorced)[68].

While Charles was the "primary-mover" of the couple's relocation to Italy, he had to react to Manon's decision to move back to France. Confronted in turn with the challenge of being the "secondary-mover", he decided to perform a "half-move" in order to maintain his own professional activities. Thus, he did not resign from his position in the labour force to follow Manon but, instead, negotiated his transfer back to France within his employing company: becoming thereby an "intra self-initiated expatriate". Generally, males as "secondary-movers" tend to refuse "total-moves" much more often than females do. This case illustrates the challenge of a "labour force work integration" under the conditions of mobility, which lead a partner – Manon – to initiate a re-relocation in order to safeguard their own position in the labour force. Manon refused to subordinate her own professional career to Charles' and thus took the initiative to return to France,

67 Je ne vais pas m'arrêter de travailler (Own Translation).

68 Et donc, je suis rentrée et lui m'a suivi six mois après il est revenue en France (Own Translation).

becoming the "primary-mover". This case shows that the analytical categories of the "primary-mover" and the "secondary-mover" are relational and processual given, for example, that these types may change. I shall analyse the power dynamics involved here in Chapter 8.

To summarise briefly the concept of a "half-move", the modalities of settling are clearly bi-local (or multi-local) when the "partner-coordinated movers" maintain ties with the former country A, as is well exemplified by Manon, who took advantage of the maternity leave program in France to follow her husband to Italy, however temporarily; by Maria, who tele-worked for two years; and by Julia, who commuted between London where she worked in the labour force and Geneva where her husband and daughter lived. Still, such strategies are for the most part temporary and less than perfectly sustainable in the long run.

6.5.4 Immobility of a Secondary-Stayer

The data I have analysed reveals a third type of move, or of non-movement rather, which occurs when the "secondary-mover" decides not to move at all, introducing a "split-family" dynamic and a "secondary-stayer". It is difficult to speak of a "partner-initiated mover" or a "partner-coordinated mover" in these cases because the "secondary-stayer" does not relocate at all. He or she decides to stay in country A, which is quite often the "country of origin". In this case, the "primary-mover" travels back and forth between country A and country B. In this constellation, it is the "primary-mover" who comes back to visit the other partner. Metaphorically, we can think of a sailor who comes back home after six months at sea. In the context of this study, I did not encounter many such cases, yet they are arguably frequent in sectors like the army, the shipping industry or the fishing industry. The coordination is diffuse because both partners continue their professional careers independently of one another. This is the case of Carlos and Raul (6.1.3 Intra Self-Initiated Expatriate, 120), as Raul never followed Carlos in his relocation first to the Dominican Republic and then to Germany:

> [Raul] owns his own business. He is really successful in Mexico City financially. He is independent. I am completely independent. We don't share a common bank account, so our finances are separate (Carlos, 44, partnered).

While his partner continues to manage his family company back in Mexico, Carlos moves extensively in his work for a marketing company. Thus, they live their everyday and professional lives in different countries, which does not mean that they do not feel close as they make extensive use of new information and communication technologies: "We call each other every day, we see each other every day", Carlos told me (Carlos, 44, partnered). Besides, for twenty-two years Carlos has travelled back to Mexico to visit his boyfriend and family at least twice a year. The immobility of the "secondary-stayer", as much as the mobility of the "primary-mover", create a split "family-strategy" in which both partners prioritise their own professional careers, thereby reducing the constraints implied by "total" or "half-moves". As it is often the case in "family-strategies" where both partners work and at least one is recurrently mobile, Carlos and his partner do not have any children. According the collective approach, a "primary-stayer" is a contradiction in the terms, as the defining criterion of a "primary-mover" is giving the initiative of a move. In other words, if both partners do not decide to move – there is no migration and when one does decide, s/he becomes the "primary-mover".

6.5.5 Access to the Labour Force

So far, we have looked at the unique challenges confronted by a "partner-initiated mover", as well as the different strategies used to circumvent these described by the position of a "partner-coordinated mover" or a partner's choosing immobility. The "total-move" suggests difficulties for the "partner-initiated movers" to coordinate their own professional career with that of their partner because they settle in a new local that they did not choose. Similarly, the "half-move" shows how the "partner-coordinated movers" may decide to maintain their position in the labour force in the former country, at least temporarily. Adopting the stance of a "partner-coordinated mover" is often only a temporary solution, as, in most cases and in the long-run, only two solutions are available; either becoming a "partner-initiated mover", as in Maria's case, or becoming a "primary-mover" in one's own right, as in Manon's case. In the following section, we will identify the elements that either facilitate or hinder a "partner-initiated mover's" access to the labour force after a migration, that is, the access of a "secondary-mover" who has opted for a "total-move" and decides to live in the same place as his or her partner has relocated to. I have already shown that a "partner-initiated mover" faces unique challenges relating to their integration of two professional careers in which that of the "primary-mover" is ultimately prioritised. The "unique challenges of the partner-initiated mover" (6.5.2) refer to the high probability of their being pushed out of the labour force and into the "domestic sphere". Thus, the aim of this section is to point out the elements which facilitate or, on the contrary, hinder, a "partner-initiated mover's" access to the labour force that also acknowledges the specificity of their position.

a. Types of Skills

In line with the literature in Migration studies, "partner-initiated movers" with technical, scientific skills and/or managerial skills tend to find professional situations after relocating more easily than do those with such "softer", more "contextual skills" as language proficiency and teaching experience. Technical, scientific and managerial skills are seen to be more easily transferable, internationally (Cornelius, Espenshade, and Salehyan 2001; Larsen et al. 2005; Liversage 2009; Schmid 2016). However, the same literature warns us that men tend to own these skills much more often than women do, who are more frequently skilled in teaching and languages (Liversage 2009, 121). As "partner-initiated movers" tend more often to be women, the odds of successful placement in a new location are likewise not in their favour. In the following, I will contrast two empirical cases.

Annisa and Sara (Starting from Minus Zero, 161) are both "partner-initiated movers" when they arrived in Switzerland. Both have university degrees, but where Sara studied Social sciences, Annisa studied Biology. They both sought a situation in the labour force in Switzerland without the benefit of support from the husbands' companies, without any prior knowledge of French, and without having any professional network whatsoever in the host country. They both, in this sense, were fully confronted by the "unique challenges of the partner-initiated mover" (6.5.2 Unique Challenges of a Partner-Initiated Mover, 159). Moreover, the similarities in the decision to move between Annisa and Sara's case are striking – they both move because of their partner and leave a position in the labour force, if not a career, behind. While Annisa did obtain a position in the labour force, Sara ultimately left for New York to find work, presumably, having given up on the possibility of ever finding anything in Switzerland. Annisa is from Indonesia. She studied in Jakarta before achieving a Ph.D. in microbiology in Germany. She moved to Switzerland, following her Adrian: "we got married and I moved here" (Annisa, 39yrs, married). Adrian is also from Indonesia and also does research in the field of biology. After her move to Switzerland for the sake of Adrian's career, Annisa found a research position at a university hospital through an employment website designed for "Life and Earth scientists":

> I moved here to reunite with my family. … So, I know it wasn't too difficult for my new employer to produce my employment documents, because I was already here. It is not like he had recruited me from abroad (Annisa, 39yrs, married).

Unlike Sara, Annisa[69] managed to find employment in Switzerland where her scientific skills were recognised and in demand. Thus, she seemed an asset to the labour force. Most "partner-initiated movers" interviewed for this study have some form of "tertiary" level education. However, the heterogeneity of profiles shows that they have not all benefitted from the same chance of finding a position after a relocation given the important role played by the types of skills play a role. What seems to be at issue, then, is not so much one's "level of education" as the types of skills that respondents have. The demand of certain types of profiles as well as the experience and skills of the candidates are major factors to take into account while discussing the elements which support or hinder a partner's post-relocation access to the labour force. In these conditions, "partner-initiated movers" with skills that are more readily transferable have an advantage over those whose skills and diplomas are either not easily recognisable or too directly linked to a specific nation-state. Nevertheless, I identify other elements that are complementary to the employment outcomes of highly-skilled migrants (Dumont and Aujean 2014; Platonova and Urso 2012; Stirling 2015) and therefore play a central role in better understanding what facilitates or complicates the success of a "partner-initiated move" into a foreign labour force.

b. Language

The role of the language is central to someone ability to find position in the labour force abroad. In the two regions where I conducted my interviews, one might have thought that high level abilities in French or German would be an asset in the process of finding a position in the labour force. Certainly, speaking the local language does facilitate the search for such a position. However, and interestingly, many "partner-initiated movers" did not really emphasise the importance of local language skills. What they did underline, instead, is the

69 Annisa uses a vocabulary which strongly refers to schemes of the "controlled immigration" side of the "migration binaries". Thus, she speaks of "family reunification" which is how she got her residency permit, as the end of the sentence confirms, "I was already here" before having a position in the labour force. As an Indonesian national, she needs a legal justification to settle in Switzerland. Her contact with a "controlling state", due to her nationality, shapes not only her experience of professional migration but also how she refers to her own migration experience reusing the language that the administration used while allowing her to settle in Switzerland. My point is to underline the variety of people behind the label of "partner-initiated mover": while the skills do play a role in finding a new position in the labour force, the way a person is categorised by the state shapes the migration experience as well, regardless the skill level.

presence or absence of a strong "international labour market", which they distinguish from a "local labour market". The "local labour market" refers to the more "traditional" positions that demand fluency in the local language as well as recognizable experience, skills, and diplomas. The "international labour market", on the other hand, corresponds to positions available in multinational companies, NGOs, and research institutes, where the language spoken is mostly English and the experience, skills, and diplomas required tend to fit rather "international" standards. Interpreting Annisa's case in the light of this distinction reveals that she found her position in the "international labour market" in part because she had done her research in English. For many "partner-initiated movers", the language spoken by employers in "local labour market" is seen as a crucial barrier that places positions there beyond consideration. The "international labour market", on the other hand, in which the language spoken is English offers many more opportunities, respondents have argued. According to the Swiss "structural survey" (2013), English is the first foreign language spoken at the workplace in the Cantons of Geneva and Vaud, as 29% of the respondents of the survey in the Canton of Geneva, and respectively 21% in the Canton of Vaud say that their primary working language is English. This variable is useful to give an idea of the size of the "international labour market". Unfortunately, I do not have related numbers for Germany.

c. *Recognition of the Diplomas and the Recognition of the Previous Professional Experience*

Even for fluent speakers of the local language, other problems arise as they try to access the "local labour market", as is illustrated by the case of Laura, who resigned from a multinational company in France to follow her husband Thomas, to the French speaking part of Switzerland. A native-French speaker, Laura studied management and had expertise as well as professional experience in human resources. At the time of the interview, she had found a position in Switzerland and was working for a multinational consumer goods company, where she spoke English. Thomas, a pharmacist by trade, found employment in the pharmaceutical industry. He came to Switzerland through an "expat-move", whereby the company paid for their accommodation and supported Laura while she sought employment. This is how Thomas presented Laura's difficulties finding employment:

> My wife has worked in two international companies, which is to say that both were non-Swiss companies. Because regardless of the number of resumes she had sent out, or of interviews done, she was never taken. … In fact, she was systematically asked for a Swiss

> diploma … a specific human resources certificate. … As for me, I have never been asked to show my diploma. My diploma as a pharmacist is French and I have never been asked for the equivalent in Switzerland (Thomas, 44yrs, married)[70].

Lacking a certificate to find employment, Laura would have had to obtain it in order to compete for positions in the "local-labour market". Without it, her profile remained incomplete. She therefore found work in a multinational consumer goods company (*i.e.* in the "international labour market"), which tended to "look more at the experience and less at the diploma" (Thomas, 44yrs, married). According to my interviewees, the recognisability of professional skills differs according to whether the position sought is in the "local" or "international labour market". Thus, "partner-initiated movers" tend to feel they have more chances of finding employment in the "international labour market", where the recognition of skills required is rather focused on professional experience than a specific diploma. Thomas contrasts the difference reception accorded to himself and to Laura. While he did not have to present any equivalence for his diplomas, Laura was confronted with an obstacle that is specific to the "partner-initiated movers" trying to access to the "local labour market". In fact, so much is the "local labour market" perceived to be either inaccessible or disqualifying, "partner-initiated movers" feel they have much a better chance of finding a position in the "international labour market".

d. Power of Place

In fact, many interviewees speak of two parallel "labour-markets", describing the difficulty of moving from one to the other. Specifically, they underline the fact that there are nearly no Swiss people in their teams. Gabriel (6.1.2 Drawn Expatriate, 139), for example, is a French pharmacist working the senior manager for regulatory affairs at a multinational pharmaceutical company in Switzerland, where he has lived for more than ten years. He speaks of the opening of very different labour markets in regions where multinational corporations have settled. When he thinks about his colleagues, he emphasises that he does not have any direct Swiss colleagues:

70 Ma femme a travaillé dans deux sociétés internationales, les deux donc pas des sociétés suisses et là malgré le nombre de cv envoyés ou d'entretiens passés, elle n'a jamais été prise. (…) En fait, on lui demandait systématique d'avoir un diplôme suisse. C'était (…) un certificat spécifique aux ressources humaines (…) Moi, pour moi, on ne m'a jamais demandé un diplôme, mon diplôme de pharmacien, il est français et on ne m'a jamais demandé l'équivalent (Own Translation).

> In my group, I don't have any Swiss employees. No, often, in the cross-company functions like IT there will be more Swiss employees. Obviously, also the human resources because one must know the local regulations. In our company, the admins are Swiss, but most people in the relatively skilled labour force, well, I do not mean that / [I mean] the specialized labour force is full of people who come from elsewhere (Gabriel, 54yrs, divorced)[71].

For Gabriel, it is clear that he works in an international milieu which is not much related to the local labour force except when it comes to the maintenance and security positions in the company buildings, and/or such positions as require a knowledge of specific local spaces. When interviewing Abigail, the head of the marketing of a multinational consumer goods corporation, she asked me, laughing, "where are the Swiss people?" (Abigail, 43yrs, Single). Only really half joking, this quote underlines the co-presence of two segments of the labour market in a local space which do not really interact with one another. When the "partner-initiated movers" arrive after a relocation, they very often lack the contacts and professional networks required to access the "local labour market". Thus, the "power of place" is central where the presence of a strong multinational fabric in the region is essential to the "partner-initiated movers'" ability to find employment in the "international labour market". Different local spaces offer different professional opportunities. In this respect, the Lake Geneva Area in Switzerland and the Rhein-Main Area in Frankfurt are two regions where the multinational fabric is so strong as to offer newcomers opportunities for employment in both the local and international labour markets.

e. *Company's Support for the "Secondary-Mover's" Inclusion in the Labour Force*

The type of contract accorded to the "primary-mover" has an impact on the means available to the "partner-initiated mover" in finding employment. In fact, when the "primary-mover" performs an "expat-move", the "partner-initiated mover" usually receives ample such support. Manon (Relocation of Headquarter, 155; Maternity Leaves, 168) is a veterinarian specialised in pet food. She worked for several major actors in the sector, developing new products. As a reminder,

71 Dans mon groupe j'ai personne de suisse, non souvent c'est les fonctions transversales genre informatique où il y aura plus de suisse, les ressources humaines évidemment parce qu'il faut connaître la législation. Chez nous ce sont les admins qui sont suisses mais la plupart des gens de main d'œuvre qualifiée enfin faut pas dire que/ main d'œuvre spécifique, c'est des gens qui viennent d'ailleurs (Own Translation).

her partner Charles is a senior manager in a multinational consumer goods company. As part of his company's strategy, the managers had decided to relocate their headquarters from France to Switzerland, transferring their whole team, which implied relocating the families, too. Thus, they proposed "expatriate contracts" to soften the impact of this process. Part of that expatriate package was an outplacement agency for the partners. Manon, therefore, received extended support in her search for employment in Switzerland; because: "the company really wanted us to stay" (Manon, 55yrs, divorced). During our interview, she described the importance of the support offered by the outplacement agency, as well as the personal investment it implied. In France, she was a national product director and finding the exact corresponding Swiss position would have required fluency in French and German. She did not speak German and it was, for her, "out of question to learn it" (Manon, 55yrs, divorced)[72]. Accordingly, she could only find something at a global or European level. Furthermore, she had already been in contact with the outplacement agency before the relocation. In order to continue working after the relocation, she sought a new position abroad while still working 100 percent of the time in her former position:

> Manon: They did everything they could to help me find a job in Switzerland, which does not mean that I relied on them entirely. I spotted all the recruitment agencies and I contacted all that could be contacted, to try/
> F.T.: /So there was also an involvement on your part/
> Manon: /Enormous (…) I was working in France, in Paris. I came to Geneva every two months to meet people, to meet the recruitment companies, to meet my outplacement agency, to do job interviews (Manon, 55yrs, divorced)[73].

This combination of challenges is recurrent when it comes to seeking employment as a "partner-initiated mover". The "power of place", and, more specifically, the structure of the "local" and the "international labour market" affects the job opportunities; as many "partner-initiated movers" find employment within the "international labour market". Moreover, the support of the husband's company is central, not solely to finding actual employment but, rather, to reorient and

72 C'était hors de question de l'apprendre [l'allemand] (Own Translation).

73 Manon : Ils ont tout fait pour trouver un emploi en Suisse, ce qui ne veut pas que je me repose sur eux. Après avoir examiné toutes les agences de recrutement, j'ai contacté tout ce qui pourrait être contacté, pour essayer/
F.T.: /C'est donc aussi une implication de votre part /anon: / énorme. (...) J'ai travaillé en France à Paris, je suis venu à Genève tous les deux mois pour rencontrer des gens, pour rencontrer des entreprises de recrutement, pour rencontrer mon cabinet de déménagement, pour faire des entretiens (Own Translation).

advise the "partner-initiated mover". At the end of the day, the outplacement agency did not find employment for Manon, but it did help her to prepare a resume and present herself effectively in job interviews. For her, the move still required an enormous investment of time and energy on her part. The support was nevertheless crucial for Manon, because it empowered her in the process of coping with such a situation:

> They asked me: 'What can you do?' To which I answered: 'What can I do? After 15 years [in the same company] I don't have a clue.' I was so into my work. So, they helped me do a skills assessment and prepare a resume. (…). So, they rebooted me/ actually it is not reboot, but rather they put me back on track" (Manon, 55yrs, divorced)[74].

In this case, the support came from an outplacement agency paid for by Charles' company. This gave Manon the tools she needed to successfully find employment abroad. In sum, she found a position in the labour force, thanks to her "hard-skills", her "uncompromising will to continue to work" as she phrases it, and the support of an outplacement agency. She did not want to stop working and, if she had not found anything in Switzerland, she would rather have returned to France.

f. Dual career Network

Professional networks are another type of support which can help "partner-initiated movers" find employment; though these are mostly oriented towards the "international labour market". Maria (Teleworking, 148) found an auditor position in a multinational consumer goods company through one of these networks. The network supports "dual-couple careers" and is born out of an alliance of a dozen of multinational companies. The goal is to facilitate the work arrangement of "secondary-movers". Interviewing the coordinator of the network shows that, on the one hand, companies support "dual careers couples", being as they say "dual careers friendly". On the other hand, the "partner-initiated movers" are often highly-skilled professionals seeking employment in the labour force which is, conversely, an opportunity for these companies in their own search for "talent". According to the statistics provided by the network, more than 80% of the "partner-initiated movers" have a university degree or the equivalent[75]. Thus,

---

74 Ben me dire "qu'est-ce que vous savez faire?" et moi de dire "Mais ce que je sais faire? Mais j'en sais rien au bout de 15 ans", je suis tellement dans mon travail que voilà. Donc à faire un bilan de compétence et à refaire un CV. (…). Donc ils m'ont rebooté, enfin ce n'est pas rebooté mais remis sur les rail pour me présenter à un entretien (Own Translation).

75 This statistic is part of an internal document that the respondent transmitted to me.

they represent a valuable recruitment pool for the company, too. Maria started to work for this network on a voluntary basis. She helped organise events for its member companies. Such events usually focus on specific topics like the recruitment process. Managers of member companies, specialists in human resources, and "partner-initiated movers" meet during these events. For Maria, "that really changed the whole game, because you get in touch with some people on a personal level" (Maria, 42yrs, married). Due to her active participation in this network, she became aware of a job opportunity in a multinational consumer goods company:

> We had a meeting because we were organising an event here at *** [name of the company], me from the *** [name of the network] side and the *** [name of the company] employee who told me about an opportunity they had in their own department, that they were growing and that they needed someone and [she asked] if I wanted to apply for the job (Maria, 42yrs, married).

Maria found a new professional occupation in Switzerland through interpersonal contacts, which were ultimately possible because she was part of this network, which is dedicated to the partners of employees of member companies (i.e. not everyone has access to it). Moreover, her husband's company financed a career coach and some language courses. In each case, however, the "partner-initiated mover" speaks of a very important personal investment in the process of finding employment.

In sum, "partner-initiated movers" access to the labour market is contingent upon the types of skills brought with them, the languages they speak, whether their diplomas and/or work experience is recognized, and upon the presence of an "international labour market". Furthermore, given that their professional and social networks are oriented towards the "international labour market", "local labour markets" are mostly out of reach for them. This combination of elements creates the conditions in which the "partner-initiated movers" have more chance finding employment in the "international labour markets". For these reasons, geography – which is to say the specific local spaces where a couple might settle – has a strong impact on the chance that a "partner-initiated mover" will have access to the labour force post-relocation.

6.5.6 Types of Moves of the Secondary-Mover

When it comes to the "secondary-movers", I have identified three different types of moves on the basis of whether the partners end up living together or apart. A "total-move" refers to two partners and their children move together and subsequently live together. This means that the "secondary-mover" follows the

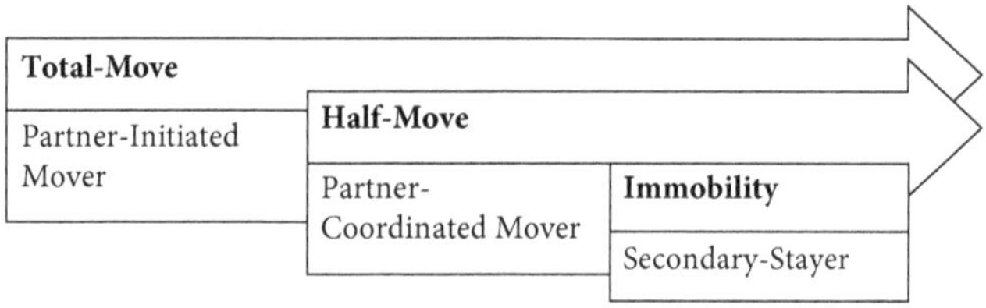

Figure 16 The Types of Move of the Secondary-Mover. Source: Own elaboration

"primary-mover" entirely to the new locale. The "half-move" identifies a situation in which the "secondary-mover" only *partially* follows the "primary-mover", maintaining ties to the former country. In the context of dual career couples, such "half-moves" are common but temporary. They compensate for the drawbacks of the "primary-mover"' relocation, by the "secondary-mover's" strategic use of mobility. Third, I present the case in which the "secondary-mover" is, in fact, a stayer, having decided to stay in the home country (Figure 16).

Each type of move implies specific challenges for the "secondary-movers", I argue. Following this logic, the "partner-initiated mover" finds him/herself in a disadvantage position as s/he starts from "minus zero" in a local space s/he did not chose because of the professional opportunities there but rather for emotional reasons. In many cases, the "partner-initiated mover" need to rearrange the care work arrangement before having the time to seek employment in the labour force. The type of "partner-coordinated mover" stresses the ways in which such challenges are circumvented, however, not without creating new challenges for the partner's "family-strategies" to respond to. In particular, "coordination" highlights the importance of mobility as a strategic tool in the integration of two professional careers. However, as exemplified by Maria, who teleworked in Japan for an Italian company, and by Manon, who took a maternity leave, being the "coordinated mover" is either exhausting and thus non-sustainable over the long run or a strictly short term solution.

6.6 Theorising the Professional Careers Coordination

Thanks to Expatriation studies, I can develop better the understanding of the different challenges that the different types of "primary" and "secondary" movers are confronted by, through a more detailed focus and precise conceptualisation of the move's initiator. In this chapter, I have described the different types of moves for the "primary-mover" and the "secondary-mover" and will briefly conclude

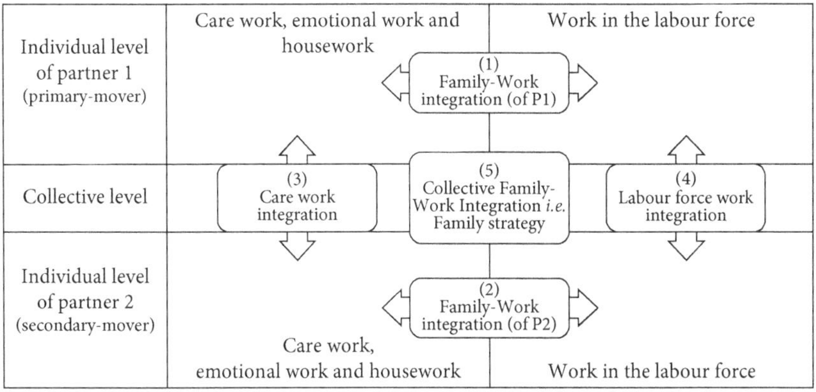

Figure 17 Family-Strategy. Source: Own elaboration

by summarising its main results. As a reminder, Figure 17 illustrates the scope of the analysis thus far as being focused, largely, on the right-hand column.

I started this chapter by showing the relevance of what I call the "professional approach". It corresponds to an analysis focusing on the relationship between the employer and the employee (6.1 Migration Triggering: An Individual Approach, 138), emphasising a professional and individual approach to the initiator of a relocation. Then, I presented another perspective by focusing on who among the partners initiates a move, what I called a "collective approach" (6.2 Migration Triggering: A Collective Approach, 142). This approach introduces a seminal distinction between a "primary-mover" and "secondary-mover", designed to account for the social and gendered dynamics involved in a move of this sort. Developing my argument around that distinction, I analysed the "labour force work integration" of highly-skilled migrants. To that end, I insisted on the continuum between "expat-moves" and "local-moves", which are defined by different perceptions of "motility". Then, I named the different types of reactions characteristic of "secondary-movers". I showed that "secondary-movers" might circumvent the challenges of relocating "totally" with their partner; however, only for a time, at which point a decision still needs to be made. Such types of "partner-coordinated mover" are only temporary. Living "one life in two different worlds" at the same time seems very difficult in the long run. Besides, I have pointed to the gender imbalance in the distribution of "primary" and "secondary" movers, where the latter are very often the female partner, which only adds a gender hierarchy to the specific challenges of the "secondary-mover". These specific challenges stress the specificity of the "partner-initiated" movers' access to the labour force, as represented in the bottom right corner of the Figure 17. I have shown that "partner-initiated movers" have a much greater chance of accessing the "international" than a "local" labour market after a relocation. I have argued, in this way, that the specifics of the locale count. One can never but move somewhere – as floating, placeless spaces do not exist and space is always somewhere located. Thus, local spaces with an important "international labour market" offer more professional opportunities to the "partner-initiated movers".

Thus, I have shown that not all relocations are equal, and the next chapter will stress that the conditions of a "primary" mover's relocation affects the whole family. In fact, not only are the conditions of the relocation as such central, but so is the way the partners themselves interpret the "primary" mover's "motility" in terms of the central role it plays among their collective "family strategies". Bluntly, the reaction of the "secondary-mover" is not going to be the same if the partners believe that the "primary-mover" is moving either for six months or six years. In the following chapter, I will switch to a discourse analysis of the discourses told by the people I interviewed in order to grasp how this interpretation of a move influences the "family-strategies" overall. While this first empirical chapter represents a "fine grained" analysis of the mechanisms involved in a decision-making process, and of their consequences, the second empirical chapter will deal with the narratives of the interviewees more broadly.

7 Representing Migration: Between Motilities and Anchors

In the previous chapter, I described different types of moves and I showed that they emerge through a relational process which considers the partners rather than solely the relationship between the employee and the employer. The shift away from a professional and individual approach acknowledges the way in which the partners coordinate two professional careers when at least one of them is mobile for professional reasons. In the current chapter, I will focus on the narratives that the partners develop when they settle in a new local space. Most importantly, I will show that the "primary-mover", whose continuum spans between an "expat-move" and a "local-move", orients the ways in which the partners narrate their experience of settling in new local spaces, as well as their ways of "displaying family" (Finch 2007). By "displaying family", Finch (ibid) refers to ways people communicate what they believe to be distinctive about their family, while relying on and (re)producing a "repertoire of what family means" (2007, 78). In this context, I will show how the notion of being "motile" (Flamm and Kaufmann 2006), which I understand as having the capacity and the will to be mobile, influences the way the partners "display their family" (Finch 2007).

Hannam, Sheller, and Urry (2006) speak of a "dialectic logic of mobility" (2006, 2) to emphasise that mobility must be conceptualised with the spatial anchors and artefacts it implies. Following this logic, I will pay special attention to the ways the partners talk about their "modalities of settling". "Modalities of settling" are the set of practices and representations highly-skilled migrants develop when arriving in a new local space as they rearrange their "family-strategy". For example, nomads have tents because the tent, the central artefact in their way of settling, enables the nomadic way of life. A Mongolian *ger*[76] can be built (and unbuilt) in a few hours. It is because of the *ger* that the Mongolian nomads maintain their "motility". This process is quite similar in the case of highly-skilled

76 "yurt, also spelled yurta, Mongol ger, tentlike Central Asian nomad's dwelling, erected on wooden poles and covered with skin, felt, or handwoven textiles in bright colours. The interior is simply furnished with brightly coloured rugs (red often predominating) decorated with geometric or stylized animal patterns. The knotted pile rug, first known from a nomad burial at the foot of the Altai Mountains (5th–3rd century BC), probably developed as a fur substitute to provide warmth and sleeping comfort in the yurt". (*Encyclopedia Britannica* 2016, "Yurt, Shelter")

migrants – even if I do not understand them as contemporary nomads. Hotel rooms and corporate flats enable faster and easier moves than other kinds of accommodation, such as owned property. However, when the partners describe their "modalities of settling", they also talk about their decisions concerning their "care work integration" – that is, how they divide the care work between them, often relying on external support like day care services.

This chapter has three parts. First, I will clarify the concept of "displaying family" (Finch 2007), as it plays a central role in my argument. Second, I will demonstrate how the narratives accepting the state of "*high motility*" contribute to justifying the process by which women give up work in the labour force to do care work. Third, I will analyse the narratives of partners who refuse the "constraints" of "motility" and are consequently able to share the care work more equally. The perceived need of "motility" contributes to justifying a traditional "care work integration". Thus, I propose the following questions: what kind of "meaning patterns" do the interviewees produce when they talk about settling into a new local space? Do these "meaning patterns" guide them while they make decisions on their "care work integration"? If yes, how do they orient their actions while making these decisions?

7.1 Displaying Family

Human beings do not live in a "cultural vacuum"; "family-strategies" are embedded in our values and the ways in which we represent them. The concept of "displaying family" (Finch 2007) underlines "the stories which people tell to themselves and to others about their own family relationships" (2007, 78). Drawing on this concept, I analyse the system of meanings and values developed by the respondents while "doing family" (Lutz and Amelina 2017). The theory of "symbolic interactionism" (Blumer 1969) offers an epistemological background to ground an analysis focusing on the narratives of the respondents. It is rooted in pragmatic philosophy (Dewey 1925; Mead 1932), but is further refined. For Blumer, "symbolic interactionism sees meanings as social products, as creations that are formed in and through the defining activities of people as they interact" (1969, 5). Scholars analysing the various "doings" ("doing gender". "doing family", "doing migration", etc.) all underline the primacy of human actions and interactions on the constitution of meaning. Thus, the respondents develop and attach meaning to what they call family, and live accordingly as their "family life". Blumer (1969) argues that interaction, signification, and interpretation form a fundamental triad. This is the heart of "symbolic interactionism", as the signification that humans give to things first comes from the interactions among individuals, and is subsequently reworked in an interpretative process. This idea is at the core of the three famous premises of "symbolic interactionism"[77]. In the context of studying families on the move, "symbolic interactionism" offers a way to understand the link between narratives and practices. I use the concept of "displaying family" as a tool to see how people imbed what they consider to be "family" into a system of signification – what I called earlier a "meaning pattern". For Finch (2007), "displaying family" refers to "the process by which individuals, and groups of individuals, convey to each other and to relevant audiences that certain of their actions do constitute 'doing family things' and thereby confirm that these relationships are 'family' relationships" (2007, 67). This concept offers a way of analysing how the notion of family is constructed as a "category of practice" (Brubaker 2002) by the family members themselves, by exploring the ways in which the respondents describe it . While as a "category of practice" the term family is meaningful for the respondents, the "category of analysis" must be explained and corresponds to the process of "displaying family". Thus, I understand "displaying family" as a processual and dynamic "category of analysis" to be explained rather than an explanatory concept in and of itself. "Displaying family" is the strategic social operation occurring when the actors deploy particular means of categorisation to show that their family "works well". Finch (2007) underlines that "a fundamental driving force in presenting families to an external audience is to convey the message 'this is my family and it works' " (2007, 70). In other words, while speaking of the family, the partners construct a discourse to valorise and/or justify their practices; it is not *just* a neutral discourse in which the partners give a sociologist a description of how their family works.

The moment of the interview is a Goffmanian moment in which the interviewee creates a description of his or her family for the sociologist (Goffman 1990). It is a *mise en scène*. Thus, the "deconstructive tools" presented in the "methodological premises" (Chapter 3) are not only useful in assessing the scientific literature on the topic but also in analysing the discourses of the respondents. One of the main objectives of my work is to "decentre the discourse" of the respondents to stress which norms about the family are depicted as legitimate and which require

---

77 Blumer defines "symbolic interactionism" through the following three premises: "The first premise is that human beings act toward things on the basis of the meanings that the things have for them. (...). The second premise is that the meaning of such things is derived from, or arises out of, the social interaction that one has with one's fellows. The third premise is that these meanings are handled in, and modified through, an interpretative process used by the person in dealing with the things he encounters" (Blumer 1969, 2).

justification. For example, I will show that frequently the respondents "display a family" in which the two partners work in the labour force, offering only a vague understanding of what "working in the labour force" could mean and blurring the distinction between hobby and professional activity. This often leads to discrepancies between their practices and their discourses. When it is obviously not possible to provide such a display, the respondents provide a justificatory discourse explaining why one of the partners left the labour force. In turn, this tells us something about the normative aspects of doing and displaying family: "dual careers couples" seem to be the discursive norm.

I not only aim to "decentre" the discourses of the respondents. I also intend to "decentre" the approach of the study itself, through the way in which I assess the interviews. In the previous chapter, I discussed the unique challenges that "secondary-movers" face in gaining access to the labour force. In so doing, I shed light on a long forgotten topic: the "trailing-spouse" [sic.], who has been considered primarily as a "burden" in many studies and certainly not as a partner with a tertiary education struggling to maintain his or her own professional activity (for a discussion of the topic, see 2.4.3 Expatriate Adjustments, 49). In the present chapter, I propose to "decentre" the approach by focusing – with one exception – on how the "primary-movers" display their family and more precisely their coordination of the care work and the work in the labour force. In other words, this chapter analyses how the partner who works in the labour force coordinates his or her professional activity with the care work. This is also a forgotten topic as studies analysing the work in the labour force of the highly-skilled migrants traditionally focus solely on the "masculine side" of the "gender binaries", namely the "productive, economic activity" (for a discussion on the topic, see 3.2 Methodological Individualism, 73).

7.2 Motile Narratives

The way the partners perceive the move of the "primary-mover" shapes the "family-strategy". The terms "primary-mover" and "secondary-mover" explain not only who initiates a move but also the reasons for the move. This point is absolutely crucial as one of the partners very often believes that they have moved because of the other. The key to understanding the effect of the move of the "primary-mover" on the "family-strategy" is the perceived need of "motility". Through three narratives, I will show that the perceived need to remain "motile" (re)produces gendered hierarchies. The narratives stress how the constant need of "motility", for the sake of one professional career, implies an uncompromising focus on the prioritised career, reinforcing gendered hierarchies in the "family-strategies". This configuration is very often to be found when the male partners perform an "expat-move"; they become an "assigned expatriate" according to the professional approach of Andresen et al. (2014), and usually the reaction of the female "secondary-mover" to the mobility and the "motility" of her partner corresponds to the type of the "partner-initiated mover".

7.2.1 Structural Constraints

The story of John and Aurelia highlights the development of care needs within a couple, a process by which the partners maintain and deepen a relationship of dependencies and responsibilities while relocating regularly. In the following section, I will analyse John's narrative. I conducted an interview with him at his office in an empty conference room, which he arranged for the interview. It lasted one hour. Aurelia and John are married and have two young children of one year old and three years old. Today, John is a senior manager in a consumer goods multinational company, while Aurelia seeks employment in the labour force following their last relocation. In addition, they are trying to find a day care solution for their children. So far, they have not found anything satisfactory. Since having children, John tells me, it has been even more complicated for Aurelia to seek employment. How is it then that it is more complicated for her to seek employment and not more complicated for him to fulfil his professional activity? How did this situation develop and how does John display it?

John finished his studies at the beginning of the 1990s and started working for a marketing company in Chicago. After three years working for them, he asked his supervisor for new challenges and was given the task of opening an office in Boston[78]. He undertook this work for one year before moving back to Chicago. During these first years in the labour force, John was in his late twenties. Young, ambitious, and without care responsibilities, he was able to respond quickly to any professional opportunity. In that sense, he was the quintessential "motile" professional. Thus, when his previous manager called him to ask if he would accept a position in Hong Kong, he did not hesitate:

> My previous manager called me and said: "Hey, we got this opportunity in Hong Kong, would you be interested?" and I said: "We pack on Thursday, let's go". I mean [snap fingers] that was literally: "I'm in, Hong Kong, never been there, done anything about it, sounds great. Let's go". I was really just right and ready for change. You know quite

78 I have already presented a "mind map" of the story of John and Aurelia in the methodological chapter (4.2.3 Analysing the Interview Corpus, 63).

> literally, the next week, I was on the plane to Hong Kong. … I was single at that point, in a relationship but not a serious one and was not worried whether that relationship was going to make the trip or not (John, 50yrs, married).

In this quote, John recalls his first international relocation and constructs a narrative in which the possible constraints that could hinder the relocation are not important enough to dissuade him. The use of the personal pronouns stresses how the decision to relocate led him and his former girlfriend to end their relationship. "We pack on Thursday. … I'm in" (ibid). In fact, what happened is that *he* packed on Thursday. At the end of the quote, he clarifies the situation as he says that he prioritised the relocation over the relationship and/or she refused to follow him. He was going to relocate regardless, as he did not perceive the relationship as serious enough, meaning that he could make this emotional sacrifice on the altar of his career.

The sentence "I'm in, Hong Kong, never been there, done anything about it, sounds great" (ibid) depicts an adventure of someone free from constraints ("I'm in") and happy to jump into the unknown ("never been there"). Retrospectively, he has some good reasons to depict it like that, as this relocation was going to be a crucial step for his professional career. It would allow him to take on a challenging position, to develop key professional skills, and to create a professional network, which would support him when he experienced difficulties. But that is not all. John also narrates a high *availability to mobility*, i.e. "motility"; by snapping his fingers he expresses the high pace at which changes happened in his life: "quite literally, the next week, I was on the plane" (ibid). He could respond almost instantly to any opportunity around the globe, because he did not see any need to integrate his career with that of a partner, and neither did he have any care responsibility as he did not have children or relatives requiring care work. A separation from one's partner and the absence of care responsibilities enable direct actions in the labour force: an unconstrained "motility". He speaks not only about a frictionless mobility but also about the speed of his agreement to relocate. Thus, John moved to Hong Kong as an "assigned expatriate" who was supported by his company, as "the notion of being left alone [is] not on the table" (John, 50yrs, married). He worked for a company which was experienced in sending employees abroad, and the "expatriate package" he received was formalised and comprehensive and contributed to his frictionless relocation.

After a few years in Hong Kong, John switched to another company, this time in Italy: a fairly bad experience for him as he felt that this new company had significant management issues. He accepted this position because it was "the best job on paper" (ibid), but it turned out to be "the worst job in reality" (ibid). Yet this was where he met Aurelia, whom he would marry a few years later. Aurelia was employed by the same company but in the North European market. She is Swedish, and was working and living in Scandinavia, and he is American, working and living in Italy. For a year, they dated each other across the continent, "where EasyJet would take us" (ibid). Eventually, they wanted to give a real chance to their relationship and they decided that she would resign from her position and move to Italy to live with him. At this point, they tried to find a position for her in the same company. She should have received a position, but the arrangement did not work out as planned. This is how John recalls the situation:

> So, my job was the bigger of the two in *** headquarter in Italy and she was a label architect at *** in the North European region. So, a lot of conversation happened before, and when she arrived that job never materialized and that is another reason that I was very happy to leave ***, that is just a company that was very willing with bracket promise and I don't think that was ok, good organizations don't work that way (John, 50yrs, married).

The circumstances of John and Aurelia's life changed as soon as they decided to live together in an atomic heterosexual partnership. At that point, they had to coordinate two labour force positions, though they only had minimal care work because they did not have any children. The decision to move in together took a specific shape: Aurelia moved to join him because his job was "bigger", according to him. In John's narrative, they made a rational decision, but it can also be interpreted as the construction of a gendered hierarchy in the newly created partnership. John is aware of this, now, and produces a justificatory narrative to contextualise the specificity of their situation as he explains what she did to maintain her position in the labour force. Expressing his frustration, John actively insists that it was not he who pushed Aurelia out of the labour force but rather the incompetency of others. The couple planned this relocation: they were not reckless, and it should have worked out; but some people were probably not frank, or were at the very least incompetent, and their plan did not work. John's argument displays two types of justification for a (female) partner's departure from labour force work for the (male) counterpart, while denying a patriarchal organisation of their partnership. These two types of justification are *the hierarchy of the positions* and *the incompetency of others.*

As John had the "bigger" job, Aurelia resigned to join him: this is the hierarchy of positions. In the interview, this crucial justification is very briefly mentioned but expresses a strong power relationship: the one with the better position maintains that position. In their case, as in so many cases, the men have the "bigger" positions. This configuration corresponds to general social and structural trends, as women still often have worse positions in the labour force, and receive less pay than men (Hausmann, Tyson, and Zahidi 2009, 64). Structural inequalities are (re)produced in John and Aurelia's partnership because their rational calculus (re)produces them. This corresponds with the Foucauldian argument in which the big strategies of power become embedded in micro-relations of power (Foucault 1994, 66). John neutralises the gendered argument, however, suggesting that he and Aurelia made a rational decision in a difficult situation, where there was no good choice. His narrative implies that it would be unfair to pejoratively assess their choice because they were coping with heavy structural constraints. In this way, John refuses to be seen as yet another patriarchal male.

John provides a second justification to underline that he was not trying to create a patriarchal partnership by stressing that Aurelia managed to find a position in the labour force before relocating. However, the company betrayed them as it did not keep its promises. This is the second argument that sees the partners struggling against what could lead to a traditional division of tasks. In sum, John underlines the external circumstances which led Aurelia to lose her professional activity once in Italy.

Later in their story, they married and Aurelia became pregnant with their first child. John resigned from his position in Italy and took up another position offered by one of his former employers in Hong Kong. He underlines that this decision took her perspective into account:

> She was personally very unhappy and that was having an impact on her and therefore on our relationship and I knew that she was the one that I wanted to marry. So, that wasn't going to be able to continue, so we both decided we go to Hong Kong. When we arrived in Hong Kong, my wife was three months pregnant, so she started looking for work again with the assistance of the company. The way that Hong Kong and I think China and part of Asia work, a lot of employers said: 'Great, we'd love to hire you, come back when you are ready to work after your baby. We are not going to hire you while you are pregnant, because we know you are going to go on maternity leave. So, great but later. Yeah, no offense, but kind of we don't want to talk to you right now' (John, 50yrs, married).

In the first part of the quote, John underlines that Aurelia wanted a job in the labour force as being out of it was a painful shift: she refused to leave the labour force permanently. John emphasises her unhappiness by adding the adverb "personally": he did not say that we *collectively* are unhappy. Here, John actively displays family as he implies that they were not unhappy partners; they were happy to be together. By specifying that she was personally unhappy (while he was not) and suggesting that this impacted their relationship, omitting to mention himself, he stresses that Aurelia's unhappiness came from the fact that she was unemployed. Her unhappiness was directly linked to the fact that she did not hold a professional position in Italy. Contrarily to what happened with John's former girlfriend in the United States, this time he took Aurelia's needs into consideration as "she was the one that I wanted to marry" (ibid). Thus, they decided to move together, but not just anywhere: to Hong Kong. At that point, I believe there was little doubt that John had to convince her: "You have to trust me on this one. It is going to be great" John told Aurelia (ibid). He asks her to rely entirely on his credibility, with no evidence that things will indeed work out. This explains his irritation when he recalls why, at first, she did not find any employment in the labour force in Hong Kong. Furthermore, for Aurelia, this new relocation is similar to the one that led her to resign from her position to come to Italy in the first place. She was – once again – going to be the one out of the labour force, which allegedly scared her. She left a familiar place and a good position in a multinational company to join someone she met a year ago in a foreign country. But that is not all: as the initial plan did not work out, she was now unemployed and their collective answer to that, if she would agree, was to relocate to Hong Kong. It took a lot of courage for her to accept the move, but she ultimately did so. John, unlike Aurelia, would not move without securing a position in the labour market, which explains why they decided to move to Hong Kong. It was important for him to secure a job, but not for her. Here is another inequality revealed. He managed to get a position in Hong Kong by relying on his professional network. Arguably, they could also have moved back to Northern Europe, but they decided to relocate to Hong Kong; clearly, John was once again going to be the "primary mover".

In the second half of the quote, John explains how it became more complicated for Aurelia to find an activity in the labour force as she was pregnant. He displays his reaction to the deepening of their relationship as that of someone who did what he could to make it possible for her to continue to work, refusing once again the patriarchal narrative in which he would push her out of the labour force. As he wanted to live with her and seemingly did not want to make her unhappy, they made the decision to move to Hong Kong. Yet this is not the logical answer to her need for a position in the labour force. Logically, to do that, they would have had to move to a place where she could find a job, which was not in Hong Kong. John acted again according to his needs and his professional career. When they arrived in Hong Kong, Aurelia sought employment in the labour force, while pregnant, but did not find anything: nobody wanted to hire a pregnant woman. Here, John justifies Aurelia's inability to find a position by underlining structural constraints: namely the sexism of employers who did not want to hire a pregnant woman. The reported speech of the potential employers who could have hired Aurelia highlights a position that he considers to be inappropriate. "We do not want to talk to you" (ibid) implies John's critique of these employers, thereby transferring the responsibility for Aurelia's unemployment to others.

After the birth of their first child, Aurelia found a position in the labour force, and she later took a maternity leave for their second child. John expresses his relief and, for once, his narrative describes the situation accurately:

> Everything went very smoothly and after the birth of our first child, my wife found work and she was hired by one of the companies she had spoken with previously. We were in Hong Kong for a little of two and a half years and she worked for the last year and a half that we were there. She took a short maternity leave when our second child was born, so we had two kids while we were in Hong Kong and then moved with two young children here (John, 50yrs, married).

There are two moments in this quote: the first one corresponds to their situation when the "order" was restored, and lasted for the time they stayed in Hong Kong. The way he wants to display his family aligns with their objective situation. The statement "Everything went very smoothly" (ibid) expresses, in John's view, this sense of normality – of what corresponds to normality in his view – where the two partners work in the labour force. It expresses his ideal display of family and reveals how he would like to live if things were only the way he wanted. He proposes a model in which both partners should work in the labour force; yet, when it comes to the care work, the narrative is more univocal. He mentions Aurelia's maternity leave but there is no sign of a paternity leave. Hochschild and Machung (2012 [1984]) show that women mostly do the care work in addition to their work in the labour force, which is not the case for men. When the two partners have a position in the labour force, it is most often the women who take up the "second shift" (2012 [1984], 24) of care work. The patterns of what family means also include what is unspoken, unquestioned, taken for granted. In John's case, the fact that *only* Aurelia took a maternity leave is one of these assumptions. Furthermore, his "order of things" – in which both partners had a position in the labour force (as Aurelia was still employed even when she was on maternity leave) – did not last long, as it was disrupted by a new relocation: "and then [we] moved" (ibid), he says. Indeed, *then* the company asked John to move to Switzerland and Aurelia resigned and the whole arrangement had to be created again, for Aurelia to have a paid position and for John to be able "display family" (Finch 2007) in a way that suited their situation. He does not mention the fact that he could have resigned too, so that she could have continued her activity in the labour force; thus he creates again the "hierarchy of position" that led Aurelia to resign in the first place. According to my former conceptualisation, John does an "expat-move", with Aurelia following him and reacting as a "partner-initiated mover" for the third consecutive time.

When they arrived in Switzerland, the circumstances had changed, as there was more care work to be done to raise their two children. Thus, this relocation implied not only coordinating two professional careers but also integrating the care work required by the newly arrived children. Under these conditions, Aurelia struggled to find enough time to seek employment in the labour force as they could not find a day care arrangement for the children. The situation was frustrating, according to John:

> We are technically repatriated but in reality we are expatriated and the way that we've been/ the way that we need to come and manage our life here is basically like we are Swiss, like we have lived here before, like we do have family that can help us to take care of the kids while my wife is looking for a job and maybe while my wife starts working while we are waiting for our number to come up on the day care list and we don't have that facility available to us. So, this move has been more personally challenging for us, but we are managing through it (John, 51yrs, married).

Now, with two children, they need external help – day care – if Aurelia wants to have the time to seek employment in the labour force. John expresses his frustration about the lack of day care opportunities in Switzerland; they are number 41 on the waiting list, he told me. He emphasises the lack of support that they have received. Since he already has a position in the labour force and because no members of their extended family live in Switzerland, Aurelia must, in John's view, take up the larger share of care work. It is as if he is blinded, as if he does not see that he could help, too. For John, they are stuck in a vicious circle, since the only way to be prioritised on the waiting list for the day care solution is if the two partners work in the labour force, but they need this day care solution so that Aurelia can properly seek employment. Thus, John shows his irritation during the interview as he remembers arguments he has with the company over spousal support. He wanted his company to pay for language courses or professional memberships for Aurelia: "You guys seriously have to put your money where your mouth is" (ibid), as he puts it. On top of that, Aurelia works in a sector which is not really developed in the city where they live in Switzerland; she would have a better chance of finding something in a larger city like Geneva or Zurich, which would imply daily commutes. Several times during the interview John emphasises that he hopes she will find a job, but the combination of constraints they are facing, and his blindness to the help he could provide, make this seem very unlikely.

His narrative shows, nevertheless, what kind of external constraints appear when it comes to integrating care work within a partnership. When they arrived in Switzerland, many challenges arose, especially regarding Aurelia's involvement with the care work and her difficulty in finding a position in the labour force at the same time, as, apparently, John does not think about reducing his working time in the labour force. Besides, the next move is never far away:

> I don't expect to be/ we don't expect to live here for all that long. You know, this is a two to three years assignment, just like my last one and at that point we'll move out of Switzerland to another geography where we'll be on an expat package again (John, 51yrs, married).

For Aurelia, the next relocation can be expressed as a "sword of Damocles" over her potential for employment in the labour force, as they will both move when the company employing John asks him to do so. On the one hand, John's narrative is the one of someone justifying himself, as his professional career is, at least partly, responsible for Aurelia's *un*professional situation. The conditions of "motile" relocations create gendered constraints, as it is very often the women who lose their professional activity in the process, and John's narrative is one example of how this is sometimes justified. On the other hand, at no point during the interview does he mention how he could help; he is blind to his scope of action. The conditions of his professional activity in the company seem to be an unspoken priority, something that cannot be touched. They came to Switzerland for the sake of his professional activity and to reduce the time he spends at the office, supposedly in order to give Aurelia more time to seek employment – which seems to contradict the actual reason for their stay. The narrative is defensive because he knows well what kind of interpretation their situation mirrors: the pejorative display of a "trailing spouse" and a "breadwinner". He refuses (and at the same time reifies) these "membership categories" (Sacks 1972; Watson 1983). The "membership categories" are common-sense designations for entities within the social world. Through them, the actors can identify individuals and social groups and attempt to (re)define a situation, while giving meanings to these individuals' or social groups' actions. The "membership categories" (ibid) of the "trailing spouse" and the "breadwinners" refer to a patriarchal organisation of a partnership, which John continually reuses in his narrative. "We are not like that" captions his argumentation. However, for him, Switzerland is only a temporary assignment. Why should they invest time and energy in a position in the labour force that she will have to quit anyway? Because, of course, they will leave for his purpose. This situation expresses a tension, if not a paradox. In the discourse developed through his narrative, John proposes an alternative to the traditional and patriarchal "repertoire of what 'family' means" (Finch 2007, 78), but he practices the very opposite. He does not accept this repertoire and thus proposes another categorisation in which structural constraints are the central elements to understanding why Aurelia does not work in the labour force. The key to understanding the tension, in his discourse, between how he wishes to display his family and their actual practice is an example of the (gendered) impact of "motility". The fact that he is the "primary-mover" blinds him to any kind of negotiation with regard to the division of the care work with Aurelia because he has to perform for his company, being an "expatriate" and being paid "top dollar" (ibid). In order to display "his" family, he provides a discourse focusing on the constraints they face and describing how the family struggles against them while, at the same time, he is inflexible regarding the prioritisation of his career. This is one way of displaying a traditional family while refusing the discourse that comes with it. John's case shows the discrepancies between discourse and practice. The narrative stresses that structural constraints – which hinder the capacity of the "secondary-movers" to find a position in the labour force after a relocation – are omnipresent. This narrative also responds to the challenges of the "partner-initiated movers" that I developed in the previous chapter, when one partner resigns from her (or his) former professional position and agrees to relocate for the sake of the "primary-mover's" career.

7.2.2 Career Men and Career Women

Stressing the structural constraints is a first element of narratives "displaying family" under the constraints of "motility"; it places the responsibility for women's loss of professional activity on the context. Some, like John, develop their whole narrative around these constraints. Others rather take these constraints for granted while "displaying family", naturalising them and thus creating a "no alternative narrative". Kim, for instance, develops this "no alternative narrative": he stresses that there is no alternative to the decision in which the female partner leaves the labour force. I interviewed Kim at his office and he started the interview by telling me that he married his company before marrying Sandra, which already offers a clue as to his priorities. Together, they have four sons and have relocated to seven different countries within the last 20 years. In fact, he has worked for the same company for more than 25 years now. He is Dutch and currently the director of the recruitment program of a large multinational company in Switzerland: a senior manager in a big organisation. His career is that of an "assigned expatriate", as he has worked the whole time for the same company and relocated many times to different countries. He accepted higher and higher positions with more and more responsibilities, being sent abroad either to develop new markets or to supervise existing subsidiaries. In other words, he, Sandra, and their children relocate at least three times per decade. How does he display "care work integration" then? Kim is very straightforward: he does the paid labour force work while Sandra does the unpaid care work for the household. In contrast to John's narrative, in which he explains Aurelia's difficulties in finding a position in the labour force, Kim focuses his discourse on the value of family and the trust needed between the partners:

> A relocation is certainly a stressful time. But the great thing is, I think it makes the family bonds stronger because the only thing which is always consistent is the family unit. No matter how many times it moves, or where it moves to, it moves together as a team, and I think you kind of go through the different challenges together in terms of picking up new languages and yeah dealing with new cultures. But I have to say that I have been very fortunate: my wife is very much very organised, and she does most of it (Kim, 49yrs, married).

The family is the sole consistent unit in a context where everything is subject to quick modifications. The stress generated by a relocation reinforces the bond within the partnership, according to him. For this equation to work, he adds nevertheless a condition: the family needs to work as a "team". The metaphor of a "team" is striking, as it refers to different players having different functions, such as defenders, midfielders, and forwards. The analogy implies a traditional division of the tasks between him and Sandra, though he does not explicitly name care work, referring to the latter instead as "it". Indeed, in a team, the players know what they have to do and how to play. Furthermore, the analogy stresses a strategic vision of the family able to function under the constraints of "motility". He explicitly links a high "motility" ("no matter how many times it moves, or where it moves" [ibid]) and the strength of a family organised along traditional lines ("it moves together as a team" [ibid]). Kim offers a narrative in which it is clear who does what. In other words, there is no "care work integration" between him and Sandra, as she does all the care work while he focuses on the labour force work.

For him, this way of not dividing the tasks offers advantages when it comes to multiple relocations. He speaks about a traditional division of the tasks, as he knows that the only way of having such an uncompromised focus on the professional career while, at the same time raising four children, is to have a spouse doing all the care work: "my wife is very organised, and she does most of it" (ibid). He needs someone to do the care work, so he can focus exclusively on his professional activity right after the relocation, as he explains it:

> When you move, it tends to be the most stressful time in your new job. You have to go training, you have to go to the market, so it's just not the right time to be spending a lot of time with the family and integrate things. That is, I think, the challenge. I think the work takes on the front role and it is going to be/ hum/ very busy at that time (Kim, 49yrs, married).

He contrasts doing "training" and "going to the market" (ibid) – which is a professional term implying doing the "real work" to increase the profits of the company – with "spending time with the family" (ibid). The latter is a euphemism, as he phrases it in a way which could imply spending free time having fun with the children. This devalues Sandra's care work, because she does not simply "spend time with the family" (ibid), but rather invests her time in a vital, yet unpaid work for the "elementary family" in order to be able to live in the new local space while her husband is absent all day long. She needs to arrange the children's integration into new schools as well as doing all the care work for them and Kim. The time just after a relocation is the busiest time in terms of care work, too. In other words, he depreciates the care work because he refuses to explicitly compare "going to the market" to sell digital marketing products and finding a school for the children. The difference of value attached to the different types of work is another way to create gender inequality, for the care work is very often underappreciated when it is compared to the labour force work. It is, nevertheless, of at least the same importance, because Kim's life would be simply impossible without the dedicated and constant support of Sandra. His discourse suggests that he does the important labour force work and Sandra does the less important care work:

> We decide on a house and the rest she can manage it there. And it works for us like that in terms of/ because I have, you know, I have full confidence in her and she is actually very decisive and knows what she wants and it works better that way when you decide, one person should focus on it because if you do it all together you get just more stressed, I think. She is the one who does most of the logistics (Kim, 49yrs, married).

"She can manage the rest" (ibid) – except buying the house, which, he implies, is a male thing, after all – is again a clue of the different values he attaches to labour force work and care work. Kim develops a patriarchal argument to display the organisation he has with Sandra. A patriarchal organisation is not only about a clear division of the tasks between the labour force work and the care work within the partnership, but also about "the domination of women and younger men by older or more powerful men. Literally the 'rule of the fathers'" (Levy 2007). Thus, it refers to a difference of rank and power within the partnership, which Kim expresses by stating his confidence in Sandra. "I have full confidence in her" (ibid) reveals the hierarchy between them; it is as if he delegates the care work to a subordinate. It shows once again his devaluation of care work.

This hierarchy reinforces (and is being reinforced by) a patriarchal organisation of the family: the labour force paid work is synonymous with financial capital, rarity, and power which outclasses the care work, which is categorised as devotion and abnegation. Thus, the father, the *pater familias*, makes the decisions, is the one who leads; this is not only about the choice of the next relocation but the choice of of how much care work he wants to assume, leaving no choice to the other partner but to agree to take on the rest – except in the case of a separation or divorce.

The constraints of "motility" and of multiple relocations become a way to justify a traditional model of the family in which everyone knows what he or she must do. Kim presents the way of dividing care work as a rule, something they have tested, which works best like this for them: "one person should focus on that" (ibid). This way of presenting the division of the tasks corresponds to the analogy of the team he developed earlier. For him, this is the model that best serves his career, as there is no need to compromise between two professional careers. Furthermore, he does not have to bother about the care work as "she does most of the logistics" (ibid). However, he does not take the last step and does not accept the full implications of such a family organisation, as he says that Sandra works in the labour force, too. In that sense, the traditional model of the family, even in a family strongly organised along traditional lines, does not seem to be fully legitimate – especially doing an interview with a student in sociology working on the topic. A sign of his discursive discomfort is the way he narrates what Sandra actually does. Each time he speaks about it, his words fall short. In the first quote, he pronominalizes her work without giving a concrete subject ("she does most of it" [ibid]), in the second quote he depreciates it ("it's just not the right time to be spending a lot of time with the family" [ibid]), and later he simply does not mention it, interrupting his sentence: "it works for us like that in terms of/ because" (ibid). When I asked him if Sandra works in the labour force, Kim provided a shaky argument:

> The company during our expat assignment supported her to become a yoga instructor. Throughout these moves she always has been able to find, I would say, employment. That is not financially that lucrative but something that she is passionate about that she loves to do, meet new people, in particular local people I would say depending on which country. Japan is very difficult to meet with new people but in Mexico … So, for her, finding a supporting profession which is flexible/ I mean if you want to be a career woman and you both want to have a career it is much more difficult I think if you want to be able to move (Kim, 49yrs, married).

In this excerpt, Kim blurs the lines between a hobby and a paid activity in the labour force. He suggests that Sandra should be thankful for a company that is kind enough to pay for her training to gain a certificate to teach yoga. Kim is not really convinced about the first part of his argument: "I would say, employment" (ibid) he told me; but this implies that others would not say so. He offers here a politically correct answer. He proposes what he thinks I want to hear, namely that the partners of "assigned expatriates" (Andresen et al. 2014) can find a position in the labour force even in the context of multiple relocations. Is not his company "a dual career friendly" company after all? At the end of the quote, however, he rejects the possibility of a dual career while being "motile", expressing a central tension between the "care work integration" and the "labour force work integration". His clause "if you want to be a career woman" (ibid) emphasises this perceived impossibility for him; yet, as we have seen in the case of John, he does not raise the possibility of supporting the care work himself. In other words, he is creating the very impossibility he refers to in order to explain why Sandra does not work in the labour force. The meaning of "career women" is central here, as it expresses a perceived impossibility. The "career woman" mirrors the "career man", the female version of the professional, uncompromisingly focused on her professional career. For Kim, these professionals do not do the care work: they focus solely on their professional advancement and do not (want to) have the time for care. Because he wants to be a "career man", he needs someone who will agree to compromise her career as he, certainly, would not do so. As his company asked him, his partner, and their children to move from Lithuania to Switzerland to the Philippines to Australia to Mexico and so on, it is difficult to see how Kim and Sandra could have developed a dual partner career without him agreeing to negotiate a larger space for Sandra to develop an activity in the labour force. Concretely, this would probably mean staying longer at one place or accepting a move for the sake of her career, maybe even resigning from his company. Would he accept such a compromise? He probably would not; after all, he married his company before marrying Sandra, as he told me at the beginning of the interview.

Without considering the "career women" option, just maintaining any activity in the labour force seems complicated for Sandra, especially when Kim depicts how fast they have had to make the decision to move: "We have a job for you in Mexico, talk to your wife about it, we'll call you tomorrow" (ibid). In this case, the time between the decision to relocate and the actual relocation was so short that they had to cancel their holidays to do an exploratory trip to Mexico. Under these conditions, how can she maintain an activity in the labour force? She does not, because her husband prioritises only his own professional career, letting her do the care work. He tries to justify his position as he mentions that the income is not so important compared to the advantages of teaching yoga, which allow her to "do something [she] love[s]" (ibid) and to "meet local people" (ibid). So, what is the purpose of this activity in his narrative if it is not to earn money? I would argue "to keep her happy" (sic). This notion represents another aspect of these narratives that I will analyse in the next section.

In sum, Sandra has sacrificed her professional career to keep up with the pace of her husband's relocations. Kim's narrative offers an assumed division of the tasks, as having a dual career was never an option for him, and even if it was, is not really an option for Sandra anymore. This contrasts with John's narrative, which proposed a different line of argumentation, underlining the way he and Aurelia have fought against difficult circumstances, trying to reverse them. Kim accepts nearly the whole package, as he admits, at the end of the last quote, that it is not possible to develop a dual career in their case. Thus, he develops a narrative valorising a patriarchal model of the family, which implies a lack of respect for the care work, coupled with an uncompromising focus on his career. Such a narrative eliminates other ways of organising the family, as the intensity of his investment in the labour force work is non-negotiable, and only his willingness to compromise could give Sandra more time to seek employment in the labour force. Furthermore, they have integrated work and family following that pattern for decades now and it is very difficult to reintegrate into the labour market. While Sandra struggles to find a position, Kim is a director, displaying a "no alternative narrative". When there is no other option, there is no reason to feel responsible for a one-sided "care work integration". In fact, it is a confirmation that the choices made in this respect were the good ones because they are the only "realistic" ones: a self-fulfilling prophecy. The drawback of such a family organisation is that it requires the female partner to agree to sacrifice her independence. That point is central because it underlines that the price of successful international careers is not paid by "primary-movers" but mostly by their female partners. This traditional family organisation takes years to become engrained, and one or both of the partners might decide to change things later. At a certain point, the (female) partner – being ejected out of the labour force by the uncompromising focus of the (male) partner on his career – can refuse to continue to follow such a scenario, in which she risks losing her independence and may divorce. I will deal with the consequences of divorce and separation in the next chapter.

7.2.3 Paradoxical Family Men

Besides the discursive elements stressing a fight against the external constraints and the ones underlining a "no alternative" scenario, I see a third way of putting into words a traditional division of the tasks within a partnership: the male partner working in the labour force underlines that he, in fact, prioritises the family. The narratives of the interviewees who mobilise the "paradoxical family men" element, in fact, combine the two former elements, showing that the narratives are dynamic and that their constitutive elements are not mutually exclusive. The "paradoxical family man" takes the external constraints for granted and develops a "no other alternative narrative", yet he does this by emphasising that his priority *is* the family. It is paradoxical: while the "secondary mover" and the children follow him for the sake of his professional career, he emphasises his status as a "family man". Dennis develops a narrative of that kind. He is married to Katia and together they have relocated several times. They have moved to many places including Germany, the United States, and Hong Kong, before relocating to Switzerland. Dennis told me straight away that he is a "family man". When I asked him how it is possible to combine his professional career with his family life, he provided me with the following answer:

> It is not difficult. I am a family man anyways, so I like to have a job, it's fun, but career is not everything for me. … I do my job as efficiently as I can, I try to be home for dinner at the latest. Dinner time at home is religion; so, we try to always be there, all the family. So, I just try to work as quickly and effectively as I can; so, do not let the organization suck me (Dennis, 49yrs, married).

Here, his argument in favour of the family is related to their organisation of the daily life. The explanation he develops is curious: he stresses that he comes back in the evening for dinner. Leaving in the morning and having a full-time job and then coming back for dinner in the evening is what apparently makes him a "family man". He starts by asserting that for him working in the labour force "is fun", implying that his job is a game, compared to the family which is the serious matter. He develops a discourse in which he diminishes the perceived importance of his activity in the labour force. He underlines that he easily achieves the integration of labour force work and family because he prioritises the latter.

However, many elements in this quote show that there is once again a tension between discourse and practice. "Dinner time at home is religion" (ibid) is the statement on which he builds his argument. Yet this is, analytically speaking, a sign of the discrepancy between discourse and practice as he uses a figure of speech: namely, a hyperbole. He implies that family is central to him and being back at home for dinner is one of his priorities, but the use of such a figure of speech is designed to increase his credibility. In fact, when he says he comes back home for dinner time, he uses the verb "to try" (ibid) two times. It may be not as easy as it seems. Though he presents "being at home for dinner" (ibid) as evidence of his prioritisation of family, one can wonder if it is not, in fact, a daily fight for him to achieve it. Maybe he even wishes he could be a more present "family man".

His words "not letting the organisation suck me" (ibid) reveal the pressure that "primary-movers" face in their labour force work. Many narratives of employees of multinational companies underline the pressures they face to invest a lot of time in the labour force. The employees' incomes are high and the benefits mentioned in their contracts are numerous, meaning that they (the expats) are expensive for the company, the pressure on them to work hard and to "perform" is strong. During the interview, Dennis differentiates himself explicitly from the "stereotypes that high level managers are terribly busy and important and that they do not have time for their family" (ibid). He deploys a narrative in which he emphasises being a "family man", and yet his argument is more oriented towards his colleagues than his family: he is actively comparing himself to his colleagues. He speaks of being a "family man" compared to his colleagues who are "career men". The "paradoxical family man" captures this element in his discourse. He cares more about his family than some of his colleagues do; yet for him as for them, the family is subordinated to professional activity – something he does not see or mention. He does not speak, for instance, about a fairer division of the care work: the topic he raises is coming home for dinner. But who cooks the dinner? He develops a discourse which provides an answer to the pressures of the workplace and displays his struggle to safeguard his modest objective to be at home for dinner. In sum, the explanation of his daily practices and his discourse – the meaning he attaches to them – do not align, and this reveals the difficulties he faces in finding time with his family. It seems that it is not as easy as he would like me to believe.

This first excerpt is about the daily organisation of time and the way in which Dennis positions himself compared to his colleagues rather than his partner, I argue. In a way, he is telling me: "I try to be a little bit better than some of my colleagues who are at the office all the time". In the second excerpt, Dennis still positions himself in comparison to his colleagues, but this time he is referring to a broader organisation of time. For him, it is important to control the pace of his professional relocation for the sake of the family and at the expense of his career. He argues:

> So every time you look at getting a different job, it also probably means that you move in the company and for me personally I think I've made a much slower progression throughout the organization than many other people have because I like the stability more, because moving family as you probably have heard from many other people is very difficult, that is why for the sake of the family, I'd rather move much more slowly and hence six years in Indonesia and five years in Hong Kong which is way over average for much of the people (Dennis, 49yrs, married).

In this excerpt, Dennis says that he relocates less frequently than his colleagues. While his discourse superficially focusses on the family, the competition he faces at work is obvious, too. The conditions of the labour force work not only have an impact on the daily organisation of time but also on the organisation of time in the long run. In this respect, Dennis, while aiming to control the pace of the relocations, perceives himself as disadvantaged compared to his colleagues who do not seem to have such priorities. His prioritisation of the family explains why he refuses to move when the company says so. In that sense, the organisation of "motility" is again at the core of the narrative. The higher the "motility", the more difficult it is to combine labour force work and care work: this is Dennis's argument. Conversely, the lower the "motility", the slower the progression in the company. Thus, the tension between care work and labour force work is exacerbated by the organisation of time at two levels: at the level of the daily life – when it comes to the organisation of the day – and at the level of the family – when it comes to decisions regarding a possible further relocation. So far, I have shown how Dennis "displays family" compared to the one of his colleagues, but how does he concretely display his children and his partner?

Speaking with Dennis about the children is a large part of the interview. He underlines a positive and a negative aspect of raising children while on the move. The positive aspect is that they are "colour blind" (ibid) and the negative aspect is that they do not have any "anchors" (ibid). These two aspects are deeply intertwined since it is the mobility of the family which allows the children to live and discover many countries while growing up. During the interview, Dennis speaks about the positive aspects of such a life for the children first:

> I have three children, to grow up in an international environment, which means that they are colour blind, they do not really understand what racism is, they are open-minded, so that nationalities are a typically different concept than for us. That is a huge reward to see that people can grow up as if they do not see any physical, ethnical, national boundaries (Dennis, 49yrs, married).

More than Dennis' career, the biggest advantage of frequent relocations is to raise the children in an international environment. However, he is afraid of not being able to offer them stability and continuity in their social lives. In fact, at the time of the interview, Katia and the children were on holidays in Germany, while he was working for his company in Switzerland. They had just left Hong Kong, but they had not yet arrived in Switzerland. They had no place to live; they were in an "in-between situation of homelessness" (ibid), as he told me. In Germany, they go to their parents' place to spend the holidays. In Hong Kong, their accommodation had been terminated. In Switzerland, they still had not moved in as their pieces of furniture were somewhere on the ocean, on a freighter. This situation is especially complicated for the children, Dennis told me. In his view, the children are paying a price for their frequent relocations because they have lost friendships and have an unstable sense of where "home" is:

> Stability for children is, I believe, very important and I can't give them that stability. So, you need to be extra sure that you have a place for them where they have an emotional anchor and that can be very dangerous if you don't have that because then they just go through life, never investing in meaningful relationships (Dennis, 49yrs, married).

Though Dennis has constraints because of his professional activity, he emphasises during the interview that he is in a better position because relocating is much more challenging for Katia and the children. Concerning the children, his biggest fear is that he will raise "superficial assholes" (ibid) who do not engage with anyone, since they know they are going to leave in a few years anyway. He is afraid because they do not have an "emotional anchor" (ibid). That is why Dennis tries to stay in touch with their former friends in Hong Kong, but it seems very complicated. Thus, they plan to go back to Hong Kong for holidays, so the children can see their friends and play soccer with them. "We don't have an anchor. We don't have a home base. We don't have a place that we go to" (ibid) aptly summarises this intense feeling of uncertainty and fear that lurks behind the smiley, welcoming, and open Dennis I interviewed. He is aware that the price of his mobile career is high for the family. Thus, he has tried to diminish the pace of the relocations to offer the children a chance to build friendships, but in the end they have all had to move anyway. "When all options are exhausted, you have to go" (ibid): this emphasises the fragility of the social networks that highly-skilled migrants create when they arrive in a new place. As soon as the position in the labour force is taken away, there is nothing left and the "modalities of settling" that they may have enjoyed become part of the past. They tried to stay in Hong Kong and no doubt if they could have done so they would have stayed.

This case shows that "motility" is not always chosen: sometimes it is a "forced motility". The children are not the only ones paying a high price as it is also complicated for the partner, as we saw in the first chapter. While proposing an explanation for the reasons that the couples find it difficult to maintain dual careers under the constraints of "motility", Dennis's discourse stresses the price of Katia's sacrifice:

> I think because [silence] it's much much much more difficult now, so because at the time my wife also used to work for *** and she quit her job at the time. I know that we support dual careers and so forth, but it is very difficult to have two working spouses who put equal weight on their work life. … So, one of the troubles that I've/the discussion that my wife and I have before we move, every now and then, we go back 15 years: "I have to quit my job for you, so we can live this lifestyle, blah blah blah, you, never forget that" and those are unfortunately the worse moments that we have to go through (Dennis, 49yrs, married).

This quote speaks to the gendered inequalities that the prioritisation of one career can create, though the "expats' narrative" displays it in a softer way. This excerpt offers insight into the way in which Dennis and Katia divide the care work and the labour force work: it is, as in the first two cases, a traditional division of the tasks, since Katia quit her position in the labour force to follow her husband. Not only have the children paid a high price for Dennis's mobility, but Katia has also seemed to suffer a lot. Accordingly, Dennis implies that it is more difficult not only for men but also for women who want to work in the labour force nowadays ("it's much much much more difficult now" [ibid]). The underlying message is that it would be so much simpler if they (the women) would not try to do so as it complicates the life of the "career men". He repeats his implicit message in the next sentence when he speaks about the "dual careers *and so forth*" (ibid):[79] these unimportant things that the company provides as if these programs were inadequate to face the challenges compared to the challenges that a high "motility" raises for the partners. He expresses a frustration which reveals the difficulty of maintaining two professional careers. A simple way to diminish the tension is when the (female) partner agrees to abandon the idea of working in the labour force. He starts the next sentence with "the problem that I have" (ibid) before correcting to "the discussion" (ibid). Dennis tries to rectify his discourse to fit an accepted narrative of what family should be. Thus, he actively "displays family" (Finch 2007) as he changes the term "problem" to "discussion". Analytically speaking, the "problem" belongs to the realm of his practices, while the "discussion" belongs to the realm of his narrative. A discussion implies a shared division of power in which the two partners can express their interests equally, while "my problem" corresponds to his own professional perspective and the problem of coordinating his professional career with Katia

79 Own emphasis

and the children. This quote reveals the many paradoxes and tensions of Dennis's narrative on the one hand, and his practices on the other.

Nevertheless, it is difficult to see Katia as a completely "happy partner"; there are indications that it is not the case. First, the temporal markers indicate that Katia's willingness to follow him and to give up her independence was not the result of a single discussion they had one time 15 years ago; rather, it is a recurrent discussion – a recurrent argument – because it is a recurrent decision to prioritise his career. She allegedly does not accept the division of the tasks. It seems that he never convinced her to fulfil the role he wants her to play. When she speaks about her pain, about what she did for him in order to enable his career, he undercuts her words by summarising them with "blah blah blah" (ibid). He answers her pain and sacrifice by mocking her. They have probably never quite agreed on this topic as she mentions that he should "never forget" it (ibid). In John's narrative, the order of things was restored when he and Aurelia both had a position in the labour force; in Dennis' case, I argue, the order of things would be restored if Katia tried not to discuss working in the labour force. This is an example in which Katia, the female partner, is being sent back to the sphere of the household, doing the care work for the family. Dennis mobilises a "no alternative narrative" to explain why Katia left the labour force:

> I think it is becoming more and more difficult in a dual working spouse relationship to have one person who is not, who does not have to take the back seat, because one person always has to make a switch. Let's say you are married and your wife gets the job and you move, so you have to start a new job, three years down the road, you have to quit your job again and start another one, which is more than suboptimal (Dennis, 49yrs, married).

Dennis underlines the tension inherent in the prioritisation of one professional over the other when mobility – and even more so, "motility" – is implied. He proposes an example in which the female works in the labour force while the male does the care work – a configuration I did not encounter in my interviews. The first sentence of the quote highlights the tension that arises when it comes to integrating two professional careers in a partnership but takes up an allegedly more accepted perspective in which the man stops working for the sake of the female partner. It is difficult for the interviewees to accept the traditional and patriarchal organisation of family within their narratives. As in the cases of John and Kim, the "accepted repertoire of what family should be" is in tension with Dennis's practices. In their views, the "accepted repertoire of what family should be" does not correspond to the division of the care and labour force work that they develop in practice. John, Kim, and Dennis develop discursive strategies – discursive tricks – to emphasise that they agree with a more egalitarian integration of the labour force work between them and their partners, but these strategies also suggest that they have difficulty finding a way to legitimate their family organisation. The path-dependency of their previous choices explains why they continue to follow this path. After a certain length of time with the same "family-strategy", they find themselves in a position in which it is difficult to change the organisation of the family. Thus, their discursive tricks reveal the difficulty of changing the "family-strategies", as they have to keep up their professional activity in order to maintain the family's standards of living. Nevertheless, the practices remain invariably the same; none of them seems to acknowledge that their partner would need support in the care work in order to achieve a more egalitarian integration of the positions in the labour force.

I have shown three types of narratives, three different ways of explaining and justifying why and how one of the partners – the woman – leaves the labour force to do the care work. All three of these narratives allege that mobility and dual careers are impossible to reconcile as the pace of the relocations is too high for the other partner to coordinate his or her professional career. Their discourse on "motility" orients their approach to settlement. The pattern they produce implies that a dual career is impossible, which leads them to impose a traditional division of tasks upon their partnership.

Up until now, we have seen narratives in which the openness to a next relocation is high, at least discursively. Another range of narratives actually refuse "motility", or to put it another way, valorise more the localisation and the development of local anchors after a relocation. In the first part of this chapter I have shown the discursive construction of the concept of "motility" from an emic perspective. Through these discourses, I have stressed that the openness to mobility for the sake of one professional career reinforces inequality of gender roles. The respondents told me their stories in good faith, kindly agreeing to answer my questions; though I am critical, my goal is to show how gendered hierarchies are constructed while "displaying family".

7.3 Anchored Narratives

In the second part of this chapter, I will analyse the narratives which express a lower availability to "motility". These narratives focus more on long term settlement in a local space although this does not mean that the partners are going to stay permanently. When the perceived need and/or wish for "motility" is low, the choices in the "modalities of settling" correspond to a long-run perspective implying other kinds of narratives to display family. These narratives emphasise the challenges that the partners face in sharing the care work, their fear of losing their position in the labour force and running out of options in the local space, or their struggles in finding a new position in the labour force. In this section, I will still analyse narratives of highly-skilled migrants who display their families in a certain way after having moved, but whose perceived lack of "motility" creates another field of possibilities as, for instance, they may consider local public schools for their children. Contrarily to the partners who develop a narrative strongly stressing "motility", the narratives emphasising localisation offer a wider range of choices in the care work integration. It sometimes implies– though by far not always – more room for the partners to manoeuvre in order to share the care work in a more equitable way.

7.3.1 Ignoring Motility

The practices and the discourses concerning "motility" may be contradictory: there is no need for coherence between the two realms; though actors aim to make them coincide, it does not have to be that way. In other words, when it comes to the frequency of their mobility and the discourse they develop the practices of the partners do not always coincide. Maria (Teleworking, 148) is a striking example of an interviewee who has developed a discourse *a priori* contradictory to her highly "motile" situation. She followed her husband, Franz, to many different countries as the company offered him positions across the globe. Maria and Franz relocated to England, to Italy, to Japan, and to Switzerland. While she found employment in the labour force after each relocation, she also resigned for the next relocation. She is an example of a "partner-coordinated mover", who struggles to maintain her professional activity due to her husband's relocations. As they do not have any children, their care work integration is quite straightforward; they did not have to deal with the increased load of care work that children create. Furthermore, she did not have to fight against the "housewifing" (Kanter and Halter 1978) pressures of her husband, in particular, and society, in general, when it came to raising children. The "housewifing" process is the process by which the female partner is pushed away from the labour force to the sphere of the household, doing the care work. Thus, Maria had time to look for paid work after their various relocations because she did not have to invest her time in care work. These circumstances, however, did not remove the "Sword of Damocles" of her husband's next relocation hanging over her professional activity, for there is still a "hierarchy of position" within their partnership. He has never resigned, and she describes his career as the "steep upward career" (Maria, 51yrs, married) of a financial manager in a multinational corporation.

Actually, the possibility that he could have left his position for her is not a topic in the interview: the "hierarchy of positions" is naturalised to such a point that it is simply not a question anymore. When I asked her about an earlier discussion, Maria told me that:

> We always discuss it together, whenever the offer came. Well, we would have a discussion and see where we both stand if it the right time for us, if the job is interesting enough, if my husband wants to do it, if I would be willing to follow (Maria, 51yrs, married).

The first clause is all about "displaying family" (Finch 2007), as Maria underlines the systematic discussions leading to a common decision of the partners. They talk on equal grounds, though always at her expense, I argue. The crucial point of the excerpt is the kind of categorisation it implies. She does not question the division of the types of the "primary-mover" and of the "secondary-mover" in their partnership. It is as if it is inconceivable for her to accept a position abroad and to ask her husband to follow. And this is the case even though they met while working for the same company, though they both started in the same company at the same hierarchical level with a similar university degree, and though they do not have children (which is usually *the* excuse to explain why the female does not achieve such a "steep upward professional career"). While all the elements in their partnership suggest that they could focus on a dual career, she develops a narrative in which the possibility that she could move and he could follow is left unsaid. Her narrative emphasises how deeply incorporated the "hierarchy of the positions" is between them. The patterns that she (co)produces orient her actions; they offer her a certain field of possibilities. This field conditions her (re) actions, as the question of knowing whether they could relocate for the sake of her professional career does not seem to be a "realistic" possibility. Thus, she is vulnerable to the "sword of Damocles" of her husband's career; this sword could be called "motility". Indeed, she develops an argument that shows the disruptive side of "motility" and how she avoids its consequences:

> We never considered any move, any move, we never considered it as being temporary. Maybe we knew, of course, it would be temporary, but in terms of integration, in terms of the job, in terms of me looking for a job, I never thought about the temporarily, about the time limitation, because otherwise, I think I would not have been able to really find the energy to start from scratch (Maria, 51yrs, married).

In this quote, she narrates how she purposefully ignores their "motility", though the practice she develops is "motile". She distinguishes between *considering* and *knowing*, which is an interesting way of depicting the situation she is in. She knows that they are going to move, but in order to "find the energy to start from the scratch" (ibid) and ultimately to get a position in the labour force, she acts as if they will stay in the same local space in the long run. In this quote, Maria reflects on how she managed to maintain her professional activity through the series of concessions – if not sacrifices – she had to make in order to follow Franz. For her, it is clear that arriving in a new local space while already knowing that she might soon leave it, would discourage her from seeking employment there; she would not have the energy to engage in this local space so much. The words she uses, "starting from scratch" (ibid), to describe each of her arrivals in a new local space, imply an exhausting process; therefore, accepting "motility" while relocating would be destructive for her motivation to continue seeking employment. The idea of being available to leave a local space at any time while trying to find a position in this specific local space creates a "double bind" (Bateson et al. 1956), I argue. A "double bind" refers to two conflicting messages, such as, for instance, "I give you the order to disobey me"[80]. Indeed, either Maria accepts that she is about to leave or she looks for a position in the labour force to stay: seeking a position in the labour force to leave it straightaway highlights the conflict between the two messages. In order to resolve this "double bind", one of the binds needs to be removed. This is the same argument that pushes many "secondary movers" out of the labour force; it is the same dilemma, the same "double bind", yet Maria has decided to ignore the *other* bind. She refuses to acknowledge the looming truth that they will eventually have to move as she steps in to find employment, in this way lying[81] to herself about how long they will stay. Only this lie can reassure her that her efforts are not in vain, as she invests a lot of time and energy into finding a position in the labour force after their frequent relocations. This is how she describes her arrival in Italy:

> I was quite excited to go to Italy, but I knew that I had to learn the language first, before I could actually approach the local job market. So, what I did in Italy: I moved and immediately went into a full-time language course for almost a year and then I started to/ well it was after 8 months, I started to look for a job when I thought I was quite comfortable with the language, and then after one year, I started working in the local market (Maria, 51yrs, married).

---

80 Example found on the blog "la boite à outil du montieur éducateur", retrieved April 13, 2018, from http://laboiteame.unblog.fr/double-contrainte-injonction-paradoxale-ecole-de-palo-alto/

81 I use this expression to underline how Maria copes with the "double-bind" that I spot in her discourse. As for the rest of my analyses, my goal is to critically assess an interview as a discourse, not to judge a respondent as a person.

In this quote, Maria speaks about what she did to find employment after she arrived in Italy. It is as if she was taking the "integration express lane", so to speak. She learned Italian in eight months, and after one year she began to work for an Italian company specialising in online translation, using her German skills. In so doing, Maria constructs a discourse to distinguish herself from the "membership category" (Sacks 1972; Watson 1983) of the "trailing spouse". Following the logic of the "double bind", the "trailing spouse" typically does not work in the labour force, thus removing the other bind: the need to seek employment in the labour force. Maria refuses this categorisation and its implications: instead, after one year, she spoke the language and worked in the local labour force. In this way, she creates a discrepancy between the narrative and the practice. Maria's situation reveals the dilemmas that "motility" can create. It also highlights that "motility" is not an abstract concept: it contributes to (re)produce a power differential within her partnership along gendered lines. "Motility" is *for* someone and it is a privilege to be the "depository of motility" in a partnership. Maria's discourse mirrors the "motility" narratives of John, Kim, and Dennis, yet in a reversed form. She implies that high "motility" in the case of two working partners in the labour force does not work; thus, she develops a discourse ignoring "motility", while John, Kim, and Dennis acknowledge it. Yet they do not have to pay its price, as all three have the privilege of being its depository within their partnerships. All four of the narratives highlight a high practice of "motility", depicting an incompatibility between "motility" and dual careers. Yet the "meaning patterns" they develop demonstrate several different possible reactions to that situation.

7.3.2 Refusing Motility

In other cases, such as Lynn and Alex's (6.2.1 Primary-Mover and Secondary-Mover, 139; 6.5.1 Total-Move of a Partner-Initiated Mover, 158), the partners develop discourses corresponding to their (low) practice of "motility". Lynn and Alex relocated once, but not again since then, even though they would have had the opportunity to do so. They both work for the same multinational company in Germany. They do not see how they could better coordinate their professional careers and the care work that their daughter requires. They both have a good position in the company while having developed a "care work integration" that allows them both to work in the labour force. To do so, they have hired a nanny and pay for a private school. I interviewed them separately and each interview lasted a bit more than an hour. When I asked Lynn if they have the possibility of relocating abroad, she gave me the following answer:

> There were a few chances for that, all within *** [company]. … I mean either we changed our mind or the situation changed, or the position changed, and it wasn't relevant anymore. So yeah, I mean but I think we've always consciously felt that in order to live here we have to have something really really good that makes a lot of sense for probably both of us and not just one of us. So, we both have a lot of earning here so and we, that would be obviously a prerequisite at this point and that does not come up every day, so I think that is why we are still here (Lynn, 51yrs, married).

In contrast to the narratives presented earlier, Lynn explicitly considers the two careers when it comes to deciding if they will relocate again. She emphasises that they "both have a lot of earnings here" (ibid) and that maintaining the same income is a condition to maintaining their lifestyle in Germany or somewhere else. Their "care work integration" requires two paid positions in the labour force as it is expensive. She focuses on maintaining what they have rather than considering where they could go. When she says that they need something that "would make sense for probably both of us and not just one of us" (ibid), she sends a message to her employer and to her husband. The message is directed towards the company, which offered them each different positions and asked if they would agree to relocate again. She wants something that would make sense for both of them, however, which the company did not propose. The message is directed towards her husband, too, as she underlines that a prerequisite for any move would be that they would not only both have to maintain an activity in the labour force, but they would also have to earn similar incomes to the ones they have now. Therefore, she argumentatively recuses the beginning of a "hierarchy of positions" between them.

Lynn also uses the first person plural (we) to speak about their professional careers, which contrasts with the other interviewees, who nearly all use the first person singular (I). In her eyes, to be convincing enough to be considered, a new relocation would need to be attractive for both of them: a situation that they have not encountered since their first relocation. It shows, once again, yet from a different angle, that frequent relocations create a context in which it is difficult – if not nearly impossible – for both partners to develop a professional activity.

The arrival of Mary, their daughter, emphasises even more the development of a sceptical discourse regarding further relocations. In Lynn's narrative, the arrival of Mary corresponds to practical and discursive shifts on different levels. She has to face (1) the pressures of displaying "being a good mum", while (2) continuing her labour force work at a high position – she is as an account director – and (3) explaining why she does not want to move higher in the hierarchy of the company, since this would imply a further relocation. This is what she answered when I asked her about the advice she would give to someone starting a career such as hers:

> I worked really, really hard for a long time to, you know, to achieve that and I think I was on a good way all along to doing that and achieving that and I think I was living this success and then once you have kids – like they say – everything changes anyway, and you start to look at things a little differently, and now I am not sure anymore what success really means (Lynn, 51yrs, married).

The first sentence of this quote stresses the shift of perspective caused by the birth of Mary. Her use of the past tense is striking in that regard. Lynn is currently the account director of the European subsidiary of an American multinational company, but she speaks as if she has given up on success. What else could success mean to her? For her, living success is about continuing to climb within a company to reach the top of the hierarchy. It means aiming at the position of an executive director. When she speaks about working hard, she means more than 60 hours a week, and when she speaks about achieving and living success she means accepting the relocation that she was offered a few years ago, which would have led her into that race. Though she uses the past tense to speak about it, she still develops a narrative of the young and ambitious professional she was incarnating, just like her male counterparts, whose narratives I analysed at the beginning of the chapter. The difference between Lynn and them is their gender and children, I argue. The relocations of John, Kim, and Dennis allowed them to continue to climb up and, for some of them, it meant effectively reaching the highest position. Lynn refuses to do so, but is it really her choice? Yes and no, I argue. She ultimately decides that it is, though she makes this decision through the lenses of the "meaning patterns" she (co)creates and uses. She decides, yes, but who would decide against being a "good mum?" She decides, yes, but who would take care of Mary? Her husband is supportive, yes, but he works in the labour force, too. He will not resign to relocate for the sake of Lynn's career and to take care of Mary. Thus, the fact that she is a woman and a mother, as well as the network of constraints safeguarding their lifestyle in Germany, orient her decision. To put it bluntly, her child limits her ascent; for Lynn, Mary was the glass ceiling. Many studies show that the arrival of children diminishes women's participation in the labour force and their subsequent chances of achieving an upwardly mobile professional career (Gerson 1986; Slaughter 2012), as statistically the fathers systematically do much less care work for their children (Imhof 2015, 33). Accordingly, their careers are not so much at stake when they have children.

"Like they say, everything changes anyway" (Lynn, 51yrs, married). Who says this? Male interviewees never say such things. Actually, most of them say "she took a maternity leave" (John, 50yrs, married). Things stay the same for them, as they manage to develop a "(non-)care work integration": a division of the tasks in which the female partner does all the care work, and which is actually free of charge, expect for their partner's professional sacrifices. In Lynn's case, blurred social pressures from her partner, colleagues, parents, me (a male interviewer), and society in general, push her to display herself as a "good mother". She speaks a lot about the notion of success and she draws a distinction between success at work and success in life:

> I think, you look at success in your job is one thing, in your career, and as you get older, I think you begin to start to think about success in life and so how you reconcile those two things. It is probably the biggest question, challenge (Lynn, 51yrs, married).

Thus, Lynn distinguishes between two scales of values which express the tensions between two opposing arguments. Such a narrative stresses the tension between the professional career and the care work. In cases in which the division of the tasks between the partners is clear-cut and patriarchal, these questions do not appear, as they seem to align. Since the female partner does all the care work, the male partner measures his success in life through the lens of his professional career. This is not the case for Lynn, who must struggle instead between these two contradictory scales of values. So, she actually has to maintain a contradiction. So, she has made the decision to give up "motility" in her professional activity. However, she speaks about a stronger attachment to the local space where they live, because under these circumstances, she can better manage the tension between paid work and care work. While comparing these two scales of value, she stresses that the price of an ambitious professional career is high. She has to be careful of the daily and the long-term organisation of time, which is practically the opposite discourse to the one I showed while analysing narratives valorising "motility". They were saying that "it's just not the right time to be spending a lot of time with the family" (Kim, 49yrs, married). Lynn has to find a compromise between these two scales of values and has to find the time to spend with her family, as she explains it:

> Once, you've hit a point when you just kind of say: "Ok, my goal now is much more around maintaining, insuring, supporting, helping, growing versus having to be the one in the front line all the time". It takes that shift today. … I am not willing to, that is just a no go, you know, if we were forced into a move which will significantly reduce my time with my family or increase the complexity of that time, I would say no. I've learned that, you know (Lynn, 51yrs, married).

This quote describes the compromise she made. It exemplifies the construction of gendered social pressures sending her into the household, what can be called a process of "housewifing" (Kanter and Halter 1978). She takes a defensive stance and refuses to aim at higher positions, as seeking a higher position would probably mean a relocation and/or longer working hours. In so doing, she expresses – similar to the narratives we have already seen – the narrated incompatibility of a "career women" taking care of her child. Narratives contribute to shaping reality, offering specific lenses to make decisions; yet they do not construct reality alone. In absolute terms, it is certainly possible to be a woman, have a career, and raise children. However, this requires the woman to overcome practical constraints, to organise time, and to manage the integration of the professional activity and the care work. Thus, the second half of the quote relates to my argument that "motility" has strong gendered implications. In contrast to the narratives in which the interviewees embrace "motility" – or at least take its constraints for granted – Lynn refuses it altogether. Her message could not be clearer, as she uses phrases such as "a no go [even] if we were forced … I would say no" (ibid). The tension between the two scales of values leads her to adopt a defensive position to maintain her current professional activity and to minimise the risks of a relocation which would considerably disrupt their "care work integration": Lynn and Alex, her husband, both live and work close to Mary's school, Mary has had the same nanny for more than five years, they have found a school which they both like for her, and they have just bought a house. A further relocation would disrupt this whole arrangement. Lynn and Alex's choice shows – once again – the disruptive character of "motility" on the capacity of the partners to integrate care work and work in the labour force. Lynn refuses this as she perceives it as a threat. Their "modalities of settling" in Germany are more and more anchored, meaning that a further move would require important reorganisation, would be time-consuming and risky. They would, for instance, have to sell their house rather than simply terminate a lease agreement.

7.3.3 After Motility

So far, I have shown the narratives of interviewees accepting, ignoring, or refusing the pressures of "motility", as well as the broad range of discourses attached to it. Chiefly, I have stressed that "motility" increases the complexity of the organisation of the care work as well as the "labour force work integration". These two processes very often take place at the expense of the women's professional careers. Furthermore, "motility" not only complexifies the organisation between the partners but it also implies an emotional price, for instance, in terms of losing one's independence and friends. The partner and the children suffer these consequences. In other words, the situation of being "motile" is an uncomfortable position and it is usually only a matter of time before the partners want to settle somewhere. It often coincides with later stages of the "life cycle" (O'Rand and Krecker 1990) as circumstances change. The fact that the children are getting older and graduate from school or that the interviewee's parents require care work are reasons expressed by the partners for the reduced pace of their relocations. Thus, discourses which emphasise the development of anchored "modalities of settling" are common, because they suggest a way to control the emotional and social costs of "motility". Dennis's narrative acknowledges these costs when he speaks about the fears and pains of Katia and the children, yet he is also saying that he and Katia do not want to stay in "orbit" their whole life (Dennis, 49yrs, married). Another interviewee, Julia, also speaks about "floating in space" (Julia, 42yrs, divorced) and the need to land. Kim speaks about "floaters" (Kim, 49yrs, married), too:

> If you can do that, it is nice to have a centre, because otherwise you become a floater. I think some people are absolutely fine with that. Others, I think later on, well, all of a sudden, they say, well, I don't even know where I would invest in real estate, where I would want to live and, yeah, to some extent you could say well, that is a shame. … I think it [silence] I mean, for us it [owning a house in Switzerland] is a key component, and also, we are a very close family. So, I enjoy, you know. Now, I also have the opportunity of living closer to my parents (Kim, 49yrs, married).

This excerpt underlines the need to develop a centre, a "home base". Kim refuses to make this a rule as there are always exceptions – and he is "absolutely fine with that" (ibid) – yet he also speaks of this "moment" when people usually want to settle down. He is nevertheless very careful about not generalising his argument: he takes a stand and argues in favour of what he thinks is best. He develops a normative argument: the normal thing to do is to settle down at one point. The normal thing is to be "integrated" somewhere. In his view, being a "floater … is a shame" (ibid), because "floaters" miss many moments with their family and parents, moments they cannot buy back. Besides, they have nowhere to go back to: they are in "orbit", as Dennis puts it. The "floaters" are not anchored to a particular place, as they stay in a liminal state between where they are now and an unknown next destination; they have nowhere to come back to, but merely the next place to go to. They have lost their sense of having a home. Metaphorically, they are like a kite whose rope is broken, having no guidance except from external constraints, such as the wind. In other words, Kim speaks of "floaters" as people who relocate where they are told to go. There is nothing bad about that, he says, until the notion that they are missing important moments in life becomes too important, and this is when the "tipping point" is reached. Kim describes this "moment" – which comes "all of the sudden" (ibid) – as the realisation of the losses that living far away from relatives implies. Later in the interview, he complains about not having been at any of the marriages of his cousins; he also missed many funerals. Thus, he implies that for him, the consequence of 'floating' between relocations has been a lack of contact with his relatives. Then, "all of the sudden" (ibid), he began to consider the price of living far away with a new perspective, no longer solely a professional one. A key factor in his decision to settle down in Switzerland was the possibility of seeing his parents more often, as they also live there. Kim implies that at a certain point, the "motility" that drove his professional career needed to be approached differently, as he and Sandra want to live closer to their relatives. Kim's argument continues as he expresses the importance of geography, but also the complexity of narratives talking about "motility":

> Neither my wife and I are Swiss, I have a Dutch passport, but I never lived there, as I said, I moved all of my life with my parents. My wife is British and we all feel that this is home. That is why we invested our money in buying a house here as well, and that is why we wanted to move here, maybe there is an opportunity to go and do another assignment, but I enjoy coming back here and enjoy living here. I mean, Switzerland for me is home, so we may do another assignment you know (Kim, 49yrs, married).

The "sedentary bias" is to be criticised in migration and mobility studies (Wieczorek, 2018), and it is not as if Kim will now enter the "sedentary order of things". His narrative is more complex and offers a reminder that there is no such a thing as settling for good ("so we may do another assignment, you know" [ibid]). Developing more anchored "modalities of settling" such as buying a house do not equal a "sedentary life" governed by immobility[82]. Kim's narrative shows quite the contrary, as settling somewhere does not mean immobility: settling in Switzerland still offers the opportunity to visit Sandra's relatives in England. Even though he has established a place to return to, Kim highlights that developing more anchored "modalities of settling" is not about being immobile. In sum, the binaries between "mobile/immobile" and "motile/immotile" are

82 State power and (im)mobility is a crucial but understudied topic. (Im)mobility is a tool to govern. Karl Polanyi, for instance, describes the relationship between the British Victorian Laws on geographical mobility of workers, industrialisation processes, and the action of the legislator to provide "social services" – the "Poor Laws" – while not obstructing the economic development of Britain.

oversimplifications, as Kim's narrative demonstrates that there is a full spectrum ranging between the supposed binaries of mobility/immobility and "motility/immotility".

In fact, Kim's case highlights that "motility" and mobility are concepts which only acquire meaning within a spatial and a temporal context; *in abstracto* they mean almost nothing. For Kim, the contextualisation about where to settle corresponds to a sense of proximity to one's extended family. The temporal element corresponds to periods of the "life cycle" (O'Rand and Krecker 1990) and refers to choices related to the children and the parents of the interviewees. Kim and Sandra's children are doing their baccalaureate and Kim speaks about living in Switzerland for a while so as to give their children better chances of success:

> If you do the baccalaureate because, hum, that was ideal for my son, because then he had one year to start of preparing for the IB [international baccalaureate] and then you have the last two years where you do the IB. Those are the three years where you keep and stay at the same school, that is the most important and I think. At a younger age, it does not really matter that much. What is very difficult is when at the middle of your baccalaureate you change schools or if you come from a non-IB standard and then you want to do the IB, I think then it is difficult (Kim, 49yrs, married).

Kim emphasises that the period when the children are doing the baccalaureate is a risky time for a relocation as being in the same school for some years increase their chances of succeeding in their studies. Thus, he implies that the age of the children matters when determining the extent of the family's "motility" ("at a younger age it does not really matter that much" [ibid]). Many interviewees corroborate his interpretation that high 'motility' is less risky with younger children. During the three years of high school – when children are usually between 15 and 18 roughly – the "motility" of the family needs to be controlled, he stresses. We have seen that it is not an absolute or final decision. However, as long as the children are doing their baccalaureate, he will not relocate, and only once the children leave to go to university might they accept another relocation.

Moreover, Kim talks about constructing a place to return to, in case they relocate again. He also speaks about periods when he considers it too risky to relocate for the sake of their children's education. Thus, I distinguish a specific form of "motility" which is difficult to maintain in the long run: a "motility oriented towards the unknown", which is different from a "controlled motility". Essentially, the "motility oriented towards the unknown" complexifies the care work organisation as it implies spatial (where) and temporal (when) uncertainties. The "controlled motility" refers to a "motility" in which the partners have spatial and temporal restrictions. They know, for instance, that they are not going to move too far away, too soon, but rather are going to stay where they are for a while, in a local space that they have chosen ("that is why we wanted to move here" [Kim, 49yrs, married]).

Another issue when it comes to more anchored "modalities of settling" is the emergence of care work directed towards the parents of the interviewees, as new care responsibilities appear when the parents of the interviewees get old and require attention. In the case of Lynn and Alex, for instance, the couple arranged a room in their house in Germany so that Lynn's mother can visit whenever she wants. They hope that she is going to come more often. It is rare that the parents move to join their children, but it is still a possibility, and under these conditions, relocating every three or four years becomes extremely complicated. More often, the children, *i.e.,* the interviewees, aim to live closer to their parents, *i.e.,* the interviewees' parents, which implies relocating to a place where they can integrate this new care responsibility with the labour force work and the care work they already have. These new circumstances lead interviewees to be reluctant to accept new opportunities for relocation as they try to stay close to their parents and relatives: a "controlled motility", I argue.

I will use Hannah's narrative to show how "motility" can be encouraged or, on the contrary, hindered at different stages of one's life; for her, the matter has grown pressing now that her parents are getting old. She is British and arrived in Frankfurt 24 years ago. Since then, she has relocated to Kiev, Moscow, and Istanbul. Hannah is one of the few female "primary-movers" I interviewed. She is now in her fifties and a group account director in a multinational marketing company. She married Hans and they relocated together for a decade. Now, they have both been back in Germany for six years. They do not have any children. They separated after they returned from Turkey, their last relocation. When I asked Hannah what motivated her to accept the relocation, she speaks of adventure and offers a discourse similar to the one I presented at the beginning of this chapter, in which the career seems more important than the relationship:

> My husband … was studying architecture actually in Frankfurt but his studies were taking longer and my career started taking off, and then in 2003 the company asked me if I would move to Kiev. … He gave up studying and he came with me and for me that was actually quite/ I would have done it without him. Well, no, I wouldn't have divorced him but if I've been single. If I have been single, I would have done it (Hannah, 52yrs, separated).

Here too, the "hierarchy of position" plays a role in the decision to relocate, as the one with the higher position acquires power in the relationship to impose his or her views. However, there is a narrative "ping pong", as a straightforward statement is directly followed by a sense of reluctance to expose the power. The discrepancy in the discourse often highlights ways of "polishing power". She actively "displays family" (Finch 2007) by highlighting a discourse focusing on the mutual agreements based on a rational choice ("his studies were taking longer and my career started taking off" [ibid]) over a pure imposition of power ("I would have done it without him" [ibid]). Thus, she corrects herself, saying that she would have done it if she were single, emphasising her reluctance to "display family" through the lens of power imposition. Nevertheless, her statement reveals her intention not to compromise and her attitude toward relocating, too. In the narratives, "displaying family" is about coordination and mutual agreement; in practice, it may be more often about power relationships. As John did with his girlfriend before his first relocation, Hannah prioritises her career and convinces Hans to come with her. They had a lot of discussions about the possibility of relocating to Kiev. Contrary to John, she was not ready to end the relationship, but similar to John, she was still very keen to relocate there as her "career was starting off" (ibid). Allegedly, the fact that her partner was not very "motivated to finish his studies" (ibid) and had no deadline to finish them convinced him to follow her, which he did for a decade, supporting Hannah with the care work. In Hannah's narrative, the challenges they faced together while abroad strengthened them as a couple. It was only when they came back to Frankfurt that they separated. Single and without children, Hannah still has care and emotional work to do, as her parents are getting older:

> My parents are very elderly, my father died 18 months ago and I just felt that it would be wrong to be on the other side of the world, because my parents are in England/ My mum now/ and for me, it just felt kind of the wrong thing to do, to go to the other side of the world, but honestly, I think if we had gone to Melbourne, we would be probably still together, because I think that the unit that you feel, like to get through life (Hannah, 52yrs, separated).

In this quote, Hannah points out that she developed a "controlled motility" so as to be able to care for her parents in England. Thus, developing a certain stance toward "motility" may change throughout one's "life cycle" for different reasons. In her narrative, it also comes with a consequence: namely, a separation from Hans. Fifteen years ago, Hannah's parents did not require any care work as they were much younger, which allowed Hannah and Hans to accept relocations to Kiev, Moscow, and Istanbul. After Istanbul, the company offered Hannah a relocation to Melbourne. At that point, she decided to refuse and to take control of where she wanted to live: Frankfurt. Her decision shows the distinction between "motility oriented towards the unknown" and a "controlled motility".

In Hannah's and in Kim's cases, I highlight the need for modifications toward "motility" throughout the "life cycle" (O'Rand and Krecker 1990); the idea of a continuum expresses the way the interviewees narrate their mobile and "motile" backgrounds, as there is no "either/or" situation. Hannah, for instance, mentions having two homes and constantly travelling between England and Germany. This situation stresses that going through the challenges implied by living abroad reinforce, in some cases, the feeling of commitment between the two partners. In sum, Hanna's narrative shows different stances regarding "motility". While younger, she agreed to move and convinced her partner to accept this "motility towards the unknown", and as her circumstances changed, she decided that she needed more control over where and when to move.

7.4 Gender and Motility

The objective of this chapter was to analyse the narratives of highly-skilled migrants in order to assess the role of "motility" in their "family-strategy". I started this chapter by asking the following questions: what kind of "meaning patterns" do the interviewees produce when they talk about settling into a new local space? Do these "meaning patterns" guide them in making decisions on their "care work integration" and once the decisions are made, how do they orient their actions?

To answer these questions, I have distinguished two stances regarding "motility" which influence the "modalities of settling", and by that the "family-strategy". These two stances correspond to two constellations of narratives: while the first one accepts and even valorises "motility", the second one stresses the disruption an acceptance would cause on the "care work integration". Furthermore, while the first stance refers to a "motility towards the unknown", the second stance concerns a "controlled motility". Yet these two stances both deal with different "meaning patterns" and both have concrete consequences for the "care work integration" of the partners. A strong availability to "motility" disrupts a more equal "care work integration" and offers little opportunity to the (female) "secondary-mover" to develop her own career in the labour force. A controlled stance towards "motility" is often the basis of a narrative emphasising the wish of the partners to maintain a more equal "care work integration".

The first stance is conveyed in narratives accepting "motility" and, at the same time, denying it, as under its constraints the partners find it difficult to maintain an equal division of the care work and the paid work. A fruitful way to engage with these narratives is to spot the discrepancies between the narratives and the practices. Thus, the interviewees emphasising a narrative in which "motility" is "oriented towards the unknown" all, in one way or another, refuse the possibility of strong dual career couples, while distancing themselves from the "membership categories" (Sacks 1972; Watson 1983) of the "trailing spouse" and the "breadwinner". They do this in a paradoxical way, acknowledging that two careers should be possible but failing to see that the prioritisation of their own professional career hinders their partner's career, they do not step in to offer support in the care work. This point creates, in the narratives, the impossibility of developing a "dual couple career", as frequent relocations force the partner to continually reorganise her professional activity – keeping in mind that she has to do the care work, too. The paradox lies precisely here, between the practices preventing dual careers and the narratives acknowledging its importance. This insight corroborates the results of studies in sociology of family emphasising that the parity in terms "care work integration" as well as "labour force work integration" in families and couples "exists in the minds but not in the family practices. Notwithstanding these transformations, the couple remains protective of a traditional gendered hierarchy" (Déchaux 2010, 49)[83]. In other words, the change in the discourses is a cosmetic change which does not seem to affect the practices.

The second stance comes across in narratives that adopt a more critical view of "motility", trying to control it and to reduce its impact on the partnership. A "controlled motility" usually implies a strong need for coordination between the partners, whether it be between two professional careers or in the division of the care work. Some interviewees purposefully ignore "motility" in order to find the energy to start from zero after each relocation, thus creating a discrepancy between their narratives and their practices. In Maria's case, for example, she distances herself from the "membership category" (ibid) of the "trailing spouse", as she underlines having been able to find a professional activity after each relocation of her partner. In so doing, she offers another perspective on the "no other alternative narrative", too. The question of whether dual careers are possible becomes, in fact, irrelevant, because the way that reality is shaped through narratives orients the realm of possible reactions. Maria manages to find a position in the labour force after several relocations because she was "lying" to herself, trying to convince herself that this time was the last relocation. Thus, she creates a specific way to give meaning to her settlement in a new local

83 La parité existe donc dans les esprits à défaut d'exister dans les pratiques familiales. En dépit de ses transformations, le couple reste le conservatoire d'un ordre sexuel traditionnel (Own Translation).

space: Maria will probably relocate again for the sake of her husband's career. In other words, "motility" is a concept oriented towards the future: it is practiced in the way it is narrated.

In that sense, the interviewees' subjective interpretation of their situation creates "meaning patterns" based on what they perceive to be possible, in a given context, but always tomorrow. Metaphorically, "motility" can be seen as a "horizon concept", one that is always perceived ahead but can never be reached. Thus, one can only act by relying on today's interpretation of what tomorrow may be. The narrative guides the action, because it creates the possibility of acting when the outcome of the action is seen as realistic. I also presented a case in which the practice and the narrative tend to align, yet not without tensions, as refusing "motility" also means maintaining the *status quo*, keeping two professional activities in the same local space. Through Lynn's narrative, I showed the effects of the tension between two scales of values, as she has to simultaneously deal between "being a mum" and "being a successful professional". Furthermore, I underlined in this section the changes that occur during the "life cycle" (O'Rand and Krecker 1990), and the ways in which these affect one's attitude towards "motility". Having a high "motility" today does not mean having it forever, as the children and elderly parents of the interviewees usually are or become reasons to aim at a "controlled motility". Thus, I argue that it is necessary to assess the concept of "motility" through the "gender lenses", as dividing care work in a "couple" or an "elementary family" becomes increasingly complex when accepting a "motility oriented towards the unknown".

8 Family-Strategies of Highly-Skilled Migrants

In the first empirical chapter, I dealt with the reactions of highly-skilled migrants after they had made the decision to migrate. I defined several types of moves corresponding to the two types of movers (the "primary-mover" and the "secondary-mover"), from a perspective that acknowledges the partners more than the employer/employee relationship. This "collective approach" stresses that migration implies different challenges for the partners, as specific constraints exist for the "secondary-mover". In the second empirical chapter, I analysed the narratives of the partners and showed that the ways in which they narrate their settlings influence their "care work integration". The partners who stress the importance of "motility" for their professional career tend to develop a traditional and patriarchal way of "doing family", while others, struggling to maintain a more equal division of the tasks between them, describe how they try to control the impacts of "motility" in their daily lives. Hence, I have developed two narrative stances regarding "motility", showing that the attitude towards a further move is a key to understanding the way in which the partners integrate the care work and organise their "modalities of settling". I have shown the consequences of their decision to relocate as well as the meaning they give to their settling, but I have not spoken, so far, about possible forms of "family-strategies" that appear in different cases. This is the objective of the third and final empirical chapter: to distinguish forms of "family-strategies" corresponding to different ways of "doing family" on the move.

8.1 Conceptualising the Family-Strategies

After considering the types of moves of the "primary-mover" and the "secondary-mover" ("expat-move" or "local-move" associated with "total-move" or "half-move") (chapter 6) and their narrative stances on "motility" (chapter 7), I have developed three forms of "family-strategies". These correspond to specific ways of "doing family" on the move at a given time in the biographies of the partners and ultimately emerge out of the empirical cases. Table 6 shows how and under which specific circumstances these "family-strategies" emerge. Each form of "family-strategy" is related to a typical constellation of moves and specific ways of making sense out of it. This model is not causal but rather emphasises the most common pattern for each combination. When a "primary-mover" performs an "expat-move" while the "secondary-mover" reacts with a "total-move", very often

Table 6 Conceptualising the Family-Strategies through the Different Types of Move. Source: Own elaboration

		Types of Move of the Primary-Mover	
		Expat-Move	**Local-Move**
Types of Move of the Secondary-Mover	Total-Move	Motile Family-Strategy	Local Family-Strategy
	Half-Move	Mobile Family-Strategy	Mobile Family-Strategy

the partners develop a narrative valorising "motility": I describe this as a "motile family-strategy". When the "primary-mover" performs a "local-move" while the "secondary-mover" still performs a "total-move", the narrative is, in most of the cases, anchored and I speak of a "local family-strategy". When the "secondary-mover" coordinates their professional activity with that of the "primary-mover", introducing the type of the "partner-coordinated mover", the narratives emphasise mobility as a way of coordinating the partnership; I call this a "mobile family-strategy".

It should be stressed that the various forms of "family-strategies" correspond to the combination of moves and the narratives produced to describe the relocation at a given time through the biographies of the respondents. I am not creating boxes to classify the respondents once and for all, but rather I have developed a framework that explains multiple forms of "integration" between the care work and the work in the labour force. The "family-strategies" are flexible and dynamic, as the partners continuously adapt them to their circumstances. In other words, the partners may very well switch from one "family-strategy" to another several times. The "family-strategies" change over time and are subject to conflict, as the interests of the partners are not always aligned. In sum, I conceptualise the ways in which highly-skilled migrants integrate professional career(s) and family life by analysing not only the relationships between different types of moves but also the ways in which they perceive their relocation. This approach combines the results of the two first empirical chapters but add a biographical perspective to emphasise the dynamics of the "family-strategies".

8.2 Motile Family-Strategy

The "motile family-strategy" corresponds to a "primary-mover" performing an "expat-move" (being supported by the employing company) linked with a "secondary-mover" who reacts with a "total-move" (facing the challenges of the type of the “partner-initiated mover”). The support of the company is extended to the “partner-initiated mover” and the children for the sake of the “primary-mover’s motility”, though this does not mean that the “secondary-mover” is “motile”, too. She is restricted in her “motility” precisely because of the “motility” of the “primary-mover” – because of the need of the “primary-mover” to maintain his capacity to be mobile for the sake of the employing company. In other words, the support of the company encompasses all the members of an “elementary family” in order to safeguard the “motility” of the “primary-mover”. This situation gives the partners the incentive to develop “motile modalities of settling”, which include, for instance, choosing an international school for their children instead of a local public one.

As we shall see, the “motile family-strategy” involves a traditional division of the tasks within an “elementary family”, as the “partner-initiated movers” are nearly always women and they often do not work in the labour force, or they struggle to find a new professional activity after the relocation (6.5.2 Unique Challenges of a Partner-Initiated Mover, 159). Instead, they do the unpaid care work, including (1) the care work for the children as well as the housework, and (2) the “homemaking” in a new local space (like finding a new house, finding a school for the children, dealing with the administration, etc.). While the company offers support for the settling process, the “partner-initiated movers” must sort out the daily unpaid care work by themselves. We shall see that this “family-strategy” does not rely much on the nation-stated “family policies” (5.2.1 Family Policy in the two Regions, 103) or on the “hidden economy of kinship” (3.2.2 The Hidden Economy of Kinship, 59), but more on an “expat-bubble” (Fechter 2007a) and a traditional division of the tasks within the “elementary family”. I identify three core aspects to describe the “motile family-strategy”: the prioritisation of one professional career over the other, the unpaid care work of the “partner-initiated mover”, and the support of the company, which allows the children to receive a private education and at the same time integrates the parents into specific networks of support.

8.2.1 Prioritising one Career

Pedro and Marta met in Barcelona where they both studied. He graduated in business administration and she in industrial psychology and they finished their studies at the same time. Pedro received an offer to work as an auditor in Germany, and as he told me, “Marta said very quickly that she would be very happy to embark on the venture” (Pedro, 50yrs, married). So, Pedro performed an “expat-move”; he was the “primary-mover”. Marta followed him through a "total-move"; she was the "partner-initiated mover". They spent two years in Germany, where Marta did not work in the labour force but took German language courses while Pedro had his first professional experience. They started to prioritise Pedro's career. Pedro's father was German and Pedro spoke German, and having professional opportunities there, their strategy was to develop the conditions for a long-term stay in Germany; hence, it was important for Marta to learn German, too. After two years, Pedro's employer offered him a position in New York which they accepted, because it was their "dream to live in such a city" (Pedro, 50yrs, married). Thus, their second relocation happened according to the same configuration: Pedro was the "primary-mover" performing an "expat-move" and Marta the "partner-initiated mover" still prioritising Pedro's career.

In New York, Marta found employment for the United Nations. At that point, the "family-strategy" changed because they decided to stay longer in New York, thus starting to prioritise Marta's career. When Pedro was asked to come back to Spain, it was too early for her to leave; she did not want to resign as she wanted to maximise her first professional experience. Besides, working for the United Nations gave her a "motile" trade. Marta and Pedro saw it as an opportunity to have two professional careers that they could more easily coordinate. Thus, Pedro declined to return to Spain even though there was no longer a position for him in his company in New York. He resigned and began to seek employment in the labour force, as they had decided to remain in New York. This shows that once the "partner-initiated mover" finds a position after a relocation, the "family-strategy" is subject to increased negotiations as the professional interests diverge, as these interests are dynamic and sometimes conflicting. After a few months of seeking employment, Pedro found a position in the consumer goods company for which he still works today. In total, they spent six years in New York and this stay coincided with a reprioritisation of their two careers.

However, two nearly simultaneous events were to reverse the prioritisation of the two careers once again, giving Pedro a decisive advantage: his employer offered him "a great position" in Switzerland, while Marta became pregnant with triplets and stepped back from the labour force in order to do the care work for the newly arrived babies. The arrival of children is a "critical moment" (Riaño et al. 2015) which can decisively affect the "family-strategies", especially when it coincides with a relocation. Marta had to deal with the combined challenges of being a "partner-initiated mover" and having an increased load of care work in the "elementary family". For the "partner-initiated movers", this combination makes it difficult to find employment in the labour force, because they are mostly alone doing the care work. In other words, the load of care work is too important to be coordinated with a professional activity without any support. When

Marta and Pedro arrived in Switzerland, neither she nor he had any relatives or knew anyone who could help them with the care work. When I asked Pedro about the support they receive from their parents or relatives, he told me that they go to visit them during their holidays or that their parents sometimes come to visit them:

> We always go in the summer at least for a week if not two and then we go easily during Easter or any other weekend we will be there anyway. It is what we do mostly. They also come here. So, I would say they also come once or twice a year (Pedro, 50yrs, married).

Thus, they cannot rely on the "hidden economy of kinship" because their own parents and relatives are not there. While in other types of "family-strategy", the partners often try to develop a more coordinated relationship with their relatives in order to be able to receive help with the childcare, this is not the case for those who develop a "motile family-strategy". Moreover, the children were born shortly after Marta's arrival in Switzerland and at that time she was not employed in the labour force. Therefore, she was not entitled to a maternity leave and could not find a day care centre. This means that she was completely out of the labour force, having to do all the care work for the children without external support, which gave her no chance of joining the labour force for a time. Thus, she was not included in the nation-stated "family policy". This situation is common amongst the partners developing a "motile family-strategy" and is emphasised by what one respondent called the "vicious circle of day care":

> In order to be on the priority list [for a day care centre in the Geneva region], the two parents must work in the labour force. But, for the two parents to be able to work or to seek employment in the labour force, you need time. If you do not have a place at the kindergarten, then you do not really have time [to seek employment in the labour force] (Christophe, 37yrs, married).[84]

The "partner-initiated movers" typically arrive in a new country without a position in the labour force. Thus, they are not prioritised when it comes to receiving a place in a day care centre. For the "partner-initiated movers", a wide range of support for the childcare is out of reach; there is no formal support and no "hidden economy of kinship". Under these conditions, they usually do not have the time to seek employment in the labour force. On top of this, as I will show in

84 Pour être prioritaire, il faut que les deux travaillent mais pour vraiment travailler ou chercher un boulot il faut avoir du temps et si on n'a pas de place à la crèche ben on ne peut pas vraiment avoir de temps (Own Translation).

the next subchapter the "partner-initiated movers" do another type of invisible care work in the context of a relocation: "homemaking".

The only person who can help is the male partner. Marta's husband did not help her because he was (over)working for the company, and being paid very well, as he told me, which created a strong "hierarchy of position" (7.2.1 Structural Constraints, 187). This is a central point because the narrative of the "hierarchy of position" justifies the "motile family-strategy" and opens the way for an undisputed division of the tasks. The combination of young children – significantly increasing the load of care work in the "elementary family" – and a relocation for the sake of the husband's career is disastrous for a balanced prioritisation of the careers: it creates a "path-dependency", as the more a career is prioritised, the harder it is for the other partner to challenge it. I do not want judge Pedro and Marta, or their division of tasks and the way they organise their "elementary family". Rather, I want to show how, for Marta, all the support she could receive became unavailable because when they relocated she was in the position of a "partner-initiated mover". The changes in a "family-strategy" can also go in the direction of a "sedimentation" of the division of the tasks, being reinforced over time. Though I have emphasised that the "family-strategies" are flexible and can change, this may not always be the case. The "family-strategies" may be flexible while the partners do not have the increased care work of raising children (as was the case when Pedro and Marta were living in New York), to then become much more rigid when children are involved.

This is similar to what West and Zimmermann (1987) understand as the construction of an "essentialisation of gender", as "once the differences have been constructed, they are used to reinforce the 'essentialness' of gender" (1987, 137). I witnessed similar process in the context of "doing family". When I speak of a "sedimentation" of the division of the tasks, I want to underline that once the prioritisation of one career becomes too strong, it is used to reinforce the stability of the division of the tasks between the partners. A few years later, Pedro and Marta moved from Switzerland to Great Britain, as Pedro was climbing up the company's hierarchy, investing a lot of time in the labour force work. Again, Marta did not work in the labour force in London but did the unpaid care work for the family. Pedro and Marta have now been back in Switzerland for some years and the prioritisation of Pedro's career is not questioned anymore (Figure 18). Though Marta has returned to a paid position in the labour force and they have found a day care arrangement for the children, the prioritisation of his career is definitive, I argue.

Frequent relocations favour the prioritisation of one career over the other and create a strong "path dependency", as once Pedro is working in the labour force

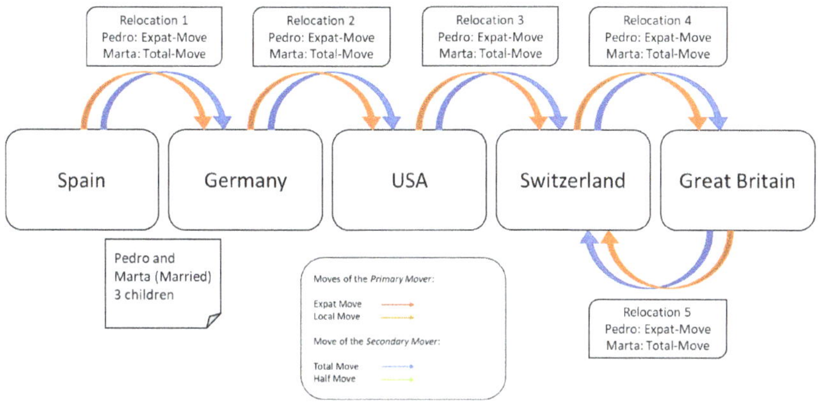

Figure 18 Mobile Trajectory of Pedro and Marta. Source: Own Elaboration

and earning good money while Marta does the unpaid care work for the family, reversing the structure is increasingly difficult, especially when there are three children in the equation and the partners are living in a foreign country. Pedro explained to me how they came to be in this situation:

> The idea was clearly *someone* would have to take care of the children and I think at the moment we embarked in the international career it was going be more *probably* me leading the professional career and she would more be looking for where the opportunity would be arising. I think we were always clear from the beginning that it was very difficult to have a very let's say strong dual career (Pedro, 50yrs, married)[85].

In my interpretation, this quote is revealing. Admittedly the division of the tasks is not going to change anymore, though Pedro phrases it as if it could have been different. After the arrival of the children, Pedro worked in the labour force and Marta did most of the unpaid care work in the family, yet he uses an unspecific language to talk about the division of the tasks within the family. This unspecific language in fact expresses an understatement. His clause "someone would have to take care" implies that there was a 50 percent chance that he could have been the one doing the care work. Metaphorically, it is as if they flipped a coin when the children arrived, and he got heads: "I'll work in the labour force". Yet it is not a 50 percent chance: most cases show that women are nearly always the ones who leave the labour force to do the care work. Thus, it was not "someone" who

85 Own emphasis.

would have to do the care work, but clearly Marta (and this point does not apply to them, but reveals a general trend). In the same sentence, Pedro is clearer when he says that this decision was taken at the moment they "embarked in the international career". Notice that he uses a singular noun here; this makes it seem as though it was never a question for him, as he was always going to be the one to have the career and someone else would do the care work. This line expresses the far-reaching consequences of the choice to embark in an international career, as it exacerbates gender hierarchies within families, especially when it comes to the chances for women to to make progress in their careers. In fact, if their husbands are not extremely supportive and do not agree to share the care work more fairly, it becomes very difficult for them. In chapter 7, I showed that this support is rare because the idea that the "primary-mover" can offer support for the unpaid care work is very often absent.

It is not a coincidence that Pedro continued to work in the labour force while Marta did not, as the conditions of international careers favour a traditional division of the tasks when the partners have children, I argue. Marta and Pedro's case is extreme in this sense as they had three children at the same time, with one requiring special medical attention. But that is not all. The fact that none of Pedro or Marta's parents or relatives live nearby – although the amount of care work increased drastically in their "elementary family" – removes the possibility of mobilising the "hidden economy of kinship". The only person who could have helped with the care work was Pedro, but he was working around the clock for the company. This is another social consequence of the "motile family-strategy": the "motility" of the "primary-mover" makes it very difficult for the partner to mobilise the "hidden economy of kinship" to help with the care work. Marta, without formal care, nor informal care, nor non-formal care, is alone to deal with the care work. Being a "partner-initiated mover" and a caregiver, Marta was combining various layers of challenge: she resigned to follow Pedro, but she did not have the time to seek a new position in the labour force because of the care work. This shows how choices regarding mobility contribute to (re)produce gender hierarchies in the professional sphere, and the absence of support in the division of the tasks only exacerbates these problems.

This division of the tasks was unquestioned in the interviews I carried out with the male "primary-movers" living in a family deploying a "motile family-strategy", as frequent relocations favour their professional careers while their partner often withdraws from the paid labour force. The difficulties that the female "partner-initiated movers" face in finding employment in a new local space (which I showed in chapter 6), the increased load of care work in the sphere of the household following a relocation (which I shall develop in the next section), and the interest of the male "primary-mover" in maintaining the *status quo* in the division of the tasks leads them to present their situation as if there were no other way (7.2.2 Career Men and Career Women, 195). The other way would be that men agree to take on a larger share of the care work, which would free some time for the "partner-initiated mover" to seek employment. Yet from the "primary-mover's" perspective, the whole purpose of the relocation is their professional career, and I would argue that it is in their best interests to believe there is no other way. That is why I speak of a naturalisation of the division of the tasks. This is usually accompanied by an ex-post justification which stresses the difficulty of "having a strong dual career" and suggests that "we knew it". Thus, in the case of the "motile family-strategy", the division of the tasks overlaps with the types of the "primary-mover" and the "secondary-mover", creating a prioritisation of one career over the other – a prioritisation which tends to solidify over time. In that sense, the "family-strategy" still changes as it fixes individuals even more deeply in traditional "gender roles".

The arrival of a child is critical when it comes to the "work family integration"; it does not always put an end to the female "partner-initiated mover's" professional activity, but it does reinforce the prioritisation of one career over the other. In fact, it is a pivotal point in the partner's organisation of their "family-strategy". Gender studies speak of a "critical moment". Pedro and Marta's children were born during their first stay in Switzerland; then, they moved to London, to come back to Switzerland a few years later. Marta was not employed in the labour force during their first stay in Switzerland and their stay in London. As Pedro told me:

> That was a very conscious choice to make sure that she was not looking for a job unless there was something which would fit easily with her ability to really take care of the children. … So, the children were born here in Switzerland, so they didn't go to school there and when we were in the UK, they joined the school in the UK, when we came back here [in Switzerland] unfortunately they could not join ISL [International School of Lausanne] at the beginning, so they had to go to St. George school for one year and then they joined ISL (Pedro, 50yrs, married).

This quote shows, once again, the quasi-naturalisation of the "hierarchisation of the careers": it was never going to be him who will do the care work. The first sentence of the quote shows the patriarchy embedded in the narratives justifying a "motile family-strategy". Interestingly, however, even when the hierarchisation is strong, the children's entry into primary school coincided with Marta finding a position in the labour force in Switzerland. Without the "hidden economy of kinship" (informal care) she could only find a position in the labour force once the children were able to join a day care centre (formal care). In the realm of the "motile family-strategy" this day care centre is very often at a private English-speaking primary school, for which the company pays (hence the importance of the support of the company). I will show later on the importance of international schools in the "motile family-strategy". For now, it is enough to note that the coincidence between a day care centre for the children and the professional activity of the "partner-initiated mover" underlines that the prioritisation of one professional career does not mean that the "partner-initiated mover" will never find a position in the labour force again. The absence of appropriate support contributed to Marta being pushed out of the labour force. As soon as private, formal care could be found for the children, Marta had the time to seek and subsequently find employment in the labour force. This does not disrupt the "hierarchy of position" in the family, but I argue that it shows the specific types of support needed in the context of a "motile family-strategy". This support is not part of the "childcare provision" of the public "family policies", but primarily uses the privatised sector of day care provision paid by the company to support the "motility" of their employees.

In this section on the construction of the "prioritisation of one professional career", we saw with Pedro and Marta that before the arrival of the children, they negotiated the integration of their two careers in the labour force in different ways. Admittedly they favoured Pedro's professional career for the first relocations, yet Marta managed to find an occupation in New York and they decided to stay longer there, emphasising the prioritisation of her career for a time. Nevertheless, when the children come, it is nearly always the woman who stops – at least for a time – her work in the labour force. In some cases, she only reduces this work in order to have the time to do the care work for the child. Either way, the man's career is still prioritised over woman's. Truth be told, the "motile family-strategy" is another example in which the result of many gender studies is confirmed: women do most of the unpaid care work when the load of care work in the family rises (World Economic Forum, 2016: 31). It is still very often the woman who takes up the "second shift" at home (Hochschild and Machung, 1989) after the arrival of children. In this context, the "motile family-strategy" depicts a non-shared "collective work family integration": a traditional and patriarchal division of the tasks to integrate work in the labour force and the "elementary family". This comes with a naturalisation of the "gendered roles" within a family which overlaps with the "gender binaries" I presented in the state of the art as well as the types of the "primary" and the "secondary movers". This situation has little to do with the level of education of the partners. In fact, in many cases both spouses had attained comparable degrees.

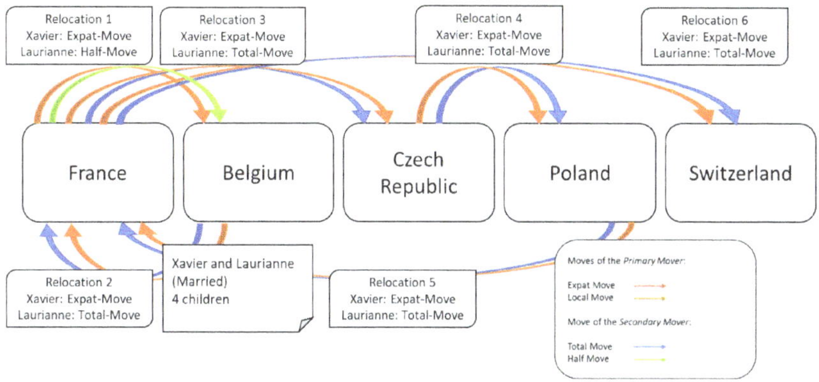

Figure 19 Mobile Trajectory of Xavier and Laurianne. Source: Own Elaboration

8.2.2 Homemaking and Caregiving

The "motile family-strategy" draws on a traditional division of the tasks, as the women do most of the care work while the men are active in the labour force. In this section, I will explain the specificities of the care work done by the "partner-initiated movers" as they face an increasing amount of care work that stems directly from the experience of "doing family on the move". I will show that this supplementary work is usually invisible but necessary. Importantly, this work provides a crucial support which contributes to the success of the professional careers of the male "primary movers". The case of Xavier and Laurianne is striking in this regard. Both are French, married more than 25 years ago, and they have four children. Together, they have lived in five different countries and relocated six times. Figure 19 summarises the history of the various relocations they have undertaken together.

In their "family-strategy", the configuration of the moves is almost always the same, introducing Xavier as a "primary mover" performing "expat-moves" and Laurianne as a "partner-initiated mover". Theirs is a constellation of moves which displays the "motile family-strategy", according to my conceptualisation. As in Pedro and Marta's case, the exception to this configuration is to be found in one of their first relocations, when Laurianne continued to work for her former employer after they relocated from France to Belgium, a "half-move" according to my conceptualisation. We shall see that in their case, too, the arrival of the first child coincided with an irreversible push towards a strong prioritisation of the husband's professional career. Xavier is a general manager in a pharmaceutical corporation and made a steep upward career move in the industry, taking him close to becoming the CEO of the company. In contrast, Laurianne does most of the care work – she has raised four children between five different countries, having relocated at least two times per decade – but she does not work in the labour force. In fact, it would have been impossible for Xavier to have such an upward mobile professional career, as well as having four children, without Laurianne doing the care work for the family. As Xavier told me during his interview, Laurianne took on the "stewardship" of the family:

> When you have a family, the success of mobility is a tacit agreement between the spouses. That is to say that the other must be perfectly convinced as well as trusting the spouse. Unfortunately, at the beginning she worked one year or two in Belgium and then we moved to the South of France and from that moment we made a life choice, we knew that I would probably have this life and she, if she agreed/ it meant that we defined our priorities. Our priorities were that we wanted children, several children and to be mobile. It meant that one of the two of us had to take care of the stewardship of the family and she did it for many years (Xavier, 48yrs, married)[86].

Xavier speaks of trust and conviction to underline the responsibilities they took on together. He told me about being a practicing Catholic, going to mass regularly, which supports the way he describes the "elementary family" as a basis for their mobility and their marriage as a pact underlying their "family-strategy". He does not see his partner as a burden but rather as an ally[87]. This means that he holds the professional career and is responsible for maintaining the living standards of the family. In his view, Laurianne has responsibilities too. Her responsibilities are the care work for four children and himself abroad, which concretely means "enabling family" in a foreign context. He proposed to me a

86 Quand on a une famille, la réussite de la mobilité c'est vraiment un accord tacite entre les conjoints. C'est à dire qu'il faut que l'autre soit parfaitement convaincu aussi, fasse confiance, en l'occurrence, c'est ce qui s'est passé, mon épouse m'a fait confiance. Au début elle a malheureusement travaillé en Belgique un an ou deux et puis on est parti dans le Sud de la France et à partir de là on a fait un choix de vie, on savait que moi j'allais sans doute vouloir avoir cette vie-là et donc elle, si elle était d'accord, ça voulait dire qu'on définissait nos priorités et en fonction de ça, nos priorités ça a été on voulait des enfants et avoir des enfants plusieurs et être mobile, ça veut dire qu'il faut que l'un des deux assure l'intendance et elle a assuré l'intendance pendant de nombreuses années (Own Translation).

87 We shall see later in this chapter the case of the divorced couples. No doubt that if Xavier and Laurianne would divorce, the alimony that he would have to pay would be substantial.

traditional view of the family which fits well with the contemporary career of a business manager. I shall come back to this apparent paradox in the conclusion, as it is a central element of the "motile family-strategy".

Laurianne and Xavier's case corresponds with the typical "collective work family integration" of couples developing a "motile family-strategy". In this context, the care work of the female "partner-initiated mover" is crucial for the male "primary-mover" as it allows him simultaneously to be mobile, to have a developing career, and to experience the joys of family life. But what does this so-called stewardship involve? In their seminal study, Hochschield and Machung (1989, 30) speak of three spheres of work: job, children, and housework. The 'partner-initiated mover' has a specific experience in each of the three spheres. I described the unique challenges that this partner faces in the labour force in chapter 6, and I will speak here of the challenges concerning the children and the housework. Unfortunately, I did not interview Laurianne, and so I will present the case of Lara and François to provide more insights about the care work of the "partner-initiated mover". The housework is specifically tied to "homemaking".

Lara and François (Gender Imbalance, 160) have been married for more than 25 years. He is an IT specialist working for an agro-food multinational corporation and was relocated to Saudi Arabia, Russia, and India. In each of these relocations Lara was the "partner-initiated mover" and each time she struggled to find a position in the labour market. This is how she describes what "homemaking" is about:

> In general, you are transferred as a cell. You arrive and "monsieur", the next day, goes to the office and you're there, I must find something to eat .... The rest, the facilities, the housing, it is "madame" who will manage.... You are looking for a school and they [the company] pay for it. You put your kid where you can (Lara, 61yrs, married)[88].

"Homemaking" is at the core of an iterative process happening when the partners relocate on multiple occasions, as the same array of problems and questions is repeated time and again with each relocation. The "partner-initiated movers" need to find a new school, eventually find a nanny, settle into the new house, carry out the administrative tasks related to the move, and so on. Though the company supports them, it is the female "partner-initiated mover" who does the actual care work, including supervising furniture removals for the move or

88 En général, t'es transférée comme une cellule. T'arrives, monsieur, le lendemain part au bureau et toi t'es là, faut que je trouve à bouffer .... Le reste, les installations, le logement, ma foi, c'est madame qui va se débrouiller .... L'école c'est toi qui la cherche et eux ils la payent. Tu mets ton gamin où tu peux quoi (Own Translation).

looking for a new school for the children. The straightforward "expat-move" of the "primary-mover" hides, in fact, the invisible work of the "partner-initiated mover", who must manage and sort things out by herself. It is not a "frictionless mobility" but a "differently tracked mobility", as Favell (2014, 136) points out. Several times during the interview, Lara mentioned that the company helps and provides information, and yet the support is perceived as a costly burden by the employees of the company. Very quickly, the "partner-initiated movers" feel that their problems and questions are not well received, at least according the narratives I have collected. This is how Lara describes the situation:

> It is in their best interests that we figure out our problems by ourselves very quickly. We are cheaper when we solve our problems by ourselves (laugh) than when we are completely lost (Lara, 61yrs, married)[89].

The "homemaking" is a time-consuming kind of care work which the "partner-initiated movers" usually do alone for the most part. Furthermore, the "home-making" work is a supplementary kind of work which comes on the top of the usual housework, such as cleaning the house, doing the laundry, ironing, grocery-shopping, or cooking.

When it comes to childcare work, the organisation of the daily routine and the organisation of time dominate, as the "partner-initiated movers" are usually the only one to do it. Lara always tried to work in the labour force when she was a "partner-initiated mover", but in some places, it was simply not possible because of the constraints of the "caregiving" for their son, Julien. She explained to me how, in New Delhi, she could have worked in an embassy, but the distances between their flat, the international school, and the embassy were too far, so she had to decline the offer from the embassy. Finding a school and/or a day care arrangement for the children is already a challenge on its own. I shall develop this point in depth in the next section.

In this configuration, in which the female "partner-initiated mover" does most of the care work, the "primary-mover" can fully dedicate himself to his activity in the labour force, which gives him an important "mobile capital" (Urry 2007) or, to put it in other words, allows him to be "motile"; this contributes strongly to his successful mobile professional career as he can dedicate himself to being "efficient" immediately after a relocation. The interviewees developing a "motile family-strategy" speak regularly of the family, the central unit for mobility, as a team. The family is a relocatable unit and its members follow the

89 Ils ont intérêt à ce qu'on se démerde très vite. On leur coûte moins chère en se démerdant (rire) qu'en étant complètement paumée (Own Translation).

lead of the "primary-mover", as they all move together, knowing that they could not do it without the crucial care work of the "partner-initiated mover".

8.2.3 Company's Support

Another characteristic of the "motile family-strategy" is the support of the company. In fact, without the support of the company, a "motile family-strategy" would not be sustainable in the long run, as it is a financially expensive strategy. This means that a "motile family-strategy" usually implies that the "primary-mover" holds an "expatriate contract". In chapter 6, I showed how the company can help the "partner-initiated mover" to find a position in the labour force. I mentioned, for instance, companies paying for a career coach or developing dual career networks (see Company's Support for the "Secondary-Mover's" Inclusion in the Labour Force, 157 and Dual career Network, 158). In fact, this is a first form of support, explicitly aimed at helping the "partner-initiated movers" to find a position in the labour force after a relocation. Yet amongst the couples relying on a "motile family-strategy", it is rare that both partners hold a position in the labour force, for all the reasons we have just seen. I argue that there are two other types of support which are nearly systematically present when it comes to the "motile family-strategy": the support to relocate and the financial support for the schooling of the children. I will deal with both of them in the current subchapter.

g. Support to Relocate

In chapter 6, I argued that the company's support is not disinterested, but rather aims to maintain the "motility" of the "primary-mover" (6.4.1 Expat-Move, 149). Pedro and Marta, Xavier and Laurianne, as well as Lara and François all received extensive support from their respective companies during their multiple relocations. The support to relocate (covered in this subchapter) usually implies three main areas: (1) help to settle straight after a relocation, (2) paid access to a relocation office (which will help the partners to find accommodation for their stay other than a corporate flat), and (3) administrative support to deal with the various state bodies. For the company, this means paying for most of the relocation process. Pedro and Marta's case demonstrates the process by which the company provided them with a corporate flat for their first months in Switzerland:

> The company has temporary flats that they make available, so you arrive the first day and they give you straight/ maybe the first day you go to an hotel but the second day you have your flat, so they give you the keys. … You have time to find your own apartment

> and even if you were not able to find it, you can rent that one out for some time until you find your apartment. So normally, they make you available the apartment, they provide you a car, so they really provide everything that you need at the beginning to get started (Pedro, 50yrs, married).

Pedro's quote underlines how the company contributes to creating the *capacity of being mobile*, i.e. being "motile". This implies not only financial capital, but also property. The company provides significant help to allow the partners to relocate quickly without having to worry too much about finding, for instance, a new flat. In fact, this practice allows the "primary-mover" to be directly available for the company, reducing the amount of time required for the move to a minimum. This is especially true if the "partner-initiated mover" does the care work tasks of "homemaking" and "care giving".

The support of the company in the Geneva region and the Frankfurt region is especially important when it comes to finding accommodation as, in both regions, the housing market is tight, if not saturated, and so employees benefit significantly from the support of the company in softening the relocation. The company not only provides a flat for the first months, but also offers the services of a relocation office to find new accommodation. Under these conditions, Xavier and Laurianne moved to the Geneva region and decided to buy a house there. They wanted to settle in the region for the long term, showing once more the dynamics of the "family-strategies". As Xavier told me:

> Now, I would say that I am trying to communicate to the company that I would like to stay here [in the Geneva region] several years. Yet I am not immune to the possibility that someone will come to me in one year and a half and tell me: "Xavier, we have a mission for you in the United States at the company's headquarters and we would like to send you". If this happens, I will have to think (Xavier, 50yrs, Married)[90].

Xavier is not sure how long he will be able to stay in the Geneva region, but he is still trying to convince his employer to let him do so by communicating informally within the company. Their decision to buy a house also implies a decreased "motility" and is thus, as Xavier perceives it, a risk. This shows that Xavier and Laurianne do not necessarily want the state of "motility" in the future. Although they want to settle for a longer period in Geneva, the risk that Xavier's

---

90 Je dirais, aujourd'hui, j'essaie de communiquer en interne que, moi, j'ai envie de rester ici plusieurs années mais je ne suis pas à l'abris qu'il y a une personne qui vienne me voir, dans un an et demie, et qui me dise "Xavier, on a une mission aux Etats-Unis au siège et on aimerait bien que ce soit toi". Bon là, il faudra que je réfléchisse (Own Translation).

employer may ask him to relocate somewhere else will always exist. They live in a liminal state, implying uncertainty regarding a further move. Nevertheless, when they first arrived, the company offered Xavier and Laurianne the services of a relocation office. For Xavier, the relocation office was not so important in finding the property, as they could have found one by themselves, he told me, but it was particularly valuable because it offered a guarantee of reliability. This increased their chances of obtaining the property. This is how he summarises how the relocation office helps employees and their partners to settle in the Geneva region:

> They [the people working for the relocation agency] take care of the logistics of the move and since it is an agency, often the renter or seller feels reassured. They say: 'it's serious.' This facilitates the relationship because when you make contact directly, you can always have people saying: 'who is this person?' 'How can I trust this person?' So passing through a third party helps, but the price did not change (Xavier, 50yrs, married)[91].

The company helps in two respects. First, it allows a more gradual relocation by providing a corporate flat and/or a hotel room. Second, it provides references. A relocation agency creates credibility and offers local contacts. Furthermore, working for the company is also a guarantee in and of itself.

The third type of support that the company offers is administrative support to deal with the local state bodies. Very often, this service is provided by the company itself, which has the know-how internally. In fact, the big companies where I did the interviews usually have a full service that specialises in the mobility, the relocations, and the settling of their employees. Pedro speaks of a kind of support that consolidates the administrative work of settling in a new country into a simple procedure:

> They prepare everything for you, your work permit and everything. They tell you: 'listen, you need to go to the commune on Monday right 8 o'clock and here are the papers and you go and you sign and present and you are good to go' (Pedro, 50yrs, married).

In all these examples, the company offers concrete support, either through internal resources (corporate flats, know-how) or by mobilising other organisations specialised in facilitating the mobility of highly-skilled migrants. The use of private, for-profit organisations which helped the respondents to settle in a new

91 Ils [les employés de l'agence de relocation] font la logistique et puis comme c'est une agence, souvent ça permet à la personne qui loue ou qui vend d'avoir des garanties. Elle se dit : 'c'est sérieux,' ça facilite le rapport (…) parce que quand vous faites en direct et bien il y a des gens qui peuvent toujours dire : 'c'est qui cette personne?' 'Quelles sont les garanties de cette personne?' Donc passer par un tiers ça vous aide mais c'est tout, le tarif il n'a pas changé (Own Translation).

local space also creates a lucrative market in which these private organisations are competing. In other words, these companies are doing business by offering services to highly-skilled migrants, and based on the ideas of Groutsis, Broek, and Harvey (2015), I suggest that such migrants operate within a 'migration industry' (Tissot 2018). In my article, I distinguish three main areas of support: the basic need to relocate (also covered in this subchapter), the support for the partner to find a position in the labour force (6.5.5 Access to the Labour Force, 171) and the schooling of the children, mostly through international schools (discussed in the next subchapter). These are the three domains in which the "migration industry" supports highly-skilled migrants.

To summarise, then, the employing company lends support by providing information, furnishing a flat, and offering access to private organisations such as relocation offices or outplacement agencies; yet in most of the empirical cases, the contribution of the "partner-initiated mover" to the resettlement is also crucial. In fact, one could say that it is a combination of the two, the unpaid care work of the female "partner-initiated mover" and the resources provided by the company, that creates the "motility" of the "primary-mover". However, not only do the "partner-initiated mover" and the employing company provide support, but so do other private, for-profit organisations. As we can see, the state of "motility" of the "primary-movers" is maintained by a specific "family-strategy" and a complex network of organisations. These organisations provide concrete support for relocations. Others provide support when it comes to the day care and the schooling of the children. This is the third, last, and most expensive way in which the companies offer financial support: the schooling of the children. The companies provide the means to the parents so that they can afford a type of schooling that maintains the "motility" of the "primary-mover".

h. *International Schools*

The choice of school for the children is a striking aspect of the "modalities of settling" in the "family-strategies". In the "motile family-strategy", the parents decide to send their children to an international school. Two elements are central to this choice: the language of the schooling and the availability of the same curriculum in other countries. This curriculum is usually referred to as "the international baccalaureate". Yet international schools are expensive. One year of tuition fees for one child is approximately 20,000 Euros or 30,000 Swiss francs in an international school (5.2 Contextualising the Lake Geneva Region and Frankfurt Rhine-Main Region, 118). The support of the company is important in allowing the family to send their children to international schools – especially when there is more than one child involved. This shows that "motility" is financially costly. Besides, the choice of the school creates a "path-dependency". It is not easy to change school systems once the decision to go to an international school has been made; this is why some families develop a "motile family-strategy" without being mobile anymore, ending up paying costly tuition fees for an international school, because the children do not have a high enough level of the "local language" to go to a public school.

Usually, the international school is the cornerstone of a "motile family-strategy". It is an important place of social integration for the "partner-initiated mover" who does not work in the labour force, as the school helps to create a community of "expatriates" after a relocation. The school offers an environment and a network of support composed of other parents who can give tips to those who are just arriving. Due to the high tuition fees, the established network is selective; not everybody can afford these types of schools. It helps to connect people with the same social status (though different countries of origin), who are going through the same challenges. As the partners arrive in a new local space not knowing anybody and having to go through the challenges of a relocation, the other parents at the school provide valuable organisational and psychological support. In the cases of "elementary families" that have a "motile family-strategy", the social network around the international school is a central element of their social lives.

Richard and Andrea met at university, both studying international business. They got married, had four children, and have lived in seven different countries. Richard has worked in the pharmaceutical industry for more than 20 years now. Like Pedro and Xavier, Richard is moving up in his career and in his sector (thanks in both cases to the support of their partners). Today, Richard is the "worldwide market president" of the pharmaceutical company which employs him. In Great Britain, he started as a sale representative at the bottom of the hierarchy, and through his many relocations he climbed the ladder within the industry. After a few years in Great Britain, he was offered a country manager position in Chile. At that point, Richard and Andrea made a key decision about the way their "family-strategy" was going to look for the rest of their careers. She resigned from her position to join him on "this adventure". At that time, they still did not have any children. During their time in Chile, Andrea wrote her dissertation and travelled extensively in Latin America. They had decided that Richard was going to be the "primary-mover" performing "expat moves" and she the "secondary-mover" reacting with "total-moves", expressing once again the sedimentation of the division of the tasks. They both did the same academic course but *he* got the offer to go to Chile and they decided to go there together.

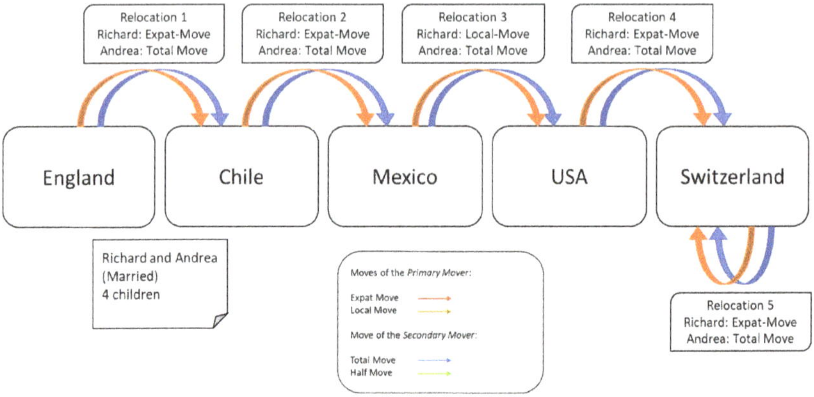

Figure 20 Mobile Trajectory of Richard and Andrea. Source: Own Elaboration

I interviewed only Richard and this is how he recalls this crucial moment of their careers:

> She was working for *** in the marketing in the head office and said: "Ok! I am good to go! So, I can give up work now and I'll come with you". … So, wherever they would send us, we said we are open to mobility. So, at that early stage we were very open to move because we've both done an international business degree (Richard, 48yrs, married).

When Richard says that they were "open to move", he means that he did not have a problem with relocating his "elementary family": both partners accepted this distribution of the tasks. Apparently, they "solved" the conflict related to the division of the tasks; at least, this is the way Richard "displays" it. I have shown in chapter 7 that this does not imply an absence of conflict or that Andrea did not suffer in the process.

After Chile, they moved to Mexico, the United States, and Switzerland, as the summary of their mobile trajectory shows (Figure 20).

They developed a strategy which makes further relocations easier – because there is only one career to consider. This strategy enhances the "motility" of an "elementary family", a "motile family-strategy", for the sake of the "primary-mover's" career. Choosing an international school for their children stresses the importance they give to their "motility":

> Because we didn't know wherever we would move again. We want to keep it flexible because wherever we would move the international baccalaureate was available so that was one of the key drivers (Richard, 48yrs, married).

Richard and Andrea describe a family in a liminal state between "here" and "somewhere else". The price is the difficulty, if not the impossibility, of maintaining a professional career and living together. Andrea did further studies in personal coaching and is now working part-time in the labour market, yet her main occupation is that of a "care giver" and a "homemaker" for the family as they have four children. Thus, "motility", like mobility, has strong gendered effects (7.4 Gender and Motility, 221). Those families, which are extensively mobile and able to remain "motile", are in many cases organised according to a traditional gender model. In this strategy, the wives represent the "social side" of the "gender binaries", while the husbands are the "economic ones". These "elementary families" are able to cope with mobility and children only because the female partners are the caretakers.

In Richard and Andrea's case, the international school is the central place where they have developed their social network and friendships during their stay in Switzerland. They developed this network mostly because of Andrea's reliance on it, for Richard works more than full time. They find it difficult to engage with locals, as they do not speak French fluently and thus they do not "experience the same thing" (Richard, 48yrs, married). As a result, they have invested much more time in the group of parents gravitating around the international school. As Richard told me:

> Yes, for all the new arrivals at school we organised a barbecue where we bring in 15 families and they just get to know each other for the first time before school starts. … My wife is on the parents and teaching association, the PTA, so she is very active in school now because we've been here for some years. She is very well, so she very much takes a leadership position in that school community, of integrating people (Richard, 48yrs, married).

Thus, the school is a place that creates contacts among people experiencing the same challenges. Yet the turnover in the group is high as there is always a family leaving and a new one arriving. Many of the interviewees who develop a "motile family-strategy" prefer the social networks constructed around "fellow expatriates", as they all know that today's situation is only temporary. "We have no time to break the ice", as one of the interviewees told me (Nick, 54yrs, married). The parents at the international school offer a social network of people who are able to give tips to those who have just relocated. This network is exclusive and helps to create a sense of a community after a relocation. When I asked the partners who rely on a "motile family-strategy" where they create their social contacts, their answers referred systematically to two places: the company where one of the partners works and the international school that the children attend. In some rare cases, the respondents also mentioned social websites like *Internations*[92]. Thus I understand the social relations of the families who have a "motile family-strategy" as an "expat-bubble" (Fechter 2007a) which is strongly structured around the poles of colleagues and children, reproducing again a "gender binary". This "bubble" works as a forum for social contacts, support, and advice for the newly arrived family.

Yet some families arrive with a "motile family-strategy" and end up staying much longer than expected, and in these cases they may adopt a "local family-strategy". In other words, not all stay in this "bubble" because those remaining in the same local area for the long term may develop other networks elsewhere. The "path-dependency" created by sending the children to an international school is high, however. Some consider sending their child to a local school, but the language and the fear of not being able to help or that the child will not succeed in a local school often convince the parents to stay with an international school – at high cost when the support of the company is not available anymore.

i. Summary of the "Motile Family-Strategy"

A "motile family-strategy" enables the partners to raise children abroad while the "primary-mover" is "motile"; yet, the "partner-initiated mover" typically has problems finding a place in the labour force. In fact, the "motility" of the "partner-initiated mover" is low, because it is constrained by the "motility" of the "primary-mover". Cangià (2018) speaks of a state of "precarity", describing the feelings of one of her respondents as follows: "Tina tries to make sense of ambivalent feelings, such as the frustration, impatience and sense of uncertainty regarding her husband's unknown next work destination and her immobility, alongside the expected excitement associated with moving to a new country on the other hand" (Cangià 2018, 25). The constant prioritisation of one partner's career creates a state of "precarity" for the "partner-initiated movers", as they are constantly in the difficult situation of creating a provisional arrangement, whether it be in the labour force or regarding the care work. And, this leads (in most cases) to a traditional model of the "elementary family" in which the male is the "breadwinner" while the female is the "homemaker/caretaker". The "work-family integration" is gendered, as the partners prioritise one career over the other; the woman does not work in the labour force, but in the sphere of the household, while the man is professionally active. A striking similarity amongst the partners developing a "motile family-strategy" is the rarity with which the

92 Website of Internations, retrieved April 13, 2018, from www.internations.org

partners mobilise non-formal care. Furthermore, the seemingly disruptive consequences of *the availability of the "secondary-movers" to the "motility" of the "primary-movers"* restrains the partners' capacity to mobilise non-formal care. In the previous chapter, I discussed the case of Maria, who managed to continue to work in the labour force while often relocating by refusing her partner's "motility", or by telling herself that each relocation would in fact be the last relocation (7.3.2 Refusing Motility, 211). By accepting their partner's "motility", the "secondary movers" find themselves in a crippling situation, in which any kind of family organisation not involving a traditional division of the tasks seems useless or unachievable.

This strategy creates a liminal state for all the members of the family. They are stuck between "here" and "somewhere else", making it very difficult for the "secondary-movers" to develop a professional career while caring for the family, as the next move is unpredictable: it could be in two months, two years, or 20 years. This strategy permits a successful career for only one of the partners. This is only possible because the "primary-movers" receive the crucial support of the "secondary-movers". Thus, the "secondary-movers" are a constitutive element of the successful career of the "primary-movers". Far from being a "burden", as they have often been presented in the scientific literature, the "secondary-movers" allow the "primary-movers" to have a successful professional career and to experience the delights and miseries of raising children. Yet the "partner-initiated movers" pay a high-price for this, sacrificing their own professional careers and independence.

In terms of support, a "motile family-strategy" combines the support of private organisations to replace (partially at least) the nation-stated "family policy" and a specific constellation of social networks; some call this constellation an "expat bubble" (Fechter 2007a). These families are (partially at least) excluded from nation-stated "family policies'" such as "maternity leaves" or "childcare provision" and do not have relatives nearby to help with the care work ("hidden economy of kinship"), and so they build a network of peers among other "partner-initiated movers" who get to know one another through company-supported private day care organisations. Through this combination, the strategy can be durable and may potentially survive many relocations. This is not a question of comfort but of making a relocation possible by maintaining the "motility" for the "primary-mover". It does not mean that the "partner-initiated movers" suffer extensively, as raising children abroad as a privileged foreigner can be rewarding, as many interviewees told me, but still the loss of one's independence and work in the labour force is very often a painful experience. A "motile family-strategy" enables further relocations (more easily), enhancing the "motility" of the "primary-mover" because it makes the "elementary family" into a complementary relocatable unit. Yet these families have social contacts and social networks. In other words, they are not an independent unit, as the metaphor of the "nuclear family" might imply. On the contrary, they are integrated in a complex network of support financed by the company. This integration creates the liminal state of "motility" and has deep consequences on the social life of the family. In this context, the international school plays a key role as it brings together families facing similar challenges when they arrive in a new local space. In sum, the "motile family-strategy" implies a clear gendered division of the tasks between a "breadwinner" and a "homemaker/caregiver" which favours a "motile" organisation of the "elementary family", in which the husband can respond quickly to any professional opportunities abroad: an unsettling "modality of settling" facilitating mobility and children but hindering a dual career.

8.3 Local Family-Strategy

The "local family-strategy", on the contrary, emphasises anchoring "modalities of settling", diminishing the "motility" of the "primary-mover." The most common combination of moves leading to this "family-strategy" is a "local-move" of the "primary-mover" while the "secondary-mover" performs a "total-move"; though in some cases the partners develop a "local family-strategy" by staying longer in the region. After 10 years in the same place, for instance, some may want to buy a house where they live; thus, they develop a more anchored "family-strategy" involving stronger bonds with the local space. The "primary-mover" performs an anchoring move, which I call a "local-move", a relocation with little or no support at all from the employing company. He or she works in the labour force and migrates under a local contract. The combination of the two creates more roots with the new local space, making a further move less likely and/or at least more complicated. Compared to the "motile family-strategy", the mobilisation of the local nation-stated "family policy" is more common in the realm of the "local family-strategy". More often, the partners opt for a local school (instead of an international school), as they typically do not receive financial support from the company, being on a "local-contract". In the "motile family-strategy", I showed that the combination of frequent relocations and young children favours the development of only one professional career. In the context of a "local family-strategy", the partners do not face the same combination of challenges. We shall see the cases of partners who receive "parental leaves" and who both managed to stay employed in the labour force. The mobilisation of non-formal care such as nannies or au pairs is also more common than in the "motile family-strategy".

Furthermore, some partners manage to mobilise the "hidden economy of kinship" (informal care). All this increases the capacity of the "secondary-mover" to have the time to seek employment in the labour force, while correspondingly decreasing the "motility" of the "primary-mover". Through a "local family-strategy", the members of an "elementary family" develop a better capacity to mobilise the different kinds of support available when it comes to the care work of the children. This subsequently offers them more possibilities to coordinate two professional careers – though not always. When it comes to the type of accommodation, they may decide to buy a house (instead of renting a furnished flat). The families developing a "local family-strategy" typically do not relocate a lot (anymore). As we shall see, they have different financial means, a different status, and typically no support from the employing company (anymore).

8.3.1 Low Support for the Care Work

Annisa and Adrian (6.5.5 Access to the Labour Force, 171) are both scientists working in biology. Their case shows how the lack of support in "critical places" (Riaño et al. 2015) influences the "family-strategy". They started their studies in biology in Indonesia, since the two of them are Indonesian. They both have a doctorate; Adrian gained his in Australia and Annisa in Germany. After Adrian graduated in Australia, they wanted to live together after years of separation. They decided that he would come to Germany, since she was finishing her PhD there. However, he did not find a position in Germany but in Switzerland – so they decided to move together to Switzerland. They moved and he started his new position in a research institute (Figure 21).

At that time, they were still without children and she sought employment in Switzerland. As we saw in chapter 6, she found a position at the local hospital until the arrival of their first child. When I asked Annisa why she stopped working, this is how she explained their situation:

> It was insane to keep two kids at the *crèche*[93] with that salary, because I wouldn't have anything at the end. It is really expensive and difficult because they were not so many, they are more now but still it is not. It is not sufficient (Annisa, 39yrs, married).

The arrival of children is a tipping point in the "family-strategies". We have already seen this. Without the support of the company, the partners cannot afford an expensive privatised day care and Annisa takes up the domestic work of the "caregiver". In this context, I follow Riaño et al. (2015), who not only speak

93 Kindergarten, in French in the original interview.

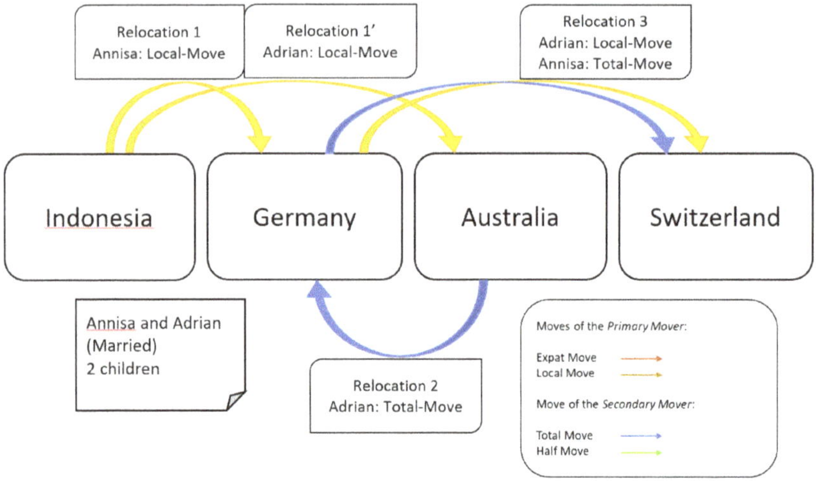

Figure 21 Mobile Trajectory of Annisa and Adrian. Source: Own elaboration

of "critical moments" reproducing gender hierarchies, but introduce the term of "critical places". The combination of a "critical moment" – the arrival of a child – in a "critical place" – the specific location where they were living – led Annisa to withdraw from the labour force to do most of the unpaid care work for the children. She points to the difficulties of finding a day care centre for the children: its costs, and the lack of availability. Though she received a Swiss maternity leave of 18 weeks, she did not find a day care arrangement, which would have allowed her to coordinate work in the labour force and care work. She therefore resigned after the maternity leave. Compared to the "motile family-strategy", the circumstances are different, but the consequences are the same: the female partner is out of the labour force. Annisa's case still contrasts with the respondents mentioned in the subchapter on the "motile family-strategy", none of whom received a maternity leave. This reflects a difference between the "motile" and the "local family-strategy". According to my conceptualisation, the "secondary-movers" in both strategies are "partner-initiated movers" (as they perform a total-move). However, under the constraints of a "motile family-strategy", the "partner-initiated mover" faces several challenges simultaneously and is typically not employed in the labour force when they arrive. Annisa found a professional activity in Switzerland before resigning. It was not the simultaneous challenges but the lack of childcare provision which pushed her out of the labour force.

Moreover, and as I stress throughout this study, the support of the husband is not questioned in either interview, neither with Annisa nor with Adrian. Adrian was not entitled to a paternity leave, as this does not exist in Switzerland; fathers receive only one day off. Without his support, without the support of the employer, without access to the "hidden economy of kinship" – their parents live in Indonesia – Annisa has only the local variation of the national "family policy" available, and this policy favours a traditional model of the family. Thus, Annisa is subject to the local "gendered" constraints of a patriarchal "gender culture" (Pfau-Effinger 1998). Her situation reflects the studies analysing the national Swiss "family policy" as well as its subnational variations (Ferragina and Seeleib-Kaiser 2015; Imhof 2015). Imhoft shows that in the Canton of Vaud, the female partners do the vast majority of the childcare for the children between zero and six years old (2015, 33). Annisa and Adrian are no exception, as Annisa does most of the care work in their "elementary family". Thus, the constraints of the "critical place" have sent Annisa back to domestic work without any remunerated working position, because as she told me, emphasising the lack of childcare options in the region, "I have to wait until they [the children] are older and then I can easily start something" (Annisa, 39yrs, married).

Another example of the impact of the subnational variation of the "family policy" can be seen in the situation of their first son, who just started school. He is enrolled in the public school and has a midday break. As there is no school canteen, one of the parents must be at home at midday. Yet they live in the countryside and the trips back and forth two times a day between the workplace, the school, and home would be extremely time consuming. Even without these midday breaks, Annisa would still have to do the care work for the second younger child. Annisa is frustrated by this situation, and she tells me that even when the two children are old enough to go to the public school, she still does not know how she will deal with this midday break. The very organisation of the day care system creates barriers preventing Annisa from joining the labour force. This point is crucial, as Annisa actually wanted to stay in the labour force and had to resign because she (not he) needed to do the childcare work. We shall see in the next subchapter that in Germany where the "family policy" is different, the parents, as they told me in the interviews, manage to share the care work and the work in the labour force in a different way.

The fact that Annisa is out of the labour force contributes to unsettling their situation in Switzerland. They have been in Switzerland for 10 years, they have bought a house in the countryside, and they both expressed their wish to stay many times during the interviews. They took out a mortgage to buy the house, however, since Annisa cannot work in the labour force, even though she would like to, and thus Adrian is the only member of the "elementary family" who has a paid position. He works on projects that last between two and three years, but their residence permits are linked with his work contract. This is how he presented to me the stressful and precarious situation they are experiencing:

> You can't be unemployed so to speak, to put it whereas now it's tied to your permit. Your permit is tied to your employment, if you cannot continue with your work then you have to leave (Adrian, 41yrs, married).

The whole family-strategy is oriented towards a local settling and relies on Adrian's capacity to maintain his position in the labour force. Their first child just started public school in Switzerland, anchoring the family further in the same local space, as he will learn French at school. I interpret this situation as a "trickle-down" effect of the lack of support from the employing company. They have developed a "local family-strategy" and their situation would become problematic very quickly if Adrian loses his position. A "dual couple career" would safeguard their status in Switzerland, but the lack of support has pushed Annisa back into the sphere of the household. Thus, only one partner can work full-time in the labour force. Their situation differs from that of the families developing a "motile family-strategy" in the sense that any further moves will be more complicated. At the same time, Adrian and Annisa are not sure that they will be legally allowed to stay in the country; their stay relies on Adrian's career as long as they do not have a permanent residence permit – the Swiss C permit. The situation is precarious because they developed a "local family-strategy" without knowing whether they would be able to stay.

When it comes to the integration of work and family, this case shows that the "local family-strategy" and the "motile family-strategy" both generate gendered hierarchies between the partners, though in different ways. Whereas it was the liminal state between here and somewhere else that was the major challenge in the "motile family-strategy", the "local family-strategy" underlines problems linked with lack of support for the partners. The lack of support and/or the lack of (extended) financial means tend to push the "secondary mover" out of the labour force.

8.3.2 Combination of Formal, Informal and Non-Formal Care Support

Let us now contrast Annisa and Adrian's case with that of Alex and Lynn. I have already presented their case twice so I will be brief here (6.2 Migration Triggering: A Collective Approach, 142; 7.3.2 Refusing Motility, 211). As a reminder, Lynn and Alex work for the same company in Germany. They moved from the US to Germany 14 years ago; Lynn had an expatriate contract and Alex a local one. In the first years, they received an expat package, which is over now. Since then, they have both been on "local-contracts" and both have good earnings; from their perspective, finding such conditions following a relocation "does not come up every day" as Lynn told me (Lynn, 51yrs, married). Initially, their plan was to stay only a few years in Germany. Alex stressed during the interview that "we were here 14 years, but the original plan was two or three years" (Alex, 52yrs, married). In other words, what was a "motile family-strategy" at the beginning has progressively become a "local family-strategy": they recently bought a house in Germany and Alex talked to me about selling his flat in the US.

Today, they have a daughter of eight, Mary. Mary was born in Germany and both Lynn and Alex took parental leaves, which allowed them to share the care work that Mary required when she was a toddler. Lynn explained to me that it was a difficult experience for her, but still, but she was still grateful that she had the opportunity to take the time off:

> When I had my child, I had some time off, seven months off, which I never could have had in the States but in Germany you can and I took seven months off to feed my daughter in the beginning (Lynn, 51yrs, married).

In fact, the time of her maternity leave corresponded with important changes within the company. During her maternity leave, one person whom she hired became her boss. Her former boss, who supported her and whom she trusted, no longer worked for the company following her maternity leave. As she told me:

> The guy who had brought me here and I could build my career with and I had a lot of trust with, he was out (Lynn, 51yrs, married).

The situation was personally difficult for Lynn, and she refers to it as the biggest challenge of her professional career. Still, she managed to maintain her position in the labour force and continued to work for the same company during and after her maternity leave. The maternity leave also meant that she kept 80% of her last income during the nine months she was on leave. It certainly helped Lynn and Alex not to spend their savings, which would allow them later on to pay for private formal and non-formal childcare for Mary. Furthermore, Alex took paternity leave for three months. He did not perceive this as a risk or something unusual to do; as he explained:

> I was sure that I was going to be taken back at the agency, I didn't really question that. … People do it all the time, it happens almost all the time, they take this time off (Alex, 52yrs, married).

In other words, he did not feel that he would lose his position in the labour force by taking a paternity leave to do the care work for his daughter. In fact, he was legally protected so that he would not lose his position in the labour force due to his choice to take parental leave. This corresponds to what Pfau-Effinger (1998) called the "gender culture" and shows that the region where the respondents settle does really play a role, favouring or hindering the capacity of the partners to share the increased care work implied by the arrival of a child. Nevertheless, both Lynn and Alex expressed the difficulties of finding a place in a public day care centre; they opted instead for a private one. In fact, Mary has gone to a private day care centre since she was one year old, and she is now going to a bilingual private school that they pay for independently. But it is not an international school, as Lynn told me. Most of the children are German and the school is subsidised by the German state. It follows that the tuition fees are less significant than in an international school. Lynn and Alex decided to send Mary there because of the language skills she would acquire through this school, as it is private German school with a strong focus on English. Indeed, the first four years of teaching are all in English with a German class; it then switches in the fourth grade, with the teaching in German and an English class. This format corresponds to Alex and Lynn's needs, as they want to stay on in the long term in Germany but also want Mary to have a native written and spoken level of English.

They also hired a nanny who takes care of Mary during the day; this is a kind of non-formal care. As I have already mentioned, Lynn and Alex are close to what we can call an "equal" dual career couple. Furthermore, both of their positions in the labour force are demanding. They do not have the time both to continue their professional activities and to do all the care work for Mary, so they hired external help. As Lynn says:

> I mean my husband says to be a modern family these days you need three parents because two isn't enough and I think that's right if you look at a lot of family these days they live close to the grandparents or they have you know have like a live-in uncle or an aunt or they have a nanny like we do or they have an au pair (Lynn, 51yrs, married).

The "work-family integration" of Alex and Lynn contrasts with that of Annisa and Adrian. In the latter, the gender roles fall within the "gender binaries" of a male "breadwinner" and a female "caregiver". In the former, they both have a position and need to delegate a part of the care work to a third person, in their case a nanny. Alex and Lynn's "local family-strategy" requires substantial financial resources because the company does not support them anymore in the way that it would support the partners under an "expat-contract". They compensate for this lack of support by both working in the labour force and by both receiving maternal or paternity leaves. This means that they did not "lose" any income when one of the parents was doing the care work for Mary. Their strategy has allowed them to coordinate two professional careers while raising their daughter. This combination not only includes the mobilisation of (private) formal and non-formal care but also informal care – that is, the capacity to mobilise the "hidden economy of kinship". Actually, when I asked Lynn and Alex about their parents, they both told me that their parents and relatives often come to Germany for extended periods of time. Furthermore, some of Lynn's relatives live in Germany, too. Lynn told me:

> We see them relatively often for the fact they are on the other side of the world. My mum is German, she just spent three and a half months with us and she'll come and spend the summer with us. So, she lives in the States. She is getting older you know, she is almost 80, so I think we will see her more and more here and we bought a home a couple of years ago and we had in mind that we may see more and more my mum. … My husband's family, we see it at least once a year, usually for three to four weeks because they come here. …Alex's parents also come to Germany for extended periods of time (Lynn, 51yrs, married).

Not only does Lynn's mother come often for extended period to live with them, but Alex's parents come quite often to Germany for long visits, too. Moreover, some of Lynn's relatives live in Germany. According to Alex, they can help with the care work, too:

> My wife's family can help with these family things, so they can take Mary for a weekend or you know help babysitting sometimes and things like this (Alex, 52yrs, married).

In Lynn and Alex's case, an extensive network of relatives and parents can help in the care work. They are embedded in an "hidden economy of kinship" which allows them regularly to mobilise informal care. Interestingly, they have consciously developed a "modality of settling" which allows then to mobilise informal care. They have done so by creating a space in their house where relatives can come and live for long period. In other words, it is not that their parents and relatives live nearby (except for Lynn's niece and nephew), but that they have created the conditions to welcome relatives and parents into their home. As Alex told me:

> When we decided that we were going to stay and decided that we were going to buy a place and so I found a place that the layout had not been determined yet and so I could say, you know put a wall here and put a bedroom there and put the bathroom there and we made a place where her mum could stay as long as she wanted. So, the idea would be that she would come and move in with us and live with us now that her husband there had died (Alex, 52yrs, married).

Indeed, it is not only Lynn's mother who comes but also Alex's parents. Thus, Lynn and Alex organise the childcare for their daughter through a combination of different forms of care available to them. They combine formal, informal, and non-formal care. Whereas in the "motile family-strategy", I spoke of a combination of nearly simultaneous challenges ("homemaking", the specific challenges of the "partner-initiated mover", and the "caregiving"); in the "local family-strategy", there are more opportunities to develop a combination of support for the care work. An "elementary family" can more easily sustain a dual career couple and have children, because the care work of "homemaking" is done once and for all, and they do not find themselves in a liminal state anticipating an ever-imminent departure, a state which requires the "secondary-mover" to focus on the care work. The members of the "elementary family" rely on staying for the long term in the local space where they live, knowing that they will not receive the support of the company as the "primary-mover" is not "motile". Therefore, the incomes of the two parents play a central role in their capacity to maintain a dual career couple and the "family policy" helps them to share the care work for their child without losing any income. As a result, the parents have more possibilities to mobilise different types of support for the care work. The contrast between Alex and Lynn and Annisa and Adrian is striking. From this perspective, pursuing a dual couple career while developing a "local family-strategy" is either enabled or hindered by the "family policies".

That said, Alex and Lynn are also bound to the region where they live, because they both have good positions there. Since they have a child, their "family-strategy" demands more financial means (for the private school and the nanny) in order for them to continue to work in the labour force, which means that the incentive to move is low. Indeed, moving would not only involve relocating but would also probably reduce their standard of living, which they do not want since it could hinder Mary's education. Metaphorically, we can see their situation as an expensive "gilded prison": they pay for their lifestyle by working a lot in the labour force, as they each work more than 50 hours per week; Lynn told me: "a normal week is between 50 and 60 [hours a week]" (Lynn, 51yrs, married). Similar to Annisa and Adrian's, Lynn and Alex's situation is hanging by a thread: their work in the labour force. By deciding to stay where they are, they aim to safeguard their professional positions. But their situation also contains risks. The situation is paradoxical, as Alex sees mobility as a driver for success – following a widespread social discourse – but their own success is built locally, thus excluding mobility and the "motility" of one of the partners. This is how Alex explained why they stay in Germany:

> Job security, *** [Lynn] is doing especially well at her job. In fact, she's been offered other bigger positions in other cities, such as Lausanne but she does not want to move

> to Lausanne. She does not want to take the whole family there and she didn't want that job anyway so. It looks like as we stay, we have our positions and they are secure but we are not so ambitious about advancement anymore. It is hard for me to advance without working in German. There is not many places where I can go. I could probably, I am a writer-creative, I could probably write in English and have a good freelance job like that but as for working in an agency and moving forward and advancing more and more it is really difficult for me and it would also be difficult for me to go back to the United-States as a 52 year-old man and a creative, to get a job. There are younger cheaper you know people who can do this (Alex, 52yrs, married).

They both told me that each of them has received individual offers to work abroad, but not at the same time. Thus, a further relocation would be meaningful only individually and not from a family perspective. Collectively, a further relocation does not make sense, since there is a high chance that they will lose one income in the process, or that one of the partners will experience a deskilling. They do not want to lose the "arrangement of care" they have today to raise Mary; as Alex told me: "I like the security of knowing that I can pay for Mary's school, I can pay for Mary's house" (ibid). Relocating is not an option but staying is risky, too; they do not have a lot of other opportunities in Germany, which could be a problem if one of them gets fired. They invest a lot in their work in the labour force because they are afraid of losing it. In other words, they diminish the risk of losing their positions by investing a lot of time in them. At that point, the "local family-strategy" becomes unstable. The need to keep their current positions turns out to be a central objective precisely because they want to maintain the possibility of living in a place they came to for professional reasons, because they know that finding another position in Germany will be difficult for them.

j. Intermediary Summary of the Local Family-Strategy

The two cases discussed above illustrate the central challenge of the "local family-strategy": the "work-family integration" of these two "elementary families" hinders further relocations because they want to keep their current positions in the labour force, either because they are afraid of losing their residency permit (Annisa and Adrian) or because they are afraid of losing the combination of incomes that allow the "arrangement of care" they have developed (Lynn and Alex). Consequently, they have all developed "modalities of settling" which will permit them to stay in the long term in the same local space. The factors within the "family policy" – including parental leaves and types of schooling other than an international school – as well as the type of accommodation, are a part of a strategy for staying in the same region: a "local family-strategy". In other words, their "modalities of settling" are more anchoring and oriented towards a long-term stay. Compared to the "motile family-strategy", the "local family-strategy" offers better conditions for raising children while having a dual career couple (assuming the parents can mobilise enough support for the childcare) but hinders further mobility. Another family organisation in which the "local family-strategy" is common is international divorced couples with children. Usually, they develop a "local family-strategy" so that both parents can still see their children.

8.3.3 Separations and Divorces

When children are involved, a divorce or a separation creates bonds to a local space. I will stress that the "local family-strategy" is a way to resolve the complexities of coordinating the care work between two former partners. Notably, in my cases I only had access to one of the partners, the one who decided to maintain bonds with Switzerland or Germany after their divorce or separation. Some of the respondents divorced or live now separated, but I did not interview everyone who decided to return, for instance, to the city or the country where they grew up. These people are invisible in my corpus of interviews because they had left. That said, all the divorced partners with children who I interviewed develop a "local family-strategy"; none developed, for instance, a "motile family-strategy".

Not all (married) partnerships function and there are conflicts in each family; in some partnerships, at least one of the partners believes that the problems are unsolvable and that they need to end the relationship. The partners decide that they cannot live together anymore and/or that they do not want to be married anymore. This is not a rare situation; many of the interviewees are divorced or separated and some have remarried. Gabriel (6.1.2 Drawn Expatriate, 139) arrived in the local space where he now lives and works as a "drawn expatriate", because he was recruited by a head hunter. He relocated from Paris to Basel and from Basel to Neuchâtel, finally returning to Basel 15 years ago. Like Alex and Lynn, his mobile trajectory differs strongly from those of the families developing a "motile family-strategy", as he has not repeatedly migrated over the last 15 years. He was married to Karen, who is American, and they have one daughter together, Martha. Martha and Karen lived in Zürich after the separation. When I asked him about his private situation, he gave the following answer:

> [I am] divorced, I live here in Switzerland with a partner who is not Swiss, and I have a 19 year old daughter who is studying in England now but before who was living in the Canton of Zürich (Gabriel, 54yrs, divorced)[94].

---

94 Divorcé, j'habite ici en Suisse avec une compagne qui n'est pas Suisse et j'ai une fille de 19 ans qui étudient en Angleterre maintenant mais avant qui était résidente dans le Canton de Zürich (Own Translation).

Gabriel decided to maintain ties with Switzerland in order to be able to see Martha while she was still living in Zürich with her mother. Meanwhile Gabriel met Irina at work, a Spanish national. They now live together in a house they bought. During the interview, Gabriel did not want to speak about his divorce, but behind his words I could detect a difficult and painful process. "I cannot comment on this" (Gabriel, 54yrs, divorced), he told me. When I asked him if he would accept a position somewhere else, this is how he answered:

> There are family criteria that come into play. I have a daughter who studies in England. I don't exclude it [to relocate abroad], but for the moment I am not looking abroad either (Gabriel, 54yrs, divorced).[95]

When he speaks about "family criteria", I believe that he is referring to his wish to keep seeing his daughter on a regular basis. At the very least, the "family criteria" motivated his wish to stay in Switzerland at one point in his life. Yet the interview with Gabriel revealed that his motives evolved as the circumstances of his life changed. He now has a new reason to stay, since he lives with Irina. Thus, his wish to stay is multifaced, his divorce and his daughter being only two elements of a broader context. His desire to be close to his daughter was probably a much stronger element when Martha was still living in Zürich, but now that she studies in Great Britain, his incentive to stay in Switzerland has decreased in that regard. In the meantime, however, other circumstances of his life changed, as he dated a colleague and ended up buying a house with her in the region. He is now starting an application for Swiss citizenship. He sees it a "testimony that he is serious guy" (Gabriel, 54yrs, divorced), and expressed many times his "cultural closeness" to Switzerland, though he still feels like a "foreigner". Thus, he aimed to stay in Switzerland close to his daughter while she was under 18 years old, but many other elements have come into play since then to explain his ongoing wish to stay where he is.

Following their divorce, Karen (Gabriel's ex-wife) had custody of Martha and he needed to find ways to continue to see her, which implied living not too far away from her, even though he was not the "caregiver" on a daily basis. Historically in both Switzerland and Germany, women more often had custody

95 Ben après il y a des critères familiaux qui entrent en compte. J'ai une fille qui étudie en Angleterre. Je ne l'exclus pas je ne l'exclus pas du tout mais pour l'instant je ne le cherche pas (Own Translation).

of the child after a divorce or a separation than men. This trend, however, has diminished in Switzerland (from 86% of the cases in 1986 to 58.4% in 2008 with the increase of the shared parental responsibility, which was attributed in 36.3% of the cases in 2008) (De Flaugergues 2009, 26) and is nearly non-existent in Germany nowadays (as in 96% of the cases a shared parental responsibility after a divorce or a separation is given) (Krack-Roberg, Krieger, and Weinmann 2016, 51). Thus, Gabriel's situation is that of someone without custody of the child.

When one of the divorced partners has the shared custody of a child under 18 years old and has migrated for professional reasons, this person needs to integrate work and family by him or herself (and, when necessary, to coordinate with the former partner). This situation creates a strong incentive to develop local anchors to be able to cope simultaneously with the work in the labour force and the care work. For these people, the situation is a real "balancing act", as the integration between work and family relies nearly exclusively on one adult. In this context, they mobilise formal, non-formal, and informal care.

Yuna is from Japan. She works for an American multinational company in the treasury department, in Switzerland. She first studied in Japan and then went to New York. There, she did an internship in a Japanese bank and was subsequently hired by the bank. She did not like the position of assistant; thus, she decided to study further and enrolled in a university in New York. After she graduated with a degree in economics, she sought employment in the labour force. At that point of her life, after 11 years in the United States, she was in her early thirties. The recruiter of a Japanese multinational offered her a position as an auditor at the company headquarters in Europe. Yuna accepted the position and relocated to France. After two years in France, she received a position in Switzerland, which she accepted. She relocated as an "assigned expatriate" to Switzerland. During her stay in Switzerland, she had a child, Kazuhiro, who is now of school age, and then she divorced.

During our interview, Yuna did not mention her former husband; I asked twice about him, but she avoided the question, and thus I have no idea who he is. I just know that he is apparently totally absent and out of her life. Yuna has full custody of Kazuhiro. The interview was much more about how she manages to simultaneously "integrate work and family", as well as the social impact of her child in her life. Though she has a mobile background and arrived in Switzerland with an "expat-contract", Yuna now relies on a "local family-strategy". Two elements are central to understanding how she has managed to develop such a "family-strategy" on her own: the availability of a "childcare provisions" for Kazuhiro, to which she has had access since he was three months old, and her employer's understanding.

Yuna's case underlines the centrality of the children in the creation of a social network in a new country. While we have seen the socialising role of the international school for partners developing a "motile family-strategy", in Yuna's case, the public kindergarten at the beginning and now the public school foster her inclusion in parent networks, which allow her to learn more about her local space by, for instance, requiring her to increase her competence in spoken French. This is how she remembers it:

> The only people I knew were just my colleagues and the majority was Japanese at that time. The first two years it was not really easy and also due to the language … But since I got the child, I was almost forced to get to the community because raising a child you really have to be in a community. For the services, for instance, my son, he was taken care since he was three months old. That is public service. He goes to the public service and he was at the day care and then of course he meets friends. So, I started to socialise with their parents and then that was the really first time I felt I was accepted. We had something in common, we had the child, we were mothers and most of them working mother. Yeah, they are doing invitation *laugh* and through that I improved my French a lot (Yuna, 46yrs, divorced).

During the interview, Yuna mentioned many times her wish to stay in Switzerland because of the quality of the public schools there. A key element of her 'family strategy'is the availability of public services. Due to the strong "path-dependency" that the schooling of children creates, the choice of the school system indicates the parents' perceived need for "motility". The fact that Kazuhiro goes to a Swiss public school reveals Yuna's wish to stay in Switzerland in the long term. In the quote above, Yuna speaks of her improvement in the local language as well as the feeling of "being accepted" (ibid). The school is a central place to socialise and it also determines the kinds of contacts that are going to be made. While those in international schools mainly self-identify as "expatriates" and believe they are not going to stay long in Switzerland or Germany (as we have seen, for instance, with Richard and Andrea), Yuna has been able to get in touch with the "local population". This implies a completely different range of social experiences, yet Richard and Yuna are colleagues and have a similar mobile and "motile" background. Yuna was also "motile" and mobile at the beginning of her career, moving from Japan, to the United States, to France, to Switzerland, but now with the full custody of a child, she needs to find "arrangements of care" which she can hold on to in the long term, as she is alone in doing the care work and the work in the labour force. A further relocation would mean for her a complete disruption of the "family-strategy" she has developed in Switzerland. Managing the integration of both a position in the labour force and the care work requires either a "partner-initiated mover" doing the care work or giving up the "motility". It is not that

Yuna does not intend to move again. She does not exclude returning to Japan, for instance, yet she does not want to (or cannot) be "motile".

The second element of Yuna's "family-strategy" is her employer's understanding of her situation. She switched companies while she was in Switzerland. Her former boss became the CEO of an American biotechnology company that had its headquarters in the Geneva region and he asked her if she would like to join the new team he was creating. What convinced her to accept his offer was the assurance that the new position would not involve further relocation or too many business trips. Holding a position which does not require too much travel is a precondition for Yuna, as she is raising her child alone:

> It [my job] usually involves relocation. But fortunately, since I get my child as a single parent, I was lucky to be offered a position which doesn't require travelling much. When I moved to Switzerland I was an auditor, an internal auditor, I travelled a lot. The boss I had, he was promoted to CEO in the company and he offers me a new position in the treasury (Yuna, 46yrs, divorced).

A professional position which does not require mobility is necessary for Yuna's balance between work in the labour force and care work. The working conditions are crucial in her "family-strategy", because without an employer who considers her challenges and allows her to overcome them, she has no other resort. Yuna works in the labour force, but is also a "single mother" in a country in which she has not mastered the local language and in which she does not have any relatives to help her with the care work if needed. The interview reveals a characteristic common to all the respondents developing a "local family-strategy": their fear of losing their professional activity by being fired, for instance, as they know it would be complicated for them to find another position in the labour force. For Yuna, the fact that the company employing her acknowledges her "work-family integration" is a necessity. We shall see below that in Julia's case the company played the same central role. In that sense, being a "family friendly" company while managing staff internationally is not only about developing programs to help the "secondary movers" find employment in the labour force after the relocation of the "primary mover". It also implies supporting employees facing complex situations while living abroad, such as Yuna's, as the challenges she faces are heightened by the very fact that she lives far from her home country.

We have already met Julia in my analysis of the "local-moves" of the "primary-movers" (Localising the Home-Base, 154) and the "half-moves" of the "secondary-movers" (Commuting between the Workplace and Home, 166) in chapter 6. She is a British senior manager in an American multinational pharmaceutical company based in Switzerland, and she specifically asked to be "localised" in Switzerland, meaning that she wanted Switzerland to be her home base. She was married to Harry, who is Australian, and now lives and has a position in Geneva. They have one boy of eight years old, Ben. Her choice to be localised in Switzerland is closely linked to her family situation, because she has shared custody of the child with her former husband. For them, their "local family-strategy" is also a legal matter, as one parent is not permitted to leave Switzerland with the child without further agreement in front of a judge; if they do not do so, it could be treated as a child abduction. Compared to Yuna, who relies on public services for the day care of her son, Julia's "modalities of settling" rely on (private) formal and non-formal actors. She has hired an au pair and Ben goes to a Swiss private school. It is not an international school, and is thus similar to the school that we saw earlier in this chapter that we saw earlier in this chapter with Lynn and Alex. The organisation of Ben's care work does not rely only on an au pair and a private school, because Julia's parents, as well as Harry, support her too. Her parents come to Switzerland every six weeks and take care of Ben during part of the summer holidays. Ben also spends part of the summer holidays with his father. Yet Julia does the bulk of the care work. As a result, Ben's school timetable and the school's location are of great importance:

> Two things, one is the timetable of the school and also because of the fact that it was central between me and my ex-husband (Julia, 42yrs, divorced).

Time management is indeed a crucial topic for Julia and she mentioned it many times during the interviews. She is constantly juggling many things in order to integrate her work in the labour force and the care work for her son. She does not want to relocate, but she does have to take some business trips; it is for this reason that she hired an au pair, in order to have someone to stay overnight with Ben when she was away. In addition, her assistant has access to her private and professional timetable and the company seems to be very understanding. This is how she presented the situation:

> So, it's a/ but it's juggling, it's very complicated, you have to be very well organised and you have to have great support in your company, so my assistant, she knows my schedule with my son, so she books my travel around the time she knows he is with his father, my boss also, will always set meetings on the days he knows my son is with his dad. So, everybody, it is a real team effort (Julia, 42yrs, divorced).

For both Julia and Yuna, this "balancing act" of being a "working mum" in a foreign country would not be possible without the flexibility of their company, which allows them to organise their daily lives in a fashion that renders "work-family integration" possible. Their situations contrast with that of Gabriel, who wanted to stay in Switzerland to continue to see his daughter, but was unable to shape his daily life in a way that would allow him to cope with both family and work on a daily basis. Nevertheless, the three cases emphasise the necessity of understanding professional life and family life together, otherwise the professional choices may not make sense at all. The last two cases also show that the employer's understanding of their employee's complex family situation – no matter how they arrived and for how long they intend to stay – is a precondition for these employees' integration of care work and work in the labour force.

k. Summary of the Local Family-Strategy

The "local family-strategy" enables ways of "doing family" in which the integration between care work and professional labour leads the (former) partners to anchor their lives in a local space, hindering further relocations. The complexity involved in coordinating two professional careers and the care work required by different levels of dependencies is not compatible with a succession of moves. In fact, the greater the complexity of the family's internal relationships, the more it is difficult to perform multiple relocations. Thus, the "local family-strategy" favours complex ways of "doing family" as well as dual careers while it hinders mobility. Thus, this "family-strategy" comes with its own costs, namely the stress and fear generated by the necessity of keeping the current position in the labour force.

The biggest difference between the "motile family-strategy" and the "local family-strategy" has to do with childcare. While a traditional and patriarchal division of tasks characterises the "motile family-strategy", a mobilisation of formal, non-formal, and informal care structures – supporting the care work implied by the arrival of a child – is a central element of the "local family-strategy". Unlike the "motile family-strategy", the members of an "elementary family" developing a "local family-strategy" are more often embedded in a "family policy", meaning that they use parental leave and local "childcare provisions." They often acknowledge the "hidden economy of kinship" while making decisions regarding childcare, and may even hire a nanny or an au pair to help. Due to the stronger bond developed with the local spaces in which they live, a "local family-strategy" reflects regional differences such as those between Frankfurt and Geneva, whereby the more developed "family policy" in the former is better able to support the capacity of the partners to maintain their own professional activities.

8.4 Mobile Family-Strategy

We have seen that both the "motile family-strategy" and the "local family-strategy" imply a specific "work-family integration" as well as various "modalities of settling". I see a third "family-strategy" in which these two elements are also distinctive, namely, the "mobile family-strategy". The "work-family integration" of the "mobile family-strategy" is characterised by a prioritising of the professional careers of both partners over the family. Indeed, a majority of the "couples" and "elementary families" developing this strategy do not have children (which is not to say that both careers are given equal weight in the balance). When it comes to the "modalities of settling", the "mobile family-strategy" underscores bi-local or multi-local anchors which span beyond the borders of a nation-state by linking different local working and living spaces to one another. The strategy itself implies frequent mobility. Therefore, the partners make a strategic use of mobility to compensate for the drawbacks of "motility" implied by the design of their careers. They are mobile and "motile", relocate often, have a dual career which they tend to prioritise over their family life.

8.4.1 Succession of Half-Moves

A first way in which the partners develop a "mobile family-strategy" is through the "half-moves" of the "secondary" or "partner-coordinated mover". In this case, the "secondary-mover" comes to an agreement with his or her current employer to remain employed after the relocation. I described three main ways of doing this in chapter 6: commuting, teleworking, and taking a sabbatical or maternity leave. Analysing the biographical trajectories of the respondents who develop – immediately or in the long term – such a strategy, through a succession of "half-moves" that allow for a dual career, creates a hierarchy among the couple's two professional careers. In other words, the "secondary-mover" invests a lot of time and energy to remain employed, often at the expense of raising children, while the members of the family still prioritise the career of the "primary-mover".

For example, Maria and Franz are both German. They were married more than 15 years ago, when they were both working for the same multinational consumer-goods corporation (I analysed Maria's narrative in the subchapter 7.3.1, Ignoring Motility, 208). They both had studied business administration and management in Germany. Franz has worked for the same company for about 15 years. He corresponds to the "assigned expatriate" type, while Maria, who followed him through each relocation, is the "secondary-mover". She found new employment in the labour force after each relocation. Thus, both their professional activities have been near continuous for more than 20 years, as Maria told me and as their LinkedIn accounts show. They do not have children. Purposefully or not, they have prioritised their professional activities over their family lives. During their four relocations, he was always the "primary-mover" performing an "expat-move", while Maria refused to stop working in the labour

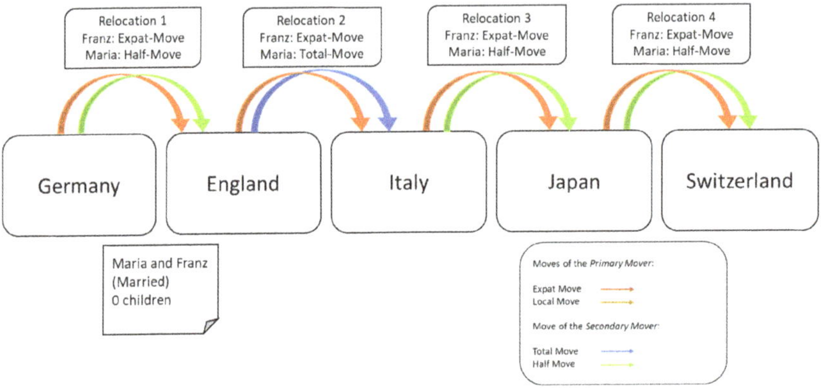

Figure 22 Mobile Trajectory of Maria and Franz. Source: Own Elaboration

force. Thus, she frequently performed "half-moves" in order to coordinate her career with that of her husband's. When they first moved from Germany to England, she continued working in Germany for six months, until she finished the project she was working on. At that time, Maria and Franz travelled extensively in order to continue seeing each other on weekends. Only after she had finished her work in Germany did she move to London to live with her husband. It is at this point that she started seeking employment and, six months later, found a position in marketing. After a few years in London, her husband was called on to Italy. This second relocation from England to Italy is the only one for which Maria performed a "total-move", resigning from her job in London in order to follow her husband. They moved together, and Maria started one year of intensive Italian lessons before successfully finding a position at an online translation company in Italy. A few years later, when they relocated to Japan, the Italian company allowed her to work for them from Japan for several months. In chapter 6, I showed how exhaustive such a working arrangement was for her. Therefore, she resigned and started doing unpaid work for a start-up in Japan. When, three years later, her husband was relocated from Japan to Switzerland, Maria once again performed a "half-move", continuing to work for the same Japanese start-up (Figure 22). At that point it was clear to her that such a working arrangement would not be possible for the long term:

> I worked for a start-up company in Japan and actually when I came to Switzerland I did the same thing again. I continued to work for the Japanese start-up from Switzerland. Although I already knew that the same problem would come again, which of course it

> did, because of the time difference, because the distance is rather large and the cultures are so different. (…) It was not really feasible to live in two worlds basically (Maria, 51yrs, married).

For the second time, Maria developed bi-local "modalities of settling" in order to coordinate her professional occupation with the imperatives of her husband's career. First, she continued to work for the Japanese start-up until she found a company based in Switzerland. She did not resign from the Japanese start-up directly, but only later on. The impossibility of living in two worlds, as she says, underlines that such arrangements are only temporary. When the time difference is so big and the distance so large, you have to choose between maintaining your professional activity or following your partner. In the long-run, there is no other choice; after one year of working for the Japanese company in Switzerland, Maria told me that she resigned because she did not see any way of advancing her career with them:

> I think, I continued for a year. Hum, also because it was quite exciting and I was very happy to support this start-up further and if I would have stayed in Japan for more time /I really liked it/ but I mean realistically I knew we would probably not go back to Japan for work. (…) I could have continued but there was no perspective in moving forward (Maria, 51yrs, married).

In fact, she felt that she was not going to return to Japan, though she enjoyed working and living there. Thus, she agreed to follow her husband from Japan to Switzerland. After having quit the Japanese start-up, she found employment as a project manager in the same company she had worked for more than 15 years ago. Though Maria maintained some form of professional activity through each of the different relocations; her career has been systematically subordinated to her husband's as she was not the one to choose either the destinations or the timing of the moves, and because she had to start over and over again in new positions with each relocation. I interpret the fact that she accepted volunteer work and felt lucky to be supported financially by her husband, as a clue to her subordination. This is how she presented her situation to me, when living in Japan, she resigned from the Italian company:

> I found something else although this was more/ I mean I was lucky that I didn't have to rely on my own salary. So, I decided to join a start-up company where I started to work first of all as a volunteer and then, when they got their first paying contracts, in a paid position. But, this took almost two years (Maria, 51yrs, married).

Thus, the succession of "half-moves" is a way for the "secondary-movers" to maintain some professional activity though not in a way that would allow them to compete with their partner's career. Some might say that the stakes involved in Maria's situation are not very high; and yet the consequences of that lack of competition within the couple can create possibly frustrating situations for the "secondary-mover", having repeatedly to leave in the middle of some project they had found interesting and enriching. Maria "really liked" her position in Japan for instance. As she resigned from the Italian company, she was left in Japan with nothing beyond the financial support of her partner. She found a professional position in a start-up which was, initially, non-paid. She had invested a lot of effort and energy into developing the company and her relationship with its founders when, at the moment the company began to generate profits so that things begin to take shape for Maria, she had to leave because Franz was being relocated to Switzerland. In this way, Maria managed to stay active in the labour force by settling in her new locale, however in a *desynchronised* way as compared to her partner, by maintaining bonds with the former country for a time before switching completely to the new one.

The settling occurs twice for the "secondary-movers", given the way they adapt their careers to that of the "primary-mover", rather than sacrificing them. Thus, the "half-move" is a first step designed to soften to impact of the relocation on the "secondary-mover's" career. After a time in the new local space, the "secondary mover" seeks other employment in the new country. The term of "partner-coordinated mover" emphasises these attempts to *coordinate* two professional careers under the conditions of mobility. This first way of developing a "mobile family-strategy" stresses a succession of "half-moves", but I see a second way in which the "secondary-movers" negotiate the divisions of labour within the family. Although the succession of "half-moves" does not lead to the sacrifice of one professional career for the sake of the other partner, it still leads to the subordination of the other career by the other first, which is not the case when the roles themselves are altered.

8.4.2 Power-Dynamics

The types of "primary-mover" and "secondary-mover" are *a priori* not fixed once and for all by the partners. One of them can very well contest a given division and have it altered. In other words, a division governed by the initiative of a move is the result of a power-dynamic between the partners and can therefore be challenged. We have seen many cases in which this division is, instead, most often not challenged but, rather, overlaps the "gender binaries" cemented into such identities as the "productive male" and the "reproductive female". The "motile family-strategy" we have been describing illustrate situations that have remained unchallenged or in which the imbalance of power between the partners is so large that the "secondary-mover" can not compete anymore; this hierarchisation can ultimately lead the female partners to sacrifice their professional activity to do all the care work. Such agreements about who the "primary-mover" is and who the "secondary-mover" often (re)produce gender hierarchies whereby the male's professional career pays more and is subsequently perceived as more important than that of his female counterpart. A minority of partners, admittedly, do try to coordinate two upward, equal, professional careers. This tendency is visible, I argue, through a recurrent challenge to conventional attributions of the roles of "primary-mover" and "secondary-mover". Most of such challengers prioritise their professional life because they are not embedded in a complex network of mutual dependencies and responsibility, including family life, which often means that they are either childless (at present, and for whatever reason), or because their children are away in boarding school).

Partners may challenge the gender hierarchy, as long as the "secondary-mover" has challenged the distribution of the roles within the partnership. The stakes are high because repeated relocations governed by the same distribution may leave one of the partners an important advantage in the power-dynamic. Manon and Charles are one of the rare cases of a dual career set in which one career was not subordinated to the other (6.5.2 Unique Challenges of a Partner-Initiated Mover, 159). As a reminder, Manon was the product manager of the European region in a pharmaceutical company while Charles was a senior manager in an agro-food company. They both had a university degree and met while they were living in Paris where both were starting their careers in different companies. At one point, Charles' company proposed to move him to Italy to manage the subsidiary branch there. He and Manon would need to relocate there. Manon accepted but took a maternity leave to follow Charles. She performed what I call a "half-move" but never went further than that by accepting a "total-move". For her, it was out of question to totally cut the links to her professional activity in France, as she puts it:

> I told my husband: "I must go or I have to find a job in Italy otherwise I go because I will not stop working". So, I returned to France and he followed me. Six months later, he was back in France (Manon, 55yrs, divorced)[96].

There is much to be said about this quote. It breaks with what we have seen thus far as the initiator of their second relocation, from Italy to France, is not the same as the

96 Je lui ai dit: « moi il faut que je rentre ou il faut que je trouve un travail en Italie ou il faut que je rentre parce que je ne vais pas m'arrêter de travailler! » Et donc je suis rentrée et lui m'a suivi six mois après il est revenu en France (Own Translation).

first move to Italy. It is Manon, who refused to subordinate (or sacrifice) her own professional career, and initiated initiated their return to France. Nor did Charles follow her directly, as he also refused to subordinate (or scarify) his career. Indeed, he needed six months to finish his work in Italy, so he performed a "half-move" and continued working for the same company. Manon challenged the division of the roles and re-established the balance between their respective professional careers. Not only was she able to continue her professional career at the same company, but when Charles needed to relocate from France to Switzerland a few years later, she obtained a year of sabbatical from her employer, which she could not have had asked for if she had resigned in order to stay in Italy with her husband. It allowed her to seek employment in Switzerland, with the help of an outplacement agency paid for by Charles' company, but in the knowledge that her position in France remained secure if she did not find anything in Switzerland. She explained to me that it was a way of protecting herself from the risks of the relocation.

> I had my own back in the sense that, until I found a job, I asked *** for a sabbatical and it was when I found a job [in Switzerland, that I resigned from my position in France]. (…) But it is true that it was anticipated. I had been working with the outplacement firm since September (Manon, 55yrs, divorced)[97].

Manon performed a "half-move" and maintained ties with the former country by keeping her actual position in France. The fact that she had been working for the same company for a decade and was entitled to a sabbatical allowed her to take the time needed to seek and find employment in Switzerland. Figure 23 summarises the mobile trajectory of Manon and Charles.

The path-dependency also works the other way around. Indeed, it need not only trigger and reinforce conditions that prioritise one career over the other one; it can also create and maintain the conditions for a non-hierarchical relation of careers among the partners. Manon's case is striking in this regard. Because she refused to subordinate her career in the first place, she refused to resign from her position with her former employer and took the sabbatical she was entitled to. In other words, if she had accepted to resign in the first place, the path-dependency of their trajectory would have lead, I argue, towards her subordination. This underlines the importance of challenging the division of the roles (when both partners want an upward moving career), for once a path-dependency leading

97 Si vous voulez j'avais assuré mes arrières parce que tant que je n'avais pas trouvé de travail, j'avais demandé à N*** un congé sabbatique et c'est quand j'ai trouvé un emploi. (…) Mais donc voilà, mais c'est vrai que ça avait été anticipé. J'avais travaillé depuis septembre avec le cabinet d'outplacement (Own Translation).

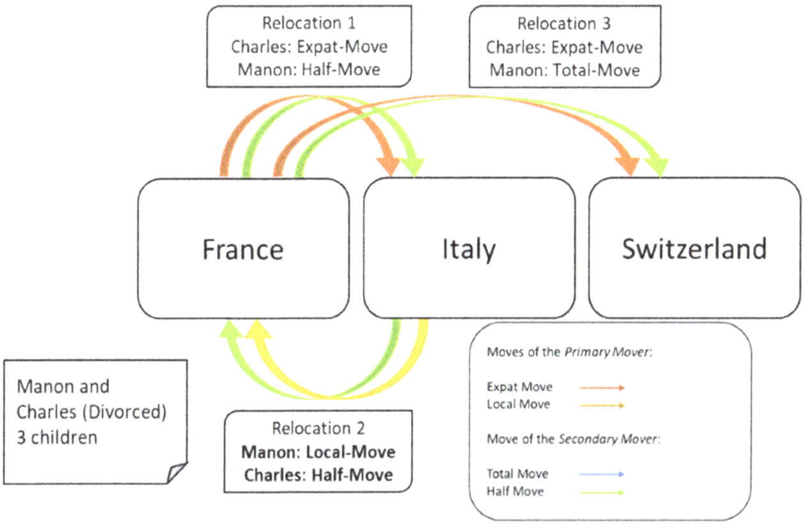

Figure 23 Mobile Trajectory of Manon and Charles. Source: Own Elaboration

towards an imbalance of the prioritisation of the two professional careers in a family is triggered, it is very hard to turn around. We have just seen how much energy Maria invested in maintaining her own professional activities. Manon, too, speaks of an exhaustive process; although she, arguably, had to take fewer risks as she was able to rely more on insurance and paid-leave in her effort to maintain some continuity in her career. Besides, while Maria had to start from "zero each time she was unplugged," as she told me, Manon managed to move up the hierarchy of the two companies she worked for. Thus, Manon and Charles provide an example of a balanced power-dynamic, where the roles are shared among the members of a family, the "secondary-mover" becoming the "primary-mover", and vice-versa. As the "primary-mover" and "secondary-mover" do not share the same privilege; pretending that such power-dynamics don't exist only hinders the career of one of the partners. Maintaining a balance in the hierarchy of the two careers implies keeping this tension alive. Nevertheless, Manon and Charles eventually divorced whereas Maria and Franz are still together.

l. Dual Career and Secondary Stayers

I already provided an in-depth presentation of Carlos and Raul in the previous chapter, where I introduced the notion of "secondary-stayers" (6.5.4 Immobility of a Secondary-Stayer, 170), as a third way of performing a "mobile family-strategy", in this case, when one partner simply refuses to move and follow the other. As a reminder, while Carlos was a global accounts director of a multinational corporation; Raul, his partner, was the director of a raw-materials trading company in Mexico. Carlos worked in Mexico, the Dominican Republic, and Germany while Raul always stayed in Mexico. Since Carlos left Mexico-city, he has returned at least once a year to see his partner, his parents and his friends; *using mobility as a means of maintaining the bonds with his partner and relatives*, what I would describe as a bi-local "modality of settling". In this case, the question of the "primary-mover" and the "secondary-mover" is clarified from the outset by a clear "no go" or "I will not follow you". The emphasis in on how the two partners decide to pursue their respective professional careers independently, rather prioritising work over family than one career over the other.

8.4.3 Mobile Family-Strategy and Children

Families that develop a "mobile family-strategy" prioritise work over the family itself. Maria and Franz, for example, do not have children and probably never will since they are now over fifty. We need to be cautious not to generalise that partners who develop "mobile family-strategies" would always prioritise their professional lives over their partnerships, as it would be inappropriate to generalise that homosexual couples would focus only on their jobs because they do not have children. The possibility of *prioritising* work in the labour force over the partnership does not, of course, have to imply a total subordination of the one by the other. Indeed, it does not have to mean that only the professional occupations count. Maria and Franz or Carlos and Raul have developed their relationships over decades, and who am I to say that their relationships are not important to them? Yet, I note a difference in the complex interdependencies and mutual responsibilities that characterise Maria and Franz' situation, for instance, who do not struggle over their "work-family integration" as much a family with three children does, in the development of their "motile family-strategy".

The case of Manon and Charles underlines the flexible nature of "family-strategies". They have three children and yet both have maintained an upward-moving professional career. How did they integrate mobility, work, and family in this way? The most crucial support, I argue, is that Manon had access to the French maternity leave system, which allowed her to follow her husband to Italy without having to resign from her position, so that she subsequently was entitled to take a sabbatical during their second relocation. Besides, their three children did not systematically follow them; meaning that they lived as a split-family.

Interestingly, Manon and Charles' way to integrate work and family reflects their "mobile family-strategy", as one of their children preferred to stay in France and attended a boarding school before going to university. Two of their children followed them. One of these two left to study in England once he was done with the French baccalaureate he completed while attending a private school in Switzerland. The other one studied in a Swiss university. Manon and Charles' case shows that "family-strategies" can be very dynamic and change over time. Age and life cycle are central to any explanation about how Manon and Charles maintained both their positions in the labour force and raised their children. Indeed, not only is the age of Manon and Charles important, but so are their children's ages. When they arrived in Switzerland, two of their children were already nearly adults and only the youngest required much care work, as Manon expresses it:

> We had one child who preferred to stay in France in a boarding school, a daughter who came through the French school of Valmont and then third too / so the eldest and youngest ones followed us while the middle one remained in France. [When we moved to Switzerland], the oldest children were semi-adults, they had something like 15 or 16 or 16 and 17 so they had almost finished their schooling in France, while our daughter was still very young (Manon, 55yrs, divorced)[98].

In other words, one of their children used mobility as tool of family coordination, too. "Mobile family-strategy" often implies a split-family situation, as is the case with Manon and Charles. The different members of the family live apart, at least for a time, using mobility to meet up. Manon and Charles have since divorced, and the children are grown up. When I interviewed her, she told me repeatedly that she wants to stay in Switzerland and enjoys the place. The third child, who was still young when they arrived is now studying at university in Switzerland. Her interview reveals the traits of someone adopting a "local family-strategy", aiming to settle in the long term. The "family-strategies" are dynamic and can change over time as Manon illustrates, who develops a "local family-strategy" now that all the children are adult and she divorced from Charles.

"Family-strategies" are dynamic and change over the life-cycle, and "mobile family-strategies", especially, are temporary and contingent upon the specifics of

98 Et puis alors, on a un enfant qui a préféré rester en France en internat, une fille qui est venue à l'école française à Valmont et puis troisième aussi/donc l'aînée et la dernière nous ont suivi et celui du milieu est resté en France. Nos grands étaient semi-adultes, ils avaient quelque chose comme 15 et 16 ou 16 et 17 ans donc ils avaient quasiment fini leurs scolarités en France tandis que la petite était encore très jeune (Own Translation).

age and life cycle. Very often partners will adopt a "mobile family-strategy" when they are young, and then change to a more "local" or a "motile family-strategy". Young people without children tend more often to develop a "mobile family-strategy", until the arrival of the first child. I interviewed Tyler in Frankfurt shortly before he was relocated to Amsterdam. He and Vanessa, his girlfriend, had been together for seven years and both were in their late twenties. Tyler is American, and Vanessa is bi-national Austrian and Dutch. They met in the US where he was studying and she was an au pair. They never lived together during the seven years of their relation for Vanessa had soon moved back to Austria in order to finish her studies. Tyler started to work for a marketing agency based in the US after he finished his bachelor degree. After two years working for this company, he asked if they would have a position for him in Europe, using what was offered by the company as a means to live closer to Vanessa. So, Tyler moved Frankfurt, while Vanessa lived in Graz, Austria, and they extensively travel in order to see on another. One client of his current employer's then offered him a position in Amsterdam, which he accepted knowing that Vanessa was about to move there, too. This is how he presented the situation when I asked him how he found the position in Amsterdam:

> It was an offer from another company that was, I mean, that was, it was like professional growth for me and also personal, my girlfriend wouldn't be able to work in Germany because the teacher, because of her degree wouldn't be transferred to Germany for some reasons. (…). [Vanessa] has a Dutch passport, so she doesn't need anything to be able to work there, so that is pretty easy, and I love Amsterdam so [laugh] this is a kind of win-win for both of us (Tyler, 28yrs, in couple).

He agreed to relocate to Amsterdam because Vanessa is Dutch and speaks Dutch. He sees the situation as win-win, given that he already has a position in the labour force there and believes that Vanessa has good chances of finding one, too. After seven years of "long distance relationship", which corresponds in my terminology to the "mobile family-strategy", they have managed to live together in the same place for the first time. They have found a place that both accept and both expect to be able to find a professional position. The "mobile family-strategy" is common amongst young and/or bi-national couples. It depends upon access to mobility as a strategic resource in the maintenance of the relation, at least temporarily. They developed a "mobile family-strategy" that lead them to live apart for a time but seem to have managed to live together now in a place where both can have a professional position. However, as this chapter stresses, things can change dramatically with the arrival of the first child, especially when the partners live abroad. In sum, "family-strategies" are dynamic and should not be seen as static.

m. Summary of the Mobile Family-Strategy

The "mobile family-strategy" favours professional career over family life. It implies bi-local or multi-local settlings, and depends upon a strategic use of mobility. I distinguish two ways of doing so, namely, a succession of "half-moves", in which the "secondary-movers" continue their professional activity, and the development of a power-struggle within the family, whereby the "secondary-mover" contests their position and takes the initiative for a further move. While the former implies the subordination of one career over the other, the latter allows both partners to develop their professional career. Of note is the fact that "mobile family-strategies" tend to be more common amongst young people who do not have children. Still, this strategy requires a constant re-organisation of daily life given the use of mobility to coordinate and meet up. It involves a lot of travel back and forth. This strategy is exhausting either because of the frequent travel or because of the time-difference between the place of residency and of work, as was the case for Maria. Consequently, a "mobile family-strategy" is often only temporary.

8.5 Theorising the Family-Strategies

Now that I have presented the three types of "family-strategies", I will conclude this chapter by developing a deeper theoretical understanding of them. I will point, in particular, to three different elements. First, I will underline various constellations of care work organisation and social networks that allow for a finer distinction between the "family-strategies". Second, I will show the dynamic and relational nature of the "family-strategies" themselves: how they evolve, change, and are subject to conflicts over time. Third, I will stress the specificity of each type of "family-strategy" in relation to the "glass ceiling effect" (Cotter et al. 2001) that women face in the labour market.

8.5.1 Care Work Organisation and Social Networks

A "family-strategy" corresponds to the outcome of the negotiation of decisions taken by the partners after at least one of them accepts a proposed relocation abroad. To analyse such "family-strategies", I articulated a "collective approach" in Chapter 6 (Figure 24). Briefly, a "family-strategy" corresponds simultaneously to the "work-family integration" practiced by each individual partner ([1] and [2]), as well as the collective nature of their discussions, negotiations and arguing about the sharing or divvying up of the care work (3) and the professional labour (4). The "family-strategy" is at the centre of the collective approach (5).

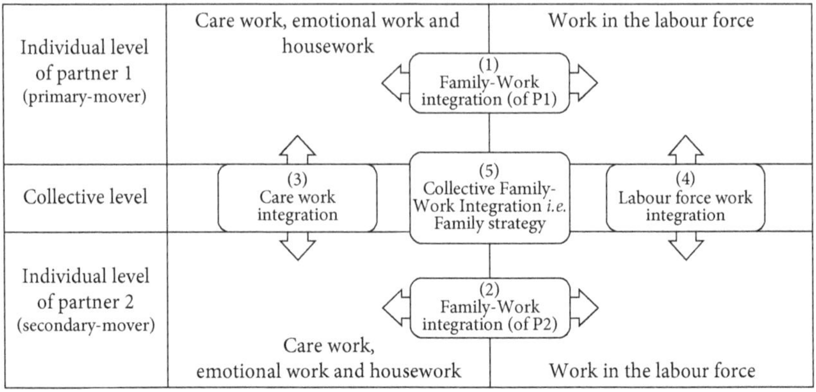

Figure 24 Collective Family-Work Integration or Family-Strategy. Source: Own Elaboration

It is the comprehensive conception of the "collective family-work integration" of highly-skilled migrants and it reflects the dynamic and relational nature of "doing family" on the move (Baldassar et al. 2014; Jurczyk, Lange, and Thiessen 2014). So far, I have shown how the "family-strategies" take shape empirically. Based on these empirical analyses, I will develop a finer understanding of them, theoretically.

I use the "collective model" (Figure 24) to analyse the process of "doing family"; but the model so far lacks any reference to the environment in which an "elementary family" or a "couple" live. The analysis of the three types of "family-strategies" show that none are developed in a social and contextual vacuum. A "family-strategy" is always embedded in a specific context. As presented here, the model remains silent about the social inclusion of the partners into the broader context. Context, clearly, influences the "family-strategies" chosen by couples. As the Frankfurt region offers a more comprehensive "family policy" than the Geneva region does, couples living or moving there are better able to integrate their professional and care work in a way which does not require the sacrifice of one of the two professional careers. Thus, each region offers different levels of access, for instance, to childcare. Furthermore, the partners can surround themselves with different people, create different networks, and mobilise different types of care within the same region without actively mobilising the district's "family policy".

Throughout the chapter, I underlined (1) the way the partners organise the care work they are responsible for and (2) how they develop social networks beyond their nuclear family. Each of the three family-strategies elaborated is specific, I argue, in these two respects. Social networks, here, include the extended "family" proper (understood as encompassing kinship relationship), friends, colleagues, the nanny, or even the members of a parent-teacher association. Partners developing a "motile family-strategy", for example, are supported by the employer of the "primary-mover", who agree/offer to pay for international schools. The "motility" of the "primary-mover" and the frequent relocations of the members of the family favours a traditional model of the family, whereby the female "secondary-mover" does the care work and the male "primary-mover" works in the labour force. Thus, the couple's social network is constructed around other parents (and especially mothers) at the international school and by colleagues of the "primary-mover". I speak of an "expat-bubble" to describe this configuration. such couples do not tend to rely on other types of care than the unpaid work of the female partner. The support of the company is crucial to maintain this type of "family-strategy" as these parents do not access the region's "family-policy", often because, as foreigners, they are not entitled to it.

In contrast, a "local family-strategy" relies much more on the region's "family policy". Such partners mobilise parental leaves and send their children to a public school or kindergarten where these options are available. Instead of the support of the company, they rely much more on the local variation of the nation-stated "family policy". Not only do they rely on the local "family policy", they also develop a more complex organisation of formal, informal and non-formal structures of care. Generally, they share the care work and/or find external support so that both partners can continue working in the labour force. The mobilisation of such non-formal child caring as a hired-nanny, or au pair, is part of such a childcare support strategy. The partners developing this strategy also tend to develop social networks with the "local populations", as we have seen with Yuna, who sent her son to a local school.

The "mobile family-strategy" is a mix of both, as it is a strategy implying a prioritising of the professional careers over the family-life. Such a strategy typically implies less care work, especially as the partners (still) do not have children. Thus, I showed that this strategy is, more often than the two others, temporary. Still, there are particular care arrangements related to this strategy, too. The boarding schools to which parents send their children for a semester are a good example (as we have seen with Manon and Charles). The use of a maternity or a parental leaves that allow the "secondary" to follow the "primary" mover on a relocation is also typical of this "family-strategy", creating a bi-local anchoring of the partnership, where one of the partners maintains a position in the labour force in a country where they no longer live. When it comes to the social network that the partners develop, I did not find a pattern which would particularly identify this strategy.

This point aims at showing that the "elementary families" and "couples" that I analyse here are not "nuclear families". I develop this concept at the beginning of the current study (3.2.3 Doing Family, 78). All the "family-strategies" imply a specific range of social networks and ways of organising care work. It shows the importance of contextualising "family-strategies". However, the partners rely on different constellations of social supports and social networks, they still always rely on some such networks of support.

8.5.2 Iterative Logic, Path-Dependency, and Conflicts

I have underlined the pivotal periods during which agreement about a "family-strategy" can change, including a relocation, the arrival of the first child, or a divorce. Such changes lead partners to re-negotiate in the hopes of developing a new common agreement; which does not necessarily mean they are going to find it. I offer two sociological phenomena through we can better understand how "family-strategies" evolve over time. Indeed, a "family-strategy" evolves along an "iterative" logic that creates a "path-dependency". In fact, the modification of a "family-strategy" is neither completely (pre)determined nor totally random, as each new relocation raises anew the same array of questions, such as, "Should I quit my job to follow you?" or "Who should care of the child after school?" Thus, a similar range of challenges emerges after each migration. Dealing with the local administration, moving into a new flat, and finding a new school for the children, or for some "secondary-movers" finding a new job, are all challenges that re-appear at each relocation. Therefore, I talk of an *iterative* logic, after the meaning of the word "iteration", "the repetition of a process or utterance" (OED 2018). This sort of repetition of the same is central to the concept of "family-strategies". For most, these questions are related to the integration of work and family and need to be reconsidered after each relocation. The same matrix of questions re-appears each time the conditions change.

These conditions refer both to "local conditions" and "biographical conditions". Local conditions correspond to the constraints and opportunities found in the new place of residence. Such notions of "gender culture" (Pfau-Effinger 1998) or "critical places" (Riaño et al. 2015), likewise, are designed to highlight how not all places are equal, recalling the importance of geography in the dynamic of "doing family". Indeed, the world is not flat; "local conditions" do matter. A couple's ability to integrate work and family is significantly impacted by the places they move to, like the "family-policies" available in the region, the quality of local public school systems, the presence of a strong "international labour market", and the availability of "mobility nodes" (Hannam, Sheller, and Urry 2006, 12).

The "biographical conditions", on the other hand, refer to the individual and *evolving* situation of the partners. In this context, the partners' age and "life cycle" (Kohli 1989; O'Rand and Krecker 1990) are central to any explanation of the dynamic of their "family-strategies". The age and number of their children, or the need of care work that the grand-parents may require are elements that change during the lives of the couple negotiating "family-strategies". I have shown that a "mobile family-strategy" tends to occur when the partners are young and/or do not have children. When young children are involved, though, the partners usually develop either "motile" or "local family-strategies". Indeed, "family-strategies" are dynamized by changes in a couple's local and biographical conditions.

Nevertheless, the renegotiation of "family-strategies" occurs under a variety of circumstances that are not, for that matter, extremely frequent. Indeed, there remains a kind of "rigidity" to the "family-strategies" chosen over time. One way to integrate two professional careers, for instance, requires the prioritisation of one career over the other. This facilitates the process of answering each new iterative array of questions raised by a new relocation until, in some cases, there is no further question to be had as the partners has fallen into a more traditional division of labours whereby the husband works in at his profession and the wife does the care work. In fact, the longer the wife is out of the labour force, the more unlikely a switch in the prioritizing of the careers is, and the more likely a sedimentation of the "family-strategy" becomes. Another such example of relative rigidity results from the choice of a school system for the children. The choice to go for an international school, a public local-school, or a private school strongly impacts the "motility" of the partners. It creates a "path-dependency" of sorts that impacts possible further migrations. In fact, in these two examples, previous decisions tend to create "path-dependencies" that over-determine further decisions. Likewise, previous organisations of the "family-strategy" influence future choices; or, to be more precise, the decisions taken in the development of previous "family-strategies" influence the kind of decisions that can be made next time round, for new decisions have to be taken in consideration the "path-dependencies" that earlier decisions impose.

Such pivotal periods (as relocation, child-birth, and divorce) impact active "family-strategy" that need to be re-adapted to new circumstances. Sociological processes like "iterance" and "path-dependency" shape these new "family-strategies". These two processes help us better understand how the adaptation of a "family-strategy" takes place. A "family-strategy" can change over time as it is not fixed once for all; although each new decision may further entrench a "path-dependency". For these reasons, "family-strategies" may as easily change over time as they may tend to remain the same; for they are neither totally random nor completely predetermined. The image of a river provides a good idea of how I conceptualise the way "family-strategies" may (or not) change over time. The riverbed (the life of the respondents) constantly orients the water ("family-strategies") while the water, simultaneously, erodes the riverbed, altering it over time which turns the river (the life-course) in new directions. In other words, they mutually influence each other.

Another element, which explains the circumstance under which the "family-strategies" change, is the appearance of conflict among the partners. There is no family without conflicts and the "family-strategies" reflect them. Having to choose to move or to remain can be a source of conflict. The way a couple shares the care and professional work can be another. As conflicts are by nature dynamic, so do "family-strategies" change over time. "I will not stop working in order to move for you," declared Manon (55yrs, divorced), referring to a situation in which the partners need to renegotiate the further integration of work and family. Such conflicts in turn can lead to a change in the "family-strategy". In Manon's case, the partners split for a time, developing a "mobile family-strategy". In order that both of them could maintain their own work in the labour force, they decided to live apart for a time, neither of them agreeing to subordinate his or her professional career to that of the other. My interviews suggest that when a man is asked to subordinate his career to a woman's, he is much less likely to accept, as Manon's case shows. Charles refused to move directly back to France with her but waited, instead, until a meaningful professional position opened upon for him before joining her; a process which took around six months. He did not resign but rather coordinated his career to Manon's, corresponding to the type of the "partner-coordinated mover". "Family-strategies" evolve as conflicts do. By emphasising the flexibility of the "family-strategy", I so not aim to place the partners in the different boxes or types of "family-strategy". In fact, I highlight the process leading the partners to develop various forms of "family-strategies" throughout their lives and according to changing circumstances.

8.5.3 Mutually Exclusive Model

In chapter 8, I have developed three types of "family-strategies" and I have just shown how these evolve during the life of partnerships on the move. However, I still have not spoken about the relationship between the three types of "family-strategies" nor discussed the "hidden form of gender hierarchy" that is visible therein. In order to do so now, I will focus on three elements that partly overlap in each "family-strategy". These three elements are (1) "motility", (2) children, and (3) dual career. I understand "motility" as the capacity to be professionally reactive and ready to answer to an opportunity abroad; to relocate for the sake of one's career. The term "children" illustrates the capacity of the partners to integrate the work in the labour force with the care work required to raise their children. The "dual career" refers to a couple's ability to develop two upwardly successful professional careers. The underlying form of gender hierarchy is that while the men can have it all at the same time ("motility", children, and upwardly mobile career), women tend to access only two of them simultaneously. This is related to the fact that the three types of "family-strategy" are mutually exclusive (Figure 25). The "family-strategy" is a collective concept accounting systematically for the relationship between the two partners while the "hidden form of gender hierarchy" refers to the effect of the "family-strategies" on each individual partner.

I argue that each "family-strategy" favours two of three elements at the expense of the third one. Figure 25 underlines this configuration. The concept of "family-strategy" drawn from the various empirical cases I have analysed in this study needs to be understood through its inherent flexibility and dynamism. In that sense, the empirical shape of a "family-strategy" follows the dynamic logic of "doing family" (Baldassar et al. 2014). Yet, it is also possible to distinguish the different types of "family-strategies" from one another. In each individual case, a "family-strategy" is not static. Indeed, it evolves over the course of a life. In the theoretical analysis that follows, however, I will analyse the consequence of each "family-strategy".

The "motile family-strategy" favours the "primary-mover's" "motility". In this configuration, the partners prioritise the career of the "primary-mover" while the "secondary-mover" does the care work of "homemaking and caregiving". The "work-family integration" follows a clear division of tasks among the partners and relies upon conventional "gender binaries". This division of labour creates an interdependency among the partners; elevating the family itself to the center of the "family-strategy". The strategy relies on a "motile family" which can be easily relocated. Thus, the traditional "work-family integration" favours the career of

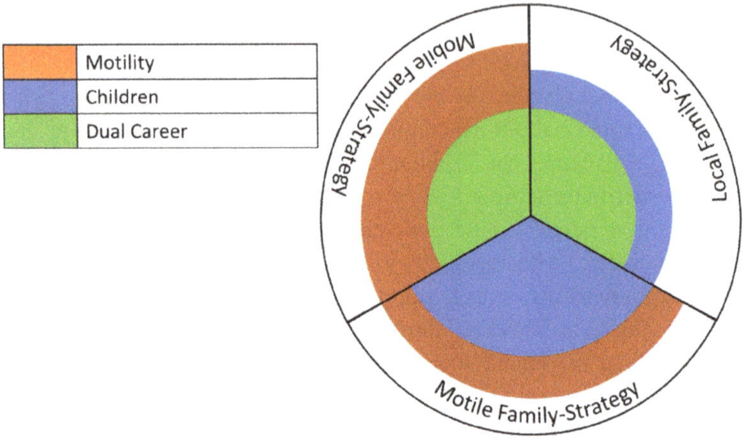

Figure 25 Mutually Exclusive Model. Source: Own elaboration

the "primary-mover" as he (or rarely she) is able to respond quickly to new professional opportunities because the "secondary-mover" takes care of the children and related care work. A dual career couple is especially difficult to develop in this context, because of the need of the "primary-mover" to be constantly ready to move, keeping up the family's "motility". Thus, the "secondary-mover" faces the same challenges that the "partner-initiated mover" faces (6.5.2 Unique Challenges of a Partner-Initiated Mover, 139). In this configuration, the man has it all, I argue: the international professional mobility, the upward professional career, and a family life with children. He can have it all precisely because it is very often the female partner who does the unpaid care work. This is the "gender imbalance" that women are most often subject to as "secondary-movers". Favell (2008) shows the same: "Spouses might "choose" to follow their partner, and feel they are completely liberated from the usual discrimination in society, but their apparent agency is locked into a structured set of constrained options further down the road that produces the same result (i.e. life as a housewife) as if their choices had been deliberately restricted" (2008, 73). The "motile family-strategy" underlines a gendered hierarchy between the partner emphasising the gendered consequences of "motility", in the "decision making process" (Chapter 6), the narratives (Chapter 7) and the "family-strategies" (Chapter 8). In fact, it appears that the men are much more reluctant to accept subordination of their own careers, either for the sake of their partner's career or to do more of the care work themselves. I have shown through the "motile narrative" stance how this hierarchy is discursively created. Why is this so? An element of the answer could be their (motivated?) "blindness" to see the help they could provide with the care work (7.2.1 Structural Constraints, 187). Another element could also be the strong expectations they have to face at their work place, not only from their superiors but also from their colleagues (7.2.3 Paradoxical Family Men, 201). The "essentialness" of the "gender binary" may also be at play here in the sense that the male partner reifies such "categories of practice" in which it is "natural" that the female partner does the care work. The narrative stance of the "career men" is in fact very close to this "essentialness" (7.2.2 Career Men and Career Women, 195). Thus, the "motile family-strategy" favours "motility" where children are had at the expense of the dual career.

A "local family-strategy," on the other hand, facilitates the doing and organising of care work and favours both partners developing professional careers, but it hinders their openness to further relocations. In this context, the "work-family integration" that each partner adopts is more nuanced, for the overly gendered constraints of "motility" do not apply here (7.4 Gender and Motility, 221). Still, the "gender culture" (Pfau-Effinger 1998) implied by the local variations of available "family policies" contributes to some degree of a gender hierarchy, such as when one partner stops working in the labour force in places where day care solutions for the children are either unaffordable or unavailable. The contrast here is striking with the amount of support that second generation female Italian migrants receive from their parents in order to be able to pursue upward mobile professional careers (Fibbi 2005). Instead, I have dealt with cases of "first generation migrants" who do not have such support available, where it is often only the financial capital of the family that prevents the (re)production of gender inequalities, and where "well off" families can pay for the day care solutions that allow them to develop a dual career and have children. Thus, I have argued, a dual career couple is a luxury. (8.3.2 Combination of Formal, Informal and Non-Formal Care Support, 252). Further, the local "gender culture" (Pfau-Effinger 1998) contributes also to (re)producing the gender hierarchy within the family itself. I have showed two contrasting cases Annisa and Adrian (8.3.1 Low Support for the Care Work, 249) and Lynn and Alex (8.3.2 Combination of Formal, Informal and Non-Formal Care Support, 252) emphasising the relevance of taking local "family policies" into consideration, for these are by no means neutral. In this context, my work corroborates studies focusing specifically on "family policies", such that couple who have settled in the Frankfurt region have access to more comprehensive childcare than those who have moved to the Geneva region.

Still, gender hierarchies are (re)produced primarily within the families, I argue; the assumption being that it is the women's role to adapt her professional occupation to the birth of a child. This assumption is not questioned by the male partners who tend to enjoy the *status quo* in this regard. Truth to be told, one of the few couples who maintained a dual upward career and lived together are Lynn and Alex: "Lynn and I are both working so somebody had to watch Mary during the day" (Alex, 52yrs, married). They developed "local family-strategy" in Germany and Alex underlines his role in doing a fair share of the care work required in order to raise their daughter. Furthermore, separated or divorced partners with children often opt for a "local family-strategy" as it allows them to have complex family relationships and two professional careers at the same time. The "local family-strategy" highlights the difficulty to maintain "motility" in both partners' professional careers when the family relationships are complex and when both (former) partners work in the labour force. In short, a "local family-strategy" favours children and a dual career but hinders "motility".

Finally, a "mobile family-strategy" favours "motility" and dual careers but renders the coordination of care work for the children more complicated. Such a strategy implies a prioritisation of the dual career couple over family life. When it comes to the "family-work integration", both partners prioritise their professional careers over children. While some (still) do not have any children, others send theirs to boarding schools if the children are not older enough and independent enough to be studying abroad. The prioritisation of work in the labour force over family and care work does not, however, mean that the partners treat their two careers equally. Thus, when the roles are fixed within the family and the same partner is repeatedly made the "secondary-mover", the family had prioritised one career over the other. A dual-couple career is possible when the "secondary-mover" (often, the wife) challenges the conventional division of roles and manages to have her own career prioritised, at least for a while. This configuration implies that the husband accepts the challenge in the first place and then the subordination of his career, even temporarily. Truth to be told, I did not encounter such a configuration in my interviews as each time I encountered a family in which the wife successfully challenged a given division of tasks, the family then split. An interpretation of this is that men tend systematically to prioritise their own professional career (and thus independence) over the professional career of their female partner. When she effectively overcomes the "hierarchy of position" and has a concrete professional offer that is better than that of her partner but that this requires him to quit his professional activity, such a man tends to prefer to separate and then divorce. From this perspective, the women achieving upward professional mobility abroad are either single or divorced. Still, I argue, the "mobile family-strategy" is often only temporary, until the families successfully develops into a dual career couple who have settled locally and constituted a "local family-strategy". The case of Lynn and Alex is striking in this regard (8.3.2 Combination of Formal, Informal and Non-Formal Care Support 252).

To conclude, in this chapter, I have analysed the formation of three types of "family-strategies" and focussed attention on their particular challenges and opportunities that each tends to face. I then developed the results of the analysis into a theoretical model to show that the glass ceiling for women is not only in the labour market but lies also – and even more centrally, I would argue – within the realm of the family itself, suggesting that the family is a central institution in which the gender inequalities are (re)produced.

Discussion Part

9 Theoretical and Empirical Insights

Two chapters structure the discussion section of the dissertation. In the first (Chapter 9) I review and summarise the main contributions of the current study. I answer the research questions posed at the outset and point towards some ideas for further research. In the second (Chapter 10) I discuss the theoretical and empirical insights of the study. I emphasise some differences that I have noted between the Geneva and the Frankfurt region, combining the contextual chapter (Chapter 5) and the three empirical chapters (Chapters 6, 7, and 8). Though this study does not develop a formal comparative design, some elements, for instance, of the "family policy", deserve further comment. Finally, I focus on the different actors I have encountered during this study to offer them some recommendations. Let us start by reviewing the crucial insights of the study with a view to answering our research questions.

9.1 Decentring the Literature and the Research Design

The main purpose of the theoretical part is to decentre the current literature on highly-skilled migration and expatriation. In other words, I develop a decentred theoretical framework, which is to say an innovative way to assess the scientific literature on highly-skilled migration and gender. Doing so, I create the notion of a "polarisation of migration" in order to express the way research opposes "*Normalfall Migration*" and "highly-skilled migration". I present two seminal theories in Migration studies, the "neoclassical theory of migration flows" (p. 37) and the "dual labour market theory" (p. 38). These two theories are usually opposed, the one being seen as "mainstream" and the other, "critical". Nevertheless, I argue, both depend upon a "polarisation of migration", opposing two types of migration that speak to to two different social processes. Opposing these two types of migration does not only refer to the skill level of the migrants in question, but implies normative categorisations that span far beyond the realm of social sciences. In fact, these categorisations are at the core of a worldview, which largely transcends social sciences: a widespread oversimplified worldview ("*Weltanschauung*" in German).

Figure 26 offers a useful way to illustrate what this worldview is all about. It shows the opposition between a "controlled migration" and a "frictionless mobility" (Favell 2014) and represents the "migration binaries" opposing "us/them", the skilled professionals who move by choice versus the unskilled migrants

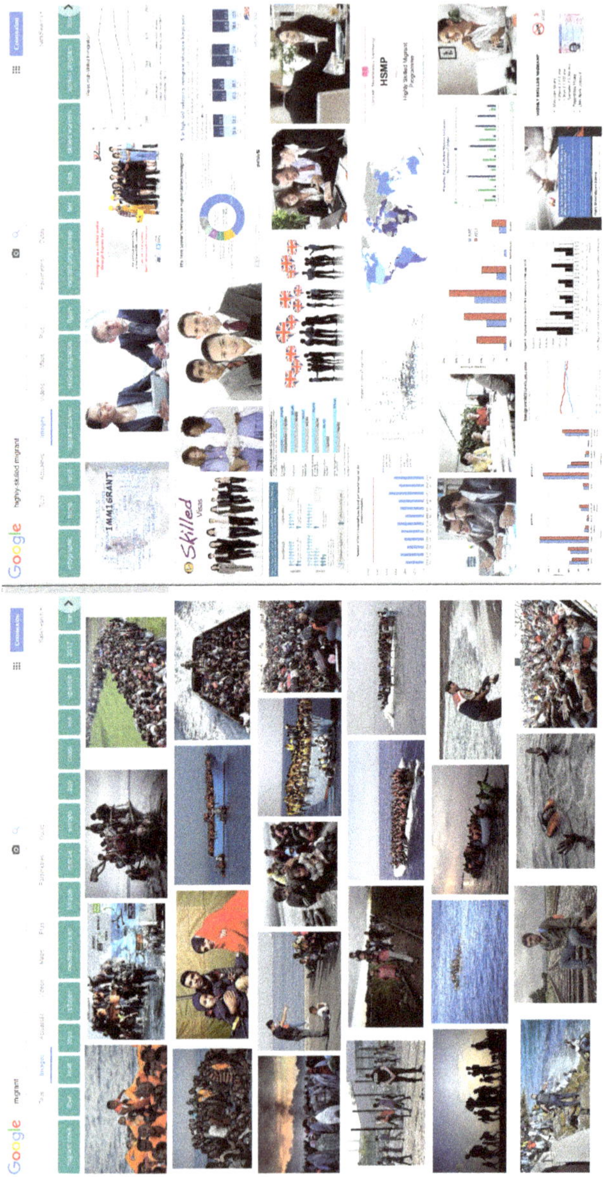

Figure 26 Opposing "Migrant" and "Highly-Skilled Migrant".Source: Own Elaboration based on Google.com

who are forced to move. In fact, it represents a seminal distinction in Western social sciences, that Edward Said discussed in his *Orientalism* (2003 [1978]). He spoke of the "Europeans [and] in front of them, the non-Europeans" (ibid., 38). The argument is close to what Bhambra (2017) describes as "methodological whiteness". For her, "it is clear that the category of 'class' is not being used as a neutral or objective one, but rather as a euphemism for a racialized identity politics" (2017, 227). Al Ariss (2010), similarly, notes that as soon an "expatriate" comes from a country of the "global South", he or she is considered a migrant. In his words, this conceptualisation "comes to replicate and support a stereotyped image of migrants who are less advantaged in terms of their originating country and ethnic origins" (2010, 80). Through the "migration binaries", I deconstruct a worldview implying "white upper middle-class mobile professionals" opposed to "racialized under-class [sic.] migrants forced to flee a scorched country". Therefore, this study develops a decentred theoretical framework able to deal reflexively with the scientific literature without reproducing a "polarisation of migration". The distinction does not only imply normative assumptions but also produces performative effects, as the collective image of a phenomena already contains, in part, its political answers. Thus, it should not be taken for granted in the scientific literature. One of these assumptions is that highly-skilled migrants will not stay in their new country of residence: they are here only temporarily. They are not a "threat" to the "imagined community" of the nation (Anderson 1991) because they have somewhere to return to, where they "belong", as if the "norm" is to live only in the place "where one comes from". My analysis challenges this assumption and shows a type of "family-strategy" which precisely allows for a long term stay in the host-country.

However, it cannot be denied that the life of a highly-skilled migrant working for a multinational company in the Geneva or the Frankfurt regions is dramatically different from that of an asylum seeker in the same regions. Indeed, the two terms refer to very different lived experiences. Yet, they not only express different lived experiences but also the different theoretical frameworks used to study them, which is where things become problematic. My work is an attempt to propose an analysis that bridges the two theoretical frameworks they presuppose; this is what I referred to earlier as overcoming the "migration and the gender binaries". In chapter 6, I developed, for instance, a distinction between the "partner-initiated mover" and "partner-coordinated mover". This analytical tool combines studies focusing on family relationships that are mostly developed along the "migrant" side of the binaries, and on the question of who is the initiator of the move, which comes from studies on expatriation (Andresen et al. 2014) refers to the "highly-skilled migrant" side of the binaries. The goal was to decentre both sides of the "binaries" in order to propose a more innovative framework. Doing so, I created a discussion between disciplines which were, thus far, almost hermetically sealed off from each other, and focused on the strong points of both, showing the possibility of a mutual prosperity. This is the first theoretical implication of my work which should encourage further research.

By exposing such a "polarised worldview", this theoretical part of the study stresses the need to acknowledge the "polarisation of migration" and to deconstruct it. This idea comes from the work of Derrida (1978) who advices us to treat the existing concepts as old tools to be used *à défaut de mieux*. I have developed the "migration binaries" and the "gender binaries" around the idea of a "polarisation of migration". Yet, my proposal for overcoming this worldview is to develop a "decentred theoretical framework" based on the "migration and the gender binaries". This decentred framework aims at deconstructing the unquestioned assumptions that the "polarisation" implies. In order to do so, I developed three "methodological premises" (3 Decentring the Research on Highly-Skilled Migration and Expatriation: Three Methodological Premises, 71). Respectively, these three "methodological premises" are "methodological individualism", "methodological nationalism", and "methodological economism". While the first two are not new and can be found in many studies, the third one, the "methodological economism" represents a theoretical insight of the current study. It relies on the "migration binaries", because it refers to the biases of opposing permanent controlled migration to temporal frictionless mobility. Wimmer and Glick Schiller (2002, 2003) coined the notion of "methodological nationalism" to denounce the biases of either naturalising or ignoring the nation-states involved in various studies: it refers to a methodological position that acknowledges the nation-states without naturalising them. I develop the "methodological economism" following the same logic and propose a position that would depoliticise migration while problematising mobility.

Table 7 summarises the main ideas of the decentred framework for studying highly-skilled migration that is presented here. Each "methodological premise" corresponds to a set of biases that I aim at overcoming in the empirical analysis. Thus, I construct an original research design that breaks with the unquestioned assumptions of the three "methodological premises". This forms the second theoretical insight and, again, demands further research.

My proposal for overcoming the assumptions behind "methodological individualism" relies on the socio-constructivist approach developed by West and Zimmerman (1987), who coined the phrase "doing gender". Many scholars use this approach to study topics other than gender. Amelina and Lutz (2017) speak of "doing migration" and Baldassar et al. (2014) speak of "doing family". Such

Table 7 Summarising the Methodological Premises. Source: Own Elaboration.

Methodological Premises	**Methodological Individualism**	**Methodological Nationalism**	**Methodological Economism**
Unquestioned Assumptions	Migrants as individuals abstracted from their family relations The economic is relevant but the social is irrelevant	Studies on migration develop "ethnic sampling" Studies on highly-skilled migration do not specify the country of origin	Frictionless mobility and controlled immigration Temporal adaptation and permanent immigration Employed skilled mobile professionals and unemployed unskilled migrants
Ways to Overcome Them	Developing a collective approach to assessing simultaneously the work in the labour force and the care work	Using two cities as entry points to contrast the lived experiences of the respondents	Differentiating the "categories of analysis" and the "categories of practice"

a perspective goes beyond the limitations of "methodological individualism", as it overturns the conceptualisation of an isolated migrant by re-embedding him or her in the social context in which they live. In fact, I am responding to Baldassar et al. when they propose that "we need to further develop our understanding of the meanings, actual practices, and obstacles related to doing family in a context of increased mobility and geographical distance" (2014, 171). Thus, my endeavour was to develop further empirical research about the process of "doing family" in the case of highly-skilled migration, and I analysed the process of "doing family" on the move by simultaneously taking into consideration the care work and professional work that gets done in the wake of a migration initiated for professional reasons.

When it comes to the "methodological nationalism", my proposal has been to take two localities as occasions to contextualise the lived experiences and narratives about professional migration. By choosing the Geneva and the Frankfurt regions, I developed an analysis that took the specificity of each region into consideration while remaining attentive to what is common to them. Glick Schiller and Çağlar (2010) develop this way of overcoming the "methodological nationalism" in their book *Locating Migration: Rescaling Cities and Migrants.* Thus, the two first "methodological premises" are not as such original, given that scholars have already proposed ways of overcoming them.

What is original is the proposal to overcome the third "methodological premise": the "methodological economism". It is a combination of the work of two scholars: Favell (2014), who denounces the opposition between a frictionless mobility and a controlled migration, and Wieczorek (2018), who points to the mobility that takes place after a migration. In fact, "methodological economism" tackles the "migration binaries". It opposes migrants, "them", who need to "integrate/assimilate" as they allegedly remain immobile post-migration, and the mobile professionals who need to "adapt" as they are a hyper-mobile part of "us". In order to overcome these biases, I underline the need to be reflexive about the "categories of practices" and the "categories of analysis" at work in the study (Brubaker 2002, 2013).

I do so by purposefully articulating the scientific discussion on expatriation and highly-skilled mobility in the semantic realm of Migration studies. This helps clarify what the "categories of analysis" and "categories of practices" are. From this perspective, I decentre the discussion of highly-skilled mobility and expatriation by emphasising that they are also forms of migration. It is never a frictionless mobility. At the same time, I use concepts drawn from expatriation studies to depoliticise the discussion about migration, hence decentring the core concepts of Migration studies.

Table 8 Implication box 1. Source: Own Elaboration.

Implications for further research:
"Methodological economism" is a tool: 1. for deconstructing the worldview that contrasts "white upper middle-class mobile professionals" and "racialised under-class [*sic*] migrants forced to flee their scorched earth" by problematising mobility and depoliticising migration. 2. for bringing together Expatriation studies and Migration studies, which had not yet spoken to each other. A fruitful approach for further studies would be based on the ability of each field to open the way to original concepts, such as the distinction between "partner-initiated" and "partner-coordinated" mover.

Instead of focusing on the "integration" of highly-skilled migrants, I focus on their ways of coping with (multiple) relocations and so on their chosen "family-strategies" for settling in a new geographical region. Decentring is a barrier against such normative concepts that are hard to define as "integration," which I deliberately avoid. Research on expatriation develops rather a pragmatic approach concretely focusing on the challenges faced by highly-skilled migrants. Such a focus allows the researcher to examine the problems that the migrants face when they arrive in a new locale, the people who can help them, and the kind of support they can receive.

Simultaneously, I continue to use the concept of migrant in order to counterbalance the "polarisation of migration" that these terms imply. In other words, a "highly-skilled migrant" is a "category of analysis" with which none of the interviewees identified. For most, they identified as "expatriate", "citizen of the world", "cosmopolitan" or "employee of their company", which are all "categories of practices". The very use of these categories, I argue, is an act of power; it is a way of creating an order by "naming the world", the goal being to differentiate themselves from others, namely, migrants. While this is quite a common effect of "categories of practice", I aim to avoid reproducing this "polarisation of migration" in my work and thus used a different "category of analysis", that is, the highly-skilled migrant. Implication box 1 (above) summarises the possibilities for further research focusing on the theoretical part.

9.2 Doing Family on the Move

While the theoretical part of this project does provide some new insights, the core of the most innovative results are to be found in the empirical sections, which offer an analysis of "doing family" on the move (Baldassar et al. 2014; Jurczyk,

Lange, and Thiessen 2014) through three different facets – corresponding to the three empirical chapters – namely, the practices, narratives, and strategies that are involved. Through these three facets, I show the variety of family dynamics deployed in a highly-skilled migration. Thus, each of the three facets corresponds to a central element of "doing family" and combines the impact of migration on the professional careers of the partners (Chapter 6: Professional Careers, 137), to the narratives that account for a couple's parsing of the care work and professional careers (Chapter 7: Representing Migration: Between Motilities and Anchors, 183), and the development of their "family-strategy" over the long term (Chapter 8: Family-Strategies of Highly-Skilled Migrants, 225). In a nutshell, "doing family" involves the decision to migrate, the narratives about those decisions, and the strategies allowing families to make the move successful.

9.2.1 Consequences following the Decision to Migrate

The empirical section started with an example of the "professional approach" (6.1 Migration Triggering: An Individual Approach, 138). Four empirical cases served to stress the variety of different professional moves being referred to by the term "expatriation". Following the work of Andresen et al. (2014), I showed the difference between the "assigned expatriate", the "drawn expatriate", the "intra self-initiated expatriate", and the "inter self-initiated expatriate". Noting the relevance of this typology in our attempts to better understand what drives "highly-skilled migration", I also developed a complementary, more "collective approach" (6.2 Migration Triggering: A Collective Approach, 142) in order to facilitate that analysis. This approach is careful to acknowledge the social embeddedness of highly-skilled migrants in order to help overcome what I called the "methodological individualist" bias. I used the same principle to distinguish different types of moves, as Andresen et al. do (2014), by attending to the question of who in the couple is the initiator of a move.

The important difference here has to do with the fact that, while a "professional approach" focuses on the relationship between employer and employee, a "collective approach" focuses instead on the partners. By decentring the "professional approach", I described two seminal types of movers: the "primary-mover" and the "secondary-mover". Each of these types is determined by its position relative to the initiator of the migration. Thus, I was able to show that the consequences of a migration for professional reasons follow different logics for the "primary" and "secondary" movers. This distinction is at the core of my work, in that it changes the way we might conceptualise highly-skilled migration (Implication box 2).

Table 9 Implication box 2. Source: Own Elaboration.

Implications for further research:
The "collective approach" aims at overcoming "methodological individualism". Further research should systematically imbed highly-skilled migrants in their family relationships while studying their inclusion in the labour market.

Consequently, I went on to analyse the way in which the experience of a professional migration differs according to the role one plays as either "primary-mover" or "secondary-mover". This leads to a differentiation of two types of moves for the "primary-mover" and three types of (im)mobility for the "secondary-mover" (Table 10). This typology of movers and types of moves is the foundation of my research. I built the whole empirical section around a recombining and detailed analysis of each separate types. In chapter 6, I analysed each individual type of move for each type of mover. In chapter 7, I showed in each type of move the power of the "primary-mover" to shape the narrative of "displaying family" (Finch 2007). In chapter 8, I combined the different types of moves in order to construct larger patterns of "doing family" (Baldassar et al. 2014): patterns that I called "family-strategies". Table 10 illustrated this conceptual bedrock of my work.

Table 10 Summarising the Types of Move. Source: Own Elaboration

Primary-Mover		**Secondary-Mover**		
Expat-Move	Local-Move	Total-Move Partner-initiated mover	Half-Move Partner-coordinated mover	Secondary-Stayer

The second part of chapter 6 (i.e. the first chapter of the empirical section) explored the different types of moves, showing that the "expat-move" implies "motility" in a way that a "local-move" does not. The analysis of the types of moves of the "primary-mover" revealed a further concept which is absolutely central to my work: the concept of "motility" (Kaufmann, Bergman, and Joye 2004; Flamm and Kaufmann 2006). I classified the types of moves of the "primary-mover" through a continuum on which the capacity as well as the openness to "motility" makes the difference between an "expat-move" and a "local-move". This distinction does not really refer to mobility as such, given that all the respondents described some level of mobility for professional reasons, but rather to an

Table 11 Conceptualised Questions and Corresponding Answers for Chapter 6. Source: Own Elaboration

Conceptualised Questions	Brief Answers
How do couples "integrate" two positions in the labour force when one has to move abroad for professional reasons?	In most cases, the "secondary-mover" decides to follow the "primary-mover" to the new location through a "total-move". Doing so, this person will face the challenges of the "partner-initiated mover". Some others prefer a "half-move" facing the challenges of the "partner-coordinated mover", and some decide against moving altogether.
Is the "secondary-mover" faced with specific challenges regarding their professional career? If yes, what are these challenges about?	Yes, the challenges vary depending on the type of move. Through a "total-move", the "secondary-mover" has to find a position in the labour force in the new location, while in a "half-move" or for a "secondary-stayer", the partners need to deal with a bi-local settling.

individual's openness and capacity to be mobile. This way of typifying the moves of the "primary-mover" through a continuum based on "motility" may initially seem harmless. However, once the perceived need to be "motile" is called into question from the perspective of the "secondary-mover", the concept makes visible the strongly gendered effects that lead many "secondary-movers" to quit the labour force. Truth be told, analyses of these types of moves by "primary-movers" are numerous, constituting the bulk of all studies that analyse professionally triggered migrations, but few of them seem equipped to account for the gendered effects that result.

Analysing the situation of the "secondary-mover", which corresponds to the challenges and reactions of the other partner, also proved to be interesting and rather innovative. I described three different types of reactions as following, coordinating, or staying. Each reaction corresponds to specific types of moves and movers (Table 10). While the "partner-coordinated mover" circumvents the challenges implied by a "total-move", the "partner-initiated mover" faces a unique set of challenges. I therefore showed what these challenges are (6.5.2 Unique Challenges of a Partner-Initiated Mover, 159) as well as what the different factors are that favour or hinder access to the labour market in the context of a "total-move" (6.5.5 Access to the Labour Force, 171).

An important point that I want to make here concerning chapter 6 is that adopting a "collective approach" specifically means that the secondary mover's professional activity is not left out of the analysis. In fact, the "collective approach" encompasses the way the partners coordinate their professional careers which I conceptualised as "labour force work integration". Though it is a complicated path, some "partner-initiated movers" do find a position in the labour force after having followed their partner abroad. Table 11 summarises the main answers to the questions I ask for the chapter 6.

9.2.2 Narratives Displaying the Division of the Tasks

The second empirical chapter (7 Representing Migration: Between Motilities and Anchors, 183) focused on the narratives respondents told. The originality of this part has to do with its adoption of a decentred perspective on how the "primary-movers" display their family. The goal was, once again, to decentre common "migration and gender binaries" by looking, this time, at how the one partner who privileges his (and more rarely her) professional career portrays their family. The two first empirical chapters respond to on another in the sense that they both decentre the analysis, however from different perspectives. While the first chapter analysed the often forgotten professional activity of the "secondary-movers", the second dealt with how the "primary-movers" display their family. In other words, the second chapter reinserted the "primary-movers" into the context of their family. There remained a small nuance to add here, resulting from my analysis the narrative of one "secondary-mover" in the second part of the chapter, namely, Maria's (7.3.1 Ignoring Motility, 208). Nevertheless, the bulk of the chapter focused on the discourse of the "primary-movers" and was structured around the concept of "motility".

I differentiated two discursive stances towards "motility" in this context. The cases in which the "primary-movers" develop a narrative that emphasises "motility" reveal a discrepancy between their narratives and actual practices. They show that the respondents avoid depicting their family as a "traditional family". Instead, they all aim at displaying a fair "family-strategy" in which both of the partners work in the labour force. Paradoxically, they also discursively devalue the care work done in the home, implying that they themselves would not do it. I noted three such stances. One emphasises the "structural constraints" (7.2.1 Structural Constraints, 187) that hinder the "secondary-movers'" capacity to find work in the labour force. Another one consists of accepting the perceived impossibility of having two upwardly mobile and motile professional careers under the same roof (7.2.2 Career Men and Career Women, 195). The last tended to underline the alleged efforts of the "primary-mover" in the sphere of the family (7.2.3 Paradoxical Family Men, 201). The common point between these three narrative stances stressing "motility" is the absence of any reference to the support that the "primary-movers" might provide even if they actually don't. They never mention the possibility of helping their partner in the care

Table 12 Implication box 3. Source: Own Elaboration

Implications for further research:
In my study, I show that the "secondary-movers" are most of the time women. Further studies should focus on the male "secondary-movers" to analyse the reorganisations of gendered hierarchies within these couples.

work so that she might have more time to develop her own professional projects. These discourses reveal the normative standpoint of the respondents *vis-a-vis* the care work. Indeed, they seem systematically to devalue it. While they adopt a narrative that implies they have wished they could be, or tried as much as they could be, more supportive of a "family-strategy" in which both partners can participate in the labour force, they remain blind to the contributions they might make themselves towards achieving such a "family-strategy".

Truth be told, while some of the respondents may indeed simply be blind, others seem intently to enjoy the *status quo* in which they get (all) they want. Nearly all the respondents in this part of the study implied that they could not invest more in the care work without consequences on their professional career. By emphasising that he is a "family man", for example, Dennis shows that he is trying to invest more time into his family, relative to other colleagues. Nevertheless, when he speaks about the daily running of the family, he shows himself to have invested nearly all his time in the labour force, referring systematically to the level of competition at work among his colleagues. In fact, Dennis is in the upper category of the middle management, and for him, as for many of the male respondents, there seems a clear choice between a more balanced "family-strategy" and their career. This point is central to understanding the reproduction of gender hierarchies within the families, given that one of the ways of developing more equalitarian "family-strategies" is the greater contribution of the male partners to the domestic and care work (Implication box 3). Again, they perceive it as an option that would hinder their careers, disadvantaging them relative to colleagues who do not do so. They perceive the situation as an "either/or", only, which is in striking contrast to they way they ostensibly value an organisation of the family in which both partners can invest in a professional activity. Indeed, they seem to make no such investment in the care work that would be required to achieve such a more balanced outcome. Even Dennis' narrative (7.2.3 Paradoxical Family Men, 201), who underlines his interest in the family, does not describe any fairer division of the tasks. I showed that while he considers himself a "family man", as compared to his colleagues, he does not talk *per se* about his actual engagement in developing a fairer distribution of the care work at home.

Table 13 Conceptualised Questions and Corresponding Answers for Chapter 7. Source: Own Elaboration

Conceptualised Questions	Brief Answers
What kind of "meaning patterns" do the respondents produce when they "display family?"	The respondents develop two kinds of "meaning patterns"; one accepting the "motility" of the "primary-mover", the other controlling it. Yet, all the respondents try in one way or another to portray their partner as working in the labour force.
Does "displaying family" guide them while making decisions on their "care work integration"? If yes, how do they orient their actions while taking these decisions?	Yes, it does. The respondents emphasising "motility" hardly ever speak about how they might help their partner with the care work, whereas those who develop a more controlled stance towards "motility" refuse its disruptive impacts on the organisation of the care work. This shows that maintaining a high "motility" for the sake of one professional career (re) produces gender hierarchies.

The second part of the chapter dealt with "anchored narratives", which is to say, narratives that adopt a stance either ignoring or refusing "motility". In this part, I referred to the singular case of Maria (7.3.1 Ignoring Motility, 208) who lies to herself in order to nurture the courage required to find a new position in the labour force again after each successive relocation. Her story underlines the difficulty "secondary-movers" have in finding employment when they migrate every four to five years. I also discussed the case of Lynn and Alex (7.3.2 Refusing Motility, 211) who refused further migrations, acknowledging that they could hardly find a better situation than the one they already had. Both are employed in a multinational company in Frankfurt, both have a position matching their professional competencies. Furthermore, both are aware that finding a better position abroad for one of them would not be impossible, doing so for both simultaneously would be difficult indeed. They do not therefore want to take the risk. In fact, they have received individual offers but always considered the other partner? Their problem is that collectively they are convinced that they could not find better and, thus, adopt a narrative stance in which they refuse "motility". I showed how their "family-strategy" becomes a "golden prison" to them as they must maintain their respective professional activities and are in the difficult situation of wanting to stay in a place they did not choose. All in all, the three narratives stage some desire to control the "motility" of the "primary-mover", in order to be able to share the care work (involving children or aging parents) and/or maintain a balanced "labour force work integration". They showed a narrative stance that refuses "motility" as it remains open to an unknown destination implied by another relocation, which contrasts strongly with the first three narratives that simply accepted "motility". Table 13 summarises the main answers to the questions I asked in chapter 7.

9.2.3 Family-Strategies

The final empirical chapter sought to conceptualise and show the inherent dynamics of three types of "family-strategies" for highly-skilled migrants. I stressed three processes leading to changes in and/or the sedimentation of a "family-strategy". First, the "iterative logic" of a "family-strategy" refers to the way the same series of questions recur at each new migration. Second, the "path-dependency" of the "family-strategies" points to the fact that former decisions have an impact on forthcoming decisions – such as when settling in a new locale, the partners have to take into consideration the consequences of their former choices. Third, I noted the possibility of conflicts arising between the partners that may lead to a change in the relative prioritising of their two careers. By this I mean that in some cases, the "secondary-movers" challenge a given "family-strategy" in order to maintain their own position in the labour force (8.4.2 Power-Dynamics, 268). In most such cases, however, the unequal nature of the "family-strategy" is not challenged, which leads to its sedimentation, meaning that the distribution of "primary" and "secondary mover" types does not switch between the partners. Through these three elements, I emphasised the dynamic and flexible nature of "family-strategies" as neither (pre)determined nor totally random.

To better conceptualise the range of available "family-strategies", I identified three different patterns, namely, the "motile family-strategy", the "local family-strategy" and the "mobile family-strategy". Each "family-strategy" both facilitates and hinders specific constellations of "labour force work integration" and "care work integration"; leading me to speak of a "mutually exclusive model". Furthermore, I showed that each strategy implies a specific relationship to the local space as the partners develop different kind of social networks and mobilise various forms of care support. I constructed each pattern from the particular mix of the types of moves (Chapter 6) and narrative stances towards "motility" (Chapter 7) that are in question.

A "motile family-strategy" makes it difficult to maintain two professional careers under the constraints of the "motility" of the "primary-mover". In fact, the "secondary-mover," who can also be described as a "partner-initiated mover," faces the challenge of redeploying the care work arrangements. In most of the cases, as care work is too important, the "secondary-mover" focuses on it exclusively without seeking external care support (whether of an informal or non-formal nature). Consequently, she does not have the time to seek employment in the labour force. This "family-strategy" corresponds to the respondents who usually self-identified as "expatriate". Their "modalities of settling" are coherent with their idea of having to move again soon, given that the "primary-mover" is "motile" and the "secondary-mover" follows. I demonstrated that the "motility" of the "primary-mover" is supported financially and organisationally by the employing company. This can result in the children studying at an "international school," which the parents have the means to pay for through the employing company. It follows that the partners and the children are included in an exclusive social network around the international school and the colleagues of the "primary-mover". I refer this situation as an "expat-bubble" (Fechter 2007a). Their "peers" face the same challenges and they usually help each other. This tradition strategy is characterised by the gendered division of the tasks between the partners, implying a male "breadwinner" and a female "caregiver".

The "local family-strategy" corresponds to a strategy which favours a long-term anchoring in the new local space. Different from the "motile family-strategy", the "local family-strategy" is preferred by partners who try as much as possible to stay in the local space to which they have migrated. This often implies negotiations with the employer to secure a long term professional position in the new local space, as we saw in the case of Yuna and Julia (8.3.3 Separations and Divorces, 258). In that context, the respondents developed a strategy allowing them to stay because they needed to deal with a more complicated "family-work integration," as is often the case with separations and divorces in which a child is involved. Another situation leading to this particular strategy is one in which both partners have a relatively good position in the labour force and do not want to take the risk of one partner losing his or her professional activity as a result of a further migration. Such a strategy, consequently, decreases the "motility" of the "primary-mover". Indeed, the "local family-strategy" favours a dual career and children at the expense of "motility". When the partners are able to develop a "family-strategy" in which they maintain two professional careers abroad, they often rely on formal, non-formal and informal forms of care support. They can mobilise the local nation-stated "family-policy"; as they worked in the labour force in the same region for a few years, they are entitled, for instance, to maternity or paternity leave and to a place for their child/ren in a public day care centre. It is also common in this context for the parents to hire nanny or au pair, or that their own parents come to help with the care work". In the case of a nanny or an au pair, they tend to delegate the care work to other migrants. This is the "global care chain" that others have discussed (Amelina 2016; Degavre and Merla 2016), which only

Table 14 Implication box 4. Source: Own Elaboration

Implications for further research:
My work deals with highly-skilled migrants. Further studies could use the "mutually exclusive model" to focus on the resident population, asking about the "family-strategies" of commuters, or even "extreme commuters" (who commute more than 90 minutes twice a day to reach their place of work)? Can this "mutually exclusive model" be generalised? Further studies could thus focus on the impact the time spent commuting has on the development of gendered "family-strategies".

underlines the privileged position of the respondents of the current study. Rather than reducing gender inequalities *per se*, they transfer them to other women.

The last pattern of "family-strategy" is the "mobile family-strategy" which corresponds to a daily and extensive use of mobility in order to maintain the partners' "family-work integration". In fact, their integration of professional work and care work is difficult to maintain, as the partners tend to travel extensively. This strategy is often temporary as it is exhausting. This strategy favours the "motility" and the "careers" but not the "children". The case of Maria working for an Italian company in Japan exemplifies the difficulty of maintaining this strategy over the long term. Though partners usually do not have children, given that the strategy implies a prioritisation of their professional careers over family-life, some do. In this context, sending the children to boarding school is an option commonly turned to.

From a "collective perspective", the three strategies offer an innovative way of tackling the (re)production of gender hierarchies within the family: what I call a "mutually exclusive model" (Implication box 4). I distinguish three elements: "motility", children, and career. I show that while men can have an upwardly mobile and successful professional career, including "motility" and children, women can often only have two of these at any one time. At the core of the model lies the recurring fact that women do the unpaid care work more often than men do and the question is, as Table 11 summarizes, what can be done to diminish this discrepancy?

Table 15 Conceptualised Questions and Corresponding Answers for Chapter 8. Source: Own Elaboration

Conceptualised Questions	**Brief Answers**
How can the "family-strategies" be conceptualised to study "gendered hierarchies" within families? What kind of model can I construct for them?	I distinguish three types of "family-strategies". Each "family-strategy" favours two elements and hinders the third one. The "motile family-strategy" favours the "motility" of the "primary-mover". Strong "gendered hierarchies" support a traditional division of the tasks between the partners given that the female "secondary-mover" does the care work, hindering any hope for a dual career couple. The "local family-strategy" favours dual career couples and a fairer division of the tasks when it comes to the care work, but hinders the "motility" of the "primary-mover". The "mobile family-strategy" favours a dual career couple and the "motility" of the "primary-movers" (if not both partners) while hindering family-life. I articulate the three types of "family-strategies" through a "mutually exclusive model" and show how the strong "gendered hierarchies" of the "motile family-strategy" allows male partners to combine a career, motility, and children. At the same time, it undermines the female partners' capacity to coordinate all three elements. This model shows that unlike their male counterparts, the female partners cannot have it all.
What is the relationship between the "family-strategies" and the region in which the respondents settle?	Each "family-strategy" stresses a specific social network as well as a distinguishable organisation and mobilisation of support for the care work. The "motile family-strategy" requires the financial support of the employing company, involving international schools and networks of fellow "expatriates". The "local family-strategy" relies more on the local variation of the nation-stated "family policy" as well as a mobilisation of a mix of formal, informal and non-formal care structures. The "mobile family-strategy" implies an extensive use of mobility and refers to boarding schools.

10 Recommendations for Practice

Chapter 10 considers recommendations to create a fairer division of care work and labour force work between partners by focusing on three elements: (1) the division of the care work after the birth of a child, (2) the childcare provision and the "family policy" available to the partners in the two regions of investigation, and (3) the support of the employing companies. Thus, the chapter is structured around three main parts. In the first part, I discuss the "critical time" corresponding to the arrival of the first child. I show how this crucial moment combined with a lack of care support leads to the hierarchisation of one professional career over the other between partners that has lasting effects. The second part deals with the "critical places". As mentioned earlier, my study focuses on the development of gendered hierarchies in two specific regions; namely the Geneva region and the Frankfurt region. I point out differences between the Geneva and Frankfurt regions when it comes to childcare by looking at the empirical results and by contextualising the two regions (Chapter 5). I stress that the "family policies" of the Frankfurt region are more attentive to the challenges of coordinating family life and professional careers. The third and last part of the chapter addresses the companies. Here, I underline the importance and the relevance of the company's support to the partners, by acknowledging the complexity of "doing family" on the move.

10.1 Migration, Children, and Gender Wage Gap

Many recent studies in economics show that the birth of a child creates inequalities in the labour market between partners (Blau and Kahn 2017; Goldin et al. 2017; Hausmann, Tyson, and Zahidi 2009; Hirsch, Schank, and Schnabel 2010; Kleven, Landais, and Søgaard 2018; Schmid 2016). Though these studies take place in a "sedentary" context (in which mobility and "motility" are not accounted for), they underline a range of gendered dynamics within couples and "elementary families" that explain the construction of the "gender wage gap" (Blau and Kahn 2017). The interruption or the diminution of the female partners' labour work force, because of child care work, is central to explaining earnings differentials between men and women[99].

99 Kleven, Landais, and Søgaard (2018) focus on Denmark, a country known for having "family friendly policies", thus, I suggest a similar trend exists, if not such a strong one, in the rest of Europe.

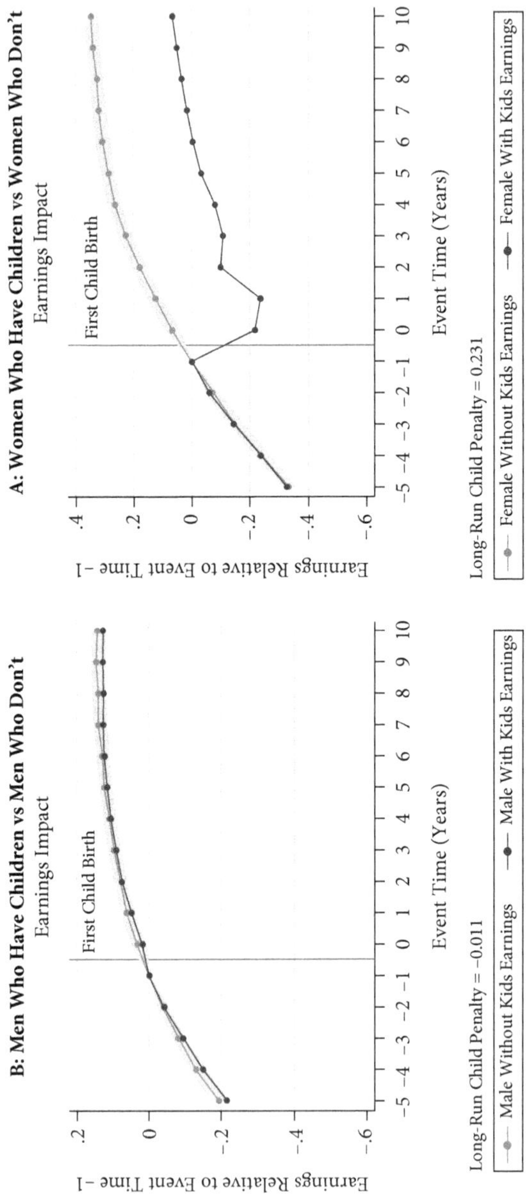

Figure 27 Impacts of Children in a Difference-in-Differences Event Study Design. Source: Kleven et al. (2018, 42)

According to Kleven et al. (2018), the impact of children on women's earnings is long-lasting; women do not catch up with the loss of income, even after ten years. This creates a critical gap between men and women, as women receive a lower income for the rest of their professional careers. Children also affect career progression; studies show that women still get a lower income than their similarly qualified male counterparts and have less chances to reach top positions (OECD 2012; Webb 2017). Here, the image of the "glass ceiling" is apt. Figure 27 shows that women reach the same level of income they had before the birth of a child only 7 years later. To put it bluntly, a child gives men 7 years advancement, contributing to the "hierarchy of position" (7.2.1 Structural Constraints, 187). Such is a "critical moment" in one's career trajectory (Riaño et al. 2015). Centrally, the division of care work between partners is the underlying generator of inequalities in the labour market. If women earn less, it is mainly because they either completely stop or decrease their working hours to do the unpaid care work. On top of that, reducing to part-time work is often a permanent and not a temporary strategy (OECD 2012, 159). Men do not change their work hours and maintain their earning when they become fathers, as the left graph of Figure 27 shows. Moreover, Hirsch, Schank, and Schnabel (2010) – focusing on Germany – speak of the "monopsonistic firms power" to explain how employers take advantage of the fact that women's labour supply is less elastic than men's. Indeed, women tend to take other considerations into account such as the necessity to do the care work for the children when considering their position in the labour force. They will, for instance, only accept positions that are not too far away from the children's school. The authors argue that this situation explains why there is up to one third of a gender pay gap in Germany (2010, 314). In other words, men are more "motile" when it comes to considering interesting positions independent of care work. The "motile family-strategy" corroborates this, showing once again the gendered impact of "motility". The fact that men and women work in different sectors is another factor explaining the gender wage gap (Schmid 2016, 462). The male-dominated sectors typically pay more than the female-dominated ones. All these factors are important to understanding the "gender wage gap" and the "glass ceiling"; but centrally, recent studies underline that "the gender gap increases with family foundation and bringing up children" (2016, 455). My study corroborates this result, as it shows the process of the construction of gendered hierarchies between partners. In the context of highly-skilled migration, the female partners, however, have to face another layer of challenges linked to the very experience of migration. My analysis stresses how "motility" (Flamm and Kaufmann 2006) is a factor leading to the prioritisation of one (and only one) professional career creating an unequal division of care work. In fact, the "motile family-strategy" often implies that the female "secondary-mover" sacrifices her career to do all the care work.

The worst-case scenario for a female partner – who not only wants to remain employed but who also desires professional advancement – is to face a resignation, a pregnancy, and a relocation simultaneously. This combination creates a strong hierarchisation of the professional careers, favouring a traditional "family-strategy" potentially leading to a "motile family-strategy". This combination of resigning and relocating while being pregnant (or having a baby) comes with another striking element: the lack of mobilisation of any kind of external care support. When the partners arrive in the new region, the female does not have the time to mobilise any kind of support, as the care work for babies is extremely time-consuming. Even though she may want to seek child care, she usually does not yet have local knowledge or access to the appropriate networks to find it. Here, the male partner and the employing company can help by providing relevant and trustworthy information. I will develop this point in the recommendation for the "primary-movers" and for companies. Furthermore, arranging child care takes time; waiting-lists for day care centres are important in both the Frankfurt and Geneva regions. In other words, the partners relocate at the moment when external care support would be of the uppermost importance so that the female partner might maintain a professional activity. As seen in the case studies, typically the "primary mover" does not help either.

In addition, the state of "liminality" implied by the "motility" of the "primary-mover" is destabilising for the "secondary-mover", as she is always trapped between one place and another. Looking for a position in the labour force is already a challenge, but when the "secondary mover" must first develop the right conditions to be in the position to seek employment i.e., to have the time to do so, the task is even more of a challenge. The Damocles sword of a next relocation is always there and is unsettling (in all senses of the word). Maria, who developed a narrative to hide the possibility of a further relocation, always convincing herself that they have settled for good (7.3.1 Ignoring Motility, 208), exemplifies just how much of challenge a relocation represents.

This array of factors, keeping "secondary-movers" from seeking external support for care work, is linked with a third aspect, which I call the "illusion of the independence of the nuclear family". When the respondents display their family as a team, as Kim does (7.2.1 Structural Constraints, 187), I argue that they imply its self-sufficiency. Sentences like: "you can move your family if it works well, it's your base" (Xavier, 50yrs, married)[100] are common in the discourses

100 La famille vous pouvez la bouger et si elle fonctionne bien (…), c'est ça votre socle (Own Translation).

Table 16 Implication box 5. Source: Own Elaboration.

Recommendations for the Female "Secondary-Movers"
The combination of a pregnancy, resigning from a current position, and a relocation – especially when the "primary-mover" is "motile" – creates a dearth of care work support. This lack of support makes it very difficult for the female partner to have the time to seek employment in the labour force. To stay employed in the labour market, I would recommend the female partner not follow her partner abroad while pregnant or with a baby, as the absence of support after the relocation creates the conditions for being out of the labour force for some time. Some women follow while being on maternity leave creating different conditions of support and subsequently different possibilities of reintegrating into the labour force.

emphasising "motility". They encourage the "secondary-mover" to do all the care work while the family settles into a new region, which keeps her from finding care support for the children. Again, the absence of support from the male partners is striking is these cases. There are, other types of "family-strategy" in which the "secondary-mover" uses a mix of different types of care support. Through a "half-move", I showed how Manon maintains her inclusion in the labour market by making use of her maternity leave. The absence of support for the care work of a small child, while being abroad, is one major reason that prevents /forbids the female partner from joining the labour force. Having to do all the care work leaves little or no time for her to develop her own projects. When the children reach school age, she has, arguably, more time to seek a position in the labour force but the "hierarchy of the position" is already established and the time of care work has created a gap in her CV.

The female partner not only loses (a part of) her income, she also loses part of her capacity to negotiate on equal terms with the male partner when it comes to further professional decisions. In the empirical part, I develop the concept of a "hierarchy of positions": a process by which the male partner negotiates to his advantage, because he earns more, "so it made more sense for us like that" he could argue retrospectively. The male partners develop a justifying discourse on how the "family-strategy" becomes unequal because it is, allegedly, the choice that makes more sense for them collectively. I speak of a Foucauldian moment (1994, 66) because the micro relations of power – in this case the male partner using his higher income to maintain his professional activity and thus maintaining his independence – reinforces the large scaled strategies of power – patriarchy in contemporary societies – which are in turn used to justify the micro relations of power (Implication box 5).

Table 17 Implication box 6. Source: Own Elaboration.

Recommendations for the Male "Primary-Movers"
The "primary-mover" can support the "secondary mover". Principally, this support implies negotiating with the employer to be able to better integrate labour force work and care work. A first step is about raising these issues in the labour force. This does not have to mean reducing the number of hours worked in the labour force per week (though it can mean that); but rather it means speaking about the integration of care work and labour force work and finding arrangements to give the "secondary-mover" the necessary time to seek employment. Sharing the private agenda with the employer or looking actively for a day care solution are helpful first steps.

Yet, many male partners work hard in the labour force, as they feel they need to maintain the family's standard of living. Many of them do not help with the unpaid care work. In this configuration, the male partners rarely acknowledge the possibility of decreasing their working hours to support their partner with the care work. They fear that this would put their careers at risk, as they work in a competitive milieu. In fact, it is exactly what happens to the female partners and this situation is widespread to the extent that it creates the gender wage gap. Furthermore, it creates a vicious circle within an "elementary family". As long as the female partner does the care work and cannot have time to look for a position in the labour force, her chances of finding a paid position in the labour force are low, if non-existent. If she had time to seek and find employment in the labour force, he would not have the only income – creating more financial security for the family. How is it possible to break this "vicious circle"?

I argue that better coordination between labour force work and care work is key. I showed some cases of respondents who managed to coordinate both. Though, these cases are the ones of divorced mothers, they stress the possibility of a better coordination between both. Yuna and Julia (8.3.3 Separations and Divorces, 258) find arrangements with their employer. They negotiate within the labour force; they use their "voice" in Hirschmann's terms (1970). Acknowledging that they the "primary movers" can help is key. They can either reduce their working hours, develop a better coordination between their work in the labour force and the care work or look for a day care solution in order to create better conditions for the "secondary-mover" to have the time to look for employment. Having more than one income in the family reduces the pressure the "primary mover" might feel to (over)work. Julia shares her private agenda with her employer, allowing him or her to know when it is best for Julia to have meetings or to plan business trips. She also specifically asked not to be relocated in the next years. By creating a better coordination and by reducing her "motility", she is able to maintain a full-time position in the labour force while doing as well as delegating care work. Her case stresses the need to mobilise care support, as she cannot rely on a partner to do it; which is coincidently the case for dual career couples. A better coordination could imply flexible home-office arrangements to fit with the schedule of a day care centre as well as flexible working hours to allow partners to share the care work. He could start earlier while she brings the children to a day care centre and vice versa in the evening. I argue that for dual career couples with children, childcare provision is a necessity, especially for families on the move. The central point is that the "primary-movers" must speak about coordinating both with their employer and generally acknowledge the value of doing so. For this to happen, a change in the mentality of both the employers and the employees is required. I will show in the next subchapter that legal provisions for paternity leave are positive in this regard, as they normalise the fact that a male reduces or stops his activity in the labour force for a time to do the care work (Implication box 6).

In the first part of this chapter, I have dealt with the "critical moment" of the arrival of a child by focusing on the partners. I will now switch to the "critical places", contextualising the regions of Geneva and Frankfurt through the lens of childcare.

10.2 Childcare in the Geneva and the Frankfurt regions

Those female partners who are able to maintain a position in the labour force mobilise external support for the care work. Here I refer to a mix of care work support to emphasise the use of formal, non-formal, and informal care support. Maintaining a position in the labour market is conditional on the arrival of a child, also on the notions of inclusion in the labour force and the availability of a comprehensive "family policy". If the mother works in the labour force in a region where the "family policy" truly supports her, the pressure to quit the labour force is small. On the contrary, if she works in the labour force where the "family policy" is conservative, the need to resign is high. For the OECD, the "family policies" have an economic significance as "gender equality and a more efficient use of skills are essential to achieving strong and sustainable growth" (2012, 23). Thus, there is an economic case for both regions to develop comprehensive "family policies". In sum, the "family policies" are essential for the regions and determinant for the parents who want to develop a dual career.

At the end of my contextualisation in the subchapter 5.2.1 (p. 124), I asked how does the "formal care" happen under the conditions of repeated professional

Table 18 Implication box 7. Source: Own Elaboration.

Recommendations for Both Regions
It is not only about developing the formal conditions to allow fathers to take paternity leave, but also about encouraging behaviours leading to a fairer share between partners of the care work required for a child. In both regions, fathers should be encouraged to take more time caring for their child(ren). The mothers who want to develop a professional career could thus have more time to seek employment in the labour force. Achieving both these objectives requires a strong childcare provision, namely through increased accessibility to day care centres for pre-school children.

mobility? The concept "family-strategies" gives some insights into this question, as the type of "family-strategy" strongly affects the reception of care work support. In the case of the "motile family-strategy", "formal care" is more difficult to facilitate because the "female partner" relocates without a position in the labour force. The situation is different for partners who make use of a "local family-strategy". Dual career couples are more common in the realm of the "local family-strategy" because the partner out of the labour force has more time to find a new position. Thus, the "local family-strategy" is a fruitful field to understand the differences between the regions of Frankfurt and Geneva when it comes to childcare.

In the contextual chapter, I showed discrepancies in terms of "family policy" between these two regions and these were corroborated by the empirical evidence. The more developed "family policy" of the Frankfurt region favours the inclusion of the two partners in the labour force. For those partners who wish to develop a dual career, maternity and paternity leave create favourable conditions for maintaining two professional careers. In fact, these insurances are even more important for highly-skilled migrants as they have less opportunities to receive informal care support as most of them cannot have access to the "hidden economy of kinship".

It is not a coincidence that Lynn and Alex manage to maintain two positions in the labour force while Annisa and Adrian cannot (8.3.1 Low Support for the Care Work, 249; 8.3.2 Combination of Formal, Informal and Non-Formal Care Support, 252). Annisa mentioned several times her wish to stay in the labour force following the births of their children, but ultimately she had to resign. The lack of childcare support in the Geneva region largely explains her situation and in that sense, Annisa lives in a "critical place". When it came to "formal care", Annisa's maternity leave was shorter than Lynn's. Furthermore, Alex took a paternity leave while Adrian did not, as the possibility did not exist in the Geneva region. A key sentence of Alex's argument was: "people do it all the time,

Table 19 Implication box 8. Source: Own Elaboration

Recommendations for the "Family Policy" in the Geneva Region
In the Geneva region, the lack of paternity leave and a short maternity leave push many women out of the labour market or force them to reduce their working hours. This situation is even more acute for migrants as they typically do not have the possibility to make use of informal care. A longer maternity leave and the possibility for the father to do his part of the care work by having access to paternity leave would create better conditions for an inclusion of both parents in the labour force.

it [fathers taking a paternity leave] happens almost all the time, they take this time off" (Alex, 52yrs, married). In fact, it is not only about the possibility to do so, it is also a matter of peoples' attitudes and openness towards paternity leave. Alex's insistence that "almost everybody is doing it" underlines a change in the "gender culture" (Pfau-Effinger 1998) within his company. The data of the OECD corroborates this and shows a general trend in Germany. The attitude towards the statement that "women should be prepared to cut down on paid work for the sake of the family" diminished slightly in Germany while it remained the same in Switzerland (OECD 2012, 210). Yet, both in Switzerland and in Germany more than half of the respondents agree with this statement. It is still far away from countries like Denmark or Sweden where less than 25% of the respondents agree with this statement. For the OECD: "the shortage of formal childcare for very young children (…) reinforce parents' attitudes towards employments and care" in which the women does the care work (ibid). At the beginning of the current chapter, I said that the key to reducing the gender wage gap is a fairer division of the care work between the parents. To achieve this, the partners need external care support as well as a change in attitudes regarding "who should do the care work". These two elements argue in favour of more formal childcare provision as it, arguably, impacts both partners (Implication box 7).

Another recurring problem is the lack of adapted day care solutions for the parents. Here too, the differences between the Geneva region and the Frankfurt region are striking. One factor which pushed Annisa out of the labour force is the price of day care in Switzerland. The combination of a short maternity leave, the absence of paternity leave and expensive day care solution were detrimental to Annisa's professional career. The waiting lists and the time spent by the "secondary-mover" in finding places for the children hindered her capacity to seek a position in the labour force. In the Geneva region, it is an oft-repeated claim by the respondents that they could not find day care solutions for small children. Or if they managed to do so, the solution was not satisfactory: either

Table 20 Implication box 9. Source: Own Elaboration

Recommendations for the Parents
For highly-skilled migrants, a successful coordination between two professional careers and the care work for a child implies the use of a mix of day care arrangements. I did not encounter a single case in which the parents found a full-time place in a kindergarten. Many of them talk of long waiting lists and as they do not know where they will be relocated, they cannot plan ahead by booking a place in advance. Thus, the solution comes with mobilising a mix of different day care arrangements.

too expensive because it is private and without subsidy or because of the lack of available places. For instance, only one child out of every two can get a place in Geneva. This situation corroborates the results of Imhof (2015) and Bonoli and Vuille (2013) that I presented in the contextual chapter. In the Frankfurt region, the respondents complain less about the day care solution for their children. Though most of the parents in the Frankfurt region send their children to a private day care centre, it also means that they can afford to pay for it (as in my empirical cases, the ones without expat-contracts are dual earners). This point is central and corroborates the recommendation of the OECD, to "ensure that work pays for both parents" (2012, 216). For Annisa, her work in the labour force did not pay enough; she made it clear when she told me that: "It was insane to keep two kids at the *crèche*[101] with that salary, because I wouldn't have anything at the end" (Annisa, 39yrs, married). This is not the case for the respondents in Frankfurt, as they have access to longer parental leaves. In the Geneva region, the female partner has to find an arrangement for day care sixteen weeks after the birth of the child (corresponding to the end of the legal maternity leave). In Germany, the partners can share 14 months i.e. 56 weeks. Thus, they can seek and organise a day care solution and the possibility to use an even more flexible parental leave which can last up to 24 months (*Elterngeld+*). I argue that the length of the parental leave creates a trickle-down effect on the capacity of the partners to share and organise the division of the tasks (Implication box 8).

That said, the partners in both regions do have the possibility of, and need to develop, a mix of care support. I showed how Lynn and Alex not only use formal care but also informal and non-formal care, and how Julia hires an au pair and sends her son to a private school. On the other hand, I showed how Annisa struggles with the mid-day breaks or how Christophe (8.2.1 Prioritising one Career, 227) has not found a satisfactory day care solution: both "elementary

101 in French in the original interview.

families" live in the Geneva region. The partners succeeded in maintaining two professional careers while doing family on the move by effectively making use of different organisations and people for the care support. In the Geneva region, for instance, there are possibilities such as day placement in a family, "home kindergarten", a nanny or au pair, a kindergarten, or a nursery. It is striking that many of the parents interviewed do not speak about combining[?] such different forms of day care. In other words, since the parents are unable to find one successful form of day care, they should aim at combining a range of care options simultaneously (Implication box 9).

10.3 Family-Friendly Companies

To understand the capacity of the partners to maintain two professional careers while being on the move is to introduce a third actor: the employing company. The employing company can be supportive in many ways but I will restrict myself only to the ways it can help in the coordination between care work and work in the labour force. In the empirical section, I noted several measures that some companies took to support the partners. I will summarise them here, treating these as examples of good practice in that they allow the partners to coordinate both more easily.

Those who relocate with small children have noted the need to be on waiting lists before a day care solution opens up. This is a common struggle for respondents in either the Frankfurt or in the Geneva region. In many cases, the absence of day care solutions creates a vicious circle for the "secondary-movers", as they do not find the time to look for employment after a relocation. Whenever possible, the company should inform their employees of a relocation well in advance, encouraging them to look for day care solutions ahead of a relocation to a new place. An easy step one that helped many of the respondents is to provide accurate information regarding the different kinds of available formal, non-formal and informal care, perhaps in the form of an information booklet. More than merely summarising information, these booklets should orient partners towards appropriate and reliable resources, persons, or organisations in advance of a relocation. Another possibility would be to ask the relocation offices to take some steps to finding a day care solution. When the partners take a two day planning trip to visit the different accommodations available, they could also start applying to or visiting some of the day care centres. The sooner they begin the application process the better, as in the Canton of Vaud statistics show that slightly more than 30% of the parents need more than six months to find a day care solution for a small child (Imhof 2015, 37).

Many interviewees emphasise that the months following relocation are the most stressful because the employee starts a new job, in a new region, with new colleagues, and new tasks. At the same time, the situation is hard for the "secondary-movers"; especially when they perform a "total-move". In fact, the moment of a relocation is critical for both partners. The employer can help to create the necessary conditions for the partners to develop an adapted care support for their family. The employer should not prevent "primary-movers" from asking for a reduction in their working time for a limited period, typically, just after a relocation; though the timing is (by far) not ideal, as just after a relocation the work load in the labour force is typically high. Yet, the conditions of an early return or a "failed assignment" are potentially exacerbated if the "secondary-mover" has to do all the care work by herself. If she had intended to continue a professional career before relocating but lacks the time to seek employment, she can also decide to return home. In the review of the literature (2 Moving with Skills: A Review of the Literature, 31), I referred to studies that showed how important the satisfaction of the "secondary-mover" is in both supporting the "primary-mover" and triggering early returns. Thus, it is in the interest of the company that "secondary-movers" happily remain for the length of the relocation. The capacity of partners to create a mix of day care support is key to increasing the satisfaction of the "secondary-mover". Yet, the "secondary-mover" needs to have the time to organise this which implies the support of the "primary-mover". Of course, no one can guarantee that a "secondary-mover" will find employment or that she will find a "dream-job". The respondents are aware of that. They underline, however, that their biggest frustration comes from not having the chance to seek it. In other words, they need the support of the "primary-movers" to have a concrete opportunity to seek employment. From this perspective, giving the "primary-movers" the possibility to either (1) reduce working hours, (2) have access to a home-office or (3) organise their time more freely with flexible working hours for a few months after a relocation, could help the partners to seek a day care centre.

The cases of Yuna and Julia, both "divorced mothers" living in a foreign country, show that closely integrating both professional and family life is possible. Julia shares her private and professional calendars with her assistant and her boss. Not everyone wishes to have such a close integration between both, but companies might take the importance of child care to an employee into account. This solution, as I have shown, works for both Yuna and Julia and does not require a diminution of their working hours. Rather, it requires flexible and/or irregular working hours with a greater freedom to work remotely

Table 21 Implication box 10. Source: Own Elaboration.

Recommendations for the Companies
– Informing the employee about a further relocation as soon as possible. – Producing information booklets summarising the different forms of care support available in a particular region – Offering the possibility to reduce or rearrange the working hours in the labour force directly after a relocation. – Favouring flexible working hours and working from home. – Being open to unconventional ways of integrating professional and family life. – Creating and/or supporting the offer of day care services in the region. – Developing dual career networks.

some days. Similarly, some companies have agreed to keep an employee on even though s/he was going to move to the other end of the world; the case of Maria working for an Italian company in Japan is striking in this regard. Being open to unconventional ways of integrating professional and family life, making an intensive use of the new technologies of information and communication, can offer (temporary) solutions. However, one has to be careful since such a strategy could be exhausting in the long term and also be a cause of isolation, which "secondary movers" precisely do not want.

Last but not least, the company can help create an environment in which both partners can work in the labour force while managing to organise the care work. This comes close to Scott's idea (2004), which gives "attention to the environment within which the organisation operates" (2004, 5). I would go one step further and argue that a company does not have to adapt or react to a static environment but can, to a certain extent, modify it. When it comes to the possible support for care work, a company can, for instance, invest in the creation of a kindergarten within its walls or nearby. This is the case of Philip-Morris in Lausanne. It is a financially expensive solution, yet it can also be done in collaboration with the local authorities. In the case of this kindergarten, some places are reserved for the children of employees and some are open to others. Another example of companies aiming to change their environment is the creation of programs that favour the dual partner career – like the International Dual Career Network (ICDN) in the Geneva region. This allows the partner who wants to find a position in the labour force after a relocation, to receive support and to be included in professional networks. In sum, as much as the "primary-mover" can be of help, so can the employing companies (Implication box 10).

10.4 Summary of the Implications for Further Research and the Recommendations for Practice

In this chapter, I gave practical recommendations for a better coordination between professional careers and care work. It is a central problem for all families who want to maintain two professional activities in the labour force while raising children, yet the challenges are exacerbated by mobility and "motility". As a conclusion for the discussion part, in Table 22 (below), I summarise the implication boxes of chapters 9 and 10.

Table 22 Summarising of the main Implications and Recommendations of the Study. *Source: Own Elaboration*

Implications for Further Research (Implication boxes 1 and 2) – Considering the "methodological economism" as a tool: 1. to problematise mobility and depoliticise migration. 2. to bring together the fields of highly-skilled migration studies and expatriation studies. – Embedding systematically the family relationships in studies on highly-skilled migration and expatriation.
Ideas for Further Research (Implication boxes 3 and 4) – Focusing on the male "secondary-movers". – Focusing on (extreme-)commuters and the development of gendered "family-strategies".
Recommendations for the Female "Secondary-Movers" (Implication box 5) – Avoiding the combination of a pregnancy, a resignation, and a relocation as it creates a dearth of care work support. – Being aware that the division of the tasks after the arrival of the first child creates a path dependency difficult to challenge.
Recommendations for the Male "Primary-Movers" (Implication box 6) – Negotiating with the employer to be able to better integrate work in the labour force and care work. – Helping with the care work and with the search for a day care centre. – Finding flexible professional arrangements to give the "secondary-mover" the necessary time to seek employment.
Recommendations for Parents (Implication box 9) – Mobilising a mix of different day care arrangements.
Recommendations for the "Family Policy" in the Geneva Region (Implication box 8) – Creating a paternity leave and developing longer maternity leaves.
Recommendations for both Regions (: Implication box 7) – Developing a strong childcare provision by increasing the accessibility of the offer of day care centres for pre-school children.
Recommendations for the Companies (Implication box 10) – Producing information booklets on childcare. – Valorising flexible working hours, home-office, and unconventional ways of integrating professional and family life. – Offering the possibility to reduce or rearrange the work time in the labour force directly following a relocation.

11 Conclusion: Motility and Mobility

From a broader perspective, "motility" and "flexibility" are close concepts. One could say that "motility" is a form of geographical flexibility. Flexibility is an ability to answer to a professional opportunity quickly without having to rearrange the "family work integration". Someone who can go on a business trip over the weekend and take two compensatory days out during the week is deemed flexible. Someone single without a child can accept a position abroad without hesitation, which requires working over the weekend without having to arrange or rearrange care work (as it is low if non-existent), is "motile" and flexible. It is the case of, for instance, John at the beginning of his career. He moved from the United States to Hong Kong in less than two weeks between the moment he learned about the position and his actual migration (7.2.1 Structural Constraints, 187). At this time of his biography, he was "motile" and flexible. From this perspective, pointing to the gendered impact of "motility" is not a trivial matter as it explains, at least in part, the difficulty of female partners to be professionally successful while raising children simultaneously and being on the move for the sake of their partners' careers. It gives a new perspective, explaining the difference in career achievement between men and women.

I show that the "motile family-strategy" favours the career of one of the partners, very usually the male partner. In fact, those who have reached the very top of these companies are, in most of my empirical cases, those who had followed a "motile family-strategy". Crossing the interviews with the "objective data" that I collected on the *LinkedIn* profiles of the respondents confirms this strategy and result. The companies are all big multinational companies employing thousands of people worldwide. Pedro (8.2.1 Prioritising one Career, 227) is the director of the planning and business development of his company, Xavier (8.2.2 Homemaking and Caregiving, 235) is the general manager (CEO), and Richard (8.2.3 Company's Support, 239) the president of marketing worldwide. In contrast, the ones developing a "local family-strategy" or a "mobile family-strategy", though they have "good" professional careers, tend not to reach these top positions and stay in the upper tier of middle management. Lynn and Alex, whom I mentioned as being amongst the rare respondents to have successfully developed two professional careers, do not hold these top positions within their employing company (which does not mean they do not have a good income). They are middle managers rather than top managers. Lynn is an account director and Alex a creative designer implying a qualitative difference with the positions of Pedro, Xavier, or Richard. In fact, during the interview and in my analysis of Lynn's narrative (7.3.2 Refusing Motility, 211), she mentions several times that she refused positions abroad at the company headquarters, where she could have continued to compete in order to reach top management positions. The way she explains how she now has another idea of what success means (7.3.1 Ignoring Motility, 208) is striking and contrasts greatly with the narratives of Pedro, Xavier, or Richard. A "traditional" and heteronormative division of the tasks between the partners allows the male "primary-movers" to develop their professional careers. They can accept any opportunity abroad, knowing that the "secondary-mover" will follow and do the care work. In fact, this model is close to that of the *bourgeois* family at the end of nineteenth century. This type of "family-strategy" not only reproduces the gender hierarchy but also contributes to a successful professional career. For these "primary-movers", such a strategy is extremely gratifying to one who makes it to the top of the company with the aid of a loving spouse and beautiful children. The ones more careful about their "family-work integration" – who integrate two professional careers – cannot compete because at one point they usually have to refuse an opportunity abroad.

My analysis leaves us with quite a pessimistic result as it shows how the respondents are locked up in seemingly binary choices. For the male partners, it is either a "winner takes all" model, in which they have to focus solely on their work in the labour force in order to compete with colleagues who do the same. Taking more time to help one's partner with the care work translates to a disadvantage in the labour market, hindering a rise to the top of a company. Thus, they have to choose between success and fairness. For female partners, the choice seems to be between children or professional advancement. Male partners who accept to follow them in a highly motile international career are a rarity. Thus, the concept of "motility" is a central and underused concept to understanding the migration, career, and gender nexus. It explains, in part at least, how some achieve and or give up on professional advancement. This combination is toxic for gender equality. Essentially, this research underlines the gendered impact of frequent migration on "family-strategies". On a more positive note, research done by the OECD (2012) shows that "family policies" positively affect gender equality between men and women in the labour force. A more important and accessible offer in terms of day care arrangements is a key policy. It has trickle down effects not only on the capacity of the female partners to better coordinate work in the labour force and care work but also on favouring fairer attitudes of the parents when it comes to knowing "who should do the care work". The context can be changed and the recommendations I develop in the current research go in this direction.

Appendix

Appendix 1: Contact Letter

unine
UNIVERSITÉ DE NEUCHÂTEL

Swiss Forum for Migration and Population Studies SFM

Institut SFM
Faubourg de l'Hôpital 106
2000 Neuchâtel, Suisse

12/05/2016

PhD on Household Strategies and Professional Careers of Highly-Skilled Migrants

Dear Madam, Dear Sir,

As part of a PhD in social sciences at the University of Neuchâtel I am studying the experiences of the households of highly-skilled migrants and expatriates in the Lake Geneva region.

My work is an empirical study, using qualitative methods of social sciences research. It focuses on highly-skilled migration and its organisational surroundings. The intense and frequent international mobility of highly-skilled professionals influences career paths and private-lives. Besides their professional activities, highly-skilled migrants, however, have also other social roles: as wives or husbands, mothers and fathers. The households face challenges which are typically linked with their localisation under the condition when – at least one of them – is mobile for professional reasons. The situation can be challenging since the chance for both partners to find a professional position in their field within the same local space is limited. In this context, I examine the different household strategies they develop. Do they both decide to come to Switzerland to work or do they choose to live apart for a time? Are they both continuing to work or is one stopping his or her professional activity in order to be able to follow his or her partner? Besides, state-bodies, employing companies like multinational corporations, research institutes, and sportive federations, as well as specific organisations, like outplacement agencies, and relocation offices are more and more aware of the challenges international careers imply. In this context, they develop programs and policies which aim at facilitating the settling of highly-skilled migrants and the coordination within the household. Do the highly-skilled migrants use these programs at all? If yes, what is the concrete help they receive and what are the social consequences for the households? My project explores the experiences and situations of highly-skilled migration by linking the everyday experience of professional mobility with potential organisational support highly-skilled migrants may receive when they settle in a new place.

This is why I take the freedom to ask you if you would agree to meet and discuss your experience of international professional mobility. In order to be able to know how this mobility is actually experienced, I intend to do interviews with highly-skilled migrants and/or expatriates settled in the Lake Geneva region. Let me add that my work is conducted by using proven scientific methods. The interviews will take approx. 1 hour. In order to evaluate my data better, I will record these interviews. However, they will be anonymized, so that neither name of people will ever appear in publications.

Would it be possible that we meet in the coming weeks? Do you have any date proposition? I will move to the place that suits you best.

Yours faithfully,

Florian Tissot

Institut SFM
Faubourg de l'Hôpital 106
2000 Neuchâtel, Suisse

Secrétariat
secretariat.sfm@unine.ch

T +41 32 718 39 20

migration-population.ch

Appendix 2: Interview Grid

This is the last version of the interview grid that I used to interview the respondents in Frankfurt during the spring of 2017.

	Interview Grid 2017
Subject of the PhD	**My work focuses on two points; first the path of your mobility and your professional career. Second, the way you dealt with your family/ private-life**
Ethics	**Respect the anonymity - I keep personally the records and I do not transfere them**

1. Experience of mobility

Biographical question	**Q**	**You're in Germany right now, how did it happen?**
	R	*How did you find a job in Germany?*
(Provide a detailed account of …/		
/… previous career and current assignments)	*R1*	*What were your different positions during your professional career so far?*
/… previous migration path)	*R2*	*Before living in Germany, did you live in another country for a period of 6 months or more?*
/… private life)	**Q**	**How difficult or easy is it to maintain a family life or a private-life next to a professional career?**
	R	*If you think of the former places you live, how did you deal with professional life and family/private-life?*
Professional careers (subjective level)	**Q**	**What have been the most important choices you have made concerning your professional career?**
(motivation to go for such a career)	**Q**	**What was your motivation to go abroad?**
	R	*Did you yourself make the decision to go for an international career?*

Choice of destination	**Q**	**When did you arrive in Germany?**
(move wanted - unwanted)	**Q**	**Did you choose yourself to come to Germany?**
	R	*Why Germany and Frankfurt?*
(Is the place important?)	**Q**	**Does your stay in Germany fit in a larger career plan?**
(reasons to stay or leave)	**Q**	**Are you intending to stay in Germany?**
	R	*Why?*
(language)	**Q**	**Do you speak German?**
	R	*If no, was it a problem when you were looking for a job in Germany?*
(employed - unemployed)	**Q**	**Is your partner working now?**
	R	*In Germany?*
Career of the partner	**Q**	**Can you tell me more about his or her professional career?**
	R	*How is the professional life of your partner going?*
(qualification recognition - blockage mobility)	*R*	*Did your partner have some trouble to get his/her qualifications recognized in Germany?*
(Stuck in the global market)	**Q**	**(If so) How did your partner find a job here in Germany?**
(language and labour market)	*R*	*Is (or was) the local language important?*
(Intra-familial strategies (pro))	**Q**	**Do you remember the discussions you had with your partner when you choose to come here?**
	R	*How do you combine professional career and private life? What are your arrangements?*
Family	**Q**	**What are the greatest challenges regarding the family?**
	Q	**How are you coping with these challenges?**

(Different types of collocations)	Q	**Are you living in the same household your partner lives in?**
		or do you have any other ways to live together?
(Living together)	Q	**How is it in the daily life?**
(Different forms of family organisations)	Q	**Who is in charge of the household tasks?**
(Children)	Q	**In what kind of school is your child/ren being tought?**
	Q	**In what language is this schooling?**
Family abroad	Q	**Do you have family members abroad? If yes, how do you keep in touch?**
	R	*How do you maintain ties in other countries?*
(NTIC)		
Daily-life in Germany		
(Bubble?)	Q	**If you think of your two closest friends in Germany, who are they?**
	R	What are they doing here?
	Q	**Have you developed new friendships in Germany? If yes, with whom?**
	R	**Do you use social media to get in touch with new acquaintances in Germany?**
	R	*Where and how did you meet these people?*
(Associationnal life)	Q	**In which groups are you active? Are you member of an association? (Germany and abroad)**
	Q	**Did you have some difficult moments in your social life in Germany (loneliness, etc.)?**
	R	How have you solved these problems?
(Discrimination)	Q	**Did you make bad experiences living here?**
advices	Q	**Would you recommend to someone of your family to come in Germany?**
	Q	**Which advices would you give him or her?**

2. Support received

(In)formal help (un) received	**Q**	**Were you helped at all to find a job in Germany?**
	Q	**Who helped you to find a job?**
(Landing in Germany)	**Q**	**How would you describe the time just after your arrival in Germany?**
	R	*Have you encountered any problems or challenges?*
(Mapping of support)	**Q**	**Who helped you since you arrived in Germany? (persons or organisations)**
	R	*What are the most difficult pieces of information to find?*
	Q	**How did you find…** … a flat? … a school for your child/ren? … a doctor?
Support of the employing organisation	**Q**	**Did the company you work for helped you in your installation process?**
	Q	**Tell me specifically what steps and aid the company offers**
	R	*Are there specific programmes supported by the company?*
	Q	**If you have been working in another country, these programs vary depending on the country?**
Glocal organisation	Q	**Have you been supported by specialized organisations such as head-hunters or relocation offices?**
[motility - inclusion]	*R+*	*Could you tell me how it happened?*
	Q	**Which concrete help did you (or are you still) receiving?**

	Q	**Have you encountered any specific problems?**
	Q	**Did you have to pay for these services?**
	R	*Are these services supported by the company?*
Relation with the state-bodies	Q	**You performed various administrative tasks on your arrival (permits, control of the inhabitants, etc.). Were you supported?**
	R	*Have you encountered any specific problems?*
(relation with specific state-bodies)	Q	**What is your experience with**… … the immigration office? … the public administration (contrôle des habitants, service des automobiles, impôts)? … the social security system? … the public school
	Q	**Is there any other problem we did not mention?**
Permit and pensions	Q	**What is your residence permit? Is it related to your employment contract?**
	R	*And your partner?*
	Q	**What about your pensions?**
	R	*And your partner?*
Summarising	Q	**To summarize, what helped you the most while arriving here?**
Self-identification (Clarify position towards key-words)	Q	**How would you define yourself in the first place?**
	R	*Why, could you explain?*
	Q	**How define yourself when asked?**

Concluding questions		
something missing?	**Q**	**Is there something you want to tell me we did not speak? Something to add?**
Interview with the partner	**Q**	**I would like to make an interview with your partner, do you think it is possible?**
Snowball	**Q**	**Would you know people who would be likely to want to participate in this study?**

Appendix 3: Data Sheet

UNIVERSITÉ DE NEUCHÂTEL

Institut SFM
Forum suisse pour l'étude des migrations et de la population

sfm
SWISS FORUM FOR MIGRATION AND POPULATION STUDIES

Thursday 23 March 2017

Identification:

Where are you born?

____

What is your nationality? (passport)

____

What is the highest diploma you achieved?

____

What is your marital status?

____

Do you have (a) child/ren?

____

Where is your partner living now?

____

When were you born?

____

Appendix 4: Code Book

Coding PhD		
Pre-set codes	A priori codes	
1. Professional activity	a. Career (Primary mover)	// Professional Career and biographical background
	b. Career (Secondary mover)	
	c. Support of the MNC	// MNC - internal support
	d. Support of the MI	// externalised support, outplacement agency, etc.
	e. Value of Mobility and Motivation to Move	
2. Private life	a. Children	
	b. Partner, Spouse	// relationship (getting married, divorce, etc.)
	c. Parents	
	d. Social life – friendships	
3. Strategy and coordination	a. Family strategy and work-life integration	// coping family life professional career, negotiations between partners
	b. Local inclusions and Modalities of settling	// motility, glocalisation, bi-local settlings, local-expatriate contracts
4. Other	a. Employees in MNC Role of Expats in MNC	
	b. Self-identification	// identification file
	c. Media consumption	
	d. Advices to young professional starting	
Emergent codes	Emergent codes	
100 Displaying Family		// Portraying family
	101 Displaying Family: Career coordination	
	102 Displaying Family: Children	// Raising the children

	103 Displaying Family: Divorce	
	104 Displaying Family: lonely bubble (/= expat bubble) (hyp.)	
	105 Displaying Family: Others have problems	
	106 Displaying Family: Social life	
	107 Displaying Family: Trailing-Spouse	
	108 Displaying Family: Education - language - open to the world	
	109 Displaying Family: Career coordination	
	110 Displaying Family: paternalist - I defend my wife and family	
	111 Diplaying Family: Home	floating, stable, etc
200 Family Strategy		// Doing family - Dynamic primary <-> secondary mover
	201 Family Strategy: Being divorced	
	202 Family Strategy: Settling	// Difficulty to settle - arriving in a new place
	203 Family Strategy: Supported by MI	// different types of support
	204 Family Strategy: Non supported by MI	
	205 Family Strategy: Accomodation	former: 205 Family Strategy: Buying a house

	206 Family Strategy: Children	use 206 instead of 943 Nanny
	207 Family Strategy: Local oriented	
	208 Family Strategy: Motility	//perceived likeliness and possibility of a further move - age of the children may diminish it
	209 Family Strategy: International School	
	210 Family Strategy: Local School	
	211 Family Strategy: Boarding school	
	212 Family Strategy: Discussion	// negotiation
	213 Family Strategy: Mobility	// Mobility as a strategy! + decision to move
	214 Family Strategy: Path-dependency	// language of education for the children e.g
	215 Family Strategy: Maintaining ties	// go back to former place with children for instance
	216 Family Strategy: A relocatable unit	//linked with trailing-spouse /=local oriented
300 Primary Mover		
	301 Primary Mover: Career	
	302 Primary Mover: Unsecure career	// From project to project
	303 Primary Mover: Upward career	// explanation how careers in MNC work
	304 Primary Mover: Type of working contract + company culture	//expat contract - local contract
	305 Primary Mover: Impact of the job	// Global impact

	306 Primary Mover: Adventure	// thrilled about the opportunity
	307 Primary Mover: Supported by MI	
	308 Primary Mover: Struggle	
	309 Primary Mover: Role of the Boss	// in decision to move
	310 Primary Mover: Expat contract	
400 Secondary Mover		
	401 Secondary Mover: Adventure	
	402 Secondary Mover: Parent	//parenting - housewifing - arriving of the 1st child!
	403 Secondary Mover: Professional Success	
	404 Secondary Mover: Strategy	
	405 Secondary Mover: Struggles	
	406 Secondary Mover: Trailing-Spouse	// supporting the relocatable unit + may look for something once settled
	407 Secondary Mover: Supported by MI	
	408 Secondary Mover: Finding a job	// process of find a job in a new local space
500 Labour Market		
	501 Labour Market: dual structure	// international or local position -> language difference!

	502 Labour Market: hierarchy within MNC	// senior manager more support
	503 MNC: Mobility Policies	//modification of the conditions
900 Others		//to be classified, incorporated in the analysis
	901 Biggest Challenge: language	//locality,
	902 Biggest Challenge: Leaving home-city	
	903 Local	//904 difference?
	904 Importance of local	//903 difference?
	905 Local friends	
	906 Power of place	
	907 Relevance of the local: Language	//problem of language in new local space for secondary mover to find a job
	908 The most difficult ("multiple choices")	
	909 Old friends	// abroad know before arrival
	910 Expat Bubble	// as a family strategy + as a barrier
	911 Expat Bubble: Media consumption	// coherent to FS
	912 Expat Bubble: Social relationships	// School as an important way to socialise
	913 Expat Network	
	914 Biggest challenge: rebuilding social fabric	
	951 Dural career couple	// Doing family? - family strategy?
	953 Nanny	// We pay – nanny: migrant, too!

954 Raising children		
955 Pregnant		
956 Mobile lifestyle as an enrichment		
960 Decision de live abroad		
961 Structure of the couple	binational	mononational
961 MNC: move of the HQ		

Appendix 5: List of the Respondents for each Chapter

Bibliography

Abrego, Leisy. 2009. 'Economic Well-Being in Salvadoran Transnational Families: How Gender Affects Remittance Practices'. *Journal of Marriage and Family* 71 (4): 1070–1085. doi:10.1111/j.1741-3737.2009.00653.x.

Adsera, Alicia, and Barry R. Chiswick. 2007. 'Are There Gender and Country of Origin Differences in Immigrant Labor Market Outcomes across European Destinations?' *Journal of Population Economics* 20 (3): 495–526. doi:10.1007/s00148-006-0082-y.

Al Ariss, Akram. 2010. 'Modes of Engagement: Migration, Self-initiated Expatriation, and Career Development'. *Career Development International* 15 (4): 338–58. doi:10.1108/13620431011066231.

Al Ariss, Akram, Iris Koall, Mustafa Özbilgin, and Vesa Suutari. 2012. 'Careers of Skilled Migrants: Towards a Theoretical and Methodological Expansion'. Edited by Akram Al Ariss. *Journal of Management Development* 31 (2): 92–101. doi:10.1108/02621711211199511.

Amelina, Anna. 2016. *Transnationalizing Inequalities in Europe: Sociocultural Boundaries, Assemblages and Regimes of Intersection*. New York: Routledge.

Amelina, Anna, and Thomas Faist. 2012. 'De-Naturalizing the National in Research Methodologies: Key Concepts of Transnational Studies in Migration'. *Ethnic and Racial Studies* 35 (10): 1707–24. doi:10.1080/01419870.2012.659273.

Amelina, Anna, Devrimsel D. Nergiz, Thomas Faist, and Nina Glick Schiller, eds. 2012. *Beyond Methodological Nationalism: Research Methodologies for Cross-Border Studies*. New York: Routledge.

Anderson, Benedict. 1991. *Imagined Communities: Reflections on the Origin and Spread of Nationalism*. London, New York: Verso.

Andreason, Aaron W. 2008. 'Expatriate Adjustment of Spouses and Expatriate Managers: An Integrative Research Review'. *International Journal of Management* 25 (2): 382–95.

Andresen, Maike, Franziska Bergdolt, Jil Margenfeld, and Michael Dickmann. 2014. 'Addressing International Mobility Confusion – Developing Definitions and Differentiations for Self-Initiated and Assigned Expatriates as Well as Migrants'. *The International Journal of Human Resource Management* 25 (16): 2295–2318. doi:10.1080/09585192.2013.877058.

Andresen, Maike, Torsten Biemann, and Marshall Wilson Pattie. 2015. 'What Makes Them Move Abroad? Reviewing and Exploring Differences between

Self-Initiated and Assigned Expatriation'. *The International Journal of Human Resource Management* 26 (7): 932–47. doi:10.1080/09585192.2012.669780.

Atkinson, Rowland, and John Flint. 2001. 'Accessing Hidden and Hard-to-Reach Populations: Snowball Research Strategies'. *Social Research Update* 33 (1): 1–4. doi:10.1177/1541204004273316.

Aure, Marit. 2013. 'Highly Skilled Dependent Migrants Entering the Labour Market: Gender and Place in Skill Transfer'. *Geoforum*, Risky natures, natures of risk, 45 (March): 275–84. doi:10.1016/j.geoforum.2012.11.015.

Avril, Alizee B, and Vincent P Magnini. 2007. 'A Holistic Approach to Expatriate Success'. *International Journal of Contemporary Hospitality Management* 19 (1): 53–64. doi:10.1108/09596110710724161.

Azar, Goudarz. 2012. 'Inpatriates and Expatriates: Sources of Strategic Human Capital for Multinational Food and Beverage Firms'. *International Food and Agribusiness Management Review* 15 (A): 73–79.

Bade, Klaus J., and Jochen Oltmer. 2004. *Normalfall Migration*. Bonn: Bpb, Bundeszentrale für Politische Bildung.

Baldassar, Loretta, Majella Kilkey, Laura Merla, and Raelene Wilding. 2014. 'Transnational Families'. In *The Wiley Blackwell Companion to the Sociology of Families*, edited by Judith Treas, Jacqueline Scott, and Martin Richards, 155–175. Oxford, UK: Wiley-Blackwell.

Baldassar, Loretta, and Laura Merla, eds. 2013. *Transnational Families, Migration and the Circulation of Care: Understanding Mobility and Absence in Family Life*. London: Routledge.

———. 2014. 'Locating Transnational Care Circulation in Migration and Family Studies'. In *Transnational Families, Migration and the Circulation of Care: Understanding Mobility and Absence in Family Life*, 25–60. London: Routledge.

Barry, Laurent S., Pierre Bonte, Nicolas Govoroff, Jean-Luc Jamard, Nicole-Claude Mathieu, Enric Porqueres i Gené, Salvatore D'Onofrio, Jérôme Wilgaux, András Zempléni, and Françoise Zonabend. 2000. 'Glossaire'. *L'Homme*, no. 154–155 (January): 721–32. doi:10.4000/lhomme.58.

Bartlett, Christopher A., and Sumantra Ghoshal. 1999. *Managing across Borders: The Transnational Solution*. Vol. 2. New York: Taylor & Francis.

Baruch, Yehuda. 2006. 'Career Development in Organizations and beyond: Balancing Traditional and Contemporary Viewpoints'. *Human Resource Management Review* 16 (2): 125–138. doi:10.1016/j.hrmr.2006.03.002.

Baruch, Yehuda, Michael Dickmann, Yochanan Altman, and Frank Bournois. 2013. 'Exploring International Work: Types and Dimensions of Global

Careers'. *The International Journal of Human Resource Management* 24 (12): 2369–93. doi:10.1080/09585192.2013.781435.

Bateson, Gregory, Don D. Jackson, Jay Haley, and John Weakland. 1956. 'Toward a Theory of Schizophrenia'. *Behavioral Science* 1 (4): 251–64. doi:10.1002/bs.3830010402.

Bauman, Zygmunt. 2013. *Liquid Times: Living in an Age of Uncertainty*. Cambridge, UK: Polity Press.

Beaud, Stéphane, and Florence Weber. 2003. *Guide de l'enquête de Terrain*. Paris: La Découverte.

Beaverstock, Jonathan V. 2005. 'Transnational Elites in the City: British Highly-Skilled Inter-Company Transferees in New York City's Financial District'. *Journal of Ethnic and Migration Studies* 31 (2): 245–68. doi:10.1080/1369183042000339918.

Becker, Howard Saul. 2008. *Tricks of the Trade: How to Think about Your Research While You're Doing It*. Chicago: University of Chicago Press.

Benveniste, Emile. 1969. *Le vocabulaire des institutions indo-européennes, tome 1 : Economie, parenté, société*. Paris: Les Editions de Minuit.

Berger, Suzanne, and Michael J. Piore. 1980. *Dualism and Discontinuity in Industrial Societies*. New York: Cambridge University Press.

Bertaux, Daniel, ed. 1981. *Biography and Society: The Life History Approach in the Social Sciences*. Sage Studies in International Sociology 23. London: Sage.

Bhambra, Gurminder K. 2017. 'Brexit, Trump, and "Methodological Whiteness": On the Misrecognition of Race and Class'. *The British Journal of Sociology* 68 (S1): 214–32. doi:10.1111/1468-4446.12317.

Biemann, Torsten, and Maike Andresen. 2010. 'Self-initiated Foreign Expatriates versus Assigned Expatriates: Two Distinct Types of International Careers?' *Journal of Managerial Psychology* 25 (4): 430–48. doi:10.1108/02683941011035313.

Black, J. Stewart, and Hal B. Gregersen. 1991. 'The Other Half of the Picture: Antecedents of Spouse Cross-Cultural Adjustment'. *Journal of International Business Studies* 22 (3): 461–477. doi:10.1057/palgrave.jibs.8490311.

Black, J. Stewart, and Mark Mendenhall. 1990. 'Cross-Cultural Training Effectiveness: A Review and a Theoretical Framework for Future Research'. *Academy of Management Review* 15 (1): 113–136. doi:10.5465/AMR.1990.11591834.

Black, J. Stewart, Mark Mendenhall, and Gary Oddou. 1991. 'Toward a Comprehensive Model of International Adjustment: An Integration of

Multiple Theoretical Perspectives'. *The Academy of Management Review* 16 (2): 291. doi:10.2307/258863.

Blau, Francine D., and Lawrence M. Kahn. 2017. 'The Gender Wage Gap: Extent, Trends, and Explanations'. *Journal of Economic Literature* 55 (3): 789–865. doi:10.1257/jel.20160995.

Blitz, Brad K. 2010. 'Highly Skilled Migration'. *International Studies Encyclopedia*. Oxford: Wiley-Blackwell.

BMFSFJ. 2017. 'Elterngeld, ElterngeldPlus und Elternzeit'. Berlin: Bundesministerium für Familie, Senioren, Frauen und Jugend.

Boeri, Tito. 2012. *Brain Drain and Brain Gain: The Global Competition to Attract High-Skilled Migrants*. Oxford: Oxford University Press.

Bommes, Michael. 2012. 'Migration in Modern Society'. In *Immigration and Social Systems: Collected Essays of Michael Bommes*, edited by Christina Boswell and Gianni D'Amato, 19–35. Amsterdam: Amsterdam University Press.

Bommes, Michael, and Holger Kolb. 2006. 'Migrants' Work, Entrepreneurship and Economic Integration'. In *The Dynamics of International Migration and Settlement in Europe. A State of Art*, edited by R Penninx, M Berger, and K Kraal, 99–132. Amsterdam: Amsterdam University Press.

Bonnet, Estelle, Beate Collet, and Béatrice Maurines. 2011. 'Carrière familiale et mobilité géographique professionnelle'. *Cahiers du Genre* 2 (41): 75–98. doi:10.3917/cdge.041.0075.

Bonoli, Giuliano, and Sandrine Vuille. 2013. 'L'accueil de jour des enfants dans le Canton de Vaud'. Lausanne: Swiss Graduate School of Public Administration.

Bonvalet, Catherine. 2003. 'La famille-entourage locale'. *Population* 58 (1): 9–43. doi:10.3917/popu.301.0009.

Bosk, Charles L. 1979. *Forgive and Remember: Managing Medical Mistakes*. Chicago: University of Chicago Press.

Bourdieu, Pierre. 1983. 'Economic Capital, Cultural Capital, Social Capital'. *Soziale-Welt, Supplement* 2: 183–98.

———. 2012. *La Distinction: Critique Sociale Du Jugement*. Le Sens Commun. Paris: Les Editions de Minuit.

Braseby, Anne M. 2010. 'Adaptation of Trailing Spouses: Does Gender Matter?' Miami: Florida International University.

Braudel, Fernand. 1979. *Civilisation Matérielle, Économie et Capitalisme, XVe -XVIIIe Siècles*. Paris: Armand Colin.

Brinkmann, Svend. 2017. *Philosophies of Qualitative Research*. New York: Oxford University Press.

Briody, Elizabeth, and Judith Chrisman. 1991. 'Cultural Adaptation on Overseas Assignments'. *Human Organization* 50 (3): 264–82. doi:10.17730/humo.50.3.22555451v6206444.

Brookfield Global Relocation Services. 2012. 'Global Relocation Trends'. London: Brookfield.

Brubaker, Rogers. 2002. 'Ethnicity without Groups'. *European Journal of Sociology/Archives Européennes de Sociologie* 43 (02): 163–189. doi:10.1017/S0003975602001066.

———. 2013. 'Categories of Analysis and Categories of Practice: A Note on the Study of Muslims in European Countries of Immigration'. *Ethnic and Racial Studies* 36 (1): 1–8. doi:10.1080/01419870.2012.729674.

Bryceson, Deborah, and Ulla Vuorela. 2002. *The Transnational Family: New European Frontiers and Global Networks*. Oxford, New York: Oxford International Publisher.

Bühler, Elisabeth, and Verena Meier Kruker. 2002. 'Gendered Labour Arrangements in Switzerland: Structures, Cultures, Meanings: Statistical Evidence and Biographical Narratives'. *GeoJournal* 56 (4): 305–13. doi:10.1023/A:1025904010911.

Bundesamt für Kartographie und Geodäsie. 2018. 'WebAtlasDE'. Frankfurt am Main: Bundesamt für Kartographie und Geodäsie.

Bürgeramt, Statistik und Wahlen. 2016. 'Metropolregionen in Deutschland'. 12. Materialien Zur Stadtbeobachtung. Frankfurt am Main: Bürgeramt, Statistik und Wahlen.

Butler, Judith. 1990. *Feminism and the Subversion of Identity*. New York, London: Routledge.

———. 2004. *Undoing Gender*. New York, London: Routledge.

Cangià, Flavia. 2017. '(Im)Mobility and the Emotional Lives of Expat Spouses'. *Emotion, Space and Society* 25 (November): 22–28. doi:10.1016/j.emospa.2017.10.001.

———. 2018. 'Precarity, Imagination, and the Mobile Life of the "Trailing Spouse"'. *Ethos* 46 (1): 8–26. doi:10.1111/etho.12195.

Cerdin, Jean-Luc, and Jan Selmer. 2014. 'Who Is a Self-Initiated Expatriate? Towards Conceptual Clarity of a Common Notion'. *The International Journal of Human Resource Management* 25 (9): 1281–1301. doi:10.1080/09585192.2013.863793.

Chaloff, Jonathan, and Georges Lemaître. 2009. 'Managing Highly-Skilled Labour Migration'. OECD Social, Employment and Migration Working Papers. Paris: Organisation for Economic Co-operation and Development.

Chang, Chia-Chien. 2014. 'Highly Educated Taiwanese Women Seeking a Self-Acceptable Social Position in Finland'. Helsinki: University of Helsinki.

Chernilo, D. 2006. 'Social Theory's Methodological Nationalism: Myth and Reality'. *European Journal of Social Theory* 9 (1): 5–22. doi:10.1177/1368431006060460.

Chiswick, Barry R., ed. 2011. *High-Skilled Immigration in a Global Labor Market*. Washington D.C: AEI Press.

Chorafas, Dimitri N., and Claude Herbette. 1969. *La Fuite Des Cerveaux. Les USA à La Conquête de Nos Savants*. Paris: Fayard.

Cieslik, Anna. 2012. *Transnational Mobility and Family Planning Decisions : A Case Study of Skilled Polish Migrant Women*. MMG Working Paper. Göttingen: Max Planck Institute for the Study of Religious and Ethnic Diversity.

Cochrane, Allan. 2006. *Understanding Urban Policy: A Critical Approach*. Oxford, UK: Blackwell.

Cole, Nina D. 2011. 'Managing Global Talent: Solving the Spousal Adjustment Problem'. *The International Journal of Human Resource Management* 22 (07): 1504–1530. doi:10.1080/09585192.2011.561963.

Collings, David G., Hugh Scullion, and Peter J. Dowling. 2009. 'Global Staffing: A Review and Thematic Research Agenda'. *The International Journal of Human Resource Management* 20 (6): 1253–72. doi:10.1080/09585190902909806.

Cooke, Thomas J. 2008. 'Migration in a Family Way'. *Population, Space and Place* 14 (4): 255–65. doi:10.1002/psp.500.

Corbin, Juliet M., and Anselm L. Strauss. 2008. *Basics of Qualitative Research: Techniques and Procedures for Developing Grounded Theory*. 3rd ed. Thousand Oaks, Calif: Sage Publications, Inc.

Cornelius, Wayne A., Thomas J. Espenshade, and Idean Salehyan. 2001. *The International Migration of the Highly Skilled*. San Diego: University of California.

Cotter, David A., Joan M. Hermsen, Seth Ovadia, and Reeve Vanneman. 2001. 'The Glass Ceiling Effect'. *Social Forces* 80 (2): 655–81. doi:10.1353/sof.2001.0091.

Crenshaw, Kimberle. 1989. 'Demarginalizing the Intersection of Race and Sex: A Black Feminist Critique of Antidiscrimination Doctrine, Feminist

Theory and Antiracist Politics'. *The University of Chicago Legal Forum* 140: 139–167.

Dabic, Marina, Miguel González-Loureiro, and Michael Harvey. 2013. 'Evolving Research on Expatriates: What Is "Known" after Four Decades (1970–2012)'. *The International Journal of Human Resource Management*, 1–22. doi:10.1080/09585192.2013.845238.

Dahinden, Janine. 2016. 'A Plea for the "de-Migranticization" of Research on Migration and Integration"'. *Ethnic and Racial Studies* 39 (13): 1–19. doi:10.1080/01419870.2015.1124129.

D'Andrea, Anthony, Luigina Ciolfi, and Breda Gray. 2011. 'Methodological Challenges and Innovations in Mobilities Research'. *Mobilities* 6 (2): 149–60. doi:10.1080/17450101.2011.552769.

Darmon, Muriel. 2005. 'Le Psychiatre, La Sociologue et La Boulangère: Analyse d'un Refus de Terrain'. *Genèses*, no. 1: 98–112. doi:10.3917/gen.058.0098.

Davoine, Eric, Claudio Ravasi, Xavier Salamin, and Christel Cudré-Mauroux. 2013. 'A "Dramaturgical" Analysis of Spouse Role Enactment in Expatriation: An Exploratory Gender Comparative Study in the Diplomatic and Consular Field'. *Journal of Global Mobility: The Home of Expatriate Management Research* 1 (1): 92–112. doi:10.1108/JGM-09-2012-0005.

De Flaugergues, Amélie. 2009. 'Les Comportements Démographiques Des Familles En Suisse - de 1970 à 2008'. Neuchâtel: Office fédéral de la statistique OFS.

Déchaux, Jean-Hugues. 2010. *Sociologie de La Famille*. Paris: La Découverte.

Degavre, Florence, and Laura Merla. 2016. 'Defamilialization of Whom? Re-Thinking Defamilialization in the Light of Global Care Chains and the Transnational Circulation of Care'. In *Family Life in an Age of Migration and Mobility*, edited by Majella Kilkey and Ewa Palenga-Möllenbeck, 287–311. London: Palgrave Macmillan UK. doi:10.1057/978-1-137-52099-9_13.

Derrida, Jacques. 1978. *Writing and Difference*. Chicago: University of Chicago Press.

Dessemontet, Pierre, Vincent Kaufmann, and Christophe Jemelin. 2010. 'Switzerland as a Single Metropolitan Area? A Study of Its Commuting Network'. Edited by Géraldine Pflieger and Céline Rozenblat. *Urban Studies* 47 (13): 2785–2802. doi:10.1177/0042098010377371.

Destatis. 2014. 'Kindertagesbetreuung: Betreuungsquoten Der Kinder Unter 6 Jahren in Kindertagesbetreuung Am 01.03.2014 Nach Ländern'. Wiesbaden: Statistisches Bundesamt.

Deutsch, Francine M. 2007. 'Undoing Gender'. *Gender & Society* 21 (1): 106–27. doi:10.1177/0891243206293577.

Dewey, John. 1957. *Human Nature and Conduct: An Introduction to Social Psychology*. New York: The Modern Library.

Donato, Katharine M., Donna Gabaccia, Jennifer Holdaway, Martin Manalansan, and Patricia R. Pessar. 2006. 'A Glass Half Full? Gender in Migration Studies1'. *International Migration Review* 40 (1): 3–26. doi:0.1111/j.1747-7379.2006.00001.x.

Dumont, Jean-Christophe, and Laurent Aujean. 2014. 'Matching Economic Migration with Labour Market Needs in Europe'. Paris: OECD, European Union.

Durkheim, Emile. 1926. *De La Division Du Travail Social*. Paris: Félix Alcan.

Eckert, Stefan, and Ulrike Mayrhofer. 2005. 'Identifying and Explaining Epochs of Internationalization: A Case Study'. *European Management Review* 2 (3): 212–23. doi:10.1057/palgrave.emr.1500040.

Esping-Andersen, Gøsta. 1990. 'The Three Political Economies of the Welfare State'. *International Journal of Sociology* 20 (3): 92–123. doi:10.1111/j.1755-618X.1989.tb00411.x.

Eurostat. 2017a. 'Commuting Zone'. *Statiscs Explained: Glossary*. Kirchberg (Luxembourg): Eurostat.

———. 2017b. 'Functional Urban Area'. *Statiscs Explained: Glossary*. Kirchberg (Luxembourg): Eurostat.

———.2017c. 'Statistical Atlas: Eurostat Regional Yearbook 2017'. Cities, road, lakes, rivers. Kirchberg (Luxembourg): Eurostat.

Eymard-Duvernay, F. 2006. *L'Economie Des Conventions, Méthodes et Résultats*. Paris: La Découverte.

Faist, Thomas. 2010. 'The Crucial Meso Level'. In *Selected Studies in International Migration and Immigrant Incorporation*, edited by Marco Martiniello and Jan Rath, 59–90. IMISCOE Textbooks. Amsterdam: Amsterdam University Press.

Favell, Adrian. 2001. 'Integration Policy and Integration Research in Europe: A Review and Critique'. *Citizenship Today: Global Perspectives and Practices*, 349–99.

———. 2008. *Eurostars and Eurocities: Free Movement and Mobility in an Integrating Europe*. Oxford, UK: Blackwell.

———. 2014. *Immigration, Integration and Mobility: New Agendas in Migration Studies: Essays 1998-2014*. ECPR Press Essays. Colchester: ECPR Press.

Fechter, Anne-Meike. 2007a. 'Living in a Bubble'. In *Going First Class New Approaches to Privileged Travel and Movement*, edited by Amit Vered, 33–52. Oxford: Berghahn Books.

———. 2007b. *Transnational Lives: Expatriates in Indonesia*. Aldershot: Ashgate.

Ferragina, Emanuele, and Martin Seeleib-Kaiser. 2015. 'Determinants of a Silent (R)Evolution: Understanding the Expansion of Family Policy in Rich OECD Countries'. *Social Politics: International Studies in Gender, State & Society* 22 (1): 1–37. doi:10.1093/sp/jxu027.

Fibbi, Rosita. 2005. 'Etre Secondo-Seconda En Suisse'. In *Racisme(s) et Citoyenneté*, edited by Monique Eckmann and Michèle Fleury, Editions IES, 211–18. Genève.

Finch, Janet. 2007. 'Displaying Families'. *Sociology* 41 (1): 65–81. doi:10.1177/0038038507072284.

Flamm, Michael, and Vincent Kaufmann. 2006. 'Operationalising the Concept of Motility: A Qualitative Study'. *Mobilities* 1 (2): 167–89. doi:10.1080/17450100600726563.

Flick, Uwe. 2009. *An Introduction to Qualitative Research*. Los Angeles, London: Sage.

Foucault, M. 1994. 'Le Jeux de Michel Foucault (Entretien Avec D. Colas, A. Grosrichard, G. Le Gaufrey, J. Livi, G. Miller, J. Miller, JA. Miller, C. Millot, G. Wajeman)'. *Bulletin Périodique Du Champ Freudien*, no. 10: 62–93.

Fourastié, Jean. 1979. *Les Trente Glorieuses: Ou La Révolution Invisible de 1946 à 1975*. Paris: Fayard.

Gammeltoft-Hansen, Thomas, and Ninna Nyberg Sorensen. 2013. *The Migration Industry and the Commercialization of International Migration*. London: Routledge.

Garfinkel, Harold, ed. 1986. *Ethnomethodological Studies of Work*. Studies in Ethnomethodology. London, New York: Routledge.

Gaspoz, Deniz Gyger. 2013. 'Une Jeunesse Au Souffle de La Mobilité Internationale Répétée. Etude Exploratoire et Descriptive de l'impact de l'itinérance Géographique Sur Le Développement à l'adolescence.' Neuchâtel: Université de Neuchâtel.

Gatti, Emanuele. 2009. 'Définir Les Expats: Le Cas Des Immigrés Hautement Qualifiés à Bruxelles'. *Brussels Studies* 28: 1–16.

Gerson, Kathleen. 1986. *Hard Choices: How Women Decide About Work, Career and Motherhood*. Oakland: University of California Press.

Giddens, Anthony. 2004. *La Transformation de l'intimité: Sexualité, Amour et Érotisme Dans Les Temps Modernes*. Paris: Hachette Littératures.

———. 2009. *Sociology*. 5th edition. Cambridge: Polity Press.

Glick Schiller, Nina, and Ayşe Çağlar. 2010. *Locating Migration: Rescaling Cities and Migrants*. New York: Cornell University Press.

Goffman, Erving. 1990. *The Presentation of Self in Everyday Life*. London: Penguin Books.

Goldin, Claudia, Sari Pekkala Kerr, Claudia Olivetti, and Erling Barth. 2017. 'The Expanding Gender Earnings Gap: Evidence from the LEHD-2000 Census'. *American Economic Review* 107 (5): 110–14. doi:10.1257/aer.p20171065.

Green, Nancy L. 2008. 'La migration des élites. Nouveau concept, anciennes pratiques ?' *Les Cahiers du Centre de recherches historiques*, no. 42 (April): 107–16. doi:10.4000/ccrh.3434.

Green, Nancy L. 2009. 'Expatriation, Expatriates, and Expats: The American Transformation of a Concept'. *The American Historical Review* 114 (2): 307–28. doi:10.1086/ahr.114.2.307.

Groutsis, Dimitria, Di van den Broek, and Will S. Harvey. 2015. 'Transformations in Network Governance: The Case of Migration Intermediaries'. *Journal of Ethnic and Migration Studies* 41 (10): 1558–76. doi:10.1080/1369183X.2014.1003803.

Gugerli, David, Patrick Kupper, and Daniel Speich. 2010. *Transforming the Future*. Zurich: Chronos.

Halpern, Diane F., and Susan Elaine Murphy. 2005. *From Work-Family Balance to Work-Family Interaction: Changing the Metaphor*. New York, London: Routledge.

Hammar, Tomas. 1985. *European Immigration Policy: A Comparative Study*. Cambridge: Cambridge University Press.

Hannam, Kevin, Mimi Sheller, and John Urry. 2006. 'Editorial: Mobilities, Immobilities and Moorings'. *Mobilities* 1 (1): 1–22. doi:10.1080/17450100500489189.

Harris, John R., and Michael P. Todaro. 1970. 'Migration, Unemployment and Development: A Two-Sector Analysis'. *The American Economic Review* 60 (1): 126–142. doi:10.1016/S1090-9516(01)00061-X.

Harrison Villalba, Cynthia, Ernesto Villalba, European Commission, Joint Research Centre, and Institute for the Protection and the Security of the Citizen. 2012. *Advantages and Limitations of Using EU-SILC for Monitoring Participation in Early Childhood Education and Care*. Luxembourg: Publications Office.

Harzing, Anne-Wil. 2002. 'Of Bears, Bumble-Bees, and Spiders: The Role of Expatriates in Controlling Foreign Subsidiaries'. *Journal of World Business* 36 (4): 366–379. doi:10.1016/S1090-9516(01)00061-X.

Hashai, Niron, and Tamar Almor. 2004. 'Gradually Internationalizing "Born Global" Firms: An Oxymoron?' *International Business Review* 13 (4): 465–83. doi:10.1016/j.ibusrev.2004.04.004.

Hausmann, Ricardo, Laura D. Tyson, and Saadia Zahidi. 2009. 'The Global Gender Gap Report 2009'. Geneva: World Economic Forum.

Hernández-León, Rubén. 2013. *The Migration Industry and the Commercialization of International Migration*. London, New York: Routledge.

Hirsch, Boris, Thorsten Schank, and Claus Schnabel. 2010. 'Differences in Labor Supply to Monopsonistic Firms and the Gender Pay Gap: An Empirical Analysis Using Linked Employer-Employee Data from Germany'. *Journal of Labor Economics* 28 (2): 291–330. doi:10.1086/651208.

Hirschman, Albert O. 1970. *Exit, Voice, and Loyalty: Responses to Decline in Firms, Organizations, and States*. Harvard: Harvard university press.

Hochschild, Arlie, and Anne Machung. 2012. *The Second Shift: Working Families and the Revolution at Home*. New York, London: Penguin.

Höfert, Andreas, and Daniel Kalt. 2015. 'Prices and Earning 2015: Do I Earn Enough for the Life I Want?' Zurich: UBS CIO Wealth Managment Research.

Hurlbert, Margot. 2010. 'Decentering Texts'. *Encyclopedia of Case Study Research*. London: SAGE.

Ietto-Gillies, Grazia. 2012. *Transnational Corporations and International Production: Concepts, Theories and Effects*. London: Edward Elgar Publishing.

Imhof, Gilles. 2015. 'Portraits Des Familles Vaudoises: Des Chiffres Pour Les Décrire'. Lausanne: Service des assurances sociales et de l'hébergement.

Iredale, Robyn. 2001. 'The Migration of Professionals: Theories and Typologies'. *International Migration* 39 (5): 7–26. doi:10.1111/1468-2435.00169.

———. 2005. 'Gender, Immigration Policies and Accreditation: Valuing the Skills of Professional Women Migrants'. *Geoforum* 36 (2): 155–66. doi:10.1016/j.geoforum.2004.04.002.

IWD. 2017. 'Bund muss Kita-Lücken schließen'. Köln: Institut der deutschen Wirtschaft.

Johanson, Jan, and Jan-Erik Vahlne. 1977. 'The Internationalization Process of the Firm—a Model of Knowledge Development and Increasing Foreign Market Commitments'. *Journal of International Business Studies* 8 (1): 23–32.

Johnson, Lisa. 2017. 'World Mobility Perspectives: 2017 Global Mobility Trends'. Hong Kong: Crown World Mobility.

Joy, Simy, Annilee M. Game, and Ishita G. Toshniwal. 2018. 'Applying Bourdieu's Capital-Field-Habitus Framework to Migrant Careers: Taking Stock and Adding a Transnational Perspective'. *The International Journal of Human Resource Management*, 1–24. doi:10.1080/09585192.2018.1454490.

Jurczyk, Karin, Andreas Lange, and Barbara Thiessen, eds. 2014. *Doing Family: Warum Familienleben Nicht Mehr Selbstverständlich Ist*. Weinheim, Basel: Beltz Juventa.

Känsälä, Marja, Liisa Mäkelä, and Vesa Suutari. 2014. 'Career Coordination Strategies among Dual Career Expatriate Couples'. *The International Journal of Human Resource Management*, 1–24. doi:10.1080/09585192.2014.985327.

Kanter, Rosabeth Moss, and Marilyn Halter. 1978. 'De-Housewifing Women, Domesticating Men: Equality between the Sexes in Urban Communes'. In *Modern Sociology: Introductory Readings*, edited by P. Worsley. London: Penguin.

Kaufmann, Manfred Max Bergman, and Dominique Joye. 2004. 'Motility: Mobility as Capital'. *International Journal of Urban and Regional Research* 28 (4): 745–756. doi:10.1111/j.0309-1317.2004.00549.x.

Kaufmann, Jean-Claude. 2011. *L'entretien Compréhensif*. Paris: Armand Colin.

Kilkey, Majella, and Ewa Palenga-Möllenbeck, eds. 2016. *Family Life in an Age of Migration and Mobility*. London: Palgrave Macmillan UK. doi:10.1057/978-1-137-52099-9.

King, Russell. 2002. 'Towards a New Map of European Migration'. *International Journal of Population Geography* 8 (2): 89–106. doi:10.1002/ijpg.246.

———. 2012a. 'Theories and Typologies of Migration: An Overview and a Primer'. *Willy Brandt Series of Working Papers in International Migration and Ethnic Relations* 3.

———. 2012b. 'Geography and Migration Studies: Retrospect and Prospect'. *Population, Space and Place* 18 (2): 134–53. doi:10.1002/psp.685.

King, Russell, Mark Thomson, Tony Fielding, and Tony Warnes. 2006. 'Time, Generations and Gender in Migration and Settlement'. In *The Dynamics of International Migration and Settlement in Europe: State of the Art*, edited by Rinus Penninx, M Berger, and K Kraal, 233–268. Amsterdam: Amsterdam University Press.

Kleven, Henrik, Camille Landais, and Jakob Egholt Søgaard. 2018. 'Children and Gender Inequality: Evidence from Denmark'. Working Paper 24219. National Bureau of Economic Research. doi:10.3386/w24219.

Kofman, Eleonore. 2000. 'The Invisibility of Skilled Female Migrants and Gender Relations in Studies of Skilled Migration in Europe'.

International Journal of Population Geography 6 (1): 45–59. doi:10.1002/(SICI)1099-1220(200001/02)6:1<45::AID-IJPG169>3.0.CO;2-B.

Kofman, Eleonore, and Parvati Raghuram. 2005. 'Gender and Skilled Migrants: Into and beyond the Work Place'. *Geoforum* 36 (2): 149–54. doi:10.1016/j.geoforum.2004.06.001.

———. 2006. 'Gender and Global Labour Migrations: Incorporating Skilled Workers'. *Antipode* 38 (2): 282–303. doi:10.1111/j.1467-8330.2006.00580.x.

Kohli, Martin. 1989. 'Le cours de vie comme institution sociale'. *Enquête. Archives de la revue Enquête*, no. 5 (March). doi:10.4000/enquete.78.

Koser, Khalid, and John Salt. 1997. 'The Geography of Highly Skilled International Migration'. *International Journal of Population Geography* 3 (4): 285–303. doi:10.1002/(SICI)1099-1220(199712)3:4<285::AID-IJPG72>3.0.CO;2-W.

Kõu, Anu, Leo van Wissen, Jouke van Dijk, and Ajay Bailey. 2015. 'A Life Course Approach to High-Skilled Migration: Lived Experiences of Indians in the Netherlands'. *Journal of Ethnic and Migration Studies* 41 (10): 1–20. doi:10.1080/1369183X.2015.1019843.

Krack-Roberg, Elle, Sascha Krieger, and Julia Weinmann. 2016. 'Familie, Lebensformen Und Kinder'. Datenreport. Berlin: Destatis/Wissenschaftszentrum Berlin (WZB)(Hrsg.).

Kvale, Steinar, and Svend Brinkmann. 2009. *InterViews: Learning the Craft of Qualitative Research Interviewing*. Thousand Oaks, CA: Sage.

Lahire, Bernard. 2006. *La Culture Des Individus: Dissonances Culturelles et Distinction de Soi*. Paris: La Découverte.

Lamnek, Siegfried. 1993. *Qualitative Sozialforschung. Band 2: Methoden Und Techniken,*. Vol. 2. überarbeitete Auflage. Weinheim: Beltz.

Larsen, John Aggergaard, Helen T. Allan, Karen Bryan, and Pam Smith. 2005. 'Overseas Nurses' Motivations for Working in the UK: Globalization and Life Politics'. *Work, Employment and Society* 19 (2): 349–368. doi:10.1177/0950017005053177.

Lauring, Jakob, and Jan Selmer. 2010. 'The Supportive Expatriate Spouse: An Ethnographic Study of Spouse Involvement in Expatriate Careers'. *International Business Review* 19 (1): 59–69. doi:10.1016/j.ibusrev.2009.09.006.

Lavenex, Sandra. 2007. 'The Competition State and Highly Skilled Migration'. *Society* 44 (2): 32–41. doi:10.1007/BF02819924.

Levitan, Déborah, Tania Zittoun, and Flavia Cangià. 2018. 'Family, Boundaries and Transformation. The International Mobility of Professionals and Their Families'. *Migration Letters* 15 (1): 17–31.

Levy, Donald, ed. 2007. 'Patriarchy'. *The Blackwell Encyclopedia of Sociology*. Oxford, UK, Malden, USA and Carlton, Australia: Blackwell Publishing Ltd. doi:10.1111/b.9781405124331.2007.x.

Lewis, W. Arthur. 1954. 'Economic Development with Unlimited Supplies of Labour'. *The Manchester School* 22 (2): 139–191.

Liversage, Anika. 2009. 'Vital Conjunctures, Shifting Horizons: High-Skilled Female Immigrants Looking for Work'. *Work, Employment and Society* 23 (1): 120–41. doi:10.1177/0950017008099781.

Lutz, Helma, and Anna Amelina. 2017. *Gender, Migration, Transnationalisierung: Eine Intersektionelle Einführung*. Bielefeld: Transcript Verlag.

Lyotard, Jean-François. 1979. *La Condition Postmoderne: Rapport Sur Le Savoir*. Paris: Les Editions de Minuit.

Mahroum, Sami. 2001. 'Europe and the Immigration of Highly Skilled Labour'. *International Migration* 39 (5): 27–43. doi:10.1111/1468-2435.00170.

Mäkelä, Liisa, Marja Känsälä, and Vesa Suutari. 2011. 'The Roles of Expatriates' Spouses among Dual Career Couples'. Edited by Jan Selmer. *Cross Cultural Management: An International Journal* 18 (2): 185–97. doi:10.1108/13527601111126012.

Malkki, Liisa H. 1995. 'Refugees and Exile: From "Refugee Studies" to the National Order of Things'. *Annual Review of Anthropology*, 495–523.

Massey, Douglas S., Joaquin Arango, Graeme Hugo, Ali Kouaouci, Adela Pellegrino, and J. Edward Taylor. 1993. 'Theories of International Migration: A Review and Appraisal'. *Population and Development Review* 19 (3): 431–466. doi:10.2307/2938462.

Maxwell, Joseph A. 1992. 'Understanding and Validity in Qualitative Research', Harvard Educational Review, 62 (3): 279–300. doi:10.17763/haer.62.3.8323320856251826.

McNulty, Yvonne. 2012. '"Being Dumped in to Sink or Swim": An Empirical Study of Organizational Support for the Trailing Spouse'. *Human Resource Development International* 15 (4): 417–34. doi:10.1080/13678868.2012.721985.

———. 2015. 'Breaking Up Is Hard To Do: Navigating Expatriate Divorce Abroad'. *StrategicAdivor*, Brookfield Global Relocation Services, 11 (109): 1–6.

McNulty, Yvonne, and Chris Brewster. 2017. 'Theorizing the Meaning(s) of "Expatriate": Establishing Boundary Conditions for Business Expatriates'. *The International Journal of Human Resource Management* 28 (1): 27–61. doi: 10.1080/09585192.2016.1243567.

Meares, Carina. 2010. 'A Fine Balance: Women, Work and Skilled Migration'. *Women's Studies International Forum* 33 (5): 473–81. doi:10.1016/j.wsif.2010.06.001.

Millar, Jane, and John Salt. 2008. 'Portfolios of Mobility: The Movement of Expertise in Transnational Corporations in Two Sectors—Aerospace and Extractive Industries'. *Global Networks* 8 (1): 25–50. doi:10.1111/j.1471-0374.2008.00184.x.

Mises, Ludwig von. 1999. *Human Action: A Treatise on Economics*. 3rd revised ed. Chicago: Contemporary Books.

Morawska, Ewa. 2012. 'Historical-Structural Models of International Migration'. In *An Introduction to International Migration Studies*, edited by Marco Martiniello and Jan Rath, 57–78. Amsterdam: Amsterdam University Press.

Moret, Joëlle. 2018. *European Somalis' Post-Migration Movements: Mobility Capital and the Transnationalisation of Resources*. IMISCOE Research Series. Wiesbaden: Springer International Publishing.

Neyer, Gerda. 2003. 'Family Policies and Low Fertility in Western Europe', 63.

OECD. 2008. 'A Profile of Immigrant Population in the 21st Century: Data from OECD Countries'. Paris: Organisation for Economic Co-operation and Development (OECD).

———. 2012. 'Closing the Gender Gap: Act Now'. Paris: Organisation for Economic Co-operation and Development (OECD).

———. 2013. 'Definition of Functional Urban Areas (FUA) for the OECD Metropolitan Database'. Paris: Organisation for Economic Co-operation and Development (OECD).

———. 2016. 'Enrolment Childcare Preschool'. Paris: Organisation for Economic Co-operation and Development (OECD).

———. 2017a. 'Childcare Support'. Paris: Organisation for Economic Co-operation and Development (OECD).

———. 2017b. 'Key Characteristics of Parental Leave Systems'. Paris: Organisation for Economic Co-operation and Development (OECD).

OED. 2018. *Oxford English Dictionary*. Oxford, UK: Oxford University Press.

Office Fédéral de la Topographie (swisstopo). 2018. 'Swiss Geoportal'. Carte nationale. Wabern: Confédération suisse.

O'Rand, Angela M., and Margaret L. Krecker. 1990. 'Concepts of the Life Cycle: Their History, Meanings, and Uses in the Social Sciences'. *Annual Review of Sociology* 16 (1): 241–62. doi:10.1146/annurev.so.16.080190.001325.

Palmer, John, and Mariola Pytlikova. 2013. 'Labor Market Laws and Intra-European Migration: The Role of the State in Shaping Destination Choices'. *CELSI Discussion Paper*, no. 9.

Papinot, Christian. 2014. *La Relation d'enquête Comme Relation Sociale: Épistémologie de La Démarche de Recherche Ethnographique*. Hermann édition. Méthodes de Recherche En Sciences Humaines. Presses de l'Université Laval.

Parsons, Talcott. 1955. 'Le Système de Parenté Dans Les États-Unis d'aujourd'hui'. *T. Parsons, Éléments Pour Une Sociologie de l'action*, Paris, Plon, 129–150.

Pecoraro, Marco. 2013. 'Gender, Brain Waste and Job-Education Mismatch among Migrant Workers in Switzerland'. *International Migration Paper*, no. 111. doi:10.2139/ssrn.2294436.

Pfau-Effinger, Birgit. 1998. 'Gender Cultures and the Gender Arrangement—a Theoretical Framework for Cross-National Gender Research'. *Innovation: The European Journal of Social Science Research* 11 (2): 147–166.

Piore, Michael. 1979. *Birds of Passage: Migrant Labor in Industrial Societies*. Cambridge, UK: Cambridge University Press.

Pires, Alvaro. 1997. 'Échantillonnage et Recherche Qualitative: Essai Théorique et Méthodologique'. In *La Recherche Qualitative. Enjeux Épistémologiques et Méthodologiques*, edited by J. Poupart, L.H. Groulx, R. Mayer, J-P. Deslauriers, A. Laperrière, and Alvaro Pires, 113–169. Montréal: Gaëtan Morin.

Platonova, Anna, and GiulianaUrso. 2012. 'Labour Shortages and Migration Policy'. Brussels: International Organization for Migration (IOM).

Polanyi, Karl. 2001. *The Great Transformation: The Political and Economic Origins of Our Time*. Boston: Beacon Press.

Radenacker, Anke. 2014. 'Family Policies: Germany'. Population Europe Resource Finder & Archive (PERFAR).

Reskin, Barbara F., and Denise D. Bielby. 2005. 'A Sociological Perspective on Gender and Career Outcomes'. *Journal of Economic Perspectives* 19 (1): 71–86. doi:10.1257/0895330053148010.

Reynolds, Tracey, Harry Goulbourne, John Solomos, and Elisabetta Zontini. 2010. *Transnational Families: Ethnicities, Identities and Social Capital*. London, New York: Routledge.

Riaño, Yvonne. 2012. 'The Invisibility of Family in Studies of Skilled Migration and Brain Drain'. *Diversities* 14 (1): 25–44.

———. 2016. 'Minga Biographic Workshops with Highly Skilled Migrant Women: Enhancing Spaces of Inclusion'. *Qualitative Research* 16 (3): 267–279. doi:10.1177/1468794115614884.

Riaño, Yvonne, Katharina Limacher, André Aschwanden, Sophie Hirsig, and Doris Wastl-Walter. 2015. 'Shaping Gender Inequalities: Critical Moments and Critical Places'. *Equality, Diversity and Inclusion: An International Journal* 34 (2): 155–67. doi:10.1108/EDI-12-2013-0112.

Rietschin, R., and R. Imhof. 2017. 'Mémento statistique de la métropole lémanique 2017'. Genève, Lausanne: OCSTAT, Statistique Vaud, Statistique Genève.

Rorty, Richard. 1982. *Consequences of Pragmatism: Essays, 1972-1980.* Minneapolis: University of Minnesota Press.

Ryan, Louise, and Jon Mulholland. 2014. 'Trading Places: French Highly Skilled Migrants Negotiating Mobility and Emplacement in London'. *Journal of Ethnic and Migration Studies* 40 (4): 584–600. doi:10.1080/1369183X.2013.787514.

Ryan, Louise, Rosemary Sales, Mary Tilki, and Bernadetta Siara. 2009. 'Family Strategies and Transnational Migration: Recent Polish Migrants in London'. *Journal of Ethnic and Migration Studies* 35 (1): 61–77. doi:10.1080/13691830802489176.

Sacks, Harvey. 1972. 'An Initial Investigation of the Usability of Conversational Data for Doing Sociology'. In *Studies in Social Interaction*, edited by D.N. Sudnow, 31–73. New York: Free Press.

Said, Edward. 1980. *L'Orientalisme. L'Orient Créé Par l'Occident.* Paris: Seuil.

Salt, John, and Jeremy Stein. 1997. 'Migration as a Business: The Case of Trafficking'. *International Migration* 35 (4): 467–494.

Salt, John, and Peter Wood. 2012a. 'Recession and International Corporate Mobility'. *Global Networks* 12 (4): 425–45. doi:10.1111/j.1471-0374.2011.00356.x.

———. 2012b. 'Shifting Portfolios of International Labour Mobility among UK-Based Business Consultancies'. *Geoforum* 43 (4): 815–23. doi:10.1016/j.geoforum.2012.01.010.

Salzbrunn, Monika. 2010. 'Rescaling Processes in Two 'Global'Cities: Festive Events as Pathways of Migrant Incorporation'. In *Locating Migration. Rescaling Cities and Migrants*, edited by Nina Glick Schiller and Ayse Caglar, 166–189. New York: Cornell University Press.

Sandoz, Laure. 2018. 'Understanding Access to the Labour Market through Migration Channels'. *Journal of Ethnic and Migration Studies*, July, 1–20. doi:10.1080/1369183X.2018.1502657.

Schaer, Martine, Janine Dahinden, and Alina Toader. 2017. 'Transnational Mobility among Early-Career Academics: Gendered Aspects of Negotiations and Arrangements within Heterosexual Couples'. *Journal of Ethnic and Migration Studies* 43 (8): 1292–1307. doi:10.1080/1369183X.2017.1300254.

Schiller, Nina Glick, Ayşe Çaglar, and Thaddeus C. Guldbrandsen. 2006. 'Beyond the Ethnic Lens: Locality, Globality, and Born-Again Incorporation'. *American Ethnologist* 33 (4): 612–33. doi:10.1525/ae.2006.33.4.612.

Schilliger, Sarah. 2013. *Transnationale Care-Arbeit: Osteuropäische Pendelmigrantinnen in Privathaushalten von Pflegebedürftigen*. Zürich: Seismo Verlag.

Schmid, Flurina. 2016. 'The Gender Wage Gap in Switzerland over Time'. *Swiss Journal of Sociology* 42 (3): 442–467. doi:10.1515/sjs-2016-0020.

Scott, W. Richard. 2004. 'Reflections on a Half-Century of Organizational Sociology'. *Annual Review of Sociology* 30: 1–21. doi:10.1146/annurev.soc.30.012703.110644.

Shilling, Guido. 2017. 'Transparency at the Top, the Management Boards of Switzerland's Privant and Public Sectors'. Zürich: Guido Shilling AG.

Shinozaki, Kyoko. 2014. 'Career Strategies and Spatial Mobility among Skilled Migrants in Germany: The Role of Gender in the Work-Family Interaction: The Role of Gender in the Work-Family Interaction'. *Tijdschrift Voor Economische En Sociale Geografie* 105 (5): 526–41. doi:10.1111/tesg.12111.

Simmel, Georg. 1950. *The Sociology of Georg Simmel*. Edited by Kurth H. Wolff. New York: Simon and Schuster.

Slaughter, Anne-Marie. 2012. 'Why Women Still Can't Have It All'. *The Atlantic*, August 2012.

Smith, J. H. 1960. 'Sociology and Management Studies'. *The British Journal of Sociology* 11 (2): 103–11. doi:10.2307/587418.

Söderström, Ola, Blaise Dupuis, and Patrick Leu. 2013. 'Translocal Urbanism: How Ouagadougou Strategically Uses Decentralised Cooperation'. In *Living the City in Africa.Processes of Invention and Intervention*, edited by B. Obrist, V. Arlt, and E. Macamo, LIT, 99–117. Berlin.

Stark, Oded, and David E. Bloom. 1985. 'The New Economics of Labor Migration'. *The American Economic Review* 75 (2): 173–178.

Statistique Genève. 2017. 'Taux d'offre en places d'accueil collectif, selon les sources de financement'. Genève: République et canton de Genève.

Statistique Vaud. 2017. 'Taux de Recours En Accueil Collectif Préscolaire (0 à 4 Ans) Par Réseau et Tranches d'âges, Structures Subventionnées, Vaud, 2010-2017'. Lausanne: Canton de Vaud.

Stirling, Alfie. 2015. 'Migrant Employment Outcomes in European Labour Markets'. London: Institute for Public Policy Research (IPPR).

Suutari, Vesa, and Chris Brewster. 2000. 'Making Their Own Way: International Experience through Self-Initiated Foreign Assignments'. *Journal of World Business* 35 (4): 417–36. doi:10.1016/S1090-9516(00)00046-8.

———. 2001. 'Making Their Own Way: International Experience through Self-Initiated Foreign Assignments'. *Journal of World Business* 35 (4): 417–36. doi:10.1016/S1090-9516(00)00046-8.

Thomas, William, Isaac. 1928. 'The Child in America: Behavior Problems and Programs'. In *The Methodology of Behavior Study*, 553–76. New York: Alred A. Knopf.

Tissot, Florian. 2018. 'A Migration Industry for Skilled Migrants: The Case of Relocation Services'. *Migration Letters* 15 (4): 545–59.

Todaro, Michael P. 1969. 'A Model of Labor Migration and Urban Unemployment in Less Developed Countries'. *The American Economic Review* 59 (1): 138–148.

Triadafilopoulos, Triadafilos, ed. 2013. *Wanted and Welcome?: Policies for Highly Skilled Immigrants in Comparative Perspective*. Immigrants and Minorities, Politics and Policy. New York, Heidelberg: Springer.

Turner, Victor. 1967. 'Betwixt and between: The Liminal Period in Rites of Passage'. In *The Forest of Symbols*, Cornell University Press, 3–19. Ithaca.

Urner, Klaus. 1976. *Die Deutschen in der Schweiz: Von den Anfangen der Kolonienbildung bis zum Ausbruch des Ersten Weltkrieges*. Frauenfeld, Stuttgart: Huber.

Van Campenhoudt, Luc, and Raymond Quivy. 2011. *Manuel de Recherche En Sciences Sociales*. 4e edition. Paris: Dunod.

Van Gennep, Arnold. 1960. *Les Rites de Passage*. Chicago: University of Chicago Press.

Wallerstein, Immanuel Maurice. 1974. *The Modern World-System: Capitalist Agriculture and the Origins of the European World-Economy in the Sixteenth Century*. New York, San Fransisco, London: Academic Press.

Walsh, Kate. 2003. 'Qualitative Research: Advancing the Science and Practice of Hospitality', Cornell Hotel and Restaurant Administration Quarterly, 44 (2): 66–74. doi:10.1016/S0010-8804(03)90019-X.

Watson, D. Rodney. 1983. 'The Presentation of a Victim and Motive in Discourse: The Case of Police Interrogations and Interviews'. *Victimology* 8 (1–2): 31–52.

Webb, Jonathan. 2017. 'Glass Ceiling Still Keeps Top Jobs For The Boys: Women Earn 75% Of Men's Salary'. Forbes. 2017.

West, Candace, and Don H. Zimmerman. 1987. 'Doing Gender'. *Gender and Society* 1 (2): 125–51.

Wieczorek, Anna Xymena. 2018. *Migration and (Im)Mobility: Biographical Experiences of Polish Migrants in Germany and Canada*. Bielefeld: Transcript.

Wilding, Raelene, and Loretta Baldassar. 2009. 'Transnational Family-Work Balance: Experiences of Australian Migrants Caring for Ageing Parents and Young Children across Distance and Borders'. *Journal of Family Studies* 15 (2): 177–87. doi:10.5172/jfs.15.2.177.

Wimmer, Andreas, and Nina Glick Schiller. 2002. 'Methodological Nationalism and beyond: Nation–State Building, Migration and the Social Sciences'. *Global Networks* 2 (4): 301–334. doi:10.1111/1471-0374.00043.

———. 2003. 'Methodological Nationalism, the Social Sciences, and the Study of Migration: An Essay in Historical Epistemology 1'. *International Migration Review* 37 (3): 576–610. doi:10.1111/j.1747-7379.2003.tb00151.x.

Witzel, Andreas. 2000. 'Das Problemzentrierte Interview'. *Forum: Qualitative Sozialforschung* 1 (1). doi:http://dx.doi.org/10.17169/fqs-1.1.1132.

Zufferey, Marie-Eve, and Eric Widmer. 2014. 'Family Policies: Switzerland'. Population Europe Resource Finder & Archive (PERFAR).

www.ingramcontent.com/pod-product-compliance
Ingram Content Group UK Ltd.
Pitfield, Milton Keynes, MK11 3LW, UK
UKHW021921120926
8556IPUK00042BA/1090

9 783034 339186